Graham Viney

Young Elizabeth

One Extraordinary African Summer in the Life of the Princess

ROBINSON

ROBINSON

First published in South Africa in 2018 by Jonathan Ball Publishers,
an imprint of Kensington Publishing Corp.

First published in Great Britain in 2019 by Robinson

This paperback edition published in 2020 by Robinson

3 5 7 9 10 8 6 4 2

Previously published as *The Last Hurrah:
The 1947 Royal Tour of Southern Africa and the End of Empire*

© Text, Graham Viney 2018
© Photographs, as credited individually

Every effort has been made to trace the copyright holders and to obtain their permission for the use of copyright material. The publishers apologise for any errors or omissions and would be grateful to be notified of any corrections that should be incorporated in future editions of this book.

The colour stills on the pages of the colour picture section are taken from a newsreel film shot during the royal tour and are of varying quality. Used by courtesy of the South African National Film Video and Sound Archives.

A CIP catalogue record for this book
is available from the British Library.

ISBN: 978-1-47214-319-8

Design and typesetting by Triple M Design
Set in 11/15pt Requiem
Printed and bound in Great Britain by Clays Ltd, Elcograf S.p.A.

Papers used by Robinson are from well-managed forests
and other responsible sources.

MIX
Paper from
responsible sources
FSC® C104740

Robinson
An imprint of
Little, Brown Book Group
Carmelite House
50 Victoria Embankment
London EC4Y 0DZ

An Hachette UK Company
www.hachette.co.uk

www.littlebrown.co.uk

IN MEMORY OF MY PARENTS
AND THEIR GENERATION OF SOUTH AFRICANS

‑ॐ‑

Contents

Dramatis Personae

Bt	Baronet
CB	Companion of the Most Honourable Order of the Bath
CBE	Commander of the Most Excellent Order of the British Empire
CMG	Commander of the Order of St Michael and St George
CVO	Commander of the Royal Victorian Order
DFC	Distinguished Flying Cross
DSO	Distinguished Service Order
DTD	Dekoratie voor Trouwe Dienst (Decoration for Devoted Service)
HE	His/Her Excellency
HM	His/Her Majesty
Hon	Honourable
HRH	His/Her Royal Highness
HSH	His/Her Serene Highness
KBE	Knight Commander of the Most Excellent Order of the British Empire
KCB	Knight Commander of the Most Honourable Order of the Bath
KCMG	Knight Commander of the Order of St Michael and St George
KCVO	Knight Commander of the Royal Victorian Order
Kt	Knight
MC	Military Cross
OM	Order of Merit
PC	Privy Counsellor
TRH	Their Royal Highnesses

THE ROYAL FAMILY

HM the King, George VI, second son of George V, Emperor of India and King of Canada, Australia, New Zealand, South Africa and the British territories beyond the seas*

HM the Queen, formerly Lady Elizabeth Bowes-Lyon, daughter of the Earl of Strathmore (Queen Elizabeth in the context of this book)*

HM Queen Mary, the Queen Mother

HRH Princess Elizabeth, the Heiress Presumptive (now Queen Elizabeth II)*

HRH Princess Margaret, her younger sister*

HRH Prince George, the Duke of Kent, the King's younger brother, killed on wartime service, and his beautiful widow, Marina, the Duchess of Kent, sister of Princess Olga of Greece

The Earl and Countess of Athlone, he HSH Prince Alexander of Teck, brother of Queen Mary, she HRH Princess Alice of Albany, a granddaughter of Queen Victoria; Governor-General of the Union of South Africa 1924–1930 and Canada 1940–1946 ('Uncle Alge and Aunt Alice' to the Royal Family)

EUROPEAN ROYALS

HM the King of Greece, wartime refugee in South Africa. Ascended the throne on 1 April 1947, the day of the royal arrival in Johannesburg

HM the Queen of Greece, wartime refugee, as Princess Frederica of Greece, in South Africa, intimate friend of Field-Marshal Smuts

HRH Prince Paul of Yugoslavia, the former Regent of Yugoslavia, living in exile in Johannesburg

HRH Princess Paul of Yugoslavia (Olga), his beautiful wife, daughter of Princess Nicholas of Greece and sister of the Duchess of Kent, living in exile in Johannesburg

HRH Prince Alexander, their son, godson of King George VI

HRH Prince Nicholas, their younger son

HRH Princess Elizabeth, their daughter

THE HOUSEHOLD

Sir Alan Lascelles, PC, KCB, KCVO, CMG, MC, the Chief Private Secretary to the King*

Major Thomas Harvey, DSO, Private Secretary to the Queen

Wing Commander Peter Townsend, DSO, DFC and Bar, Battle of Britain fighter ace, Equerry to the King*

Lieutenant-Commander Peter Ashmore, DSC, RN, Equerry to the King, who attended Stansbury's (Western Province Prep)

Lady Harlech (née Gascoyne-Cecil), Lady-in-Waiting to the Queen, wife of the former High Commissioner for Southern Africa*

Lady Delia Peel (née Spencer), Lady-in-Waiting to the Queen*

Lady Margaret Egerton, Lady-in-Waiting to the Princesses, subsequently married to Jock Colville, appointed Private Secretary to Princess Elizabeth (and previously Chamberlain's and Churchill's wartime Private Secretary)*

Captain [Sir] Lewis Ritchie, CVO, CBE, RN, the King's Press Secretary, scribe of the Tour Diary, also popular author of maritime stories under the pseudonym 'Bartameus'

THE PROCONSULS AND THEIR LADIES

HE Gideon Brand van Zyl, the Governor-General of South Africa, the King's representative in South Africa, and his wife, Marie*

Lady Duncan (Alice), widow of Sir Patrick Duncan, the former Governor-General of South Africa

HE Sir John Kennedy, Governor of Southern Rhodesia, and Lady Kennedy

The Hon Sir Evelyn Baring, KCMG, the High Commissioner and his wife, Lady Mary Baring

Lord Harlech, former High Commissioner and husband of the Queen's Lady-in-Waiting

HE Lady Moore (Daphne), wife of the Governor of Ceylon, intimate friend of Field-Marshal Smuts

Viscountess Milner, influential widow of Viscount (Alfred) Milner, High Commissioner for Southern Africa and Governor of the Cape colonies and later the Transvaal and Orange River colonies ('Aunt Violet' to Lady Harlech), editor of the *National Review*

SOUTH AFRICAN POLITICIANS

Field-Marshal the Rt Hon Jan Christiaan Smuts, OM, Prime Minister
of South Africa, Minister of External Affairs and Defence, a former
Boer War general, intellectual giant and now an imperialist and
internationalist, head of the ruling United Party since 1939

Isie Smuts (née Krige), his wife

The Rt Hon Jan (Jannie) Hofmeyr, Smuts's wartime deputy, and a great
hope among South African liberals; bachelor

Mrs Deborah Hofmeyr, his formidable mother, who kept house for him

Major the Hon Piet van der Byl, MC, Minister of Native Affairs, and Joy,
his beautiful, imperious wife

The Hon Harry Lawrence, Minister of Justice, and of Social Welfare and
Demobilisation, and Jean, his glamorous wife

Dr the Hon Colin Steyn, Minister of Labour

Mrs Rachel Steyn, his mother, widow of the last president of the Orange
Free State

The Rt Hon EF Watermeyer, the Chief Justice, and his wife, Nellie

The Hon JG Carinus, Administrator of the Cape Province, and Mrs
Carinus, his wife

Dr the Hon SP Barnard, Administrator of the Orange Free State
(United Party)

The Hon DE Mitchell, Administrator of Natal, and Mrs Mitchell
(United Party)

General the Hon JJ Pienaar, DTD, Administrator of the Transvaal, and
Mrs Pienaar

General the Hon JBM Hertzog, former Boer general, head of the Fusion
government of the 1930s, ousted by Smuts in 1939 over the neutrality
issue.

Dr the Hon DF Malan, leader of the Gesuiwerde Nasionale Party
(Purified National Party), the Official Opposition, and Maria, his
second wife

The Hon Nicolaas Havenga, leader of the Afrikaner Party

Margaret Ballinger MP, trenchant liberal member of the white Native
Representative Council (NRC) in Parliament

Senator Edgar Brookes, Native Representative for Natal and Zululand

Senator Hyman Basner, co-founder of the African Democratic Party, elected senator to represent the Africans of the Transvaal and Orange Free State

Senator Major the Hon George Richards, Natal senator and *éminence grise* of various Empire Leagues in South Africa

ARMED FORCES AND POLICE

Vice-Admiral Sir Clement Moody, RN, Commander-in-Chief, the South Atlantic Station, Simon's Town, and Lady Moody

General Sir Pierre van Ryneveld, KBE, CB, DSO, MC, Chief of the General Staff, Union Defence Force, and Lady Van Ryneveld

Major-General RJ (Bobby) Palmer, DSO, Commissioner of the South African Police

Major G Bestford, DSO, Officer Commanding, Police College, Pretoria

Brigadier HG Willmott, CBE, Officer Commanding, Western Cape Command, and later military attaché at the South African High Commission, London, later still twice Chief of Staff of the South African Air Force (SAAF), and his wife, Alison

Colonel Toby Moll, DSO, Officer Commanding, Air Force Base Ysterplaat

Group Captain Adolph (Sailor) Malan, DSO and Bar, DFC and Bar, South African fighter ace of the Battle of Britain, later leader of the Torch Commando

Mrs Edith O'Connor, impressive National Secretary and Chief Executive of the South African Women's Auxiliary Services (SAWAS), formerly instrumental in setting up the South African Women's Agricultural Union, which had similar ideals and aspirations to the Women's Institute.

AFRICAN REGENTS, NATIONALIST LEADERS AND CIVIC AND OTHER PERSONALITIES

Mr Abe Bloomberg, Mayor of Cape Town, and Miriam, his wife

Councillor Ahmed Ismail, Cape Town City Council

YM Dadoo, President of the South African Indian Congress

Mahatma Gandhi, leader of the Indian independence movement against British rule

Mrs Vijaya Pandit, Jawaharlal Nehru's formidable sister

AB Xuma, President-General of the African National Congress (ANC), and his wife, Madie Hall, an African American

*Albert Luthuli, Representative Chief of the Zulu at the *Ngoma Nkosi*, later ANC leader and Nobel Peace Prize winner

Tshekedi Khama, Regent of Bechuanaland

Prince Cyprian Bhekuzulu ka Solomon ka Dinuzulu, heir to the Zulu Royal House

Mr Howard Glover, Mayor of Queenstown, and his wife, Edith

Mr JG Benadé, Mayor of Bloemfontein, and Mrs Benadé

Mr Rupert Ellis Brown, Mayor of Durban, and his impressive wife, Clare

AI Kajee, Chairman of the Durban Indian Reception Committee

Mr DP van Heerden, Mayor of Pretoria

Mr James Gray, Mayor of Johannesburg, and his wife, Ethel

Sir De Villiers (Div) Graaff, Bt, future leader of the United Party, and Lady Graaff

Sir Ernest Oppenheimer, Kt, financial genius, who controlled Anglo American Corporation and De Beers, and Lady Oppenheimer, his second wife

Sir Alfred Hennessy, Kt, Chairman of the Colonial Orphan Chamber, Chairman of the Cableway Company, and Lady Hennessy

Lady Jones, wife of Sir Roderick Jones, Chairman of Reuters, and better known as Enid Bagnold, the popular English novelist; visitor to South Africa during the tour and correspondent of Lady Diana Cooper

Frank Gillard, CBE, in charge of the BBC coverage of the royal tour of southern Africa

Elsa Joubert, Paarl-born, teenage niece of SP Barnard, Administrator of the Orange Free State, later a celebrated author

Note: For a fuller description of entries marked with an asterisk (*) the reader is encouraged to visit www.1947royaltourdp.com.

꽃

Introduction

This is a tale of long ago now. Almost all the players have left the stage although, phenomenally, one of the leads, Queen Elizabeth II, still survives in the central, pivotal role for which the tour must surely have been a partial preparation and a formative experience. The Empire has vanished and Britain and the Commonwealth have changed out of all recognition.

The South Africa it describes has gone too. Physically, a little remains, often much altered, brutalised or neglected, but the photographs, documents and above all newsreels provide a window on the setting of these extraordinary and momentous months and the events that played out within them. Added to this there are contemporary accounts – like gold dust for the researcher – and there survive too the memories of old people: some vivid, others also vivid but alas not always supported by the evidence of hard fact. They record a world that was essentially middle class in its values, and a deferential one at that.

But images, memories and manners are not enough. They do not generate the authentic whiffs and stenches of an age, and the reader is asked to conjure up the pervading smells of heat and dust, of acrid railway-engine smoke and cinders, of eucalyptus and pepper trees, of Yardley's Lavender and the friendly tang of the Indian Ocean on a summer's morning; of human sweat and horse sweat and saddle leather; of well-watered English annuals and rain on the parched African veld; of Scotch and Dutch baking, African beer, braaied meat and coffee with scalded milk; of wicker and *stoep* polish and teatime silver in the sunshine, of African thatch and drinks trays in the evenings; of Drakensberg and Highveld air alike like wine, and the uniquely pungently scented Bushveld night, as a background to it all.

This book attempts to place the royal tour in its post-war context of the history of South Africa and the Commonwealth. The Union of South Africa then was an autonomous Dominion in what was still called the British Commonwealth, and Jan Smuts, by far its most celebrated prime minister and internationalist, clearly saw it best served and best able to serve the wider international community in this status. At that date, therefore, despite being made up of many tribes and races, the country bore the unmistakable imprint of *Pax Britannica*. Aside from what G Ward Price, a senior journalist following the tour, euphemistically described as 'minority politics', the social character of white South Africa was, he considered, the closest possible overseas reproduction of English provincial life. 'The average Englishman,' he wrote, '[when] asked where he feels most at home in the Empire, says South Africa.'[1]

English-speaking South Africa gave a decided flavour to the era; with hindsight, some Afrikaans-speakers who grew up then will also now admit this. Its history has subsequently tended to be swept under the carpet. For, in spite of its immediate success, the tour would be the swan song of that age in this land. In attempting to reinforce the concept of a constitutional monarchy as the binding force of the British Commonwealth, it could not fail to focus attention on the issue of a revitalised and aggressive Afrikaner ascendancy with an emotive aim to transform the Union back into the Boer republic out of which its supporters felt they had been cheated in 1910. And although their proposed boycotts mostly failed, it was hardly surprising that emerging black and Indian politicians attempted to use the tour to highlight the issue of inequality and racial segregation.

This issue now hovered, unresolved and incrementally resented, like a storm cloud on the horizon of a seemingly endlessly sunny land. DF Malan, the leader of the Nationalist opposition, knew his predominantly white

Royal Garden Party, Westbrooke, Rondebosch. In the foreground is Queen Elizabeth, with Governor-General Gideon Brand van Zyl to her left, and the King and the Princesses behind. IAN SHAPIRO COLLECTION

electorate well. If the success of the royal tour had succeeded in significantly neutralising the urgency felt among his followers to break with the imperial connection, he had up his sleeve another far more potent neurosis to appeal to. This was race and their fear of being swamped by a black majority.

The telling moment would come a year hence at the general election. For now, from February to April 1947, much of the Union, together with its neighbouring territories, gave itself over to participate in, and follow avidly through the media, the royal progress: "The King and Queen's every breath and movement', as the visiting novelist Enid Bagnold put it in a letter home, was being 'blown through Africa at all hours on the wireless'.[2]

In spite of a background of a Britain diminished by the crippling cost of the war and the welfare state experiment, coupled with enduring a catastrophic winter, the heraldry, the mounted police escorts, the triumphal arches, the great military march pasts, the glittering balls and garden parties, the *aSozizwe*-ing and ululating tribes and township dwellers, the gloved salutes and curtsying ladies all combined to provide a spectacle South Africa has never seen before or since. It was brilliantly staged and enacted by the leads with grace and glamour, and the majority of South Africans, of all races, enjoyed themselves thoroughly and cheered, as a bemused American reporter from *Life* magazine felt constrained to put it afterwards, 'as if the parade of Empire was just beginning'[3] and not, in fact, just beginning to fade.

In a racially torn country, no single event will ever be the cause of national pride, celebration and joy. Nevertheless, despite its detractors among the various nationalist politicians with their respective agendas – Afrikaner, Indian and black – this event, uniquely, seems to have come the closest to being just that in the long and disputatious history of South Africa.

Many of the ideals, mores and manners of that era seem foreign in today's world. Some may even be construed as offensive. Certainly it is a mistake to over-romanticise times gone by. In the middle of the twentieth century, LP Hartley began his celebrated novel *The Go-Between* with a sentence that stands as one of the most loved opening lines of twentieth-century fiction. It is at once highly evocative, distancing and very telling. 'The past,' he wrote, 'is like a foreign country; they do things differently there.' By this light we should try and judge it, as we peer through history's telescope, not blind to its shortcomings but trying to understand what is now, after all, not one but two South Africas ago. And what followed it.

CHAPTER I

⇥⟨§⟩⇤

Arrival

Cape Town, 17 February 1947

The southeaster, which seemed to have blown all summer, singeing the oaks and hydrangeas, flattening the wheat before the harvest, spoiling the crayfish catch, the surf riding and the holiday season at Muizenberg, spoiling the opening day of the cricket at Newlands, spoiling much of the racing season at Kenilworth and Milnerton, and spoiling, really – as the Cape ladies remarked to one another, in tones not entirely devoid of satisfaction – spoiling, *really*, the Centlivres–Warr-King wedding[1] – blew itself out on the evening of 16 February. A great calm suddenly fell across the land and even the pounding waves of the two great oceans that surrounded it seemed suddenly stilled.

It was the break in the Cape weather patterns for which those who lived there held their very breath, for when it came they knew for certain they lived in an Eden. Of course they wanted the Royal Family to think so too. Only twenty-four hours before, everything planned for the big day would have been ruined. The arrival at the docks, the State Entry into the city, the flags and bunting, the planned garden party at Westbrooke the day after, the floodlighting of the mountain and the fireworks – all would have been seriously jeopardised by the gale; it was even doubtful if the great battleship would have been able to enter the harbour.[2]

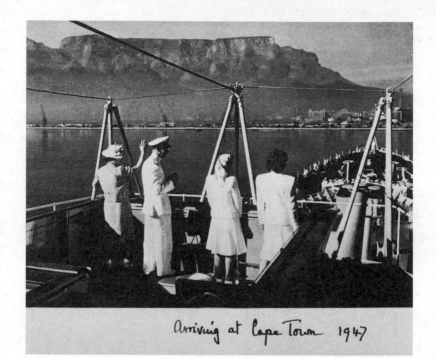

arriving at Cape Town 1947

HMS *Vanguard* approaches the newly completed Duncan Dock. The caption is Queen
Elizabeth's; the photograph was used as the Royal Family's Christmas card for 1947.

IAN SHAPIRO COLLECTION

Everyone had dreaded such an eventuality; now, their prayers seemed
to have been answered. All over the Cape Peninsula and the Boland men
stared up into the still, bright, starry heavens surrounding the Southern
Cross,[3] and said to their wives: 'They'll have a fine day of it tomorrow.'
'King's weather!' came the happy replies, for in those days the Cape, or
at least the Anglo-Cape, was well versed in such royal lore, handed down
by oral tradition and kept alive in the popular imagination by the daily
papers, the cinema and the historical novel.[4]

And so it was, after all, a perfect summer's day. The sun, the great, hot,
Cape February sun, rose on the dazzling set-piece that nature had devised:
the tremendous triumvirate of mountains beneath which nestled a city that
could still just be called beautiful – proudly though erroneously held by its

citizens to be the second oldest in the Empire. That morning, freed at last from the lashing wind and invested in the Cape's as yet unpolluted, ivory, Mediterranean light, the setting presented a sight that reminded more than one observer of a Canaletto. Before the city lay the glassy, blue bay, covered in a fine morning mist. 'It'll burn off,' said everyone (weather bores all to a man), and so it did and just before nine 9 am HMS *Vanguard* hove majestically into sight over the Eastern Mole – or so at any rate *The Cape Argus* put it that evening, employing centuries-old English maritime jargon, and knowing full well that in such a context their readers would expect it.

At 52 250 long tons (deep load), with a complement of 1 975, it was, at that date, the biggest battleship ever built.[5] In the still morning air, the Royal Standard barely fluttered from the masthead, and as the great warship slowly moved forward towards the newly completed Duncan Dock, its bugles sounded out across the water. It was a magnificent sight.

All central Cape Town had been closed to traffic since 9 pm the previous evening and was to remain so until midnight that night. Since 4.30 am that morning, with the street lamps still burning, special trains had poured into its main station, at times at barely two-minute intervals. This terminus was still a marvellous Victorian edifice, all teak ticket booths and arched iron girders and glass, with a Renaissance façade on Adderley Street. From Simon's Town, Stellenbosch, Paarl and Touwsrivier the trains steamed in; from Caledon, Worcester and Somerset West still they came, teak-shuttered and green-leathered, on time, clean and segregated, disgorging their expectant passengers into an already crowded town. That night, an extra 14 trains were added to the already well augmented service to take Capetonians back to the suburbs. By the time the Royal Family departed five days later, the station had handled an unprecedented 1 500 000 passengers.[6]

A great tide of motor traffic had inched towards the city from the outlying suburbs and *dorps* (villages). Those with priority passes displayed were waved forward by the specially deployed traffic constables; policemen, still dressed identically to London bobbies, directed the streams of pedestrians to vantage points along the route. Some, like the Vintcent family, who had happily set out 'to be there to welcome them', got no further than De Waal Drive and, giving up, parked their car alongside hundreds of others for a bird's-eye view of the proceedings.[7]

A similar view greeted two thousand schoolchildren clad in white from all the schools in Sea Point who, on the initiative of Cape Town's Joint School Board, now stood up to attention along 100-foot (30-metre) paths specially cut into the Cape heath on Signal Hill; for those on the decks of *Vanguard* these spelt out WELCOME. By command of the King, the ship at once signalled a response that was relayed up to the children and WELCOME erupted, suddenly acquiring a life of its own as they waved and cheered back delightedly as loudly as they could.[8]

Excitement on board was apparently just as great, or so reported the special South African Press Association (SAPA) correspondent covering the outward voyage, in a technically advanced ship-to-shore phone call made as the battleship finally swung to starboard to pass through the harbour's narrow entrance, leaving the three South African frigates – their local naval escorts – behind. Overhead, Venturas and Sunderlands of the South African Air Force did a fly-past in close formation.[9]

'It was a wonderful day as we approached Cape Town,' wrote Princess Elizabeth later to her grandmother, Queen Mary, 'and when I caught my first glimpse of Table Mountain I could hardly believe that anything could be so beautiful.'[10]

Every window on the processional route was given over to the fortunate and well connected, and many a favour had been called in to secure these. The balconies of the department stores and the handsome buildings of the financial district – gay with flags, bunting, crowns and loyal greetings – were jammed. The remaining third of the unallotted seats on the specially erected grandstands along the half mile (0.8-kilometre) of road that linked the docks to the foot of Adderley Street – crossing the wasteland that was still the newly reclaimed Foreshore and now proudly named Kingsway by the Cape Town City Council – had changed hands for £8. The rest had been given out free to municipalities as far afield as Namaqualand, where they were awarded by ballot, often with greatly reduced train tickets. Interestingly, in that pre-apartheid age, both Europeans and Non-Europeans were eligible for these.[11]

Before J Berth a specially built, giant reception arena had been erected – a triumphal arch ('The Gateway to Africa'), flanked by crown-topped masts, sweeping stands and a royal pavilion, all executed in that

The King greets the Governor-General, while Mrs Van Zyl curtsies in front of
Jan Smuts and General Sir Pierre van Ryneveld salutes. At right is the
triumphal arch leading to Kingsway. IAN SHAPIRO COLLECTION

curious synthesis of a medieval tournament and British post-war modern
design. A new age had dawned, and no one – whether courtier or member
of the Palace Advance Party,[12] Admiralty, Dominion Office or the Central
Committee coordinating the visit in South Africa, all of whom had had a
hand in this – wished to be seen to be behind the times.

As *Vanguard* approached yet nearer, a cry went up from among the
tens of thousands who lined the docks: 'There they are!' And there
indeed, on the specially built saluting platform that had replaced the
anti-aircraft mount on top of 'B' turret as part of the battleship's temporary conversion into the royal yacht, stood the Royal Family – the
King with his tall, athletic build in the white uniform of Admiral of
the Fleet surveying the scene through a pair of field glasses, the Queen
and Princesses deliberately still in simple day dresses. Nervously, a
smattering of applause broke out, for the reality of royal occasions was
unknown to the crowd, except for newsreels shown in cinemas. The
Queen at once responded with the charming, twirling royal wave that

The State Entry into Cape Town, seen from Garlicks department store. The procession moves up Kingsway towards Adderley Street. In the background is HMS *Vanguard*.

THE CITY OF CAPE TOWN MAYORAL MINUTES 1947

was her trademark, and responsive cheers seemed to spread like wildfire along the quays.

The order to 'dress ship overall' was given. Up, as in the age of Nelson, went the line of flags and the crowd gasped audibly in approval of this stylish piece of Royal Navy spectacle. *Vanguard* was made secure and the gangplank lowered to meet the waiting red carpet and potted palms. Striding up it went the Prime Minister, Field-Marshal Smuts, once Boer guerrilla leader, now the great imperial statesman of the age – friend of kings and queens, presidents and prime ministers, accompanied by His Excellency, Gideon Brand van Zyl, the rather less distinguished-looking Governor-General. Both were dressed in morning coats and black silk top hats.

Minutes later the King descended, to the accompaniment of a twenty-one-gun royal salute from the 1/5 Heavy Battery of the South African Artillery on Signal Hill. The King wore the breast star and sash of the Order of the Garter and was followed by the Queen, now magnificent in her feathers, pearls and diamonds and a powder-blue *robe de style* by Norman Hartnell; the two Princesses followed, dressed by Captain Edward Molyneux, the English-born Parisian couturier, in more fashionable frocks, though clearly designed with the upper-class Anglo-Saxon (rather than Parisian) market in mind.

Princess Elizabeth, whose looks seemed almost to belong to an earlier age, had a stiff formality about her, especially when her face was in repose – 'pretty too ... if there only wasn't so much Queen Mary promise about her', as Diana Cooper put it.[13] At 21, many commented that her flawless complexion appeared to have a light beneath it. Princess Margaret, at 16 and a half and barely out of the schoolroom, was on the cusp of becoming a ravishing beauty.

Immediately, the Royal Standard broke on the flagpole alongside the Union Jack and the South African flag, which had joined it, in equal status and in the teeth of bitter controversy, in 1927. The Governor-General bowed, the barrel-shaped Mrs Van Zyl was seen to curtsy, repeatedly – 'Oh! up and down, *constantly*,' as Jean Lawrence recalled, years later, waving her hand in mock slow motion, 'just like a buoy in the Hermanus swell.'[14] In the now soaring February temperatures – 'real Bombay weather', as Sir Alan Lascelles, the King's Private Secretary, described it to his wife – two members of the South African Naval Forces Guard of Honour, lined up for inspection by the King, fainted while standing stiffly to attention, one breaking his jaw in the process.[15]

The band played both national anthems – 'God Save the King' and the official alternative, *'Die Stem van Suid-Afrika'* – and the party moved up onto the circular royal pavilion where Sir Evelyn Baring, the High

Commissioner for Southern Africa, and Lady Mary (Molly) Baring;
General Sir Pierre van Ryneveld, Chief of the General Staff, and Lady
Van Ryneveld; the members of the Diplomatic Corps and their wives;
Vice-Admiral Sir Clement Moody, RN, Commander-in-Chief, the
South Atlantic Station, and Lady Moody; the Administrator of the Cape
and Mrs JG Carinus; the mayor of Cape Town and Mrs Bloomberg; and
finally the Cabinet ministers and their wives were presented.

Even for that age, the last-mentioned were a fairly remarkable group.
There was the unmarried Jan (Jannie) Hofmeyr, child genius, a Rhodes
Scholar at 15, Chancellor of Wits University at 25 and, after the outbreak
of war, Smuts's invaluable and hard-working lieutenant. Only 53, but over-
weight and unhealthy-looking, he was, as always, accompanied by his old
mother, Deborah, known to everyone – even her son – as Mrs Hofmeyr.
Strong-willed and unpleasant, and with a stammer she employed to devas-
tating effect, you didn't want to mess with her. 'What an old tartar she was,'
recalled the nonagenarian Queen Mother, long after her more famous son's
name had slipped her memory. 'I remember she bawled the King and me
out for doing something on a Sunday we should not have been doing!' There
too, in his element, and as if born in his morning coat, was Major Piet van
der Byl, Minister of Native Affairs and, together with his beautiful, imperious wife, Joy, perhaps the *beau idéal* of the anglicised Cape landed gentry.

Alongside him was Sidney Waterson, the tall, distinguished-looking
former High Commissioner in London, with his wife Betty, another
'burra mem' well known to South Africans for her broadcasts from
London during the Blitz, encouraging them to send money and food and
clothing parcels, in the old Empire spirit of hands-across-the-sea, to the
beleaguered people of Britain. There too was Harry Lawrence, Minister
of Justice and Welfare and also responsible for the demobilisation of
South African forces since the war, and his glamorous wife, Jean (privately loathed by Betty Waterson, a sentiment returned with interest), all
flashing blue smiles and veilings and draped crêpe to match, who, in her
much-admired cork-soled platform shoes towered above the royal ladies
and was in stylish contrast to the more frumpy parliamentary wives.

And there were others too, among them Sturrock, Minister of Railways
and Harbours, and Steyn, son of the last President of the Orange Free

State and now Minister of Labour. All, all were of consequence in that moment and many were shortly to come to dust.

There was some studiedly informal chat and then the public procession formed up. Now it was the Queen who subtly took centre stage. Before the fascinated gaze of the onlookers, she regally adjusted one of the feather-trimmed panels that fell from her shoulders and purposefully left the platform with the King. As one, and seemingly choreographed, the distinguished guests and their ladies remaining there bowed and curtsied in unison and were rewarded with a gracious, gloved royal gesture of acknowledgement. In the shimmering heat across the asphalt they walked, toward the vast new eight-cylinder Daimler, 18½ feet (almost 6 metres) in length, an open tourer that was one of a total of 11 ordered the year before from Hoopers, the famous coach builders in England, to convey the royal party and provincial administrators during the tour.[16]

These vehicles, as Pathé News was quick to point out, were intended as impressive examples of British workmanship and to show that postwar Britain was back in business. The Queen climbed into the specially designed flat-based back of the car and, thus elevated, waved to the stands before her. Then, taking her seat, she gave a backward wave to the crowd and the naval ratings who lined the decks of the *Vanguard* towering above the arena. These gestures were received with roars of approval by the crowds: this now was royal theatre, and this is what they had come for.

Even with the temperature reaching 102 degrees (39°C), car rugs were, as customary, arranged across the royal knees, and, as the Daimler moved forward, Major Bestford, Officer Commanding of the Mounted Police Escort, summoned up his men on their gleaming bays to ride ahead. The waving Princesses, excited to be out of England for the first time in their lives, followed in the second Daimler, getting a similar but smaller escort riding behind.

The Queen's Lady-in Waiting, Lady Harlech – 'Mima' to her intimates, wife of Sir Evelyn's predecessor – was assigned to the car immediately behind them. This also carried Sir Alan Lascelles and the prime minister who, she observed, got a 'tremendous greeting from the crowd who cheered and cheered and kept on shouting '*Onser* [sic] *Jannie*'. 'I think he was pleased,' she noted, perceptively, 'but just gave some rather absent-minded smiles and waves.'[17] Smuts, who could enchant anyone from kings and queens to strangers climbing Table Mountain by discoursing on subjects ranging from Cape flora to philosophy, was not at his best in such circumstances.

Up Kingsway they drove and clattered, past Tweed's statue of Jan van Riebeeck, past Herbert Baker's cenotaph to the South African fallen of two world wars, and on up Adderley Street past the then famous department stores that lined it – Garlicks, Markhams, Cleghorn & Harris, Fletcher & Cartwright and Stuttafords – past the columned Standard Bank with Britannia on its roof, Barclays Bank with its vast banking hall in the New Delhi imperial style, right into Wale Street past the newer Anglican cathedral (again Baker-designed) and the older one of 1832 – a copy of St Pancras Church in London – whose columned portico and spire still terminated the civic axis of St George's Street. Eastwards, down into the canyon of that once-handsome thoroughfare, they turned again, the Queen delighting the crowds by opening her blue silk sunshade against the glare.

By now the cheers of the biggest crowds Cape Town had ever known[18] had become deafening. These were described by the local coloured press as being mixed and happy;[19] sourly, in an effort to further disenchant its readership, the Afrikaans Nationalist press swiftly described them in scandalised terms as *gemeng* (unsegregated). In the mounting excitement, when the procession turned once more into Adderley Street, the police had to link arms to contain the surging masses. This continued uninterrupted until the motorcade reached and traversed the Grand Parade, where 5 000 ex-servicemen, including 500 ex-members of the Cape (Coloured) Corps,[20] all wearing their campaign medals, on being given the order 'hats off' by their commander, Brigadier Hearn, gave out three thunderous cheers that rose above the general roar.

To the consternation of the police, their cordon had by then been breached and there were youths running after the cars. Officialdom looked on aghast, but they had reckoned without the Queen. With characteristic perfect timing, she was seen to turn to smile and wave at them, almost encouragingly, and such by then were the scenes of wild enthusiasm that the lady commentator on the SABC, losing her head in the excitement of the moment, cried out to her listeners-in on their wirelesses all over the Union, the Protectorates of Basutoland, Swaziland and Bechuanaland and the Rhodesias to the north: 'But she's *lovely. Oh ... she's lovely ... lovely ...* Oh the princesses! Oh they're *lovely! lovely!* What *lovely* English girls ... Oh! ... *Oh! ...*' etc, exactly, it was thought later, rather sniffily, like someone at a football match.[21]

The Grand Parade witnessed the only 'untoward' reported incident of the State Entry. As the car bearing General Smuts and the members of the Household travelling with him passed by, there was some booing from a group of coloureds and Indians, separate from the ex-servicemen.[22] This was a general political statement from non-moderates within these groups, and does not appear to have been repeated during the tour. Almost all calls from non-white bodies for boycotting the tour for political reasons carried with them the caveat that no disrespect was intended for the King and the Royal Family.

It was a day packed with events. To Government House they drove, where they were to stay. As at Government House, Pretoria and Bloemfontein, and King's House in Durban, an elaborate programme of refurbishment had been put in hand. Naturally, it was put out that this was due anyway after six years of wartime austerity and parsimony. To this end, Mr Terry, the state decorator,[23] had been dispatched to England in 1946 by Mrs Van Zyl. While the Afrikaans press grumbled about the expense, English papers all over the country waxed lyrical to their avid female readership with mouth-watering descriptions of his finds and commissions placed there – Donegal rugs and close carpeting woven in Ireland and Scotland, chintzes printed from blocks not used since the outbreak of war, even a hand-blocked linen from Scotland featuring an image in repeat of Glamis Castle, intended by Mrs Van Zyl and Mr Terry to make the Queen feel at home.

Indeed, homeliness was a recurring theme in all this. Ruth Prowse, the celebrated Cape artist and Keeper of the Michaelis Collection, had been asked to hang a selection of pictures by South African artists in the private quarters: a Bowler, a Gwelo Goodman and a Francois Krige in the King's bedroom, and a Bowler, a Naudé and a Leng Dixon in the Queen's. Her study had an Irma Stern. 'I hung the pictures to make it look like a home,'

Prowse told the press. Maybe. But on a stifling February day, the Queen's bedroom, with its old-fashioned built-in fittings executed by Herbert Baker for the visit of the Duke and Duchess of York in 1901 and a monstrously ugly new ball-and-claw stinkwood bed,[24] the mosquito net, electric fan and Mrs Van Zyl's welcoming bowl of gladioli,[25] must have seemed a long way indeed from the Royal Lodge in Windsor Great Park.

As far as the Household were concerned, Mrs Van Zyl's domestic arrangements were evidently not up to much either. 'This is one of those incredibly uncomfortable Government Houses, with some good rooms but lacking all the essentials like writing tables and tooth glasses, etc,' wrote Lascelles, testily, to his wife, 'and staffed by a scratch lot of servants who don't know if it's Christmas or Easter.'[26]

No additional pictures were needed in the white and gold ballroom, which was hung with the massive state portraits of Edward VII and Queen Alexandra, though new and sumptuous red and gold brocatelle curtains, made from 120 yards (110 metres) ordered from the Gainsborough Silk Weaving Co in Carlisle, had been installed as a foil to the white and gold décor that survived from the 1840s. Here it was, half an hour after their arrival, that the King received a Loyal Address from both Houses of Parliament. Margaret Ballinger, one of the three Native Representatives in Parliament, was given a prominent seat in the front row of the House of Assembly members, between two ministers. Edgar Brookes, one of the four whites elected as senators to represent the black population, was likewise placed in the front row of the Senate body.[27]

Not a single Nationalist senator was present, however. Although the wording of the Loyal Address had been agreed by all parties in advance, it was noted, too, that despite all the efforts to present the King as a non-partisan, constitutional monarch, of the 46 members of the opposition pro-republican National Party, only 11 had put in an appearance. Dr DF Malan, leader of the party, was conspicuous by his absence.

After the address, the King, sitting on a throne placed beneath the orchestra, conferred on his prime minister the Order of Merit – restricted to 24 living recipients and in the monarch's personal gift. It was a singular honour.

That evening, there was a State Banquet for 504 guests in the City Hall. This imperial Edwardian baroque edifice had been gallantly outlined with

The State Banquet in the Cape Town City Hall. The Chief Justice and
Mrs Watermeyer flank the King and Queen; Smuts stands in the middle.
TRANSNET HERITAGE LIBRARY PHOTO COLLECTION

fairy lights. The royal cypher and the city's coat of arms blazed on its façade,
and the building, like many others in the city, was floodlit. The coveted
invitation read 'White Tie and Decorations'. The King, like his guests,
wore his miniatures;[28] across his chest was the sash and star of the Order
of the Garter. The ladies were décolleté in their evening dresses, with long
white gloves up to their armpits. As Major Piet van der Byl recalled, an
audible murmur was heard as the Queen arrived wearing one of Hartnell's
famous crinolines[29] – cyclamen satin flounced with lace and heavily boned
to accommodate her decided tendency since the war towards *embonpoint*
('Alas, the silhouette not all it should be,' as Clementine Churchill put it,
carefully, at the time[30]) – created to augment her ostensibly austerity-era
wardrobe.

None of this in any way detracted from her remarkable appeal. Ablaze with the crown jewels, the famous fringe tiara, the diamond and pearl necklace and earrings given by Edward VII to his beautiful Danish bride 90-odd years before, the cascade brooch across her sash and the Garter on her upper arm, she looked every inch a Queen. She had a dazzlingly flawless complexion and blue eyes. These she had passed on to her daughters, who were similarly gowned in evening dresses embroidered with sequins, and looked, as everyone excitedly said to one another, exactly like Princesses from a fairy tale.[31]

By now royal fever had gripped the entire city. There were dances arranged by the South African Women's Auxiliary Service (SAWAS)[32] for the officers and ship's company of HMS *Vanguard* at the Bohemian Club and the New Drill Hall, respectively. As the Civic Fireworks Display began on Green Point Common, Table Mountain was dramatically floodlit as never before by military searchlights that only two years previously had been deployed to sweep the surrounding seas at night in search of German and Japanese warships and submarines.

The good-natured – 'ebullient' was the term most often employed by the overseas journalists – Cape coloured population of District Six and the Muslim citizens from the Bo-Kaap poured down to the Grand Parade to join the throng of citizens who were reluctant to leave the city that was so spectacularly *en fête*. Indeed, the Grand Parade would be packed for all five nights with crowds who had waited patiently for hours for a sight of the sovereigns.[33] They watched the well-dressed guests alight with fascination. Among the onlookers were friends of Matilda, the Lawrences' cook, who, thrilled to catch sight of their friend's 'medem' in a glamorous Evangilides gown with orchids in her hair, pronounced her to all they spoke to afterwards as 'the Belly of the Ball'.

Breaking away from the programme, the King and Queen appeared on the floodlit balcony to acknowledge the delighted cheers from the crowd. Presently, they went inside. The main auditorium had been cleared and set with dining tables. Yards of curtaining of a modernist design (cost £390)[34] had been employed to help soften the daunting civic atmosphere, and it 'looked really lovely and in such good taste', thought Betty Waterson, the stage massed with potted palms and ferns and Cape heaths and proteas. The great coup, however, was the ugly, gold wrought-iron chandeliers overhead, which had, with a master stroke, been rendered glamorous with cascades of ostrich feathers, supplied by the farmers of Oudtshoorn.[35]

The Royal Family and the prime minister sat at the top table. Curiously, as he was openly a republican, Dr Malan attended this event, 'with his sour face' as Smuts put it,[36] after his pointed absenteeism that morning, and sitting, as Grahamstown's *Grocott's Mail* reported in slightly shocked terms to its English readership in Upper and Lower Albany, no more than 'a dozen feet from the Queen'.[37] He was, however, badly placed between two United Party wives who, to Lady Mary Baring's consternation, addressed not one word to him throughout the dinner.[38] This to her would have seemed bad-mannered and antagonistic; she also saw it as a missed opportunity.

Menacing looks had been directed at him for only joining in the singing of '*Die Stem*' and not 'God Save the King', as Molly Baring, sitting opposite him, later reported to her friend, Mima Harlech.[39] And there would certainly have been more menacing looks in his direction when, in his speech, the King firmly thanked all South Africans who had answered the bugle call in 1939, many of them now wearing their medals before him, together with their wives and families who had contributed so energetically to the war effort. Malan had bitterly opposed South Africa's participation in the war.

'Thank God victory was won and that I can at last tell my South African people, in person, how deeply I honour them for the splendid contribution they made ... When peace at length returned,' he continued, 'I counted very high among its blessings the freedom that it brought me to travel in the Commonwealth and pay you a visit.'[40]

Malan, the early architect of apartheid, can surely have been less than enchanted by the rest of what *Inkundla Ya Bantu*, the normally hard-hitting black newspaper, described as the King's 'inspiring speech', referring to where he made 'special and sympathetic reference' to the need for finding solutions and ways of life which would produce greater harmony among the many different races and colours that made up the Union.[41]

There was more to follow. With reference to the challenges facing the country, the King expressed his confidence in Smuts's statesmanship to guide (the Union) 'steadily towards a just and contented relationship between all dwellers in your many-peopled land'. Finally there followed what must have been hoped would be a sweetener for the less enthusiastic believers in this Utopia, if such it could be described: success in this would show a troubled world how peoples of different race and colour may live and work together for the common good.

In between courses, the Cape Town Municipal Orchestra played in the gallery (Mozart's Overture from *Figaro*, Bach's *Gavotte in D*, Scotch airs arranged in honour of the Queen, *The Fairy Tarapatapoum* by John Foulds and something, now forgotten, called *An Evening on the Veld* by William Pickerill). The eight-course menu, chosen by Mrs Van Zyl and a gastronomic feat of endurance in the February heat ('went on and on', thought Princess Elizabeth[42]), was typical South African banquet food of the day:

WINES	MENU
Sherry/Fruit Cup	Hors d'oeuvres
	Clear Soup
La Gratitude	Grilled Salmon
Nederberg Riesling	Babootie and Rice (Cucumber Sambal and Chutney)
	Iced asparagus and Mayonnaise
Alphen Burgundy 1937	Roast Stuffed Turkey
Chateau Libertas 1940	Green Peas
	Roast Potatoes Salads
Pommery 1937	Ice Cream
Port Liqueurs	Fruit
Cigars cigarettes	Coffee

The fourth item, a popular Malay supper dish, served with Mrs Ball's celebrated chutney (even at that date stocked by Fortnum & Mason, the royal grocers in Piccadilly), and intended to give a local flavour, was eyed suspiciously by the King. 'What is it?' he asked his neighbour, Nellie Watermeyer, wife of the Chief Justice, dubiously. 'Left-overs, sir!' came the prompt reply and everyone guffawed appreciatively at this piece of royal banquet repartee.[43] The City Hall chairs were cruelly hard, the salmon was of course Cape geelbek, the asparagus would have been tinned, the mayonnaise almost certainly Crosse & Blackwell. The turkey, apparently, was well cooked and carved, its gravy handed separately. The ice cream, however, looked astonishing. It was in the design and colours of the Union flag, with a large springbok head shaped in coloured biscuit surmounting it.[44]

The fruit cup was served in deference to the many teetotallers then found in all levels of society; the wines were the best that the then relatively unsophisticated Cape wine industry could produce, although the Alphen Burgundy (not a true Burgundy, but an amalgam of several different varieties: Hermitage (Cinsaut), Shiraz, Gamay, Malbec, Pontac, Petit Verdot and one other) was excellent and ordered by discerning palates in England.[45] It, and the vintage champagne ordered from a recently liberated France, can only really have pleased the sovereigns' palates, loyal though they were to Empire products. The Cape February fruit, set in silver trophies on the tables, and including the celebrated Hanepoot grapes, was of course world class. And it would have been the Queen's first taste of Van der Hum, the sweet South African liqueur made from naartjie peel by the Bertram family.

Despite all the effort and trouble, the occasion did not find unqualified approval. Lascelles wrote home the next day describing 'a terribly slow and dreary dinner ... on very hard little chairs' and that although the Royal Family appeared to enjoy themselves, 'in thirty years of public dinners I can't recall one which caused me greater misery'.[46]

Maybe for him. But when the party finally left, the royal Daimlers had to inch their way through an undispersed, cheering crowd, and so dense and demonstrative was it that, instead of taking the normal five minutes, the journey back to Government House took almost half an hour. It had been Cape Town's supreme day of joy.

In London the next morning Queen Mary, anxiously waiting for news back at Marlborough House, was relieved to find a cypher telegram in response to one she had sent to wish the family good luck at the start of their tour: 'Many thanks for the telegram. We are delighted with our reception which was friendly and enthusiastic in a temperature of 105 [sic] in the shade. Everyone is most kind. Fear you must be very cold. Best love Bertie.'[47]

The following day the Administrator of the Cape and Mrs Carinus, and the mayor, Abe Bloomberg and his chic wife, a former ballet dancer,[48] again received the family outside the City Hall for the official civic welcome. Another royal pavilion had been erected, its modernist design this time closely inspired by that built for the great Victory Parade in London the previous year, and with a similar public address system, it was proudly said. The Council had voted £2 000 to have it built.[49] It was cream-coloured and blue-carpeted and banked with flowers. Before it in radiating circles were arranged 2 750 seats; some were for invited dignitaries and mayors and mayoresses from the surrounding countryside, and the rest sold by the Council to defray expenses. Beyond these were packed more than 20 000 of the diverse citizens of Cape Town, looking on.

Again the sun blazed down, and again, miraculously, the wind did not blow. The Administrator, an upcountry farmer and well known to be a Nationalist, spoke first, briefly, in unaccustomed English. Anxious ears were tuned to detect disloyalty, but his address was gracious and correct enough, even if slightly unenthusiastic, considering Cape Town's tumultuous welcome the previous day. It included what would nowadays be regarded as somewhat disingenuous historicism and ended wishing the visitors an enjoyable and happy journey.[50]

Bloomberg, the mayor, spoke next. There was no such holding back here: the Jewish community in South Africa had thoroughly identified with South Africa's war effort and Britain's standalone position against the Nazis. Since the uncovering of the horrors of the concentration camps in 1945, this admiration had only multiplied. The fact that many Afrikaners had openly sided with the Nazis and remained unrepentant[51] cannot but have helped.

The Jewish Board of Deputies had wired an unequivocal greeting to the Royal Family on their arrival in Cape Town 'as [the] representative body of the Jewish community of the Union with assurances of profound loyalty [and] with warm wishes for a successful tour'. All affiliated synagogues held special services on the first Sabbath of the visit, with special prayers composed by the Chief Rabbi: 'Now that the day hath come for which we had waited and hoped, the day of the visit of our Sovereign ... to our beloved land. And we the children of Israel who dwell in safety under his shadow take part in the national rejoicing and greet them [the Royal Family] with praise and thanksgiving.'[52]

Bloomberg's speech was 'absolutely first class', thought Lady Harlech.[53] With well-rounded vowels (the product of elocution lessons, it was uncharitably said by the fashionable Cape), he piled it on: 'It is my honour and high privilege to welcome ...' etc. And when he mentioned how the King and Queen had bravely stayed on in London during the Blitz, a great cheer interrupted him. This was the very stiff-upper-lip, backs-to-the-wall sort of heroism that was expected of the British sovereigns in their darkest hour and the crowd burst spontaneously into 'For They Are Jolly Good Fellows'. The mentioning of this, and the cheering in response, was to be a leitmotif in the addresses of welcome in all the predominantly English-speaking towns of South Africa,[54] and also in the welcomes from tribal chiefs. Even SP Barnard, the Administrator of the mostly pro-republican Orange Free State, chose to mention this in his speech of welcome in Bloemfontein.[55]

The Loyal Address, in beautiful calligraphy on parchment, was handed to Lascelles. Now the King rose to speak. Everyone braced themselves, for his stammer was well known through rumour and broadcast; even the Queen was seen to tense herself. However, it went perfectly. In his beautiful speaking voice, he delivered his thanks 'on behalf of the Queen, myself and my daughters to the people of the Cape Province and the beautiful city of Cape Town'. Such was the relief that when the Town Clerk, Mervyn Williams, called for three cheers for the Royal Family, the spectators roared themselves hoarse and the cheers and applause continued as the royal party left the dais.

What was it, then, that these thousands upon thousands of such diverse people who made up the population of Cape Town, and indeed of every city of South Africa, were cheering? For the English-speaking population, the reasons for the cheers were unequivocal. Primarily, it was essentially a matter of tribe-ism and the reinforcement of a sense of *belonging* – 'a King was necessary if we have an empire', as even a prickly commentator like Nancy Mitford put it.[56] Stalin too, as Churchill told his doctor, Lord Moran, thought the monarchy bound the Empire together.[57] Tribe-ism extrapolated easily into an espoused political reality. As Victor Norton, the editor of the (locally) very influential *Cape Times*, saw it: 'For the first time in our history South Africa will welcome her reigning sovereign ... to-day ... the long, slow process of South Africa's national evolution is complete ... The King and the Royal Family are no longer over the water; they are here amongst us. When they are sustained by South African soil ... and above all when the King opens his South African Parliament, the sacrament of the kingship of South Africa will have been fulfilled.'[58]

Norton was not beating about the bush here, and the great majority of his readers would have unquestionably warmed to such sentiments. And this was not all. In his leader the next day, referring to the welcome the Royal Family had received, he trusted that it had given them the assurance that they had not landed on strange soil, nor come among people British only by constitutional title, but 'that they are here among their own kins-folk, that they have come home'.[59]

A love of continuity and stability, almost amounting to Shintoism, played a part too. Decades on from the perceived excesses (to Anglo-Saxon eyes) of the French Revolution, much English literature of the nineteenth century helped to foster chivalrous sentiments such as Norton's, from Sir Walter Scott's novels to the many works that drew on the Arthurian legends for inspiration. Most notable among the latter was Tennyson's hugely popular *Idylls of the King*; in addition, there were the many new editions of Malory's equally loved *Le Morte d'Arthur*, expunged of lewdness for that age and given an essentially English touchstone. Together, these gave rise to a vivid, almost quasi-religious myth: an ordered world of a hereditary monarchy, with a strong, honourable king at its head and a beautiful queen at his side. They in turn were surrounded by courtiers with romantic-sounding titles together with gallant and noble knights and their lovely, resourceful ladies, these being finally positioned above loyal subjects with whom they were on benevolently familiar terms.

This mythology had entered into the psyche of English-speaking peoples around the globe and remained there for generations to come, only to be finally tarmacked over, it is suggested (though this can hardly have been her intention), by Mrs Thatcher's era of politics. In the immediate post-war world, however, it remained a potent force.

For most English-speaking South Africans in that era then, the Royal Family stood as an ideal – something apart from and above criticism. The quasi-religious aspect was not played down by commentators. 'The Royal Family,' thought 'The Pilgrim', who wrote a regular and rather impressive column in the Johannesburg *Star*, 'represent a standard of grace which we gain by knowing, even if it is only by virtue of a fleeting glimpse.'[60] To this end, their Christian family values, skilfully portrayed by design in newsreel and film footage and verbally espoused in her speeches and radio broadcasts by Queen Elizabeth, had provided an additionally strong and compelling message in the Bagehot ideal, both in the aftermath of the abdication crisis of 1936 and in the lead-up to war. Hitler had been quick to spot this, and not for nothing had he described the Queen as 'the most dangerous woman in Europe'.

The values the Royal Family represented found a broad appeal across the Empire and even resonated in the still mostly Anglophile, middle-class United States both in peacetime and in war (where they were vividly depicted by Hollywood in hugely popular films such as the Oscar-winning *Mrs Miniver*), among what is nowadays termed by some historians as the Respectable Tendency, that is, family men and their wives who lived or aspired to live decent lives and thereby subscribed to the values that the sovereign represented.

But what made this ideal all the more potent was that the Royal Family were clearly such a happy family unit. Peter Townsend analysed this particular aspect of the Royal Family's appeal, and set down for the record the astonishing affection that such a small family – 'Us Four' as the King put it – was able to generate, and the effect it had on the general public: 'Perpetual currents of it [affection] flowed between them, between father and mother, between sister and sister, between parents and their daughters and back again. Then it radiated outwards to the ends of the world, touching thousands of millions of hearts who sent, rolling back, a massive wave of love to the Royal Family.'[61]

There was undoubtedly, too, a strong element of prestige, for however friendly and in however homely a light the Royal Family were portrayed, they were never to be seen as ordinary. Indeed, in an age where the majority still aspired upwards, they represented the last word in 'pukka', that is, how things were properly (as opposed to flashily or vulgarly) done. English people of all classes at home and in the Empire saw this at once; those from other nationalities and races saw this too, sometimes despite themselves. In this regard, it was gratifying to Smuts's supporters to see the ease with which the humbly though respectably born prime minister, who had carried South Africa's name with such honour to the highest levels on the international stage, mixed with them, in a very real sense fulfilling one of the credos of Kipling's then still often-recited poem, 'If'.

Allied to this, of course, was a strong element of local pride, right across the board – at a national, provincial, city, town and even district level. This, in the context of the tour, pertained particularly to English-speaking South Africans, although undoubtedly Indians, Africans and even Afrikaners must all at times have felt moved by it. This pride manifested itself through a particularly strong English characteristic that, much later in her life, Queen Elizabeth II explained when describing the minutiae of preparations for a state visit to England: 'We like to put on a good show.' This was countered, for the benefit of modern viewers, with 'of course, we don't live like this *all* the time'.

A royal visit in the post-war years was undoubtedly an occasion for putting on a good show: the arrangements made – sometimes almost amounting to stage direction and choreography – in conjunction with the Palace Advance Party and the Central Committee, the military parades and indabas, the decorations in the cities and *dorps*, the food baked and tables set for morning tea parties, right down to a railway sidings painted and gardened – everyone seemed keen to put their best foot forward for the royal visitors and to show their corner of the country at its best.

And there was something more to it: the element of giving and deriving joy. In a colonial, just as in a provincial, world where a social high point in the calendar was a local wedding or a New Year's Eve ball at the country club or town hall, rare royal occasions such as this represented a day of great happiness to participants and onlookers alike, to be remembered for a lifetime. Those who deprecated such sentiments as what would nowadays be called 'uncool' were generally held to be curmudgeonly.

Additionally, for United Party supporters everywhere, of whom since the 'khaki' election of 1943 technically at least a third were Afrikaans – the so-called *Bloedsappe*, with additional wartime adherents – and who had thereby endorsed Smuts's execution of the South African war effort, there was here an undoubted element of a deferred Victory Parade – *We Have Won the War!*[62] For the first three years of the war, when the fortunes of the Allies were at their nadir, this had seemed far from certain. Nationalist politicians had taunted Smuts and his party across the floor of the House of Assembly, and their supporters made no secret of the pleasure that news of any Allied reverse or deaths provided.[63] The fall of Tobruk and the capture of 10 722 South African troops was a case in point. Now, with victory two years behind them and with the King in whose name they had gone off to fight in person before them, they let loose their pent-up feelings.

This aspect of the visit was to be subtly underscored again and again during the tour by impressive military parades, reviews of ex-servicemen, and investitures at which South Africans received awards earned during the war from the King. Again and again, the King and Queen were to thank South Africans for their contribution to the war effort. It was a message that was spelt out in a spirit of togetherness and camaraderie. And in those days this went further still. Preserved at Windsor Castle are letters from ex-servicemen in England, writing to the King as he prepared to embark, asking him to thank South Africans 'for the welcome and many kindnesses shown to us troops during our stay there [which] made us glad and proud to belong to such a Christian Empire'.[64]

For the Cape coloureds and Muslims, who numbered 928 484 (mostly in the Cape, and 54 000 of them still on the electoral and municipal voters' roll),[65] there must have been, apart from the cheerful, happy-go-lucky delight in all festivities that set the Cape in a party mood, a vaguely held notion that the imperial connection was their last bulwark against the rampant racism and separatism then being espoused by the Nationalist Opposition. If so, this was a hollow belief, for since the Statute of

Westminster of 1931, the Union had been thoroughly independent of London, even though a rarely used right of criminal appeal to the Privy Council in London was retained until its abolition in 1950.

And although coloureds and Malays still lived in pockets among whites in the various electoral wards in Cape Town, and although a robed official from the Muslim community was invited onto the dais on the Grand Parade, it would be hard to describe the celebrations even in the more liberal-minded Cape as being unsegregated as we understand the term today. The neatly marshalled schoolchildren lining the long drive south to Simon's Town on the third day were separated by colour, as indeed were their schools.

The Civic Ball held in the City Hall on day two was an all-white affair; on the third night there was a Coloured Ball – at least held in the same venue – that began with 'prominent members of the Non-European community being presented in the mayor's parlour'.[66] The ball itself included the old-fashioned State Quadrille, the Lancers and what Princess Elizabeth and the London press described as old-fashioned Barn Dances. The latter was in fact the old Cape '*tiekiedraai*' (threepenny turn); these were watched with delight by the Royal Family from the royal box. This separate event was not generally regarded as offensive at the time.[67] Having loudly cheered the Royal Family standing above them (the Queen now in a gold sequin-encrusted crinoline and her diamonds), the coloured community, a significant body of ex-servicemen among them, acknowledged both the man who had defied Hertzog in 1939 and the man who had made the civic gesture the ball must have represented to them. They called for Smuts and Bloomberg; the King motioned them forward and they were cheered vigorously.

'The main thing,' wrote *The Sun* (a newspaper with a generally conservative coloured readership), 'is that the Coloured people are still intensely loyal as they ever have been and full of the old tradition that cannot be rooted out, as witness the fact that in wars they are ever ready to offer their services wherever these may be required.'[68]

Between four and five thousand members of the coloured and Muslim communities attended the ball in force, among them the Van der Byls' five housemaids,[69] whose tickets had been secured for them by their employers, and who, after hours of preparation, were sent off in the ministerial car 'mad with excitement'.[70] To cope with the numbers, the City Hall – itself 'packed to suffocation'[71] – was linked to the Drill Hall. Peter Townsend later recalled 'a dense throng, gaudily dressed, [who] swung with frenzied enjoyment', typically greeting the amused royal guests with unabashed, shrill cries of 'Hello, you darlings!' and 'Oh, you're so pretty!'[72]

There were coloureds and Malays on the Cape Town City Council in those pre-apartheid days. The Queen, having met Councillor Ahmed Ismail, had adroitly expressed her wish to see and hear the Cape Malays singing their traditional airs and songs; this was arranged at the last minute as a surprise for the Royal Family. The City Hall presented 'a remarkable study for the ethnologist', thought Captain Lewis Ritchie, RN, the Royal Press Secretary, who nightly wrote up the official Tour Diary.[73] Ismail and the other non-white councillors attending the ball were given their own box or bay in the City Hall; other white officials attending were merely allotted seats in a roped-off section of the gallery. Of course, many of the dancers, like the Van der Byls' maids, are unlikely to have been very politically minded; Cissie Gool and her activist colleagues of the National Liberation League had probably not, at this date, greatly impinged on the minds of the generality of such people.

Ismail, anyway, had sent a very dampening telegram to Yusuf Dadoo, the more radical President of the South African Indian Congress, saying that in view of the immediate and widespread response of loyalty from every quarter, 'my advice to my people is not to drag politics and grievances we suffer from into the royal visit'.[74] This, as we shall see on pp 167–176, is not what Dadoo wanted to hear. The threat of boycott and disturbances remained, for the time being, a real one. The more politically prescient among these communities had drawn hope from how, at the first session of the United Nations, a few months previously, the prime minister, who had actually rewritten the preamble to its charter, had been hoist with his own petard by Vijaya Pandit, Nehru's sister, who had successfully censured South Africa for its policies of segregation of its Indian population.

Being arraigned by Indians before the newly formed international body with which their prime minister had been centrally involved had sent shockwaves through much of white political post-war South Africa, where a majority of the electorate still felt comfortable with the norms and ways of a Commonwealth composed of white-run Dominions. Many of them regarded it as a double treachery.

First, that the (local) Indians, who had prospered so nicely under the South African sun, had taken a matter of domestic politics to uppity politicians from a not-yet-independent India in order that they might raise it, not in Commonwealth conclaves in Whitehall, but at the United Nations, was considered bad enough. It smacked of washing one's dirty linen in public. Second, that that new body, where the prime minister had seemed, until recently, to be such a revered figure, could criticise a member state on a matter of internal policy and then, with the support of the United States (until recently, too, an ally in war), successfully pass censure on their country, was nothing short of shocking. They thought the whole business deplorable.

White liberals did not agree; others saw it for what it was. Smuts, as we shall see in Chapter 5, was far too intelligent not to spot the apparent dichotomy which had raised its head so ominously, between his role as an internationalist at the United Nations and his domestic role as prime minister of a segregated South Africa. And yet if few of his supporters in South Africa had as yet grappled with this conundrum, particularly fraught as it was to them in the developing new world order, it has also to be said that many of the technically oppressed were evidently happily swept along by the heady presence of royalty, rather than showing any great willingness to obey their political leaders' wishes to make the occasion of the visit one for voicing their dissatisfaction.

The cheers of the black population are still less easy to understand. Their number in Cape Town then was small – 34 408 in all, although up from a mere 14 317 before the war,[75] for Smuts had relaxed the statutory influx control in order to man the factories as part of the war effort.

Yet elsewhere, of course, they were by far the largest sector of the Union's total population. And elsewhere too they were to turn out in great numbers to cheer, making the tour the last occasion for an outpouring of black loyalty in South Africa.[76] Again, there was a belief that the Crown was a last bulwark against racist policy, and the general democratisation

The King invests Prime Minister Jan Smuts with the Order of Merit in
the ballroom at Government House.
TRANSNET HERITAGE LIBRARY PHOTO COLLECTION

process resulting from the war years had certainly raised expectations for a
more egalitarian future. For the time being, however, blacks remained dispossessed. Fully disenfranchised like the Indians in 1936, their respective
political arms – the African National Congress and its Youth League and
the South African Indian Congress, buoyed up by the great events at the
United Nations and the plans for independence being rolled out by the
King's cousin in India itself – sought to boycott the tour for political gain,
while insisting (for form's sake) that this was not intended as disrespect

to Their Majesties.

In the event, as we shall see, it is clear these boycotts failed to spoil the tour significantly; Indians and Africans were there in their tens of thousands, both at the planned indabas, arguably intended in part to reinforce the relationship between tribal chiefs and the House of Windsor, but also in the urban areas, where no such political agenda could possibly be suggested. Since the days of Victoria, the Crown had been generally perceived as a beneficent and colour-blind power, and, despite a patent (constitutional) inability to act as such, a protector against white rapacity. The Crown generated a remarkable amount of black loyalism during the war and up to and beyond 1947. In terms of the tour itself, it had its less abstract appeal – not only because of the edifying family values it embodied, but also through pageantry, glitter and, it must be said, social consequence then not routinely available in an already very segregated society.

For many die-hard Afrikaner Nationalists, however – conservative and inward-looking by nature, bitter through years of being politically out-manoeuvred by the English, and who comprised just over half the white population – the tour was a deep affront. Indeed, in some quarters, it could be said that it came close to waving the proverbial red flag at a bull.

Smuts to them had long been seen as a *hensopper* (hands-upper, or defeatist) at the end of the Anglo-Boer War, and subsequently as a lackey of their long-standing foe, the British. Appearing too clever by half to the insular and poorly educated – *Slim Jannie* (Clever Jannie, but also by implication tricky and manipulative[77]), as his Afrikaner opponents and detractors sneeringly called him – they despised his formidable intellect and his ability to walk the international stage as a great man.

Having narrowly led the country into a war they opposed and many hoped would end in Britain's defeat and sever the imperial connection forever, he had emerged from it seemingly triumphant and temporarily, at least, on a high moral ground, with his international reputation greater than ever before. It must have been galling in the extreme. Now, with an election approaching in 1948 and facing, as his opposition, a revitalised Afrikaner Ascendancy with a strong republican sentiment, his welcoming of the Royal Family was seen as political manoeuvring to gain electoral support.

It was the last straw. The right-wing Nationalist press inflamed this opinion, at times waxing catatonic, as Evelyn Baring put it,[78] in their unrelenting hatred of the British connection. They either ignored or downplayed the tour or wrote unobliging and uncomplimentary articles about it, doubtless goaded further by the enthusiasms of the English-speaking press.

There was, however, in the mid-1940s, no general cohesion among Afrikaans-speaking South Africans on the issue of a republic, and the royal tour was to throw this vividly into relief. Many Afrikaner officials and their wives readily accepted the gilt-edged invitations to gala events, bowing and curtsying to the sovereigns, and many others flocked to road and railway to stare in fascination in a pre-celebrity, pre-television age. Yet this did not necessarily correspond to vote changing. Indeed, as Baring declared flatly at the end of the visit, 'The royal tour will not change any votes.'[79]

Nor did it, significantly. But the royal tour, with its royal banquets and garden parties, its gloved waves and handshakes, its military parades and its undoubted celebration of Englishness and the imperial connection in a colonial setting, was and remained for many South Africans of that generation, a defining moment in their lives. For many Anglo-South Africans too, as we shall see, it was to be a last hurrah before they were eclipsed, in political terms at least, for ever.

⊰§⊱

CHAPTER 2

The State Opening of Parliament and the Question of the Imperial Connection

21 February 1947

Four days after the State Entry into Cape Town, on 21 February, the King was scheduled to perform his most important engagement of the tour. This was the opening of the South African Parliament, in which all laws were promulgated in his name as constitutional monarch of South Africa. The South Africa Act of 1909 specifically stated that 'the legislative power of the Union is vested in the Parliament of the Union and that Parliament consists of the King, the Senate and the House of Assembly'. In some ways, the Statute of Westminster of 1931 made this more immediate; in 1937 George VI had been crowned at Westminster Abbey not only King of England, but King of the Union of South Africa too.

The King's state portrait in oils by Sir Gerald Kelly was destined to hang in the House of Assembly; in photograph his image hung everywhere – in government buildings, in men's clubs, sports clubs, scout halls and schools. It appeared in profile on coins and medals, and in full face on bank notes and commemorative stamps; his cypher G VI RI appeared on everything from government documents to pillar boxes on street corners.

As in matters temporal, so in matters spiritual. This was still a church-going age. Every Sunday, prayers were offered up across the Union during Anglican matins (then a more popular service than communion) for the

King's Majesty from the Book of Common Prayer, whose beautiful and, to many, reassuring words and phrases had echoed unchanged down the generations:

> Almighty and everliving God ... We beseech thee also to lead all nations in the way of righteousness and peace; and so to direct all kings and rulers, that under them thy people may be godly and quietly governed. And grant unto thy servant GEORGE, our King, and to all that are put in authority under him, that they may truly and impartially minister justice, to the punishment of wickedness and vice, and to the maintenance of thy true religion, and virtue.

Prayers were also said for the Royal Family: 'Elizabeth, Our Queen, Mary, the Queen Mother.' It was not only Anglicans but also Methodists and some other Nonconformist sects who prayed thus; similarly, the various mission churches who all used the same prayer books. Jewish congregations, too, used words that were very similar – and equally beautiful – in their morning service for sabbaths and festivals, calling on God to bless:

> ... Our Sovereign Lord, George, Our Gracious Queen, Elizabeth, Mary the Queen Mother, The Princess Elizabeth, and all the Royal Family. May the supreme King of kings in his mercy preserve the King in life, guard and deliver him from all trouble and sorrow. May he put the spirit of wisdom and understanding into his heart and into the hearts of all his counsellors, that they may uphold the peace of the realm, advance the welfare of the nation and deal kindly and truly with all Israel. In his day and ours, may our Heavenly Father spread the tabernacle of peace over all the dwellers on earth; and may the redeemer come unto Zion.[1]

No such prayer pertained in the Dutch Reformed Church congregations, although the Cape branches had, in the nineteenth century, matched their loyalism to Queen Victoria with prayers for Her Majesty on important occasions. When, during the tour, the Royal Family attended the Dutch Reformed Church service in Pretoria, prayers were said for the guidance of the King as head of state.[2] Notwithstanding this, out of a total population of 11418349 in 1946, at least 70 per cent of South Africans and possibly more, if questioned at that date, would have unhesitatingly recognised the King as their head of state.

Although the Royal Family emerged from the war more popular than ever, and the King's enemies were indeed scattered and fallen, their politics 'confounded' and their 'knavish tricks frustrated' (in the words of the rarely sung second verse of the national anthem),[3] the Empire looked rather less invincible. Where possible, therefore, a subtle reaffirmation of the imperial order of things was seen as essential post-1945.

After the defeats and the loss of face in the first years of the war – Hong Kong and Crete, for example, and most especially Singapore – the voyage out on the *Vanguard* had been orchestrated by the Admiralty to trumpet, via newsreel, the all-important issue of imperial defence through the continued strength and benefits of the Royal Navy. This was showcased by the ceremonial departure from Portsmouth, the escorts from England impressively handing over to those of the South Atlantic Station off Freetown, mid-Atlantic visits to inspect the escorts and other passing Royal Naval vessels,[4] and so on. Even the weekly mailboat and passenger service, the *Cape Town Castle* of the Union-Castle Line, passed *Vanguard* in the South Atlantic with its flags flying, its crew and passengers all lining the decks and cheering, and receiving a royal salute in return.

In a similar vein, the royal opening of Parliament was designed to underscore, unambiguously, the issue of the imperial connection, which, since the outbreak of war, had become openly divisive within the Union. Republican noises were a cause for alarm among several other countries in the post-war Commonwealth and Empire, too. Pathé News was at this time shown weekly around the world as a curtain-raiser to the public of the great cinema-going age; at a more popular level, its commentaries were regarded almost as influential as the leader page of the London *Times*. A list of the then board members of the Pathé News company – Lord Rothermere among them – provides a useful clue to its Reithian, calming and pro-establishment reporting.

Over impressive footage of *Vanguard* entering Table Bay, the emollient and persuasive tones of the famously patrician voiceover explained to his viewers around the English-speaking world that the tour was, for the Crown, 'a mission of the greatest significance. Consider the state of the Commonwealth and Empire today ...' he asked the audience, rhetorically: 'India after two hundred years of British Rule, regains her independence; British troops leave Egypt; Palestine sets the Middle East ablaze. Against this background, South Africa assumes its real importance.'[5]

The timing of the tour had therefore been deliberately planned to coincide with this annual February ceremony, when Parliament reassembled in Cape Town, the Union's legislative capital. It was normally performed by his representative, in the person of the Governor-General; now the King was to appear in person to emphasise his role as King of South Africa and to follow, to some extent, the precedents set at Westminster, where a non-party, constitutional monarchy was seen to work effectively in the birthplace of parliamentary democracy. As if to make the point more strongly, the Governor-General was absent from the Senate Chamber that morning.

This was the first time a reigning monarch had performed this ceremony in one of his dominions. There was a ceremonial as well as a constitutional aspect to the February ceremony in Cape Town. Sir Patrick Duncan, the former Governor-General, always dreaded it, and the prospect of a speech from the throne must have made the King dread it too – 'repeated spasms of stage fright which gave me great trouble', as Lascelles noted.[6] Yet he and the Queen were aware of this double significance. Again they drove from Government House in state, down the cheering streets lined with the old Cape regiments – The Duke of Edinburgh's Own Rifles (The Dukes) and the Cape Town Highlanders and schoolboy cadet detachments – the King once again in his Royal Navy white tropical uniform trimmed with gold braid. The Queen was now seen to wear the third tiara since her arrival, this time a high affair and one, it was learnt, lent by her mother-in-law Queen Mary, and made up of the South African diamonds given to her during the royal visit of 1901. This, the two Queens believed, would give pleasure locally.

Once the car had pulled up at the Senate, the full extent of the planned royal pageantry was apparent. The entrance was through a pair of splendid Victorian cast-iron gates, and on up a long flight of stone steps, lined by

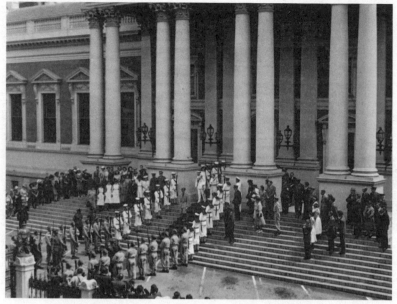

Royal pageantry: the King and Queen leave Parliament, preceded by
Wing Commander Peter Townsend, the King's Equerry, flanked by
the South African armed forces on the steps.

men from the South African Air Force and the Navy, to the door of the
imposing edifice, whose sober red-brick façade was offset by white plaster
columns and drip mouldings. Against this and the new, specially ordered
red carpet, the royal couple appeared dazzling, both wearing white in the
sunshine. Here again, Hartnell's talent for designing gowns for state occasions was seen at its best. The Queen's figure-fitting dress, much described
in the newspapers of the day, was of chalk-white silk crêpe, embroidered
with aquamarines and paillettes of crystal and blue which toned with her
blue sash of the Garter and set off her vivid Celtic colouring.[7] From her
shoulders her cape sleeves fell to the floor and beyond, so that they trailed
behind her up the entrance steps and down those from her throne, showing to great advantage on the newsreels of the event.

Inside, the Senate Chamber was crowded and extra seats had been
placed in the Queen's Hall which adjoined it and in the gallery beyond.

The King and Queen at the State Opening of Parliament. Lady Harlech stands to
the left of the Queen, with the representatives of the Union Defence Force
flanking the thrones.

TRANSNET HERITAGE LIBRARY PHOTO COLLECTION

Even the Nationalist Opposition attended, though JG Strijdom – a future
prime minister – remained outside throughout, ostentatiously smoking.
The invitations stipulated 'Dress: Formal'; in 1947, this meant the men
wore morning coats or lounge suits and the women long day or, occasionally, in the spirit of austerity, short, dresses, hats and gloves.

At forty seconds to noon, two Air Force trumpeters stationed at the door
of the Senate Chamber sounded a flourish that echoed through the Houses
of Parliament. From Signal Hill came the sounds of guns firing the royal

salute. Holding the Queen's hand in his right at shoulder height, the King processed slowly up the aisle to the thrones, behind the Gentleman Usher of the Black Rod, JP du Toit – *Swart Roede*, it said, in translation, on the opposite page of the Order of Ceremony – in his tail coat, knee breeches and buckled shoes and bearing his gold-topped staff of office.

They were followed by Sir Alan Lascelles, KCB, KCVO, CMG, MC (Private Secretary to His Majesty) and Lady Harlech, the Queen's Lady-in-Waiting, also wearing a tiara; Wing Commander Townsend DSO, DFC (Equerry in Waiting to His Majesty) and Major General J Mitchell-Baker, CB, CBE, DSO (Honorary Aide-de-Camp to His Majesty); General Sir Pierre van Ryneveld, KBE, CB, DSO, MC (Chief of the General Staff, Union Defence Force); Major General RJ Palmer, DSO, and Lieutenant Colonel PG de Wit (representing the South African Police); Commodore FJ Dean, OBE, and Commander WJ Copenhagen, OBE, VD (Sea); Brigadier JT Durrant, CB, DFC, and Colonel BG Viljoen, OBE (Air); and Major General WHE Poole, CB, CBE, DSO, and Brigadier P de Waal, CB CBE (Land).

Having handed the Queen to her throne, and keeping his head covered, the King took his seat and announced, 'Gentlemen, please be seated.'[8] With a rustle of barathea and silk, the assembly took their seats. The rest of the procession arranged themselves in strict order behind them.[9]

He then read his speech from the throne. As was constitutionally correct, much of it was written by his prime minister, who was well aware of the difficulties it might present. ('We have made the Speech as brief and simple as possible, so as not to impose on His Majesty too much of a strain in the reading of it,' he wrote to his Quakeress correspondent, Margaret Gillett.)[10] Smuts needn't have worried on this score. The King delivered the speech in a clear and ringing voice. He did not hesitate to thank South Africa for its contribution to the war effort, though he naturally passed over the fact that just under half the white population had technically voted for neutrality in 1939. Doubtless, Smuts's impressive electoral win in 1943 made it easier for him to do this. He did not, and could not, say – as he was to do in his reply to the Native Address in Salisbury – that he wished 'to thank you [all] in person not only for your loyalty during the war, which I never doubted ...'[11]

As was customary, he mentioned legislation due to be passed in the forthcoming session – 'additional estimates of expenditure for the current financial year and estimates for the coming financial year will be laid before you' – and declared Parliament open. Then, to the astonishment of everyone, the King spoke in Afrikaans. The Royal Family had been given Afrikaans lessons in London by Mr BJ Fourie from the High Commission, though this could obviously have not progressed far beyond *goeiemôre, dankie* and *totsiens*. The sentence had been learned onomatopoeically. A note in Lascelles' files in the Windsor Archives shows its content, arranged through correspondence between Lascelles and Fourie ('a phonetic version of this sentence showing how an Englishman ought to pronounce it' was how the request was put[12]), thus:

> Eck ferrklähr tonce hirdee feearde serrie fon der neachinde parliament fon der Unie fon Säyd Afrikah behoorlik gue-oopen.[13]

It was a stout effort. He struggled through it, recalled Major Piet van der Byl, where most people would have been tempted to garble through the Afrikaans wording.[14] The Queen smiled at its completion and a murmur of delight and even a smattering of applause broke out in the Senate, though the next day the virulent Nationalist press was quick to pour scorn on the attempt.

The proceedings over, the couple left the Senate, the ladies and gentlemen of both the government and opposition bowing and curtsying deeply as they passed. Even Mrs Malan did. Again, the Nationalist press derided this particularly alien and offensive (to them) form of obsequiousness. Republicanism had been an open part of the platform of the Herenigde Nasionale Party (HNP) since 1942 and its supporters were anxious to emphasise this attitude in their reporting of such an occasion. Indeed, the very ceremony that so delighted Anglo-South Africa, with its strong echoes of Westminster procedure and flummery, merely succeeded in rubbing salt in the wounds of many of the die-hard HNP Opposition and their supporters, wounds that had festered since the outbreak of war and whose causes lay a long way back before then.

* * *

The Union of South Africa had emerged from the Second World War much as Smuts had hoped: with honour and as a nation enhanced at many levels in the eyes of the world. It was richer, greatly more industrialised, and occupied, along with other Allied nations, a high moral ground. It even had the edge over them, for it was well known that in 1939 it had almost, like Ireland, voted for neutrality, only narrowly committing to support Britain because of the deft actions of the man now its prime minister, in living memory a Boer enemy of England. Smuts, as we shall see presently, had cleverly avoided presenting his declaration of war as an obvious, general show of imperial support, but had cited instead the danger of world domination by the Nazis and the more immediate risk of Germany demanding the return of South West Africa, governed by the Union as a C-Class Mandated Territory in accordance with the Treaty of Versailles. By then many South Africans regarded it as a de facto fifth province.

In the world conflict, South Africa had fought gallantly in East and North Africa and in Europe, the Middle and Far East, and its harbours and citizens had vitally welcomed Allied shipping laden with troops and supplies, denied a passage through Gibraltar and the Mediterranean. Medals and citations for bravery had showered down on South Africa's sons and daughters. There had been no conscription in the Union and all its soldiers were volunteers.[15] Just over half of the 210 000 whites were Afrikaans-speaking. There were, in addition, 45 000 coloured and 123 000 black servicemen.

Material aid in the form of money, food and clothing parcels had flowed to England from the civilian population. At the height of the Battle of Britain, even Spitfires had been funded by public subscription; East London, for example, had presented one, as had the industrial giant Iscor. Durban sponsored an entire squadron.

Abroad, South Africans in or out of uniform were popular as never before. 'Gentlemen, we have a South African in our midst to-night; drinks all round on the house!'[16] was an oft-repeated chestnut heard across South African dinner tables by the chattering classes of the day, delightedly quoting a wartime English publican's purported utterance. And so it went. One of the heroes of the Battle of Britain had the very

South African heroes: Sailor Malan (*left*), the Battle of Britain fighter ace who
later led the Torch Commando campaign against apartheid,
and Roger Bushell (*right*), a leader of the Great Escape.

DITSONG NATIONAL MUSEUM OF MILITARY HISTORY AND IMPERIAL WAR MUSEUM

Afrikaans-sounding name of Adolph Malan (fortuitously, perhaps, with
the very English-sounding nickname of 'Sailor');[17] one of the heroes of
the Great Escape was Roger Bushell, the good-looking son of a popular
mine manager from Springs; the family were well known socially and had
a holiday house in Hermanus.[18]

Thus, as the war progressed, the flagging spirit of Union – that is, the
1910 union of the two predominant white races – was held to be working
once more. Indeed, the 'khaki' election held in 1943 appeared to have dramatically changed the political landscape. Instead of the slender margin
of 13 seats by which the Union had voted to go to war in 1939, Smuts was
returned with a comfortable overall majority of 67.

This, at any rate, was the official version and it was a true one in so
far as it went. English-speaking South Africa basked in patriotic self-
satisfaction; the royal tour was widely and gratifyingly seen as a thank-you
by the monarchs for the South African war effort and to set the seal on the
country's future as a Dominion under the British Crown. But the reality
was far more complex. Writing in 1942 to Lady Selborne, widow of the

Governor of the Transvaal and Orange River colonies and her husband's chief political correspondent, Lady Duncan, the Governor-General's wife, described how proud South Africa could be of its war effort, but honesty compelled her to add what was painfully evident to her in her position: 'although we are a very divided country'.[19]

In truth, the divisions were there for anyone (not only Lady Duncan) remotely politically prescient to see.[20] South Africans – even white South Africans – led curiously parallel lives, knowing little of their fellow countrymen's ways, and disliking and distrusting what they occasionally witnessed. To the Afrikaners, the English seemed superior and stuck up (*opgesmuk*), patronising ('My dear, Afrikaans, but *perfectly* nice,' was a typical whispered aside of the era) and annoyingly confident; women of the type of Lady Duncan, Joy van der Byl and Jean Lawrence – the 'burra mems' we have already encountered on the royal pavilion in Chapter 1 – were their particular *bêtes noires*.

There was, however, an overriding grievance. English-speaking South Africans were seen as having divided loyalties. This was perfectly true, for well into the twentieth century, the majority of English-speakers regarded themselves as part of the British world and saw South Africa as an integral part of it.[21] And they were proud of it. When great crowds of South Africans from predominantly English-speaking towns such as Cape Town, Port Elizabeth, Durban and Johannesburg loudly sang 'Land of Hope and Glory' before the Royal Family, they did so because they felt they were spiritually and emotionally encompassed by the 'wider still and wider' set bounds of Great Britain. Canadians, Australians and New Zealanders felt the same way too, they knew, and no amount of voiced Afrikaner dissatisfaction on this score would cause them to let up on this one.

This absolute belief would be succinctly defended by BK Long in the famous war debate in Parliament in September 1939. Referring to English-speaking South Africans' sentiments towards the country of their origin, he said: 'That does not mean that we do not love this country, that does not mean that we put the interests of Great Britain first, but it means we have a love for Great Britain and the British Isles that does not transcend but which is part of our love of our own country.' He then expressed an old-fashioned, patriotic sentiment that all those he spoke to would have understood: 'We would be craven, cowardly and despicable if we did not hold those sentiments towards the country of our origin.'[22]

Not surprisingly, in the republican era that began in 1961 there was a concerted, official attempt to attach a feeling of unpatriotic shame to such sentiments. This was markedly assisted by Britain's cultural boycott of the country at that time and a generally held perception of Britain's diminished status under successive Labour governments.

In the New South Africa, the opprobrium attached to the very term 'colonial' has made such an Anglophile standpoint, even if only residually retained, undesirable and actually offensive. This would have been met with indignation and even scorn back then. Before the war, English-speaking South Africans referred constantly to 'Home' (Britain), an idealised country where everything from Shakespeare to broad beans and brogues was held to be better. Many of them would visit it only once in a lifetime. And sometimes never. Of course it was an old colonial prop. If English-speaking South Africans accepted in their hearts that as colonials they passed as second rate, they consoled themselves with the belief that being British colonials they passed at least as first-class second rate. There is no need to suppose an issue of low self-esteem here. Generally speaking, in the world of British middle- and lower-middle-class values then pertaining, foreigners began at Calais, Germans were trouble-makers, while Americans were vaguely understood to live in an undesirable world of skyscrapers, gangsters, divorce, hot dogs and Hollywood. There was an additional grievance that the United States had entered the First World War late and had tried to take all the credit for victory. The rest of the nationalities of the world occupied a lower status still.

The term 'Home' passed out of common usage in the 1950s.[23] Nevertheless, England still remained the standard against which all was compared and judged. An excellence in many fields that would be difficult to equal is naturally an uncomfortable one. This therefore remained an endless source of annoyance. To the old Boer term for an Englishman living on the veld – *rooinek* – was added a cruder one that referred to this especial grievance – *soutpiel*, suggesting that Englishmen had one foot in South Africa and another in England, their male organs thus dangling in the sea. (*Rooinek* referred to their propensity to sunburn, and should not be confused with 'redneck', its literal translation, which in the United States has an entirely different meaning.)

To the English, on the other hand, the Afrikaners therefore seemed not only chippy on this score but also boorish, uneducated (by which they really meant uncultured or unsophisticated) and incompetent. They were dismissive or, worse, snubbing. It did not help that most urban Afrikaners they came across in the early twentieth century were classified as 'poor whites'. This was an underclass. As the open frontier disappeared and as farms were divided among huge families in accordance with Roman-Dutch law, many Boers were unable to make the transition from subsistence farming to a cash economy and market-related agriculture. This, combined with successive disasters – the rinderpest plague and the devastation brought about by the Anglo-Boer War among them – resulted in a rapid and largely traumatic urbanisation that many Afrikaners were ill-equipped to weather, finding businesses in the towns almost exclusively controlled by the English and Jews.[24]

Yet such issues, significant though they were, were not the sole reasons for the divide. As education became more widespread, some Afrikaners embraced metropolitan standards. Not all of them were poor whites, anyway, just as not all Englishwomen were Joy van der Byls or Jean Lawrences, either. Religion, a sense of humour and points of reference all played a part in fostering these separate identities and apartness; at a less esoteric level, so too did cooking, clothes and even the way people furnished their homes.

As always, the women set the pace in much of this, as sport sometimes allowed for fraternising among the men. Children might learn to play together if allowed (this occasionally went for playmates across the colour line, too, in rural districts), but if the young of that era were actually quizzed about the difference between their home and that of an English or Afrikaans counterpart, their reply would invariably be 'It *smelt* different'. Many English children of the period remember Afrikaans homes as being strangely darkened and overly polished.[25] The celebration of Christmas in English-speaking homes, with its customs of carols, spruce, flaming plum puddings and listening to the King's broadcast, must have then contrasted almost tribally with that in Afrikaans-speaking households.

It must be said at once that these of course are generalisations.

Intermarriage was not as uncommon as might be suggested here, although frequently accompanied by parental misgivings or dismay. At official political levels a polite tolerance – Good Behaviour – was required,[26] and in some country districts the two tribes learnt to rub along together well enough.[27] Yet even so, Doris Lessing vividly recreates the very real strains of such a relationship, necessitated by country distances, in the opening pages of *Martha Quest*. It also goes without saying that such a gulf was only amplified across the colour line, where contact was almost exclusively confined to officialdom, that between individuals almost all being on the basis of master-servant relationships.

Insular and suspicious in a magnificent yet generally harsh land they all believed to be their own, each sector of the population created worlds within worlds for themselves, their families and their tribespeople, and, despite all political efforts, remained generally as unmixable as oil and water.[28]

Post-war visitors from England, delighting in a land of sunshine and plenty (and themselves from a highly class-conscious society), were much struck by this. 'I never saw a country where everyone disliked everyone else so much. Afrikaners hated the English and vice versa and both hated the Jews; whites hated the Indians and Blacks, the Blacks hated the Indians and this was all returned in kind,' recalled businessman Sir John Carden in early 1948. 'I saw at once it would never work.'[29]

Even Queen Elizabeth, always a great optimist, saw this as a real problem: 'such a complex country, with the white races quarrelling and hating each other'.[30] And the King certainly did too. One evening, looking down furiously on the country's motto embossed on the tablecloth of the White Train, *Ex Unitate Vires* (From Unity, Strength), he was seen to hit his fist on the table and heard to remark crossly, 'Not much *unitate* about this place!'[31]

The roots of the nation's divisions – that is, particularly between English and Afrikaans speakers – were not merely of twentieth-century origin; they went all the way back to the start of the nineteenth century, when the world's then most powerful nation took over the Cape of Good Hope to secure the sea route to its empire in the east. In doing so, it inherited not only warlike black tribes within, on and beyond its borders, but an indigenous white population of Dutch farmers who were both backward and fiercely independent.

The new governing class was determined to introduce policies in line with current thought and usage in Britain and elsewhere in the Empire. And thus it was not long before the new administration fell out with the more intransigent, backwoods members of this white tribe who, faced with what they considered outrageous new laws – the emancipation of their slaves, equality before the law (that is, between a master and non-European servant), and many other related and imagined grievances that seemed to threaten their traditional ways – decided to quit the Cape altogether. A small but significant group packed up and, in a movement that repeated on semi-organised lines their century-old haphazard advancement of the frontier, trekked north out of the colony.

Although numerically a small percentage of the total Cape Dutch population, the migration and its subsequent triumphs and disasters came in time to be elevated in folklore as the epic of the entire race – The Great Trek. This, until history was rewritten by more liberal minds in the mid-twentieth century, disguised its real calamity for the country, for with them the trekkers took their primitive Calvinism and an outdated, bigoted belief in a preordained, inexorably segregated way of life. Thus, for another 60 years and more, they recreated and fostered, in their rural, backward-looking, independent republics, the sensibilities of a wild frontier society based on predestination and where the indigenous population was to be forever kept in its place.

It couldn't and didn't last. What was initially for British officialdom a small annoyance beyond the frontier became, in the age of more aggressive imperial expansion, a great thorn in its side. When diamonds and gold were discovered in unimaginable quantities, and immigrants swarmed into these underpopulated lands, the stage was set for a major clash. The Anglo-Boer War (1899–1902) was seen as a Second War of Independence by the Boers. The British saw it as a war to address, ultimately by intervention and conquest, the grievances of the Uitlanders, the unfranchised English-speakers living in President Paul Kruger's Transvaal Republic and who were now its main taxpayers. In the aftermath of the war, Jan Smuts saw its causes quite clearly and philosophically: 'the Boer fought for his independence, the Englishman for his Empire'.[32]

Inevitably, the war ended in a British victory. But it came at a terrible price. Britain, which prided itself on the advancement of civilisation around the globe and fair play, had, in the war's causes and course, exposed herself to accusations of bullying and sharp practice. The Boers, at home on the veld, had proved, despite their inferior numbers, to be a resilient foe, and their adoption of guerrilla tactics prolonged an increasingly expensive and unpopular war long after the Union Jack had been hoisted in Pretoria.

For the British high command, dealing expeditiously with this necessitated a scorched-earth policy of the farming areas and the rounding-up of Boer women and children who had been supplying the commandos, and were thus rendered homeless on the veld, and housing them in temporary concentration camps. These, despite the name associated with Hitler's death camps of 40 years later, were intended for the protection and not the extermination of their occupants. But administrative incompetence, ignorance and disease resulted in an appalling death rate and provided a genuine grievance and trauma that was never to be forgotten or forgiven by a vanquished people.

The surrender, known as the Treaty of Vereeniging, the ultimate humiliation for the Boers, who had survived years of hardship creating their republics and way of life away from British interference,[33] was eventually signed at Pretoria in 1902. It was Jan Smuts, one of the great Boer leaders, who persuaded, with words of great courage and truth, the many who wanted to fight on to face the facts: the end had come. It was by no means easy. Smuts was assailed as a coward and a defeatist by his own friends, and told Churchill, years later, in the train taking them back to London after visiting Eisenhower on the eve of D-Day, that it had been the most difficult hour of his life.[34] Sir Alfred Milner, the British High Commissioner, was inflexible; there was no scope for negotiation – the Transvaal and Orange Free State republics were to be incorporated into the British Empire. Milner and his team of talented young administrators (dubbed 'The Kindergarten') put in hand a reconstruction which, if autocratically executed, was vigorous, generous and modernising.

Presently, however, Britain had a change of heart. The Conservative government that had prosecuted the war was voted out, and the Liberal

Party's victory bought a government into power that made an addition-ally generous offer to an already generous peace. This was Sir Henry Campbell-Bannerman's pledge of self-government. For Smuts, particu-larly, the moment was epiphanous: 'They gave us back our country in everything but name. Has such a miracle of trust and magnanimity hap-pened before? Only people like the English could do it. They may make mistakes, but they are big people.'[35]

Suddenly, everything seemed to have changed. The offer of self-government came on top of generous reparations and reconstruction grants made by the victors, and they now were eager to make friends. Far-sighted Boer leaders, Louis Botha and Jan Smuts in particular, surveying the wreckage of the Boer republics, saw this for what it was – and where it was leading. Inevitably, the more educated among them came round to realising as ultimately improbable the survival of their small, frag-ile republics in a vast, predominantly black continent, and, having been dragged kicking and screaming into the modern world, saw too a world where the benefits of being part of the British Empire were immediately and immensely apparent.

Of course, it was not to be hoped that all Afrikaners would see it like this. Nor did they. The die-hards and conservatives, the *bittereinders* (those who wanted to fight to the bitter end, whatever the cost) and the less educated and – significantly for a strongly matriarchal society – their implacable womenfolk were outraged. This is not what they had fought and died for, and bygones were not going to be let be bygones. Politically unsophisticated and disorganised, poor and displaced in an unfriendly and unfamiliar new age, they were, however, coerced by conciliatory forces temporarily beyond their control into the new Union of South Africa, along with the two older British colonies – the Cape, with its roughly equal populations of English and Dutch,[36] and Natal, whose white voting population was predominantly of British descent.[37]

It was not an easy forging. The Cape, from which the trekkers had set out in the 1830s, had, during the hundred years of British rule, anglicised and softened. Significantly, the settled Dutch and Germans there had ben-efited from a century of prosperity resulting from free trade with Britain. Some – like the Van der Byls, whom we have met, the Melcks and the

Joostes[38] – had become completely anglicised, as mastery of the English language became considered a hallmark of good breeding and an entrée to polite, colonial society. For the rest there were at best multiple identities and loyalties as law-abiding, God-fearing colonists and supporters of the *Bond* – the so-called Queen's Afrikaners.

But there was more to it. The liberal voices of the nineteenth century, against which Piet Retief, Gert Maritz, Anna Steenkamp and their ilk had so determinedly turned their backs in trekking away, had, in 1853, adopted a qualified franchise with no colour bar at the Cape. This was anathema to the Transvaal and Free State. (It was also something of anathema, though they were less vocal, for the rank and file of Natal colonists who, while priding themselves on being in all things British and, until 1896, officially possessing a similar, if stringent, qualified franchise as the Cape, proved, with the advent of responsible government, opposed to adopting a form of universal franchise that could one day threaten their very existence.)

Unification of disparate peoples requires constant compromise. Paramount for English-speaking South Africans was the idea of being welded into a large new Dominion, which, along with Canada, New Zealand and Australia, would play a major role in the British Empire, believed by them to be a force for good in the world and a benefit for all mankind. When Dame Clara Butt, and her many equivalents of that era, sang on stages across a quarter of the globe – then proudly coloured pink on all maps – Arthur Benson's words of Edward Elgar's stirring new anthem, 'Land of Hope and Glory':

> Wider still and wider,
> Shall thy bounds be set
> God who made thee mighty
> Make thee mightier yet!

her audiences saw this as an axiomatic ideal. These consisted not only of English-speaking colonials but also many, many others of diverse race and creed who had bought into the idea of Britishness. They had done so secure in the knowledge that, as British subjects, they had thereby scaled the top of life's tree and were the envy of the rest of the world.

If this union had to be achieved, as it certainly had to be in southern Africa, by accommodation with forces and ideals opposed to much of what the British Empire officially espoused – in this case not only continued Boer intransigence, but kicking into touch the thorny subject of the advancement of the non-white population towards some form of equality – then so be it. Union was a way forward, and once unity was achieved, all would be attainable. And if the future held obvious uncertainties, well, the British prided themselves on their negotiating expertise and their ability to compromise – skills undoubtedly helped at that date by holding most of the good cards in their hand.

It did not work out quite like that. As we shall see in Chapter 5, British promises of equal rights for all civilised men south of the Limpopo would be a major casualty on the compromising road to unification.

The Document of Union was signed in 1910. Louis Botha – only eight years previously Boer commandant-general of the Transvaal forces – became prime minister and leader of the South African Party, which advocated an amalgam of Afrikaans and English South Africans. This, on the face of it, was a startling surprise. But the British, determined to make the new Union work, had jettisoned the more experienced (and liberal) Cape elder statesman, John X Merriman, knowing that a popular Afrikaner head of state was an essential in this new order. Smuts, cleverer though less obviously popular with the *volk* (people), became Botha's deputy.

Almost at once the idea of union was tested, and it became apparent that the political dynamic of the new nation would not initially be one of a struggle between black and white supremacy, but between Afrikaans and English. JBM Hertzog, another Boer leader, and less accommodating than Botha and Smuts, was aware of the deep dissatisfaction among large sections of the *volk*. This was particularly acute in the almost wholly Afrikaans-speaking Orange Free State and the more rural districts of the Transvaal.

In these parts of the country, the supporters of Hertzog and his key ally, former Free State president Marthinus Steyn, were angered by what they saw as Botha and Smuts's sell-out to the British. As early as 1908, Botha had attended the Inter-Colonial Conference in London; he had also masterminded the presentation of the Cullinan diamond to Edward VII as a token of loyalty from the Transvaal Colony. These moves were eyed by many of his people at best suspiciously or more generally with total disgust. Worse, however, was the Cambridge-educated Smuts's declaration that Dutch should only be taught in schools until Standard 4 (the class for 11-year-olds). Thereafter, English was to be the language of education.

Hertzog knew his audience and, in 1913, he seized the political opportunity, forming the breakaway National Party, far more openly geared to Afrikaner nationalism. He was helped at this early juncture of nationhood by the outbreak of the First World War. Botha and Smuts saw the conflict as an opportunity to prove South Africa's mettle as a Dominion within the Empire. They believed it to be a point of national honour: Britain protected South Africa internationally, therefore South Africa had a moral obligation to fight with Britain. There was also the question of payback for the generous post-Boer War peace terms.

It was rapidly apparent, however, that a sizeable proportion of Afrikaners saw the outbreak of war in Europe as an opportunity for a payback of a very different kind. There was rebellion among the recalcitrant old Boer leaders – Christiaan de Wet, Koos de la Rey, Jan Kemp and their militant followers. There were protest meetings, unlawful declarations, shootings and deaths – notably of General Beyers and Jopie Fourie, who joined the ranks of martyrs murdered down the years, so it was held by the die-hards, by the duplicitous British.

Hertzog was not above fanning the flames. And with success. In 1924, after the untimely death of Botha in 1919, and in an unlikely alliance with the then significant Labour Party, his National Party beat the SAP at the polls and came to power. Though outwardly avoiding openly republican sentiments, Hertzog's aim was to test repeatedly and skilfully, through constitutional means, the divided loyalties (as his followers never tired of pointing out) of English speaking South Africa. To this end he was greatly assisted by the changes taking place in the imperial tide, many made at his own urging. With the Balfour Declaration of 1926 and the promulgation of the Statute of Westminster in 1931, South Africa, like all the other Dominions, became independent of Westminster, with only a common loyalty to the Crown uniting them.

It was easy therefore to propose a South African flag to fly alongside the

Union Jack and a new national anthem, '*Die Stem van Suid-Afrika*', to be sung along with 'God Save the King'. Most of English-speaking South Africa was appalled. They saw these steps as nothing so much as the start down the slippery slope on the road to becoming an Afrikaner republic. Despite Hertzog's strict adherence to constitutional forms and niceties, reading the regular correspondence between Patrick Duncan and Lady Selborne, which records the shifts and gear changes throughout the 1930s, it is hard now not to believe that he was not subtly moving in that direction. At the time, the wags thought so too, placing the following jingle on his lips:

> Quoth Hertzog: My bias is such
> I don't think I care very much
> If we all go to hell
> And the country as well
> Provided all Hades is Dutch.[39]

The Great Depression of the 1930s had, as in other countries, necessitated the formation of a national government. Hertzog, finally forced to abandon the gold standard and let the South African pound float to save the country from economic ruin, needed one to save his political skin. Smuts, in the opposition, had been co-opted into this, and thence into a 'Fusion' government as deputy to Hertzog. As in 1910, the idea of English and Afrikaans South Africa pulling together was promoted as a national political ideal. *Hereniging* (reuniting) was the Afrikaans term for this, and the party thus created was called the United Party. This time, however, it was plain to see that the boot was now on the other foot; even within the Fusion government, Afrikaners appeared to have the upper hand.

Moreover, aiding Hertzog further was the presence of yet another growing, breakaway Afrikaner party to his right, repeating in a very real sense the history of his very own actions of 1913. These were the *Gesuiwerde* (purified) Nationalists under the leadership of Dr Malan, who espoused more openly republican (and anti-Semitic) sentiments, and who for the time being represented if not exactly the lunatic fringe then at least a vociferous minority of right-wing Afrikaners. Hertzog was thus skilfully able to represent his own United Party and his political manoeuvrings to his uneasy English-speaking voters as a bulwark against the Afrikaner far right.

Acting as a deputy to a man of Hertzog's middling stature must have been galling enough for a man of Smuts's vision, intellect and capabilities. 'There is little, if anything in common between his mental equipment and outlook and that of General Hertzog,' as Sir Patrick Duncan, the Governor-General, wrote in his diary, '... It is a hard trial for a man of his capacity and experience.'[40] The trial involved swallowing many bitter pills, most notably the Representation of Natives Act of 1936, which removed black voters from the common roll and, possibly even worse for Smuts, having to vote at the time of the Munich Crisis in favour of South Africa's remaining neutral in the event of a European war.

At the time of Fusion, this issue had seemed academic, Hertzog believing that the League of Nations would order a peaceful world. Now, however, with a major conflict looming, it became the very crux of the vexed but hitherto untested issue of the Imperial Connection: was the Crown divisible or not? In other words, could the King of England be at war and the King of South Africa remain neutral? Hertzog argued that he could, and made neutrality in war the final test of the Union's independent status.

Smuts, as both an imperialist and an internationalist, believed in the benefits of the British Commonwealth and the Empire as a world force and in the country's obligation to support it and the world order as one of its members. He was obliged, as Hertzog's deputy, to go along with the government's statement of September 1938, namely, that in the event of Britain going to war with Germany, South Africa would remain neutral but would honour the agreement, in place since 1922, allowing Britain to maintain its naval base at Simon's Town. Few understood that he was merely biding his time. English-speaking South Africans were now horrified to find themselves thrust into this position – hoist, as it were, on a constitutional petard of their own making – by a population group they had traditionally discounted, and by and large felt were inferior. Afrikaner South Africa, on the other hand, was smugly triumphant.

And doubly so. For the year of the Munich Crisis witnessed an astonishingly powerful Afrikaner renaissance. This was the centenary of the Great Trek. Its organisers had imaginatively conceived a countrywide pageant involving the setting-out of wagons from all major points of the Union, timed to converge on Dingane's Day – the sacred Day of the Vow to the Afrikaner, during which they commemorated their decisive triumph over the Zulus – on the ridge south of Pretoria where Moerdijk's massive and monolithic monument to the Voortrekkers was due to rise.

The upwelling of Afrikaner Nationalism this symbolic trek occasioned was extraordinary. All along the way, the wagons were met with weeping men and women arrayed in traditional Voortrekker dress. There were braais, *volkspele* and inflammatory speeches, almost all containing a litany of Afrikaner grievances down the years at the hands of the British. Teachers in Afrikaner schools (Hertzog had firmly resisted the idea of dual-medium schools as a natural follow-on of *Hereniging*) instilled a violent form of new nationalism in their pupils. Dutch Reformed ministers, similarly powerful in town and rural districts alike, inveighed from their pulpits: the hour had come for the *volk* to arise and take its rightful place in the economic and business life of the country, which they saw as the poached preserve of the English-speakers and the Jews, to their exclusion.

Fusion, the Purified Nationalists now argued, threatened Afrikaner identity, and they drew onto their side Afrikaner cultural and educational organisations such as the Broederbond, a secret, Masonic-type organisation for years aimed at forwarding the power of 'pure' Afrikaners in every area of South African life, the Federasie van Afrikaanse Kultuurvereniginge (FAK) and the Afrikaner Nasionale Studentebond. Concurrent with all this was the founding of the Ossewabrandwag, a secret, semi-military organisation with many sinister overtones of Nazi Germany and which swiftly garnered membership. Significantly, the centenary celebrations had been aimed to bring a message of hope to the poor and discouraged – specifically the urbanised 'poor whites'.[41] They responded almost to a man.

Looking back down the years, author and journalist Rian Malan sees this resurgence, and its cause and outcome, clearly: 'Foreigners often ask [me] why my late father joined the National Party and the *Ossewabrandwag* in 1939, expecting to hear stories of anti-Semitism and anti-black bigotry. No ways. My father grew up barefooted in a small town. In his childhood, Afrikaners were the object of ridicule by their English-speaking betters. They were ill-educated and often poor, earning around 60 per cent of the average English wage, a statistic that put Afrikaners in much the same socio-economic position as blacks in white America of that period.'[42]

This is not to say that anti-Semitism and anti-black bigotry did not exist; they were major platforms of these organisations. But epigeneticists suggest that a feeling of oppression, past injustices and unprocessed trauma by a people is often carried forward down generations as a multi-layered neurosis. A new breed of historically-minded psychologists believe that this can lead to fostering a new, radical identity accompanied by a collective anger.[43] If this is so, it is obvious that such factors can be readily exploited to political ends.

Not surprisingly, therefore, the Voortrekker Centenary was essentially Malan's big moment. It didn't suit Hertzog's view of himself as the leader of a supposedly united party to be seen to be too closely associated with the very partisan outpourings it evoked. He had proved, or thought he had proved, or even pretended that he thought he had proved, to the Afrikaners that the majority of the English-speaking voters were now fully South African, finally freed from the spectre of divided loyalties. He saw, or chose to see, the United Party's support for his Neutrality Bill in Parliament as evidence that they no longer put England's interests above those of their own country. The impact of war on the still-patriotic English-speaking South Africans would, however, prove him deluded in this regard.

Moreover, if Hertzog genuinely believed he had (as he claimed) won this final political battle by declaring for neutrality, he was mistaken on another front. Malan now stepped forward with a new goalpost: there would be no real victory, he said, until South Africa was independent of the British Crown. In his speech at Blood River on the Day of the Vow in 1938, moreover, he threw down the gauntlet unequivocally: 'The Afrikaans-speaking man of the New Great Trek meets the Non-European at the New Blood River, half armed, or completely unarmed, without an entrenchment between them and without the protection of a river between them, defenceless in the open plains of economic competition ... Afrikanerdom now finds itself again in this year of commemoration. Risen out of the dust of humiliation and self-contempt, it now demands full recognition of itself, for its noble ancestry and their descendants ...'

To this he ominously added the final thrust to the burden of his argument, in essence repudiating all liberal attempts – however small, hitherto – to find a way to accommodate non-white South Africa in the country's political future: 'Have you the patriotism and sufficient power ... to use this God-given opportunity also to demand something infinitely more important – the assurance that white civilization will be assured?'[44]

In that last sentence the terrible die for the country's future was cast. As the trekkers had done a century before, he was saying, the Afrikaners were facing once more the same enemy: the non-white and the Briton. His voice resonated across the land, appealing to fiery patriots and bigots alike in a way that the ostensibly bi-racial voice of Hertzog, the internationalist voice of Smuts or even the white humanitarian-liberal voices of Hofmeyr, Ruben, Ballinger and their like never could. Alan Paton, a liberal and the future author of *Cry, the Beloved Country*, who had innocently gone to attend the centenary celebrations in a spirit of unity, only to be harshly rebuffed,[45] witnessed this national shift and saw it quite clearly for what it was:

> Afrikaner universities were [now] turning out, not Smuts men and women, or Hertzog men and women, but Malan men and women. The Afrikaner schools were turning out Malan boys and girls. The Afrikaner scout movement and cultural movements were not excited about the Commonwealth of Nations or the bi-racial policy, but about being Afrikaners, about the day when Afrikaners would govern, about the time when all the wickedness and looseness and liberal sentimentality of the last hundred years would come to an end, and all the people of South Africa would be ruled firmly and resolutely by the Afrikaner people whom God had sent into Africa for a purpose ... It was [about] being an Afrikaner and belonging to a people who, after years of struggle, were drawing nearer to the Promised Land.[46]

Without doubt, it was this burgeoning group of young Afrikaans-speaking South Africans who would most resent, and be antagonised by, the cheers, the flag waving of Union Jacks and the half-hearted singing of '*Die Stem*' along with the other outpourings of loyalty that accompanied the royal tour in 1947.[47] Malan spoke most directly to them.

Thus was the South African political stage set in mid-1939. Hitler invaded Poland. Britain declared war. The Empire and India automatically went to war. The Dominions had to answer for themselves. On 3 September, almost all English-speaking South Africans listened to the King's speech, broadcast on the BBC Overseas Service down the swooshing airwaves, and addressed, as they saw it, to themselves among many compatriots around the world: 'In this grave hour, perhaps the most fateful in history, I send to all my peoples, both at home and over seas, this message ... We have been forced into a conflict, and we are called, with our allies, to meet the challenge of a principle which, if it were to prevail, would be fatal to any civilised order in the world.'

It was unthinkable, the King continued, 'that we should refuse to meet the challenge. It is to this high purpose that I now call my people at home and my peoples across the seas, who will make our cause their own.'[48]

Opinion among them was unequivocally for war. Among the Afrikaans-speakers it was a different story, and when the King asked his peoples 'to stand calm and firm and united in this time of trial', many, though not all, had no intention of doing anything of the sort. The same cannot be said for the blacks and coloureds and Indians; in South Africa and the Protectorates they were to prove loyal to the Crown, and many were prepared to go to war.

By a constitutional oversight (and some said a stroke of good fortune) the South African Parliament had been briefly recalled, out of session, back to Cape Town on the very day Hitler invaded Poland. The next day, 2 September, Malan demanded that the prime minister make a statement. This was promised for Monday 4 September.

That weekend, Hertzog was shocked to learn that Smuts would depart from the support he had previously, in 1938, given for neutrality. It was also rumoured that Louis Esselen, his colleague and secretary (and *éminence grise*) of the United Party, had organised a majority for war. A Cabinet meeting was called at Groote Schuur, the Cape Town residence of South African prime ministers given in perpetuity by Cecil Rhodes. Ironically, in view of their personal and political animosity, Hertzog was of course assured of Malan's support in a division. Smuts, aware of this, nevertheless stated openly his conviction that Hitler threatened the peace and liberty of the world and that he therefore would oppose neutrality. Fusion was at an end.

In the spirit of the day it was natural that English-speaking South Africa – those who were in the United Party, or the remains of the Dominion Party or those still in the Labour Party – would support the political leader who enabled them to fight for King and Country or, as the latter was sometimes now commuted into, the Commonwealth. This sentiment particularly prevailed during the Battle of Britain, when England itself seemed threatened by invasion, and volunteer numbers increased significantly. However cautiously Smuts would tread in the war debate, they would privately have agreed wholeheartedly with the declaration by the Australian prime minister at this time that 'there can be no doubt that where Britain stands, there stand the people of the entire British world'.[49]

English-language newspapers confirmed this sentiment. 'Every hour of upbringing, every ounce of sentiment, every drop of blood cried out to be on the side of those who are, through no fault of their own, faced with an ordeal in which they will need the support and sympathy of everyone who is British,' read the leader of *The Natal Mercury* on 5 September 1939.

They knew, however, that they were in a minority – at that date roughly estimated at 800 000 out of a white population of more than 2 000 000 – and needed to cooperate with reasonably minded Afrikaners. And Afrikaners themselves were divided. Some – between a quarter and, midway through the war, a third – might support Smuts's line of argument, which he was clever enough to present without a hint of jingoistic phraseology or sentiment. The majority, Hertzogites and Malanites, were forcefully opposed to going to war with their former conquerors.

It was a cliffhanger. For a full day the debate raged on in the House of Assembly. Hertzog might have won the day had he confined himself to the issue of neutrality stemming from independence, and arguing that the fusion of white South Africa was more important than the fate of Poland. He didn't. Instead he defended Hitler, using the worn-out argument that blamed it all on the Treaty of Versailles, likening the humiliation of the German people to that of his own: 'I know what it is to be driven by humiliation and belittlement and insult to a point where you say, "Come what may, everything is subordinate to wiping out that humiliation which we suffer from day to day ... [I] will rather sacrifice my life instead of tolerating this condition any longer,"' he exhorted, petulantly, putting himself in the shoes of the Nazis. It was an emotional speech; worse, it was a foolish one. Many of his more moderate supporters heard in its tenor all the paranoia of old Afrikaner grievances, now so inflamed by Malan for political advantage, and were put off.

Smuts rose in reply. Whatever could have been said for Hitler, he reasoned, could no longer be said after the rape of Czechoslovakia. It was not simply a matter of Poland; Hitler was bent on world domination, he told a spellbound House, and would soon demand the return of South West Africa. This, in itself, was a telling argument for the Afrikaners, who by this time regarded the former German colony as practically part of South Africa. Others spoke, and the day seemed alternately lost and won. Heaton Nicholls, the MP for Zululand, for example, was considered disastrously jingoistic; BK Long altogether more reasoned. To loud cries of 'Aye' and '*Nee*' all over the House, a division was called. When the count was taken, Smuts had a narrow but decisive majority of 13.[50]

Hertzog at once called on the Governor-General, Sir Patrick Duncan, to dissolve Parliament and call an election. Duncan, one of Milner's Kindergarten, and pointedly selected in 1936 by Hertzog himself as the first 'South African Governor-General' now summoned up all his constitutional abilities.[51] He reminded Hertzog that the question of neutrality had already been prominently raised in the election of 1938 and that he, as prime minister, and other ministers had consistently declared that the question would be decided, if the occasion arose, by the elected representatives of the people in Parliament. And as prime minister he was now in a minority in his own Cabinet and in the House of Assembly. It was a bold move, and though the outcome was welcomed with relief in London, the constitutional implications were, at the same time, viewed with some consternation.[52] Smuts was invited to form a government, which he did with alacrity. War was declared.

Smuts moved swiftly and with an energy that belied his 69 years. Over 2 282 of the card-carrying members of the Nazi party within the country's borders (including South West Africa) and more, whom he had identified while Minister of Justice, were arrested and interned; more dissidents were to follow. All weapons were called in, ostensibly for use in the war effort. The Defence Force was purged of Hertzogites; Te Water, the High Commissioner in London, a Hertzog man and an open supporter

of neutrality, was recalled and replaced by Sidney Waterson. Radar instal-
lations were ordered to be put in place to track shipping around South
African waters; the lamentable state of the Union Defence Force was put
on a war footing.

They would say of Churchill, cometh the hour, cometh the man. Many
now said the same of Smuts. English-speaking South Africans who, now
that Britain was at war, would have been mortified by a second vote for
neutrality in their Parliament, flocked to enlist and express loyalty to Smuts
and his purged party. So did some Afrikaners. But the majority were aghast.
They had been tricked again. The membership of the Ossewabrandwag
rose dramatically. The Broederbond went into secret session.

Good Behaviour, which only just held on the surface in times of peace,
evaporated. There were cheers and boos at railway sidings all over the
country for the returning MPs of both sides as they made their way home
to their constituencies by train. Hertzog himself was greeted at every
stop by crowds of supporters waiting to pay homage; he and Malan were
now the heroes of 'true Afrikanerdom'. Pro- and anti-war demonstra-
tions erupted across the country. At cinemas where 'God Save the King'
habitually ended the performance, typically accompanied by footage of
the sovereign, his gracious Queen and the smiling little princesses (and
their corgis), there were fisticuffs as militant Afrikaners refused to rise
or tried to leave the cinema during the anthem. Fury replaced a general
dumbfounded anger for the majority of Afrikaners. If the First World
War proved divisive for white South Africa, the Second was even worse.

As she journeyed home in the ministerial coach that would now no
longer be hers, the vitriolic Mrs Kemp, wife of the Hertzogite Jan Kemp
– former Boer general and First World War rebel, and now bitter and
openly pro-republican, deprived of his Cabinet post – sent a furious and
rude message to the Governor-General's wife: 'Tell Lady Duncan that she
had better buy everything she wants because we will soon be back in office,
when they will be turned out. We mean immediately to abolish the position of Governor-General.'[53]

The country appeared disastrously divided, though to Smuts not hopelessly so. Hertzog, after a failed coalition with Malan, retired disillusioned
and died shortly thereafter. For the rank and file of Afrikaners now, the

spirit of *Hereniging* that he had espoused had been shown to be a myth. Going into the war had proved unequivocally to them that English South Africans still had divided loyalties. They now focused on the British Crown and all it represented as the major obstacle to their dream of a restored Afrikaner republic, and, emotionally, as the root of many of their problems.

In January 1942, Malan, now leader of the Official Opposition, noisily put forward a motion to withdraw from participation in the war, which was in fact a motion of secession from the Crown. He stated clearly that his objective was a republic. Although it was defeated by 18 votes,[54] it was, like his Blood River speech of 1938, another ominous portent of things to come.

None of this was lost on the major protagonists of our story. The Royal Family saw Smuts regularly throughout the war and were apprised of his difficulties at home, loftily though he appeared to them and his colleagues to dismiss them. Churchill, who, uniquely for him, listened to Smuts with respect, and doted on him too ('They were a tonic to each other,' thought Smuts's son, Jannie[55]), was also aware of Smuts's domestic political difficulties, and made every effort to include him in high-powered conferences and meetings in London and the Middle East. These received full publicity both at home and internationally.

These were far from being empty publicity gestures; Smuts's counsel was widely sought at the highest level. When announcing the changes in the Middle Eastern command, including Montgomery's appointment to head the Eighth Army after Gott's death, for example, Churchill acknowledged the 'massive judgement of Field-Marshal Smuts, who flew from Cape Town to Cairo to meet me'.[56] This statement provides a further indication of the South African prime minister's enhanced stature for, the previous year, on Smuts's 71st birthday, the King, who, like his father, regarded Smuts as a 'great man',[57] had made him a field-marshal. In October 1942 he was invited to address both Houses of Parliament in London.

And Churchill's cable to Eisenhower, preparatory to the General's meeting with Smuts for the first time, in Tunis, unequivocally sets out the high regard he had for him· '[Smuts] possesses my entire confidence, and everything can be discussed with him with the utmost freedom. He will stay some months in London [Smuts's second wartime visit], taking up full duties as a member of the British War Cabinet. He will carry great weight here with

The Cairo Conference, August 1942. Seated (from left): Smuts, Churchill, Auchinleck
and Wavell. Standing (from left): Tedder, Brooke, Harwood and Casey (Australian).

the public. I shall be grateful if he is treated with the utmost consideration.
He is a magnificent man and one of my most cherished friends.'[58]

It was against this background that the royal tour was conceived. The
Canadian tour of 1939, undertaken just before the outbreak of war, had
been an immense personal success for the sovereigns, increasing the
popularity of the monarchy; politically it was a great success too, boosting support among French Canadians and perhaps helping to soften US
isolationism. At some stage, possibly during a weekend at Windsor Castle
in 1943 and certainly again in October at an all-male dinner of the War
Cabinet at No 10 Downing Street at which the King, Smuts and Lascelles
were also present,[59] a South African tour, doubtless with a similar agenda
in mind, was mooted.

By then, things had appeared to have settled down in South Africa. Not
that there wasn't still hatred and animosity. Malan and his cohorts saw to
it that there was. But the war was at last going the Allies' way. Waverers
among the Afrikaans-speaking electorate now turned to Smuts. His
thoughts must have turned back to the dark days of 1940 and 1941. 'None

so keen as those who come up when the fight has [already] been won,' he noted wryly.[60] Many Afrikaners had lately joined the forces – some, like the Irish volunteers, simply in search of (well) paid employment which offered adventure and manly pursuits.

Certainly in the 'khaki' election called in June 1943, many of these soldiers' parents, hardly typical United Party supporters, must have endorsed Smuts's prosecution of the country's war effort with their ballot papers. Others merely abstained. There was also a belief held at the time that Afrikaans soldiers had seen a wider and more enlightened world through serving overseas. At any rate, the vote in the election went substantially Smuts's way and he was returned with a majority of 67 seats. It seemed a triumph and a vindication of his internationalist views. The climate seemed ripe as never before for a royal visit, as soon as the war was over.

Smuts saw this clearly. Much was, and has been, made by his detractors of his so-called love of royalty, along the lines of one of old Mrs Hofmeyr's famously tart remarks: 'At his age, he sh-should know b-better.'[61] Many of his biographers have tried to pass over this in an embarrassed sort of way at best. They have surely missed the point. For a man of Smuts's intellect and ability, such commonplace royal sycophancy would indeed have been unseemly. But Smuts saw in royalty – and particularly the English Royal Family, then popular as never before – something unique. It would be a binding force in the Commonwealth. And in a successful constitutional monarchy he saw, further, a real force for good in the world, and a balm, as he put it, 'to our divisions [ie, in local politics] ... and playing its part in softening party strife'.[62]

There was too, perhaps, something more in all this: the fascination for men like himself and Hofmeyr, both of a simple Afrikaner background and upbringing, with grandee Englishwomen of the likes of Lady Harlech and Lady Mary Baring, the wives of successive High Commissioners for Southern Africa. Alan Paton touches briefly on this. These were strong women with a quiet charm – an inner peace, as Hofmeyr saw it[63] – and conviction, using their strengths to exert influence in a still male-dominated world. This was a genus not typically found in Afrikaner society, where the strong women tended to be of the feisty or rebarbative (*moeilike*) personality type of the Mrs Hofmeyrs and Mrs Kemps.

Queen Elizabeth was the grandee Englishwoman-type *par excellence*, an aristocratic charmer with tremendous self-assurance and ability. And a seriousness of purpose, as Lady Donaldson would later perceptively note, yet with the skill and ability to wear her purpose lightly.[64] Smuts had quickly perceived her to be the spiritual driving force behind the family[65] and came to see in her not only a friend and ally but also a tremendous asset. She was, moreover, the perfect counterpoint to her diligent husband, who, though he had, since his accession, as Smuts observed, increasingly grown in stature,[66] possessed a less obviously populist personality. Here, he was sure, was a weapon to hand that could work magic on many levels, and he seized it.

For who could resist it, he reasoned, as he sought the furtherance of a post-war, white-led Dominion South Africanism, with himself and his party at the helm, and blessed by the many virtues and benefits of the Commonwealth connection? Certainly not the English-speaking South Africans, who would anyway have cheered a less impressive royal couple, but surely his own people – *ons mense*, his 'Good People', who supported him in the *platteland* (rural) constituencies – could be made to see those benefits, through the Crown made flesh, as it were, and in such an appealing form?

Smuts's early education in the Cape Colony, like Malan's, though conducted in the Dutch medium, had been an essentially Victorian one. This had been so even in Riebeeck West. We know for certain that the tales of the Arthurian legend had been part of it, and that chivalrous dreams of kings and queens and knights had touched his psyche, even in the remote, rolling wheatlands of the Swartland.[67] These he now articulated and transmuted for his purposes in the modern, political world. A royal progress was the sort of thing, he actually said, that kings and queens do and which give them a blessed and fruitful function in our human society. 'Nowhere,' he went on, 'is it more wanted than in this land of races and colours, and nowhere can it render greater service. Politics runs too high with us, and as the King is above politics, he becomes the reconciler and peacemaker.'[68]

During the royal tour, interviewed at the annual service on the top of Table Mountain, when the White Train had already departed, he claimed an almost saint-like quality about the King: 'There is not one of us who could see the expression on the face of the King and his family as they greeted South Africa, without feeling their charm and their spiritual quality which is acting in a wonderful way on us ... We in our youth tend to exaggerate our difficulties and to exaggerate mistakes that are made.'

This last, surely, was an attempt to quash the constant harping on of old Afrikaner grievances. 'All over the country,' he went on, 'the King, by his bearing and spiritual qualities is having a soothing effect.'[69] The effect of the presence of the Royal Family was already evident throughout the country; 'already there is more gentleness, more unity apparent'.[70]

As for the Queen, he knew that in her he had a star. Besides her, he would say, we are all small potatoes.[71] And in a moving valedictory speech, when a doctorate was conferred on her at the University of Cape Town at the end of the tour, he acknowledged his admiration for her: 'Something of your gracious personality has gone out to us and entered into the spirit of our land. It has been and will remain an abiding presence with us and a healing influence to sustain us in our difficulties and endeavours.'

Smuts was only partly right here. Many Afrikaners were indeed to be charmed by the Royal Family, and the combination of pageantry and their informality, simplicity and a displayed interest in their country came as a pleasant surprise.[72] Dyed-in-the-wool Nationalists, however, were not disposed to view the monarchy thus, and suspiciously saw the whole thing as a vote-catching effort on the part of the prime minister. It would stand in the way of their re-establishing the Boer republic out of which the British had cheated them 50 years before.

Romantic ideals were not entertained. Tellingly, Malan, their leader, appears, as a boy, to have been unresponsive to accounts of the Arthurian legend and the historical romance that the monarchy offered up in a constitutional form. Indeed, well into adult life he carried a resentment (apparently both social and intellectual) against Smuts,[73] ostensibly centring on a youthful incident when the latter had expounded to him on this theme in his capacity as his Sunday school teacher.[74] At any rate, Malan now had political reasons to be impervious to such ideals too.

When the tour was announced, Malan said in Parliament that he regarded it as a delicate situation that was of some concern to the republican-minded section of the South African population. He trod carefully here, not wishing to antagonise possible English-speaking support. Those of a republican persuasion, he went on, could lay claim to a 'specific history' and that the sensitivities of the past should be realised. He then switched tactics to respect constitutional niceties. The Nationalists were fully aware, he continued, that the monarchy was above party politics and they would accord the King the necessary respect as the head of the British Empire.[75]

As we have already seen, Malan would fail to do this, absenting himself and many of his MPs and all of his senators from the ceremony of the Loyal Address to the King from both Houses of Parliament on the first day of the tour (see page 16). He would, however, attend the State Banquet in Cape Town.

Nationalist Afrikaner response to the visit is further dealt with in Chapter 4. It was not a logical or even a cohesive one. Indeed, even as the visit got under way, a missive from the propaganda office of the HNP Federale Raad (penned by none other than PW Botha, the future president) complained to Malan that the government was scoring points over the Nationalist press's lack of a concerted response to the tour.[76] This says something for the sort of control the Nationalists considered essential to have over their press, even then. This lack of cohesion appeared to have left the door open for many Afrikaners to participate happily in the various royal occasions. Such participation did not, however, translate into vote-changing, and when the next election came around there was the more pressing issue of race to excite the voters. Smuts's dream for postwar White Dominion-ism would be jettisoned, only to be taken up, in a convoluted form, by his great political enemy and fellow pupil from long-ago schooldays, DF Malan.

For now, it was a dream that seemed to be well within Smuts's grasp. After the success of the Cape Town visit and the seal set on his government and all it stood for by the King in person, performing the opening of the Parliament as the reigning sovereign and head of the British Commonwealth, Smuts and his Cabinet went down to the Foreshore to wave the King and his family on their way as they boarded the white and gold train specially designed to take them on a tour of his youngest Dominion.

CHAPTER 3

꒰ ꙮ ꒱

The Whistlestop Tour:
A Mid-century Royal Progress
Across the Veld

21 February to 20 April 1947

Pulled up before HMS *Vanguard* on 21 February, just a few hours after the State Opening of Parliament, stood a wonderful new train, its spotless ivory and gold livery glittering in the afternoon sunshine. This was the famous White Train, 14 carriages and a third of a mile (530 metres) long, designed to convey the royal party 7 000 miles (11 260 kilometres) around South Africa, the Protectorates and Southern Rhodesia (the route is shown on the map at the beginning of this book). It was described as a veritable 'Palace on Wheels', and indeed Ministers in Attendance, Ladies-in-Waiting, Second and Third Footmen, dressers, valets, lady's maids, cypher clerks, secretaries, speech writers, the King's hairdresser and the Queen's, Equerries, flower arrangers and many other attendants would have constantly brushed past each other, hurriedly, along its corridors, as it rattled and swayed its way northwards.

In those days, harbour quays, railway platforms and even fledgling airline terminals were routinely packed at departure times, with family and friends making an occasion of waving goodbye to departing travellers. These, by their very nature, were accepted to be emotionally charged occasions, and were enshrined in that age on stage in epics such as *Show Boat* and *Cavalcade* and in films such as *Casablanca*, *Waterloo Bridge* and *Brief Encounter*.

'Wish Me Luck as You Wave Me Goodbye': the White Train, with HMS *Vanguard* dressed overall behind, leaves the Foreshore at the start of the royal progress across southern Africa.

TRANSNET HERITAGE LIBRARY PHOTO COLLECTION

The opportunity had been grasped by the tour organisers. Here now were gathered a crowd of Cabinet ministers, the Diplomatic Corps, dignitaries and senior railway officials, all of whom had received a gilt-edged invitation bearing the logo of the South African Railways & Harbours (SAR&H) and bidding the recipient to be present at the Departure of the Royal Family.

The party arrived to a roar from the crowd and in a gay mood, clearly freed from the tensions of the morning's ceremony and relieved that the speech from the throne in Parliament had gone off so well.[1] Divested of their grand attire and now in smart travelling clothes, they posed for the newsreel cameras, boarded the train and then appeared at the open windows of the Royal Saloon car. At the press of a button, the windows dropped as if by magic into the chassis to create a modest balcony, replacing the old concept of a viewing platform at the rear of the train.

This was another great scene writ large in the imperial vocabulary. The setting, in that great sun-drenched amphitheatre, with Table Mountain behind them and the bulk of the enormous grey battleship looming above the splendid train standing on the tracks, leading off and 'up away to the north' to their right, was not lost on those assembled. At precisely 4 pm, the signal, or 'right-o-way' as it was then known, was given for the engine driver to pull off.[2]

At once, with a hiss of steam, the train clanked into life. The Police Band housed on the royal pavilion struck up the wartime favourite 'Wish Me Luck as You Wave Me Goodbye', and, as the locomotive started puffing cautiously forward along the newly laid tracks right before the battleship – again dressed overall and with its ratings lining the deck – and the ivory and gold carriages slipped smoothly after it, the crowd spontaneously burst into cheers. The men lifted their hats and the women waved their handkerchiefs; there were cries of 'Godspeed' and '*Totsiens*' as they waved them on their way. Many, some quite involuntarily, felt a lump in their throats.

The South African Railways (SAR) then was a vast, state-run enterprise which, in the days before macadamised highways or frequent airline services were available to the many, carried the bulk of freight and passengers with amazing efficiency and economy over the vast distances of southern Africa. Its network was extensive; railways were one of the very tangible engineering achievements of the British Empire and the distant chug-chug of a locomotive or the mournful whistle of a goods train as it clattered off down the tracks and into the African night was part of the warp and weft of everyday South African life, often even in seemingly remote country districts.

The railways employed over 178 000 people. As an organisation it was a source of pride to its employees, and there was even a kind of *esprit de corps* among them. And there was more to it than that, for, in the decades of railway expansion following the Anglo-Boer War, the SAR had too with its timetables, signalling, workshops, supply lines and essential efficiency been a beneficial means of bringing many a rural, displaced, poor white Afrikaner employment in a systematic workplace that was patently part and parcel of the modern, mechanised world. This process accelerated particularly under the Fusion government, when the proportion of unskilled white workers rose from 10 per cent in 1924 to 40 per cent by 1933.

The White Train was described by one foreign correspondent as 'sweeping across the ochre veld like an ivory and golden arrow'.
TRANSNET HERITAGE LIBRARY PHOTO COLLECTION

The exactly worded, finely detailed manuals and timetables for the royal tour issued to all personnel involved for every section of route, still preserved in the Transnet Museum, must at least stand as an impressive monument to the residual colonial efficiency of that era.

The Railways Administration had been informed only in February the previous year of the impending royal visit. Plans were swiftly put in hand, for, apart from the prestige involved in conveying the Royal Family around the Union, the tour would undoubtedly showcase the abilities and style of this sprawling organisation,[3] and would publicise the network and the country it crossed to the outside world. Two precedents were there to study – the royal train in England, which had routinely conveyed the Royal Family in peace and wartime (serving in the latter case as somewhere to sleep on visits to bombed cities), and the train designed in 1939 for the royal tour of Canada and the United States. It is evident that there was also reference to the plans made for the Prince of Wales' 1925 tour of the Union[4] and that of Prince George (later Duke of Kent) in 1934.

Eight new air-conditioned coaches were immediately ordered from Metro-Cammell Carriage & Wagon Co Ltd in Birmingham, England; J Stone & Co provided the up-to-date air-conditioning equipment. Two senior SAR draughtsmen and a senior electrical engineer were dispatched to England to supervise the construction of the coaches; five were to be specialised luxury saloons for the Royal Family and for VIP accommodation on board.

Under normal conditions, such an order would have taken two and a half years to complete. Now they were given a mere nine months. That this was achieved was a source of pride both in South Africa – ordering, as a Dominion, the best available British rolling stock – and in England, as the manufacturing nation, struggling to get industry back on its feet after the years of war. In December, in a blaze of publicity, including an inspection visit by the Royal Family, the carriages – transported on special bogeys to negotiate the bridges and tunnels designed for the different-gauge English trains – took over 15 hours to travel from Birmingham to Birkenhead[5] where they were loaded on board the British freighter *Explorer* for the voyage out to South Africa.

In addition, six carriages were drawn from stock already in South Africa to make up the 14-car consist. These were already in use on the Blue Train, the *über*-luxury train service that ran between Johannesburg and Cape Town, and were sent to the SAR Pretoria Mechanical Workshops where they were completely stripped and refitted. Photographic records of the White Train's interiors show the Birmingham-supplied carriages to be decidedly *moderne* in concept, a combination of austerity-era late Art Deco design with an emphasis on ship-shape comfort provided on clean, no-nonsense lines.

The Pretoria workshops, however, excelled themselves in a late flowering of South African ball-and-claw stinkwood crossed with Department Store Queen Anne. Needlework covers of historic designs worked in petit point[6] continued this latter theme, though with the startling inclusion of a springbuck or protea as a central motif; the unnecessarily ugly

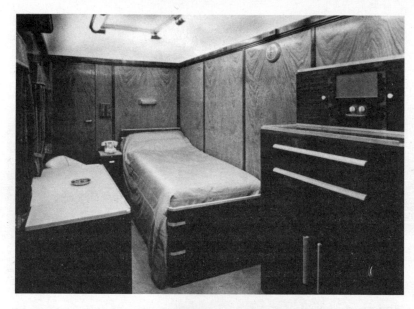

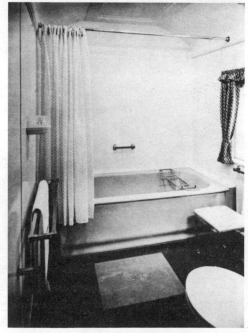

The Palace on Wheels. Shown here are Queen Elizabeth's stateroom (*above*), the King's bathroom (*right*) and the Royal Saloon car (*opposite top*), with its ball-and-claw, Queen Anne needlework and the 'misty blues' damask curtains and close carpeting. The dining car (*opposite bottom*) could seat 24 people.

carved casing of the very up-to-date radiogram supplied for the lounge car was the workshop's pride and joy. There was an overall emphasis on wood panelling, with figured chestnut for the King's stateroom and study, quilted maple for the Queen's stateroom, bird's-eye maple for the Princesses' staterooms, being employed. The corridors were of English walnut. Only the bands of diffused, cornice-level lighting and the toning grey blues, chosen by the Queen, of the fringed damask curtains and remaining upholstery suggest the lingering glamour of pre-war travel.

The bathrooms were all in apple green and cream and boasted the soaps the family preferred: Bronnley's Eau de Cologne in the bathrooms ('The King likes it oval, the Queen likes it round,' wrote Buckingham Palace in advance); Yardley's Lavender in his bedroom and Roger & Gallet's Violet in hers. The Princesses both preferred Bronnley's Sandalwood in their bathrooms and Yardley's Lavender in their bedrooms.[7] The King's bathroom additionally contained a very up-to-date electric gadget that heated his shaving water in a flask, and there were heaters behind the mirror to prevent it from steaming up.

The flowers supplied were all of a serviceable, long-lasting variety and arranged regularly by two rather *opgedol* (dolled-up) SAR stewardesses on board in Linn Ware vases supplied, with their cones, by the Cullinans' Olifantsfontein pottery studio; they look truly a mess in the photographs, though they were augmented by dismantled presentation bouquets and even freshly picked garden bunches offered up through the carriage windows by farmers' wives at stops along the way.

There was a splendid dining car containing two tables which, if joined, could seat 24. The white and gold crested china services were all supplied by Minton. Food was provided by four chefs headed by Spiros Mextaxas – 'of Greek extraction' as the Queenstown *Daily Representative* helpfully informed its readers – head chef of the popular restaurant on Cape Town Station, and who, with three assistants, worked non-stop in appalling heat (no Stone's aircon in the galley) providing meals for the party.

So keen was the Railways Catering Department to put their best foot forward that an eight-course meal was produced on the first night. For the English visitors from a still-rationed Britain and now facing 35 days cooped up on a train ('well, a lovely train, *but still a train*,' as Princess

Elizabeth's Lady-in-Waiting, Lady Margaret Colville, put it, somewhat shortly, years later),[8] the prospect of this avalanche of railway food, with radish rosettes on top, as it were, was dismaying. After the first meal the Queen walked up the tracks to the kitchen galley and, after some tactful banter, asked for the forthcoming menus and firmly put a line through several of the proposed courses. 'Pruning' is how she later described it.[9]

By 22 April – two months into the tour – these had become whittled down, as she had suggested:

LUNCHEON	DINNER
~~Fruit Cocktail~~	
~~Potage Garbure~~	Consommé Andalouse
Omelette Rossini	Fillet of Sole Otoro
~~Lamb Cutlets Chasseur~~	
Pigeons en casserole, Paysanne	Roast Turkey and Ham
Baked Beans, Green Peas, Boiled Rice,	Green Beans Celery
Chateau Potatoes	
Asparagus Princesse Green Beans Celery	Chip Potatoes
Cold Buffet: Chicken Salad, Pressed Beef,	
Boiled Ham, Ox tongue	
Assorted Salads	
~~Peach Flan~~	
Vanilla Ice Cream	Apple Tart and Cream
Coffee Dessert	Dessert Coffee

It didn't end there. In those days, when even quite modest South African homes kept a maid, and reasonably comfortably-off households had cooks, baking was the culinary skill on which housewives of all classes prided themselves. And tea – unthinkable without something to eat – was taken as a matter of course, without fail and with some ritual (varying according to background and purse), twice daily, by the majority of the nation. It was then the most common South African form of hospitality. At every stop the results of favourite family recipes were therefore loyally offered up onto the train for the party to enjoy with their 'elevenses' or mid-afternoon tea.[10]

'We are given so much food,' wrote the King despairingly to Queen Mary, his mother, '... morning and afternoon tea when we are regaled with all sorts of rich cakes.'[11] Nothing would stop this, off or on the train: vanilla cakes decorated with icing and glacé cherries, coffee cakes decorated with walnuts, fruit cakes and Victoria sponges, freshly baked cheese scones and homemade shortbread, and so on – all were passed up in cardboard cakeboxes lined with paper doilies or wax paper. And there was also a positive avalanche of *melkterts*, which every Afrikaans housewife then baked, though the English visitors, reminded too vividly of the milk puddings of their nursery childhoods, failed to acquire a taste for these.[12]

How much of this can actually have made it to the royal tea table is debatable (there were, anyway, enough hungry mouths to feed on the three trains). Yet Queen Elizabeth, with her Scotch background, understood the generosity of countrywomen, and supported the concept of the

Life on the train: the post office.
TRANSNET HERITAGE LIBRARY PHOTO COLLECTION

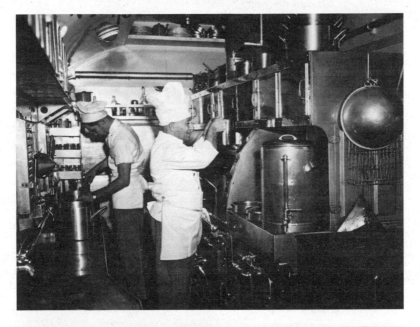

Life on the train: the kitchen car (*top*), requisitioned from the Blue Train, and the telegraph office (*above*). TRANSNET HERITAGE LIBRARY PHOTO COLLECTION

Women's Institute, with its emphasis on 'Jam and Jerusalem' ('*Konfyt* and Confinement' being that of the VLV [Vroue-Landbou Vereniging], the Afrikaans equivalent, according to the wags) and the associated home-making skills; she was for years president of the Sandringham WI. Mrs Carinus, the wife of the Administrator of the Cape, admiringly noted that the Queen always made a point of asking to meet the women responsible for preparing the teas at the various stops.[13]

Bottled drinking water was supplied from the Albion Spring at Rondebosch; of the total of 2 000 gallons (9 092 litres) of milk supplied to the train during the tour, only 10 went sour, on an especially hot day in Livingstone, Northern Rhodesia (now Zambia).[14]

Serving all this food was a team of 18 young men – the most capable stewards that the catering department of the SAR could muster, and, like footmen in a grand pre-war English house, all of approximately the same height and weight. They had undergone a strenuous training regime under the Railway Health Officer, Mr FC Holland, in Johannesburg, with daily physical jerks getting them in shape for the long trip ahead. They also received special instructions in deportment.

'Deportment in a ballroom and deportment on a train are two different things,' barked Mr Holland to the press. 'The most important thing for a train steward is to keep his balance and his dignity at the same time.' Training for such a proficiency was apparently terrifying. A 'Swedish bar' three inches wide and fifteen feet long (7.5 centimetres and 4.5 metres) was suspended high above the gymnasium floor. 'If they can walk along that without faltering,' volunteered Mr Holland a trifle harshly, '[then] the swaying of a well-sprung dining car becomes a minor hardship.'[15]

Separate bedrooms and en-suite bathrooms were provided for each member of the family and the royal ladies' dressers. The King's carriage carried his valet and his valet's workroom; his Equerry and doctor shared a bathroom and lavatory. It also contained his study, suggested officially to be the hub of the train. Though on tour, this was still a working monarchy. By a miracle of modern technology and pre-planning, His Majesty could connect by telephone via the travelling phone exchange to London, all the Dominion capitals and even Washington at every official stop. In love, but not yet officially engaged, Princess Elizabeth was observed to avail herself of this phone service to speak to Lieutenant Philip Mountbatten in England.[16]

A staff of cypher experts[17] accompanied the King to receive and pass on confidential and strictly coded messages between the British prime minister, Clement Attlee, and the prime ministers of Canada, Australia and New Zealand. Such messages would have kept him abreast of the plans of his cousin, Lord Louis Mountbatten, then Viceroy in New Delhi, for Indian independence in the latter part of the tour.

There were offices for the pernickety Sir Alan Lascelles – 'more habitable than I feared it might be, and really quite roomy', he wrote to his wife.[18] There were compartments for the royal ladies' extensive wardrobes; 'God knows where we will put all the luggage,' as he had put it querulously beforehand, gloomily surveying the mountain of cabin trunks and hatboxes deposited at Government House, Cape Town, on their arrival.

These were the domain of the royal dressers, Miss Willcox and Miss King, the Queen's First Dresser and Second Dresser, respectively, and 'Bobo' and Ruby MacDonald, the no-nonsense-get-on-with-it daughters of a Scottish domestic coachman, originally engaged as nursery maids to the Princesses and now elevated to this role. The trunks had been made to fit the longer carriages designed for the narrow South African rail gauge. And so that the dressers should be able to swiftly unpack the appropriate garments without ransacking a dozen trunks, each one was labelled 'Hartnell dress No 1', 'Thaarup hat No 1', 'Gloves and shoes No 1', and so on.[19] There was a safe for the magnificent royal jewels.

At the rear of the train was a separate carriage with its own dining room and kitchen for the Minister in Attendance – for, as in England, constitutional custom required a member of the Cabinet to accompany the King on his travels, ready to tender him with advice that would carry the authority of the government. Van der Byl, Sturrock, Lawrence, Steyn, Conroy, Waterson and others all fulfilled this role, together with their wives, 'those nice Lawrences' (as the Queen described them[20]) proving the most helpful.[21] Together with the Steyns, they were 'the nicest', according to Lady Harlech, who included the Van der Byls with them as being the 'ones who really know their job'. The added implication here was that these couples were the most socially congenial to the Royal Family.[22]

A pilot train, with its chocolate-brown and cream livery, preceded the White Train by half an hour. It carried the Administrator of the province through which they were travelling – JG Carinus for the Cape, Dr SP Barnard for the Orange Free State, Mr DE Mitchell for Natal and General JJ Pienaar for the Transvaal. By travelling ahead, they were ready on the platform to make presentations when the White Train pulled in. The pilot train also carried supplies in a refrigerated wagon and had an extra baggage van.

The pilot train also carried other railway officials and the press corps, who were regularly invited onto the White Train as part of a charm offensive. The pressmen and women covering the tour (there were a total of 18 press, newsreel and broadcasting representatives from the United Kingdom alone) were housed and fed in comfort, and could use a high-speed Morse transmitter to telegraph their reports directly from the train. Frank Gillard, in charge of the BBC's coverage of the tour, shared his compartment with George Rottner, who was making BBC history as the first television cameraman to cover a royal tour.[23] There was a darkroom for processing film and a post office dealing with thousands of letters a day – both to and from the royal party, and for sending out hundreds of envelopes stamped with the 'Royal Train/*Koninklike trein*' franking mark, coveted by philatelists and souvenir hunters alike.

Together with the post office was a telegraph office enabling wireless communication with the White Train and, astonishingly, with the general international system, for use even while the two trains were moving. The pilot train also housed the King's barber and the royal hairdressers.

A third train – the so-called Ghost Train – carried spare parts and repair mechanisms. A fleet of cars accompanied the trains everywhere to meet them at official stops; they were sometimes obliged to travel at least 200 miles (320 kilometres) over mostly unmade roads in every 24 hours to keep up.

Additionally and among the unsung contributors to this royal progress were the operating staff, stationmasters, signalmen, engine drivers and shunters, and a corps of 24 cleaning staff, under the Foreman Coach Cleaner[24] who at every opportunity descended on the train with ladders and buckets to wash its white and gold paintwork free of the dust of the veld. They groomed it like a racehorse. Magnificently modern, the White Train was an impressive and beautiful sight, sweeping through the ochre-coloured plains, as James Cameron of the *Daily Express,* put it, 'like an ivory arrow'.[25] People drove and walked for miles just to see it pass.

Every building and shed along the way had had a new coat of paint. These were the days when many stationmasters passed their lonely spare time gardening, providing floral displays that softened the swept, spick-and-span appearance that the public expected at all stations. Such efforts were done with the additional hope of receiving the annual prize awarded for the best station garden in the country – a far cry from their state today. And so it was, as the South African summer of late 1946 advanced towards Christmas, every station along the route was planted with flowers and shrubs supplied by the Railways' horticultural department. Some, like Worcester's ambitiously conceived rock garden, were spectacular indeed and drew delighted exclamations from the royal couple, both keen gardeners themselves.[26]

At every official stop, the Railway Police – resplendent in their dark uniforms and white pith helmets – were formed up to attention on the platform. They were responsible, in conjunction with the South African Police, for the safety of the Royal Family while on railway property. It is evident that these men were at times over-zealous in their task, harshly marshalling the crowds back as they pressed forward too eagerly for what would prove their only possible glimpse of the Royal Family in a lifetime. Despite the efforts of Major Van der Byl to counter adverse overseas press comments on this, it was inevitable that in some of the country areas, non-European crowds sometimes got particularly short shrift. Occasionally this led to complaints, especially in the less deferential press.[27] Buckingham Palace was even ordered to firmly deny the unhelpful claim by James Cameron, that there had been a ban placed on photographs of the Queen smiling at her black subjects.[28]

The royals, used to the efficient forbearance of London bobbies in crowd control, were not unaware of this zeal, and a reporter, waiting for his photo opportunity in the long grass beside the stationary train, overheard the King's aside to the Queen as they set out for their evening constitutional across the veld: 'Thank God, Mother, we've managed to

The Queenstown platform. In the foreground is Piet van der Byl, Minister in
Attendance. Patty Shannon, whose father had been killed in the war, stands in front of
Lascelles, the King's Private Secretary. The Administrator of the Cape Province and
Mrs Carinus watch the mayor's granddaughter make her curtsey.

TRANSNET HERITAGE LIBRARY PHOTO COLLECTION

throw off the Gestapo!'[29] Needless to say, this contrasts markedly with
the official letter sent through the Private Secretary at the end of the tour
to the Minister of Police, praising his men: 'Wherever he went, the King
was greatly impressed by the admirable way in which all members of the
Force discharged their duties and their unfailing consideration both for
the comfort and security of the Royal Family and for the welfare of the
large crowds which they were called upon to control.'[30]

The itinerary and arrangements – the work of an Interdepartmental
Central Committee – in close cooperation with provincial and local
committees – planned for 33 official stops along the way. One such, typically, was Queenstown, in the Border territories south of the Transkei,
laid out in 1853 around a central hexagon and which agricultural prosperity had provided with several attractive sandstone buildings: a town hall,
Anglican, Methodist and Dutch Reformed churches and Queens College

Princess Elizabeth pulls the locomotive's whistle, while Princess Margaret
smiles at Peter Townsend, the King's Equerry. Sturrock (second from right)
was often described as the engine driver in this iconic photograph; in fact,
he was Minister of Railways and Harbours.

TRANSNET HERITAGE LIBRARY PHOTO COLLECTION

and Queenstown Girls' High, where the headmaster and headmistress
were habitually recruited from England.

The schools, both well regarded, were an important feature of
Queenstown, many of the farming community for miles around sending their children there. Some of the more prosperous and broadminded
Afrikaans farmers sent their children there too, to avail them of the good
education and the sporting-minded, tough English public-school ethos
offered;[31] these were the core – though not solely – of the local Afrikaans-
speakers in the community who had joined up in the war. Hangklip, the
town's Afrikaans-medium school, was known locally as the 'Bare Foot'
school; at that date, it was not even considered for inter-school sports
fixtures.

In 1947, Queenstown presented a smiling but sleepy face to the rolling
eastern Cape bush that surrounded it – exhilarating countryside when

viewed from the windows of the White Train, as it double-chugged on towards it, now pulled and pushed by three separate steam engines,[32] two coupled leading and one banking, to climb the escarpment.[33] Peter Townsend so fell in love with what he saw – 'A countryside of green hills and broad pastures, full of horsemen, leather-faced old farmers and boys and girls, hair blowing, shirts billowing, sitting their horses with ease as they rode to school or market'[34] – that he began to weigh the possibilities of coming out and settling there.

The town itself, with its small population of 8194 whites, was not unlike a nineteenth- or early-twentieth-century English market town in a colonial setting; Mrs Gaskell and EF Benson would have felt at home here. Its mores and manners and its very heartbeat, as recorded by its newspaper, *The Daily Representative*,[35] were geared almost entirely to its English-speaking inhabitants and those in the surrounding farming community, many of whom were descended from the original 1820 settlers. In the town, at any rate, they were in the majority. 'English was spoken in the shops,' is how one resident puts it, firmly. Girls' High put on an annual Shakespeare festival and Gilbert and Sullivan's D'Oyly Carte operettas were frequently staged.

At that date, a good two-thirds of the reportage in *The Daily Representative* consisted unabashedly of news directly syndicated from England – Beefeaters pictured at the Tower of London, the first day of the Chelsea Flower Show, the opening of Noël Coward's new musical comedy, and so on. It also ran a specially written and extensive weekly London Letter 'on matters of interest in the Old Country'. The rest was given over to South African news, aimed at an intelligent readership and well reported: support for the United Party, enthusiastically but not blindly given, sport, the price of cattle at the local show, rainfall, and so on. Weddings and social events were described in detail by the indefatigable 'Priscilla', the *nom de plume* of Ruth Green, the editor's wife.

There was a small Jewish community, with their own synagogue, though in other ways rapidly assimilating within the English-speaking community and remembered for promoting concerts and visiting art exhibitions. And a generosity of spirit. When Patty Shannon needed her tonsils removed, Dr Rudolph Schaffer refused to present her war-widowed mother with a bill. There were 3727 Afrikaans-speakers in the town, 46 people of German descent, 2159 coloureds, 90 Indians and 13157 non-whites, mostly Xhosa, living apart in the location.[36]

Queenstown was allotted only an hour of the royal itinerary. No effort had been spared to secure an extension of this, but to no avail. Despite this the town, like so many others, threw itself into a frenzy of preparation, strictly adhering to the instructions laid out for a one-hour stop sent from the Central Committee.[37] There were meetings between the mayor and the councillors, heated exchanges in the newspaper about the plans or lack of them, plans for who would meet the Royal Family, plans for the decoration of public and private buildings ('we want dignity rather than flamboyancy [sic] to be the keynote') and plans for a royal ball to be held in the town hall that night, 'Under the patronage of the Mayor and Town Clerk for which a guinea is charged for double tickets and 1/6 for the poorer people for the privilege of viewing the spectacle from the gallery'. This was, of course, to take place long after the Royal Family had departed.

Shops advertised 'ensembles and costumes' which might be purchased for 'Queenstown's Great Occasion' and model hats imported from England and the Continent. Elsewhere under the heading 'For the Royal Visit' were advertised kid gloves – full length, elbow length and gauntlet. 'If you wished to be correctly dressed,' cautioned Messrs Morum Brothers of Cathcart Road, the local department store at whose haberdashery and glove counter these items were to be found, 'these are essential accessories for your ensemble.' A lot of snobbery attached itself then to being 'well-shod' and, priced at 31/6 to 47/6, the gloves represented a considerable outlay for women in a farming community.

Of course, as with other English-language newspapers in the Union, the doings of the Royal Family were staple newspaper fare and much reported upon. Once the South African tour began, this increased exponentially as their progress was followed with detailed reportage. Some families, unable to wait for the town's brief visit, went to Cape Town and Port Elizabeth in the hopes of better things. They phoned their impressions back to the paper's regular reporters, who duly passed these on to their eager readers: the clothes, the hats, the cheers of the crowds. The King looking 'suntanned and relaxed', Princess Elizabeth 'serious but obviously interested in everything', Princess Margaret 'smiling and vivacious', and so on. The Queen's smile, reported Queenstonian Mrs Mills, was one 'of pure loveliness'.

Finally, at 9.30 am promptly on Thursday 6 March, the White Train pulled into Queenstown station. On the platform was the mayor, Mr Glover, in his robes and cocked hat,[38] the town clerk and their respective wives, and with them the local dignitaries to be presented. There was also Mr Du Toit, the stationmaster, whose bright green tubs of asters and cockscombs were much admired. The bouquets for the Queen and Princesses had been grown and made by Walter Everitt, curator of the Queenstown Parks & Gardens; everyone was much struck by the fact that a late delphinium, included in the Queen's, exactly matched her eyes.

The actual presentations of these were made by three little girls in party frocks, rehearsed in their curtsies and required backwards walk by Edith Glover, the mayoress, who in her youth had trained at RADA in London. One was the mayor's granddaughter (this was locally considered a shocking case of nepotism, as she *wasn't even at school in Queenstown*), one was Christine Kruger (another surprise, even in the spirit of inclusiveness encouraged by the Central Committee, for her father, though a councillor, was darkly believed to have been a secret member of the Broederbond), and one was Patty Shannon, whose father had been killed in the war[39] and whose widowed mother now stood proudly by. Patty Shannon's borrowed dress had been made in Madeira; it was lent by Ruth Green whose sister, it was murmured locally over the teacups, *was married to a Blandy*.

At 9:40 sharp the Royal Family entered the Daimler to drive in a procession of eight cars the short distance to the Recreation Ground, the route gay with bunting, flags and garlands of oak and other greenery. There, already lined up, three deep, were ex-servicemen of the local regiment, the First City Regiment – European, Coloured and Native. There were also a good number of ex-SAAF members, for Queenstown had had an RAF training station built there early in the war. All the many local bodies who had contributed to the war effort were represented; seats for the next of kin (of soldiers who had died in the war), the elderly and infirm had been reserved on the Pavilion.

Schoolchildren of all races, who had been given the day off, lined the perimeter, some in their Scout and Girl Guide uniforms (the non-white Girl Guides were called Wayfarers; Brownies were called Sunbeams[40]), along with the townspeople and others who had poured in from the surrounding countryside. As the royal cars approached, the sun appeared from behind the rain clouds ('Oh kindly Providence!' averred *The Daily Representative*); these, after the drought, were much needed, but not on that particular day. All the town's church bells pealed. Mr Preston, a local pigeon fancier and Secretary of Queenstown's Caged Bird and Pigeon Club, released three flights of pigeons in groups of seven, with long red, white and blue streamers attached to them. All at once there came from all sides a spontaneous outburst. Queenstown went wild.

'The crowd is one long multitude of cheering faces; flags are waved, hats flung sky high ... tears are rolling down cheeks,' wrote the reporter. Although the council had invested in a newfangled loudspeaker system, only those close to the King heard what he had to say. The continued waves of cheers and roars – the latter identified as coming from the black ex-servicemen – seem to have drowned him out.

There were more presentations and a general walkabout, the Royal Family engaging here and there with members of the various groups. 'The King,' it was reported with satisfaction, is 'never happier than when he is among his people.' In the face of such loyal enthusiasm, there must have been more than an element of truth in this. The King, and particularly the Queen, recognised the great effort that had been expended in their honour in small towns and communities, and they and the Princesses endeared themselves by chatting naturally to those they had personally singled out in the crowd. Sometimes these encounters proved fascinating. Mrs Maclear, wife of the general manager of the local Standard Bank, for example, told them how, as the Sister-in-Charge of the 5th Casualty Station serving in France, she had led her staff of women and men under fire across country to the beaches at Dunkirk before making their escape back to Dover aboard a little, flat-bottomed, Hebridean craft.[41]

From the Recreation Ground the return route was via Frost Street (five mph, said the planning committee), down Peacock Street, over the railway, along Grey Street, down Griffiths Street (four mph), along Cathcart Road, the main street (three mph), through The Hexagon and up Shepstone Street, and so back to the station and onto the train. Driving time for the 3.2 miles (5 kilometres) was 40 minutes (the eight-cylinder royal Daimlers were designed for processional purposes and could drive at one mph in top gear without any sign of snatch or drag[42]), allowing the flag-waving, cheering townspeople who had been asked to spread themselves out along the route to be assured of a good view. The south side of Grey Street, the east side of Griffiths Street and the south side of Cathcart Road had been reserved for blacks, who shouted '*A Sozizwe! A Sozizwe!*' (Father of the Nation! Father of the Nation!), and the south side of The Hexagon had been reserved for the coloured community, who waved Union Jacks and sang 'God Save the King'.

Although brief,[43] it clearly wasn't disappointing: 'All too soon the great moment had passed, but on a sea of expectant faces there was a look of complete contentment. There was only one topic of conversation – the beauty of the Queen and the two Princesses and the grace and charm and bearing of the Royal Family. And so it went on – strangers, friends and relatives, all involved in animated conversation.'

To ensure that no one felt flat after the excitement, there was a Children's Fancy Dress Party that afternoon at the Recreation Ground, a Native Feast in the location for which the town council had paid for 30 head of cattle to be slaughtered, and finally the Royal Visit Ball in the town hall. Under a committee convened by Mrs RB Bennett and Mrs AS Chisholm (two capable local bossy-boots) and willing helpers, the town hall's drab interior had been transformed with bands of red, white and blue crêpe paper, crowns and strings of coloured lights.

Dinner parties had been held beforehand in the Hexagon Hotel and private houses; later there was a cold collation or supper buffet of cold meats, salads, trifles and fruit salad laid out in an adjoining room. Unlike the big cities, there was no question of imported blooms being used; the flower arrangements here were all garden-picked and described as being of 'autumn tints'. The Bongola Serenaders, accompanied by two of the best local pianists, provided the music until 1 am and several days later, descriptions of the women's evening dresses filled four columns of

The Daily Rep, under a heading simply stating 'The Frocks'. The greatest day in Queenstown's history had come and gone.[44]

In addition to such official stops, there were 203 stops scheduled for the three trains to take on water, a requirement in the age of steam, and an absolute necessity considering the amount of ablutions performed daily on all three. Although often at remote and rudimentary sidings, typically consisting of a few corrugated-iron shacks, and one or two pepper and gum trees to provide a scant shade over the asphalt, there were at these unpromising locations very often to be found knots of people from 50 miles (80 kilometres) away or more, who had gathered there in the summer heat for a better view of the marvellous train, and perhaps with the hope of a glimpse through a window of one of its illustrious passengers. More often than not, and to their amazement, they were rewarded when the Royal Family climbed down to talk to them.

Sometimes, too, at such wayside stops, wrote Townsend, there were gathered crowds of Africans bearing banners of welcome who had often waited all day. These were spontaneous gestures on the part of the King's black subjects and, like much else, cannot be explained away by revisionist historians. As the train steamed in they would break into haunting, melodious airs, drifting, as he recalled, on the night air, under a starry sky. The royal party was much moved by these impromptu performances and the African skill at harmonising – swaying, 'dreamy-eyed, carried away by ... their own voices'.

One song often sung to them was '*Nkosi Sikelel' iAfrika*', not then considered the subversive anthem it would become under apartheid: 'the lisping treble of the children, answered by the refrain of the male voices, a low murmuring hum, sounded like the wind murmuring in the trees'. As the royal Daimler drove slowly through the pear tree-lined streets of Beaufort West, the small Karoo *dorp* that was one of the last stops on the tour,[45] for instance, blacks strategically positioned in groups from street to street seamlessly took up the beautiful anthem from where the others had left off. The King was so taken by this anthem that he asked for a recording to be made to take home.

At Sannaspos, by way of contrast, a group of black schoolchildren, after singing 'lots of Native songs', burst into Handel's 'Hallelujah Chorus',

An unscheduled stop: the Royal Family greet the crowds on the platform at
Cookhouse in the Karoo around 9 pm.

TRANSNET HERITAGE LIBRARY PHOTO COLLECTION

At Wonderkop, in the Orange Free State, 10 March. Behind the King,
Minister of Labour Colin Steyn, son of the last president of the Free State republic,
is delighted by the response of his 'fellow countrymen'.

TRANSNET HERITAGE LIBRARY PHOTO COLLECTION

'which you must say was unexpected', wrote Lady Harlech to her husband, adding, 'they sang it extremely well'.[46] Coming into Bethlehem, in the Orange Free State, another group gave them 'Loch Lomond' rendered in a Scotch accent.[47]

But officially planned stops, and those to take on water, were not all. In keeping with the experience gleaned on the Canadian tour, if a mayor or town clerk had telegraphed ahead to the White Train with loyal greetings, and a request, 'with humble duty', that the Royal Family stop and meet the people of a town, or if the stationmaster or even the pilot train signalled back that there was a sufficient number of people gathered and waiting on a platform, there was a chance that the train would stop.

Considering the pressures of the official timetable, the Royal Family were remarkably responsive to these requests. There was a good reason for this. This part of the tour was very much a modern version of the royal progresses made by Queen Elizabeth I through her realm; 'We have to be seen to be believed' is an oft-repeated adage of the Royal Family, then and now. It is estimated that by the end of the tour 60–70 per cent of the people of a vast and often sparsely populated country had seen or even spoken to the Royal Family.[48]

'We find that the stops every two hours are rather exhausting,' wrote Queen Elizabeth to Queen Mary on the White Train stationery, 'but we try to get out & talk to the people because they *are* so nice & some have come a very long way, carrying babies, & standing patiently for hours, & one meets the ordinary citizens that way.'[49]

But, once they had left the predominantly English-speaking littoral, there was an added impetus to greet these hopeful, loyal gatherings. By then, what appeared to be the runaway success of the tour in the Cape coastal areas was inciting anger and anxiety among the strong republican elements up-country. Afrikaners in rural districts came under pressure from their local Broederbond, Ossewabrandwag and clergymen not only to boycott the tour but also to actively campaign against it.

Stories began to circulate of railway gangers living in wretched shacks on remote stretches of the route resolutely covering the windows with blankets lest their wives and daughters attempt to watch or, worse, wave to the glittering spectacle as it passed by. At Bethlehem, for example, despite a rousing welcome from a crowd double the normal population of the town, the local MP, CJ Wessels, and the member for the Provincial Council, Mrs H Hofmeyr, absented themselves from the welcoming party, along with the mayor and mayoress of nearby Fouriesburg and Kestell.[50] This put the English-speaking community – invariably numerically smaller in these areas – along with loyalist Afrikaners, on the back foot.

A case in point was Wepener, a few miles into the Orange Free State. It was nearly 10:45 pm and, to the surprise of those on board, the train suddenly stopped. It was pouring with rain, and courtiers and officials peered out into the darkness in some consternation. They knew they were now inside a republican stronghold; a stop was not scheduled – not even to take on water. Could the stationmaster have possibly dropped his signal to halt the train?

This was a quandary. The Royal Family had already retired for the night and the train was running late. It had to move on. But in the darkness were to be seen several thousand people on the decorated station platform,[51] braving the rain and braving, too, the sneers of their republican Nationalist neighbours for their now almost certainly forlorn, soaked vigil in the hopes of seeing their King.

This, at the very start of the Free State leg of the tour, might have proved a public relations disaster. Major Piet van der Byl, the Minister in Attendance, was at his wits' end, attempting to placate the disappointed local mayor, Mr CJ de Jager, and vainly trying to coax the King to come out. At first he failed to materialise; then, after a nerve-racking delay, he suddenly appeared, very bad-tempered indeed.

'Why was I not warned?' he asked crossly.

Suddenly behind him there was a movement. In a moment the Queen, in full evening dress and her jewels, had appeared, perfectly serene. Van der Byl had time for only a few hasty words of explanation. She evidently took the situation in at once and, summoning her daughters (still in evening dress; they had been dining with the Van der Byls in their ministerial carriage) to put on their jewellery, she followed the King down the steps and along the muddy platform. It seemed to a vastly relieved Van der Byl that she walked more slowly, and appeared to 'stop more frequently and talked longer than usual', the King often being several metres ahead and having

When time did not permit even an informal stop, the train merely slowed down,
giving the waiting crowds a glimpse of the Royal Family.
TRANSNET HERITAGE LIBRARY PHOTO COLLECTION

to pause, turn around and wait for her. It was a consummate performance.
'Her Majesty, though very tired after a long day, did it wholeheartedly,'
he wrote afterwards. 'I have never been so grateful to anyone in my life.'[52]
Twenty minutes later, the White Train pulled out to deafening cheers and
singing.[53] There were to be 164 of these unofficial stops in all.[54]

At other times, when they were running behind schedule, the train could
only slow down, and the Royal Family, dressed in full fig, would wave
from the lowered windows to the small crowd gathered. This was not for
nothing. Consider the case of Miss Lucy Green, an elderly spinster from
Maritzani (now Maritsane) in the dun-coloured wastes of Bechuanaland
(now Botswana), and who lived alone in her remote cottage after her store
had failed, fighting loneliness, terrible pain and poverty with marvellously
high courage, 'determined never to lose prestige amongst the neighbouring Afrikaners'. Her only companion was her beloved mare, Chessie, who,
on Thursday 17 April, she had inspanned onto her ramshackle buggy to

drive eight dusty miles (13 kilometres) to see the Royal Family pass by, just as night was falling.

For Lucy this was something of an act of faith. In 1897 she had ridden miles to see the local celebrations of Queen Victoria's Diamond Jubilee: 'Now, fifty years after, I rode to the station to see her grandchild and her great-grandchildren.' She glimpsed them only briefly through the lit window of the White Train. She wrote afterwards that she thought the King looked tired, but that he kept on saluting and smiling; the Queen, she thought, looked radiant, and the Princesses were smiling too.

After that, just as suddenly as it had appeared, the White Train would have picked up speed and vanished down the line, leaving the African night pierced eerily by one or two of the newly installed electric lampposts on the platform and its roaring silence by the sound of the cicadas in the thorn trees. Perhaps, and we can only hope, there had been a few moments of general camaraderie among the disparate gathering on the platform in the happy aftermath of the royal sighting, such as it was. Then Lucy and Chessie would have clip-clopped off into the darkness for the eight-mile drive back to the lonely cottage on the veld.[55]

Thus it was that, by the end of the journey, there had been 410 stops in all. It must have made it both arduous and repetitive, as G Ward Price, following the tour, noted in a fairly hard-hitting article in *The Star*, Johannesburg's evening paper.[56] Yet the very repetition (or apparent lack of imagination on the part of the authorities concerned) he complained about – the 'same scarlet-robed mayor, red carpet, presentations, drive to the town hall or central park, loyal address and waving flags' – simply represented small-town pride and what they could offer. The sovereigns understood this,[57] even if the journalists didn't.

They also good-naturedly put up with interrupted meals, 'mouthfuls of soup often hastily swallowed', as Lady Margaret Egerton recalled,[58] and much more besides. 'Heavens, we haven't got to get out again?' Van der Byl records the King saying as the train ground once more to a halt.[59] 'They never could be sure of a quiet family meal on the train,' Lady Margaret recalled elsewhere,[60] and even – in the case of unofficial night-time stops such as the one at Cookhouse – much needed, undisturbed rest. 'You couldn't even put on your dressing gown and get on your bed.'

The Queen, especially, never seemed to flag. Smiling and always royally dressed, by day in the hydrangea shades and feathered or flowery hats that she favoured, by night in evening dress, jewels and furs – 'If they have driven hundreds of miles to see you, it's up to you to give them what they have come for,' she told her grandson years later[61] – she would appear behind the King at the door of the carriage, pause for dramatic effect for a moment and then descend the steps, radiating a sense of excitement and pleasure, suggesting, as one reporter put it: 'O Bertie do you see this is Hicksdorp. You know we've always so wanted to come to Hicksdorp! ...' etc.[62]

It says much for her people skills that she made this seem a reality. She led by example and intended the tour to pass these skills on to her daughters. She enjoyed meeting people and took pleasure in the joy a royal occasion gives. Besides, she and the King were at their best with country people, asking what they farmed, what the rainfall had been like, what the price of beef was, and so on. They were well trained by example. George V and Queen Mary, despite their awe-inspiring appearance, were notably good at putting ordinary people at their ease; surviving footage of the Strathmores (the Queen's parents) talking with their estate workers shows similar, exemplary behaviour.

No hint of condescension was ever in evidence as they greeted every mayor or stationmaster of every town or *dorp* or siding across the veld, and then slowly passed down the line of expectant people, often excitedly clapping in delighted appreciation or simply wonderment, and stopping and talking to individuals along the way. Indeed, Kitty Muller was so carried away by the Queen's charm and friendliness on the platform at Glenconner that she was overheard to blurt out: 'You and your hubby are welcome to visit the farm at any time!'[63] And the Koos van der Merwes, on whose farm beyond Worcester the train had overnighted, and who had indeed served coffee to the Royal Family on their *stoep* the next morning,[64] were so delighted by their encounter with the Royal Family that they were subsequently felt to have got a bit above themselves in the district. Royal anecdotes were repeated once too often, and locally the farmer became known, behind his back, as 'Koos Koning'.[65]

Future royal biographer Theo Aronson, putting himself in the role of Creevey at Victoria's court, captures for us the sort of polite, stilted, yet charming conversations that ensued, for example on the little siding platform at Glenconner, now in the Eastern Cape. After a few words with the highly nervous stationmaster, sweating in his serge suit, the Queen stepped forward to greet the little crowd: 'In her light, well-modulated voice and her head enquiringly tilted she would ask questions. Had they come far? Where did they live? Oh yes, Kirkwood, where the oranges come from [the royal homework provided for the journey had been diligently attended to]. Had there been any rain? Yes, it *had* been very hot. The veld certainly looked very dry. How interesting that the station should be called "Glenconner"; it reminded one of Scotland,' and so on. As always, ex-servicemen wearing their medals were specially singled out, but so too was anyone who looked old, shy or shabby. These she would greet warmly. 'I'm so glad to meet you. How very kind of you to come and see us.'[66]

It couldn't amount to much, except the hope that they themselves would appear, as the Queen was later to write 'as nice, ordinary people'. Although they relied on those in attendance, the family seemed to have a sixth sense for spotting those holding back – the ex-serviceman at Umtata with the ghastly burned face, obviously rebuilt by plastic surgeons; the three little girls with bouquets standing 100 yards (91 metres) away and too shy to come forward; the old lady of 88 at Uitsig who had travelled 40 miles (64 kilometres) from Thaba'nchu;[67] the palsied boy with his father on the other side of the barriers. Or those unlikely during a brief stop to get a look in. Naturally, in some country areas, the coloured and black communities sometimes found themselves subjected to subtle bullying by officialdom, often ignored or corralled into disadvantageous positions. Without hesitation, the Royal Family would walk over or even back towards them, tripping straight over the railway lines, signal wires and asphalt, to be greeted with roars of delight and singing.[68]

If the tour was, officially in part, intended as a holiday for the sovereigns after the strenuous years of war, it is hard to see how it could have succeeded in this respect. Relaxation, such as it was, was sporadic. At every overnight stop, a local farmer with a good stable would provide mounts for the two Princesses to enjoy an evening or morning ride, usually accompanied by

The Princesses riding on the beach at East London, with Peter Townsend between them.
All along the way, local farmers provided suitable mounts for exercise.

GREATSTOCK / SHUTTERSTOCK

Adeane and Townsend. In a more equestrian age, this was an honour that
carried much prestige; a typical example was Mrs Cecily Niven, daughter
of Sir Percy FitzPatrick, whose horses provided mounts for the 7.30 am
ride at Sandfontein, the stop outside Port Elizabeth where the Nivens
had a farm in the nearby Sundays River Valley.[69] Other newsreels and
photographs show the Princesses riding before breakfast on Bonza Beach
at East London or across the Highveld.

'We sped in the cool air, across the sands or across the *veldt*,' remembered Townsend; 'those were the most glorious moments of the day.'[70]

The King and Queen, for their part, would take a brisk evening walk for
exercise, sometimes for as long as an hour.

Once the King walked alone. This occurred before the Grahamstown
visit, when the lightly laid secondary tracks that wound up Howison's Pass
from Alicedale were deemed unsafe to carry the White Train. The party
had transferred to the royal Daimlers for the long and dusty drive into the
old settler capital of Upper Albany and for the journey back to the train.

The King, feeling unwell, had one of his temper tantrums – known in the family as his 'nashes'.

Queen Elizabeth was particularly adept at dealing with these. Telling him that they had time in hand and that a long walk would do him good, he was persuaded to set off, shadowed by two detectives but otherwise on his own, up the winding, unmade road that followed the hazardous railway line to the top of the pass. Having reached the silent summit of this lonely location, with the Eastern Province bush stretching out as far as the horizon on the plains below, he was amazed to see a lone Boer farmer standing by the side of the road. This scene must surely have had an element of Stanley's meeting with Livingstone about it.

'*Goeiemôre*,' said the King, practising his Afrikaans and politely doffing his hat.

He received an ungracious grunt in reply.

'What are you doing here?' persisted the King.

'No man,' replied Mr Raademeyer, in his thick accent, 'I've been standing here a long time; my wife and daughters have gone to Grahamstown to see the *bleddie* royal family, but they said if I wait here I might see them go past.'

'Well, how do you do,' said the stranger extending his hand, 'I *am* the King!' And a few minutes of man-to-man conversation ensued.

Apparently, the story of this unexpected royal episode was picked up in the neighbourhood (presumably repeated by an astounded Mrs Raademeyer and her daughters) and, in the happy afterglow of the Grahamstown royal visit, was broadcast far and wide in the district to the general merriment.[71]

There were three weekends actually off – one at Drakensberg Gardens, which they all enjoyed, part of Easter at Government House in Pretoria, which didn't amount to much, and one at Victoria Falls, where the whole hotel was commandeered for the royal party. The weather there, even in April, was 'boiling', preventing the King from relaxing,[72] although in a rare private photograph both Princesses can be seen in bathing suits lying around the pool with the younger members of the Household. Princess Margaret later recalled the Drakensberg and the Falls impressing her most in the land of wide horizons, sunshine and plenty.

There were other infrequent, semi-private and delightful interludes; the picnic up-river after the open-air church service on Sunday 23 February at the picturesque Ebb and Flow near Knysna is recorded by Townsend in some detail and with pleasure.[73]

And one of the more imaginatively planned overnights was the two nights spent at Port Elizabeth, where a siding had been created on an S-bend, surrounded by spreading, mown lawns and flowerbeds just above the beach. Harry Lawrence was the Minister in Attendance, and he and his wife, Jean, took the King and the Princesses into the warm waters of the Indian Ocean with wooden surfboards and introduced them and the aides-de-camp to the exhilarating sport of surf riding. Lawrence, who had grown up bathing in the surf at Muizenberg, was emboldened to take the King and later Princess Margaret firmly by the hips and give them a good shove onto a promising wave he saw coming in, while the Queen and her ladies-in-waiting paddled in the shallows.[74]

The crowds were kept back and no photographs permitted, one of the reporters having infuriated the King with a piece of lese-majesty describing the Heiress Presumptive in her bathing costume as having curves in all the right places.

Not surprisingly, they loved these evenings. Peter Ashmore, one of the Equerries, said afterwards that this was the most enjoyable relaxation of the whole royal tour for them.[75] But it is clear that such occasions were few and far between. Endless days and nights chatting with ministers and staff, engaging with the tongue-tied or over-enthusiastic, rattling around on the notoriously narrow standard South African gauge ('this comfortable but very wobbly train', which 'shakes and sways', as Queen Elizabeth described it in her letters to Queen Mary[76]), summoned again and again so as not to disappoint, regularly faced with sections of the crowds who remained uncommunicative and others who clearly had only a vague idea of what or who they were looking at ('That is Mr King, that is Mrs King and that is Princess Elizabeth King and Princess Margaret King,' Peter Townsend overheard a local official explaining to a crowd of black children)[77] – it all took its toll. The King lost weight alarmingly, though whether this was the strain of the tour, as was conveniently claimed in its aftermath, or the early onset of the cancer that would eventually kill him remains in doubt.

On the return trip from the Rhodesias, many people along the way remarked that the King was looking drawn, and Enid Bagnold witnessed even the Queen, still in her garden-party dress, seated, give a sickly wave out of the train window as it chugged away from the packed itinerary of Maseru, 'like the dying duck [sic], a sketch of her other waves. She looked as though she would die if she saw just one more woman to wave to.'[78]

Always on duty – always on show. 'It is one long grind of unselfish labour,' wrote an admiring Cabinet minister, 'with never a break from work or duty, never a let-up. Work, work and again work, under almost unbelievable physical and psychological strain.'[79] At the end of a particularly gruelling day, Major Harvey, the Queen's Private Secretary, witnessed, to his amazement, the King suddenly shout out: 'Off parade at last!' And with that he threw his hat in the air and the Queen, spontaneously and triumphantly, kicked it into the dining room.[80]

It is a revealing story about the sovereigns: he mostly living off his nerves, and she gently but skilfully managing this with humour. Along with her refusal to be hurried, which drove courtiers such as Lascelles crackers,[81] spontaneity was one of her charms. It must have been a useful one on a whistlestop tour such as this. After the open-air church service at the Ebb and Flow, when the boats were being got ready to take them up-river, she leant over to Townsend and asked: 'Do you know where we are going, Peter?'

'No, Ma'am,' came the reply.

'Oh, how lovely!' she exclaimed. And then she broke into a song in which soon the whole family joined: 'I Wonder Where We Are Going to Be Tonight!'[82]

CHAPTER 4

ꯙꞏꞏꞏꞏꞏ

Bloemfontein and the Braai at Bultfontein: Afrikaans vs English-Speaking in the Free State

7 to 9 March 1947

Bloemfontein was the first experience for the Royal Family of a large, predominantly Afrikaans-speaking city in the interior. The visit to the game reserve and the accompanying braaivleis, scheduled for its second day, would be the quintessential experience of what Afrikaners would regard as an ideal day out.

The royal party all thought the city attractive. In its modest way, it was. Handsome sandstone public buildings terminated street axes; everywhere tall cypress trees and orange roof tiles were outlined by perennially sunny blue skies. It was the judicial capital of the Union. Like Pretoria, Bloemfontein was an imperial city, though this time a very minor one, laid over the dusty former capital of a small Boer republic. It had a charm; the family all said that they would have liked to stay there longer.[1]

Their reception had been odd, however. There seemed, wrote Captain Ritchie in the Tour Diary, 'to be an atmosphere of nervous excitement unlike anything we have met before'.[2] Newsreel footage seems to bear this out. It shows the police holding back hysterically cheering crowds, and old ladies fainting and being carried off by grim, no-nonsense paramedics. Except for the garb of the spectators – neatly uniformed Boy Scouts and schoolgirls and respectably dressed women – it's the sort of

The King and Queen greet the Bloemfontein Caledonian Society pipe band on arrival.
Some of the city's handsome sandstone buildings can be seen in the background.

TRANSNET HERITAGE LIBRARY PHOTO COLLECTION

welcome that anticipates the kind that would be given to pop stars in the future.

There is, of course, no way of telling the mother tongue of the cheering crowds we see. Certain it is that they cannot all be English. Of Bloemfontein's white population of 30 005, only 10 390 were English-speaking and this figure was partly accounted for by their strong representation among the members of the judiciary. Of course, their numbers on the day would have been bolstered by English-speakers who poured into the town from as far afield as Tweespruit to witness the royal visit.

The English-speaking sections of the city, however, provided no more than a veneer of Britishness, even in an essentially British age. It just accounted for the usual posses of English-speaking schoolchildren waving Union Jacks and South African flags, a mounted police escort, the pipe band of the Bloemfontein Caledonian Society and ranks of ex-service-men (a good number of them *tweetalige* [bilingual] or Afrikaans-speaking *Bloedsappe*), all wearing their medals and standing by to cheer the sover-eigns. Both the King and Queen were easily able to engage with them, and the pipe band was invited to play to them again on the lawns at Government House.

The black population, roughly equal in number to the whites, lived apart in the location. The remaining whites were Afrikaners, numbering 26 631. They now controlled much of civic Bloemfontein. Two years before the White Train steamed into the main station, they had wrested control of the city council after decades in English-speaking hands;[3] Bloemfontein was a great centre of support for Dr Malan.

This meant that the Royal Family faced not only strong prejudice but also active anti-monarchical campaigning. Smuts, who perhaps wisely chose not to accompany them on this part of the tour, could field only one Free State Cabinet minister to be In Attendance here. This was Colin Steyn, the Minister of Labour, and fortuitously the son of the last president of the Orange Free State Republic, together with an able Administrator, SP Barnard, who was also a member of his party.

Barnard's story was an interesting one. As a result of Britain's scorched-earth policy during the Anglo-Boer War, Stephanus Barnard had gone to one of the concentration camps with his mother at the end of the war. After the Treaty of Vereeninging, the family found themselves completely impov-erished. He was forced to find work, becoming a ganger building the national road between Bloemfontein and Cape Town. His good looks caught the eye of a regular passerby, who put Stephanus through school. Being very clever, he managed to pass matric in a few years.[4] He was then sent to university in Heidelberg, won a scholarship to Gröningen and eventually read history at Leiden. He returned with a PhD and became a lecturer in history and later a professor at Grey University College. An enthusiastic United Party sup-porter, he was, to the surprise of all, appointed Administrator of the Orange Free State in 1940, replacing Hans van Rensburg, who became leader of the Ossewabrandwag. Barnard's skill in keeping the university education sys-tem from becoming a 'true Afrikaans and Christian institution' had stood him in good stead during the divisive war years.

As for the rest, as Queen Elizabeth noted, practically the whole town council and administration were Nationalist. Indeed, the mayor, JG Benadé, was staunchly republican, having in his public career been a vociferous advocate of Nationalist principles. The members of the Provincial Council were all old Boer farmers – 'men of iron', as the Queen described them, 'but fine old men'; six of them had actually 'fought against us in the Boer War and were proud of it'. The King and Queen went on a charm offensive, Queen Elizabeth especially enjoying such a challenge. She found them all rather suspicious to start with, though later, she thought, 'we all got along very well'.[5]

Despite this, the Afrikaans-speaking press went out of its way to downplay any obvious signs of success during the visit. This was in line with a widespread pro-republican editorial policy, in place certainly since the late 1930s. It followed the lead of the unsentimental, even harsh, reporting in the pro-republican Cape Town paper, *Die Burger*, at the start of the tour.

There must have been an element of retaliation, too, against the enthusiastic, often effusive accounts from the English-speaking press of the tour's success, even in Afrikaner strongholds such as Paarl and Graaff-Reinet. Fresh reports that morning of the excited, cheering crowds of two thousand to three thousand who, only the night before, had packed the tiny stations at Rouxville, Wepener, Zastron and the like, cannot have helped either.

These were all unofficial stops for the White Train, but they were considered to be deep in the heart of the republican Free State. It was astonishing that there were crowds at these places at all. Unquestionably, thought *The Friend*, Bloemfontein's English-speaking daily, the Royal Family was endearing themselves to Free Staters of all political convictions. At Rouxville, the nonagenarian Mr Fouche, who welcomed the Queen to the province, had been rewarded with one of the by-now-famous smiles and a '*Baie dankie*'; at Zastron, the Queen had spoken words of sympathy to Mrs Van der Merwe, whose husband had been killed at El Alamein.[6] And so it went. Colin Steyn later told Lascelles that he was 'astounded by his fellow countrymen'. He expected that they would be polite – they were a courteous people, he said – but he never imagined they would show anything like the enthusiasm that was seen

The royal Daimler arrives at the Raadsaal, with the mounted police escort
drawn up in front. TRANSNET HERITAGE LIBRARY PHOTO COLLECTION

everywhere, even from 'the back-veldt farmers' who drove miles to some
wayside station.[7]

It is difficult to gauge whether the reaction was an expression of loyalty,
or curiosity, or what Lascelles defined as The-Circus-Comes-to-Town-
type excitement. Whichever way you looked at it, however, the turnouts
must have been maddening. Further, Malan's supporters cannot have
relished the repeated reports and images of large coloured and black communities greeting the Royal Family, all waving Union Jacks alone; the
South African flag was conspicuously absent among these groups. This
can only have been intensely annoying and provocative In short, none of
this was what the Nationalist press wanted to hear.

While *The Friend* gave the visit impressive front-page headlines and
enthusiastic reporting:

CITY'S MEMORABLE WELCOME TO
THE ROYAL FAMILY
Crowds Line Streets from Early Hours
Presentation of Addresses from Province and Citizens

Bloemfontein yesterday gave the King and the Queen and Princess Elizabeth and Princess Margaret Rose a Rousing Welcome to the Free State Capital ... when the Royal Family drove from the station all the main streets were packed with an excited multitude. From then on, until late last night, when the Royal Family left the civic ball in the City Hall and the illuminations which converted Bloemfontein into a fairyland of lights had been switched off, the city was an indescribable sight – flags waving, cheering crowds, tremendous enthusiasm.[8]

the Afrikaans newspapers took another line, articulating a political response that probably did not even exist cohesively among their readers.[9] The complex issue of South Africans' parallel lives, described in Chapter 2, is well illustrated here, underscored by newspaper editorship.

Die Volksblad, for example, was determined to tell a very different story. They claimed that the reception given was the most muted the Royal Family had received thus far: '*Op geen plek wat die Koning-hulle tot dusver aangedoen het, is hulle so stemmig ontvang as hier nie.*'[10] '*Stofwolke en Aangapery*' (Dust Storms and Gawping) was how they put it in their headline.[11] The newsprint war[12] culminated in the publication of a picture in *Die Volksblad* of the royal Daimler driving down an almost empty street, purporting to illustrate Bloemfontein's disinterest. '*Vir die Bloemfontein publiek het dit nie lank gevat om klaar te kyk na die koninklike gesin nie*' (It didn't take long for the Bloemfontein public to be done with looking at the Royal Family).[13]

Watching the surviving Pathé News footage, this seems patently absurd. The car shown does indeed contain the royal visitors, but it is probably driving down a suburban street taking the family to pay a call on old Mrs Steyn, widow of the last president of the Orange Free State. Such editorial dishonesty offended even a magazine like *Die Patriot*, which felt obliged to refute such reportage by publishing contrasting pictures of large crowds lining the streets to watch the parade and dispersing again afterwards.[14]

Although there is an unedifying tenor of snide one-upmanship in much of this, *Die Volksblad* was pandering to a large section of its readership who were, at heart, strongly opposed to staging any sort of welcome at all. There had been a steady barrage of criticism in advance of the visit. No angle had been left untried. The cost of the tour was criticised,[15] then the wisdom of the trip considering the crisis in England was raised,[16] then even the lack of enthusiasm in the British press was held to foretell the reception here.[17] Nearer the time, the decorations were also held to be too elaborate; South Africa, thought *Die Volksblad*, was about to look 'like a Christmas tree', its public buildings transformed into an 'over-decorated circus tent'.[18]

There was a general attitude of it being nothing at all to do with us; Smuts, like Botha before him, was depicted as a turncoat. 'If a person realises that all this is done under a government with a Boer General in charge, then you don't know whether to be offended or ashamed,' said *Die Volksblad* in an editorial.[19] On 25 February a letter from a correspondent pointedly asked if the tour was going to the Vrouemonument, the monument and museum beyond the city to commemorate the fate of the Boer women and children in the concentration camps. The *Ossewa Brandwacht* (the publication) went so far as to state that there should be no reportage at all. They felt readers were being seduced by even the sporadic coverage in the Nationalist press, which encouraged them to look eagerly for news and then hasten to the nearest point 'to pay tribute to the Conquerors'.[20]

On the day, however, Benadé, the mayor, played his part 'with the utmost courtliness', as the King's speechwriter Dermot Morrah put it.[21] Newsreel footage shows a rather bemused incredulousness; Mrs Benadé looks fairly sour throughout. Other Nationalist officials were polite, too. Nevertheless, there had been openly hostile letters to the Afrikaans papers condemning Afrikaners' playing any part in the planned welcome. Those who publicly refused were praised. One woman, misconstruing old Mrs Steyn's refusal to attend the official welcome at the Raadsaal as a snub, congratulated her publicly in *Die Volksblad*: 'Thank God for your example. May the Lord bless you for the lead you have given the waverers amongst us. Many thanks. I went through the First English War, the Anglo-Boer War, and the First World War [not the war itself but the rebellion among the *bittereinder* survivors that it precipitated], *and I know.*'[22]

The Queen is greeted by the mayor of Bloemfontein, JG Benadé, as she arrives for
the Civic Ball. Princess Margaret is between the two.

PHOTOGRAPH FROM SOUVENIR BOOKLET PUBLISHED BY CNA, 1947

The King and Queen were made thoroughly aware of all this, and it is
to their credit that they did not shy away from potential confrontations or
opportunities for point-scoring. As always, the Queen's personality and
charm were singled out by both sides as a remarkable emollient.[23] One
picture published in *The Friend* shows her actually linking arms with Mrs
Benadé at the garden party and eliciting what could almost be described
as a smile.

At least in Bloemfontein they were able to sleep in a house again.

The Royal Family at the newly completed Government House, Bloemfontein:
'very pretty and conveniently arranged, though too small for a large party
such as ours', wrote Queen Elizabeth.

Government House, Bloemfontein, was their first night away from the
White Train since their journey in it began. In 1947 it was newly built. As
Princess Elizabeth noted, it was 'charmingly sited on a high hill (Signal Hill)
overlooking the town, and where it gets all the breezes that blow'.[24] Painted
white with Mazista tiles (more modern than the pinky-orange Marseille
tiles hitherto used on houses of similar design), it was gabled and detailed
very much in imitation of Baker's Cape Revival style, with lots of teak and
scrolling Cape plasterwork. There were strong echoes of Government
House, Pretoria. It was designed in 1935 by William Mollison, head architect of the Department of Public Works, and completed in 1941.

The Duncans had been due to open it in 1942 and stay there for the
first time. Sir Patrick Duncan, then not long for this world, regarded it
gloomily as a white-elephant-in-the-making. The project, conceived back
in the mid-1930s, did not have his backing. Hertzog, the prime minister at

The Royal Family call on Mrs Steyn (*centre*), widow of the last president of the
Orange Free State. At far left is Mrs 'Rae' Steyn, her daughter-in-law, and at far
right is her son, Colin.

the time, and Havenga, his Minister of Finance, both – as Duncan noted
wryly – 'good Free Staters', had received a deputation from Bloemfontein
querying why the Free State alone had no Government House, to which
they replied 'Why indeed? We shall build one at once.'[25] And so it had
come into being.

On the day of the official opening, Duncan, mourning the death of his
son, recently killed serving with the SAAF, was too ill with the onset of
cancer to travel, so Alice, his wife, deputised for him. She knew the building
well, having been involved in its planning and furnishing and in the layout of the new garden, all of which met with the Queen's approval.[26] The
Queen had met Lady Duncan previously at a weekend at Sandringham in
1937. The royal ladies thought it all very pretty and conveniently arranged,
though small for a large party such as theirs.[27]

Many of the Household were thus obliged to sleep on the White Train.
Typically, Lascelles complained at *not* being one of them, writing irritably
that he had been 'torn out of my comfortable little cabin and moved up

to Government House, Bloemfontein, for a couple of nights. A Bore ...'[28]

All things considered, the first day in Bloemfontein had, to the Household's relief, gone reasonably well. There had been cheering crowds, bunting and illuminations. Much of the behind-the-scenes operations – the decorations, the lights, even the red carpets, together with the smoothness with which the programme ran – owed their success to WK Hartley, the Town Clerk.[29] Generally, the verdict is against *Die Volksblad*; Pathé News might be cleverly spliced, but even Hollywood at that date could not have faked crowds like this. The garden party was well attended and the Queen had dazzled in her feather-trimmed, full-skirted picture frock.

Furthermore, Mrs Steyn had now put it out that she had declined the invitation to attend the official welcome at the Raadsaal simply owing to the fatigue involved for a woman her age; she added that she looked forward to entertaining the party to a private tea at her son's house on Sunday.[30] Only the visit to the black township had gone off badly. There had been large crowds, but Benadé had clearly seen no reason to put himself out over this and there was an evident lack of effort and organisation.[31]

It always seemed to be the older Afrikaners who mellowed on contact with the Royal Family. The younger ones, much inspired by the Voortrekker Centenary, were less susceptible. One such, up from the Cape to attend the braai at Bultfontein on the Saturday, was Elsa Joubert. Her family was a politically divided one. Her father was a member of the Paarl branch of the Ossewabrandwag; her uncle on her mother's side was Stephanus Barnard, the United Party-supporting Administrator. His welcome address would certainly not have been echoed by the Paarl branch of his family:

> I find how inadequate words are when I try and express an appreciation of your presence in our midst ... To a Christian people, the throne is symbolical – it is a symbol of a greater Throne and we are indeed happy in the knowledge that you, sire ... set the highest standard of personal integrity and public honour.
>
> In the midst of great difficulties and during many dark trying years, you sir, and the Queen, faithful to your high calling, stood steadfast and were an example to your people. The nobility of your

character and the great simplicity of your home life have ever been an inspiration to us all.[32]

On the face of it, Elsa Joubert was not an ideal choice as an invitee to the royal braai. She may, however, fairly be said to represent another side of white South African youth. At this stage in her life she was a rabid Nationalist, very much the product of the Voortrekker Centenary. She grew up in Paarl, which, although it still returned United Party candidates (and did so until 1953), was a lively centre of the Ossewabrandwag movement. Her parents were both members. Elsa was a member herself, finding its crypto-Fascist aims, methods, rites and secret rituals exciting. She was young and her upbringing made her susceptible to such doctrines. She even had a boyfriend in a senior position in the movement and thought him glamorous in his uniform and gauntlets.[33]

This was a natural progression. In her schooldays, Elsa and her friends, all dedicated Voortrekkers (Afrikaner Scouts and Guides), would remain firmly seated while 'God Save the King' was played at the end of cinema performances,[34] and later, during the war, many of her contemporaries from Stellenbosch University would habitually take the train into Cape Town to disrupt the two-minute-silence when, following the noonday gun, the city daily froze to attention in honour of the South African fighting forces 'up north'. Elsa herself, though she had cousins and friends in the army, would deliberately walk on at these times, clicking her heels loudly. Despite their political affiliations, her parents deprecated such behaviour. In this her mother's small-town respectability came to the fore; she told her daughter that she was 'making a spectacle of herself'.

As for the royal visit, Elsa had deliberately not availed herself of the public holiday to go into Cape Town to watch the State Entry. This accorded with her political convictions. Her Uncle Stephanus, however, always had a soft spot for his niece, who, it is only fair to add here, later rebelled against much of her 'pinched and fenced-in' background, changing her political views entirely and writing an international bestseller, *The Long Journey of Poppie Nongena*, about the effects of the pass laws on her domestic servant.[35]

For now, the Administrator invited her to come to Bloemfontein for the festivities. He believed, he said, that the Princesses would, by that stage of the tour, have had enough of old men and would enjoy having some people of their own age to talk to.[36] When she wavered, Sarah Goldblatt, the poet Langenhoven's secretary, from whom she rented a room, persuaded her it was an opportunity of a lifetime.[37]

Elsa claimed afterwards that what persuaded her was not so much the invitation to the braai or even the chance of meeting the Royal Family, but rather the invitation that went with it, namely, to the civic ball at the City Hall the night before. Again, this was not so much because of the promised presence of royalty. She loved ballroom dancing. Typically for that time, her dominee did not approve of this. Though her mother had engaged a dancing teacher to travel out from Cape Town, several of her friends had to go to the classes in Paarl in secret, hiding the fact from their grandparents. The dancing at Elsa's matric dance was restricted to *volkspele* (Afrikaans folk dancing) alone.

Moreover, there was the happy prospect of two bands at the City Hall – the SAAF band alternated with Edgar Peterson's Jazz Musicians[38] – permitting continuous dancing without a break. More important, she had a new evening dress to wear – a midnight-blue velvet affair she had only recently worn as a bridesmaid. In addition, a journalist friend of hers was on the pilot train, covering the tour for *Die Burger*; another worked on the newspaper in Bloemfontein. The latter was in love with Elsa; it was unreciprocated, but he danced very well. In her Barnard cousins she had a ready-made party to go along with to the ball; these partners were now a clincher. In the end, it was impossible to resist.

The Saturday braaivleis in the game reserve had been planned as an attempt to soften Afrikaner intransigence. The King, however, was apparently furious at having to attend, as he said there would be nothing to see. Someone must have warned him. Lascelles insisted, however, saying to refuse would make the Free Staters angry.[39]

The Queen rightly saw it as an opportunity to make friends. During the first morning of the Bloemfontein visit, in the room at the Raadsaal where both the old Volksraad and the Crown Colony Government had once convened, the King and Queen had met the Administrator and the Provincial Council over tea. Afterwards, a jovial Dan van der Merwe, chairman of the Council, smitten by the Queen's charm, had said goodbye,

The Royal Family leave the Vickers Viking aircraft at Bultfontein airfield,
on the way to the game reserve and braaivleis.

expansively, with the words: 'Adieu, Your Majesty, until the braaivleis tomorrow,' to which the Queen had smilingly replied: 'Surely, Mr Van der Merwe, not adieu, but *totsiens?*'[40]

So it was that the morning after the ball (which the Household thought well organised, with the Bloemfontein youth well behaved)[41] everyone made their way early to the Bloemfontein aerodrome. There four Vickers Vikings of the King's Flight waited to convey them on the bumpy, 20-minute flight to Bultfontein. A Dakota and two Venturas of the SAAF flew the rest of the guests.

For the King and Queen this was not a pleasure. Although the King had been the first member of the Royal Family to get his wings, both sovereigns disliked flying. They distrusted it. In the 1930s they had lost cousins and friends in plane crashes. Then, in 1942, the King's own brother, the Duke of Kent, had been killed in a plane crash while on a wartime mission. It was whispered in official circles that he had been decapitated on impact.

With these incidents in the background, the Royal Family split themselves between the two planes. The King and Princess Margaret travelled in one plane, Queen Elizabeth and the Heiress Presumptive in the other. All the other passengers were divided between the aircraft, having first, as Elsa Joubert recalls, been made to sign their lives away on a no-claims form.

A fear of flying was not restricted to the sovereigns; each and every member of the Household evidently suffered from it too. Even Peter Townsend, the air ace, thought it dangerous, and said so. Princess Elizabeth did too.[42] It must have made for a tense 20 minutes in the air. Only Princess Margaret was left to enjoy this, her first flight, writing to her grandmother (who had certainly never flown) in a letter which was in general to tell her how they were getting on in this 'lovely country': 'Paying no attention to what the rest of my family said about flying, I enjoyed every minute of it.'[43] Edward 'Mouse' Fielden, Captain of the King's Flight, told Wheeler-Bennett, the King's biographer, that it was not until after the South African tour that the King began to enjoy flying. Queen Elizabeth became a rapid convert, later enjoying using helicopters too.

A crowd of 3 000 farmers and their families from far and wide[44] were waiting on the specially constructed Bultfontein airstrip. Curiosity, not loyal sentiment, had brought these predominantly Afrikaans-speaking Free Staters there, believes Elsa Joubert.[45] The town of Bultfontein itself must have been deserted; the crowd was still there five and a half hours later, happy to wait to witness the royal return, camping out and making a day of it.[46]

The King was seen for the first time to be wearing his South African casuals, a tweed jacket over an open-necked shirt, khaki shorts and long socks. 'This,' notes the Tour Diary, briskly, 'can be regarded as the rig that will be worn on all similar occasions.'[47] The Queen was simply dressed and the Princesses, sporting sunglasses, were in identical linen sun frocks and hats – the one pink, the other blue – looking, thought *The Friend*, 'fresh and cool'. These again were the products of Captain Molyneux's atelier, recommended by the two notably chic royal ladies – the Duchess of Kent and Lady Mountbatten – who dressed there. Understatement was here raised to an art form and sought after by stylish women the world over. Elsa Joubert, who was working for *Huisgenoot*, the Afrikaans women's magazine, was, however, unimpressed; she thought the garments girlish.

The King and Queen walked over and chatted to the gathering. They found amongst them a few ex-servicemen, and several *oudstryders* (veterans), one of whom had a son who had served in the last war, and one who had fought against the British at Paardeberg, surrendered with Cronje, and then been sent as a prisoner of war to St Helena.[48] Such were the strange, chance encounters that the royal visit seemed to occasion and which were apparently weathered so successfully all round. Everyone seems to have come out of such incidents rather well. Thereafter the party set off for the Free State game reserve.

It was a dry and dusty 14-mile (22-kilometre) drive to the old Somerville Estate. Away from the modest imperial architectural setting of the city's sandstone columns, varnished teak and cypress trees, the royal party would now confront the *platteland* Free State in what 'The Rambler', *The Friend*'s weekly columnist, noted bleakly, was its true setting.[49] It was a harsh and disheartening one. These were the very *ver verlate vlaktes* (distant, lonely plains) enshrined by Langenhoven in the words of '*Die Stem*', the Afrikaner national anthem.

The western Free State countryside was then in the grip of a drought. The sandy dirt road, recently graded by the province's Roads Department, led the royal Daimler, together with the cars following it, on and on in choking dust through the flat terrain, occasionally passing a lonely African figure on a horse, the odd maize lands badly in need of rain, two solitary Boer women in their *kappies* (traditional Boer sun bonnets) standing near a tumbledown house, a thorn tree here and there on the sparse veld. Once or twice a group of Africans cheering from the back of a lorry broke, most untypically, the overwhelming atmosphere of utter loneliness and desolation (*eensaamheid*).

Once reached, the game reserve was, in reality, nothing more than a non-hunting concession of 13 000 morgen (11 000 hectares). Game had not been imported; the era of the 'Big Five' and walkie-talkie signalling was decades away. It was understocked even by the standards of the day. Buck was really all that could be hoped for. In the drought, even these were not much to be seen.

Some time later, in a cloud of dust, the cars pulled up at Doornpan, the site chosen for the braaivleis. Here a lapa of sorts – described as a 'rustic shelter' and joylessly constructed out of corrugated iron (*sinkplaat*) – had been erected under the shade of a giant thorn tree. Several thatched rondavels with reed sides stood round about. These included four lavatories or earth closets, known in that era throughout South Africa as 'long drops', two being reserved for the Royal Family's exclusive use.

The heat beneath the *sinkplaat* and the ubiquitous flies must have been terrible. There were 80 guests in all and possibly up to half that number again as cooks and domestic workers and security police. Considering the inherent awkwardness such an occasion presented, the arrangements seem strangely ill-considered. Only a small number – the Royal Family, the members of the Household and a few chosen guests – were seated at a long trestle table; the rest remained standing in the hot sun to eat their food.

Not surprisingly, the atmosphere was strained to begin with. Most of the guests were, again, Nationalists and not particularly disposed to make a go of a royal occasion. Queen Elizabeth, however, tirelessly worked the crowd, 'with a smile plastered all over her fat face', as Elsa Joubert would later record (this is in sharp contrast to Mrs Mills of Queenstown's description of the Queen's smile being one of 'pure loveliness'), and gamely inspected the chops and *boerewors* (spiced sausages) laid out to be grilled, asking for the recipe for the marinade used for the *sosaties* (kebabs).

According to Elsa Joubert, who had been led to believe that she and her cousin were there to talk to the Princesses, she was sharply warned by a Lady-in-Waiting not to initiate conversation with members of the Royal Family. Sitting opposite the Princesses, Elsa felt that she had thereby been rendered mute.

She soon witnessed their being defeated by the eating of the first course. This was the *sosaties*. No one seems to have suggested how to handle the wooden skewer. Princess Elizabeth watched Elsa eating hers with curiosity, and then quietly laid down her knife and fork. Princess Margaret gamely used her knife to try to dislodge the last piece of meat on the skewer. It shot off, however, landing on the undesirable pink frock from which it was skilfully removed by a Lady-in-Waiting with what Elsa recalls as 'a serviette'.

The next course was easier to handle. It was a venison pie, doubtless delicious, but which now strikes a curiously inappropriate culinary note on a hot and dusty day. The conversation never really seems to have got off the ground and went no further than the stilted tourist-experience sort.[50] It was apparently constantly filtered through the Lady-in-Waiting, Lady Margaret Egerton, though no such thing is recorded by guests who spoke to the royal sisters at, say, the Watersons' private dance in Cape Town or the Johannesburg Ball.

The discussion covered the progress of the White Train. Elsa was keen to know the Princesses' impressions of the vast country through which they had travelled. The replies were pretty standard stuff. They involved an observation about the nakedness of some of the African children ('we were surprised'), the game they had just seen, the bad roads and the heat. Also, the tidal wave of *melkterts* that had engulfed them all along the way. They hadn't liked these, which reminded them of milk puddings, to which Princess Elizabeth, in particular, had had an aversion.[51]

Pudding was now served. Alas, it proved to be yet another *melktert*. A long, unwanted, egg-filled, perfectly pastry-lined row of these must, by now, have stretched all the way back down the line, through Rouxville, Zastron, Dewetsdorp, Stormberg, Cookhouse, Kleinpoort and Vondeling, to Worcester and even beyond. This one sat there, Elsa recalls with a chuckle, on its thick, white plate, its skin heavily dusted with cinnamon, which, to the uninitiated, probably looked like dust blown in from the surrounding veld. Both Princesses left their slices untouched, quietly replacing their forks. Lady Margaret was seen to gamely tackle the cinnamon/dust-free tip of her slice.

At the main table things had started to thaw a bit, and, as at other similarly and potentially awkward occasions, skilled royal badinage and the sound of laughter from the top table had the desired knock-on effect. A convivial atmosphere settled in, thought the English press.

Even the Afrikaans press were persuaded to think so too. Satisfied that they were now reporting an essentially Afrikaner occasion, with '*al die informaliteit, al die vriendelikheid en al die lekker gesels van 'n ware braaivleisfunksie*' (all the informality, all the friendliness and all the nice chat of a true barbecue function),[52] they reported it unstintingly. Suggesting, hardly fairly, that this was unusual practice, they were pleased to note that the individuals on this occasion made their separate ways (*'op sy of haar gemak 'n eie koers gevat'*) to talk to the groups of guests.

A game drive followed the braaivleis. This time Uncle Stephanus drove ahead, Elsa having scrambled into the passenger seat beside him. Even at that age, she was aware that, for her uncle, leading the King and Queen through the game reserve was a big moment in his life. He had an exhibitionist streak in his make-up, she thought, and he was determined to give them the spectacle of their lives. He roared along the dirt road behind the steering wheel of his huge black official car with OB 1[53] on its numberplate. As mile after dusty mile passed with still no sightings, there must have been a certain disappointment and even tension inside the cavalcade of cars.

Suddenly a herd was seen on the horizon. It was not on the road. Without warning, Uncle Stephanus swung the steering wheel and the Buick went bucketing across the veld, bumping violently over the tall veld grasses, dongas and mole holes towards the herd. The buck took fright and ran off, but the car swerved again to head them off, and for a moment or two only, the Royal Family must have sensed the exhilarating thrill of the unspoilt African bushveld, seeing 'the whole horizon silhouetted with thousands of game – springbok, blesbok and wildebeest'[54] – which then raced and pranced down to cross the road a few feet in front of them.

With that, it was back to the refreshment area for tea and coffee, *boerebeskuit, koeksisters* and, surprisingly at this juncture, green mealies. Everyone now watched the sovereigns carefully; it was almost a replay of the famous hotdog episode at the Roosevelts' picnic at Hyde Park just before the war. It did not, however, prove the cultural stumbling block that some apparently gleefully anticipated. Corn on the cob was not unheard of at smart pre-war English summer luncheons, almost certainly it had made its culinary way across the Atlantic with the American hostesses of that era. As with asparagus, it was correct in the polite world to eat it with your fingers; this was also the traditional Afrikaans way.

Whatever was hoped for, the Queen was not about to let the side down. She was seen to use her fingers – '*sonder enige gesukkel met mes en vurk*' (without any struggling or messing around with knife or fork), noted *Die Volksblad* approvingly[55] – and asked that she might have some more to be served on the White Train.

Queen Elizabeth afterwards described the braaivleis to Queen Mary as 'meat broiled over an open fire', adding that 'we became quite friendly and I think they softened towards us. It was hardly worth flying out to see a few buck,' she continued, 'but it was worth the friendly picnic atmosphere and a chance of making friends.'[56]

Elsa Joubert carried away no such warm memories of the day, even though she found it exciting to have everything 'laid on'. She had arranged to meet her brother, a lawyer in Welkom, at the airstrip and took her leave. She made no curtsy. While for most English-speaking women, the curtsy represented the very consummation of a royal encounter, performed with carefully rehearsed skill and grace, the Afrikaans press had been strident in its claim that this obeisance (*kniebuiging*) was foreign to them.

Not all Afrikaners would have accepted this. Many had learnt to curtsy to the popular Princess Alice during her reign at Government House in the 1920s, as old news footage shows, some of them doubtless having taken on board the oft-repeated claim, by upper-class Englishwomen, that to make a fuss about doing this or, worse, not to do so at all, was simply a sign of ill-breeding.[57] Famously prickly old Mrs Hofmeyr curtsied, for example, and even ticked off Kathleen Mincher, Smuts's adopted daughter, for turning her back on the King in the drawing room at Government House at the 21st-birthday ball.[58] This was only a minor breach of royal etiquette; doubtless, however, she relished the opportunity of upbraiding the young woman too.

After another dusty drive, the royal party clambered back into the Vickers Vikings for the flight back. 'Soon after 5.30 pm the Royal planes were specks in the southern sky and Bultfontein's great day was over,'[59] as *The Friend* put it, elegiacally. They returned to Government House for a quick, much-needed bath and change. That evening they had in to dine the Chief Justice, several senior members of the judiciary and the widowed Lady Duncan, who had driven in from her farm, Fortrie, near Westminster, which lay in the more English-speaking and less harsh part of the eastern Free State.

The Bloemfontein Caledonian Society pipe band, encountered the day before, had come to perform as requested; this was scheduled for 6.30 pm. The King and Queen had selected the programme, which included a reel and a march ('My Native Highland Home'), allowing *The Friend* to delightedly write it up as 'the first command performance of the Royal Tour'.[60]

The concert took place before the Royal Family, their guests and the immediate Household on the well-mown, emerald-green lawns of Government House as daylight began to fade. It was not a formal party; the men wore black tie and the ladies their simplest, long evening dresses. Petunias, alyssum and heliotrope scented the evening air.[61] It must have all seemed reassuringly familiar again. Afterwards, refreshments were handed round by uniformed staff, and the band congratulated. Thereafter, they marched off proudly, with the poignant tune of 'The Green Hills of Tyrol' wailing mournfully from the pipes into the gathering dusk of the Free State night.

Evening, as a time of day or even at an advanced stage in life's span, is often a moment for reflection and memories. Nostalgia, sadness, regret and even tearfulness often accompany such moments; they are the emotions akin to those of exile. The skirling of the bagpipes, especially in foreign parts, famously enhances these for Anglo-Saxons, even those from very different backgrounds. Some Afrikaners had Scottish blood in their veins, yet on the whole few could or would feel moved by bagpipe music. There is no reason why they should have been; it meant nothing to them other than as a distinctive rendition of a memorable tune, any more than it might have done to the black schoolchildren singing 'Loch Lomond' on the platform at Bethlehem as the White Train pulled in.

None of the royal party would have been immune to this, however, more particularly perhaps after the events of the day. The Queen, partly raised in Scotland, was often seen moved to tears during the tour; Scottishness was part of her appeal, and bagpipes and all matters Caledonian struck a genuine chord with her. Princess Margaret had actually been born at Glamis. Balmoral, too, held a very special place in the Royal Family's hearts, making the Highlands a significant part of the royal psyche.

Thus, however attractive the flower-bordered lawns of Government House, Bloemfontein, with their 'lovely views across the veld for miles and miles',[62] might have been, the day's experiences must surely have brought home to them that they were now standing in a very foreign field – and an indifferent, if not actually unfriendly or hostile, one at that. It is doubtful to imagine that when Princess Elizabeth came to deliver her

Lady Duncan (*left*), widow of the former Governor-General of the Union, and her son, Major Andrew Duncan, DFC (*right*), shot down over Libya (oil on canvas by Neville Lewis).

famous 21st-birthday broadcast speech six weeks later (see Chapter 10), and stated that '... although I am six thousand miles from the country where I was born ... I am certainly not six thousand miles from home,' she could possibly, at that moment, have had Bultfontein in mind.

Lady Duncan, also standing on the lawns, would not have been immune to such emotions either. In her case they were not hers by birthright, but she felt them all the same. Alice Duncan was not English. Of German parentage (the Dolds farmed near Kokstad), she had become anglicised by osmosis through growing up in the South Africa of those days. She had later bought wholeheartedly into the idea of Britishness, morphing, along the way, into a typical proconsul's wife, not only in appearance and accent[63] but also in sharing the requisite sentiments that went with such an image. These would have been absorbed from her husband. She was 23 when she married the 45-year-old MP, the son of a Scotch crofter, who had risen, via scholarship and ability, through Balliol, Milner's Kindergarten and South African party politics to be Governor-General of the Union.

Now, however, Sir Patrick was dead, hastened, it was said, to an untimely grave by the stresses of serving King and Empire at a critical moment in its history (see pp 60–61). In 1942, a prior, equally terrible blow had befallen her. Andrew, her second and favourite son, named after the patron saint of his father's native land, and from whom all traces of his maternal German antecedents had been expunged, was reported missing on a war-time mission with the SAAF over Libya. Oberleutnant Otto Schulz of the Luftwaffe had shot him down. For months, the parents had prayed that he had survived and been taken prisoner; in the end they realised that there was 'no room for hope';[64] no wreckage was ever found.

So here she stood, before the lovely house and gardens she had created[65] and would never occupy, widowed, bereaved and ageing. Despite a strong adherence to her Christian-Scientist principles, she must have known in her heart of hearts that something was very wrong with her health; she had lost weight alarmingly. Like the King, it was the onset of cancer. Hers was far more advanced, however, and would finish her off the following year, aged just 56. Much of her life had been spent putting her best foot forward in what had often been a thankless task; now it was all behind her. Small wonder, then, that there were tears in her eyes.

She was not Ruth amid the alien corn, exactly; Fortrie, named after Sir Patrick's Banffshire home, was comfortable and its garden pretty, and she played the part of the lady of the manor in the district to the hilt.[66] She must, how-ever, at least have known that she was at Government House only as a kindness from the thoughtful sovereigns, who were unlikely in her time to pass that way again. Alice's days 'in wonderland', prophesied by Smuts and whose starry-eyed commencement we witnessed around the tea table at Sandringham, were over; she would amount to little more than a piece of flotsam left behind by the retreating imperial tide. Nellie Watermeyer, the wife of the Chief Justice, and the others of similar, comfortable, proto-colonial backgrounds and sentiments who stood there with her as the music finally died away and night fell, probably had moist eyes too.

Then the King and Queen turned back into the Cape-Dutch-gabled house, and took their guests in to dinner. It was a small party. Apart from Lady Duncan, there was Ernest Watermeyer, the Chief Justice, Justice BA Tindall, Justice O Schreiner, Justice L Greenberg and their respective wives. None were Nationalists. Politics could therefore have been discussed openly, either across the new 27-foot (8.2-metre) stinkwood dining table,[67] by the men over their port or perhaps in private afterwards.

They would now have heard Lady Duncan's current political hobbyhorse. This, Alice Duncan's final sally into a world that she was leaving behind her for ever, had already been expounded to Lady Harlech, who had visited Lady Duncan in her hotel room late on the Friday night after the civic ball, at her urgent request.[68] The two women, who had known one another in their former, official lives, had crossed paths briefly that afternoon at the crowded garden party.

In those days this would still have counted as petticoat politics. Late and tired as she was after the dinner on the Saturday night, Lady Harlech lost no time in setting down all she had heard in a letter to her husband.[69] She thought it of sufficient merit to record.

The burden of Lady Duncan's political prognosis for South Africa was as follows: that Smuts should retire now – she felt he should – and that 'Hoffie' (Hofmeyr) would be wise to try and form a coalition government and get some of the less extreme Nationalists to work with him. Lady Duncan rightly saw that Hofmeyr was not a leader in the way Smuts was, but that, owing to his extreme intelligence, she felt he would be able to manage a coalition very well.

Living in the Orange Free State, Lady Duncan, who had endured the political slings and arrows of her husband's governor-generalship (many aimed at her in particular), was perhaps able to appreciate more clearly than others the way the political winds were blowing in the Union. The rocks she saw, if they did not exactly loom ahead, were, nevertheless, very visible to her just below the surface. The surprising success of the tour in the Free State, and even in places like Graaff-Reinet, where the Nationalists had fully cooperated, suggested, she believed, that such a coalition would succeed. It was an opportunity the tour's success seemed to have highlighted. It was a valid one.

Many saw Havenga, formerly a Hertzogite, who headed the Afrikaner

Party, as holding the key that would deliver these less extreme Nationalists. They had been trounced in the 1943 election, but the party remained active, at Havenga's insistence, as a meeting ground for Afrikaners of moderate political beliefs. According to Arthur Barlow, however, the party had, by that date, already made a secret, tentative approach to Smuts in late 1946 or early 1947, via 'Kalie' Rood, MP for Vereeniging.[70] Havenga's terms were discussed at a United Party caucus in early 1947. They were a tall order: a guarantee of eight seats in the House of Assembly for former Afrikaner Party MPs; Havenga's admission to the Cabinet; and recognition of Havenga as Smuts's successor following his retirement.

The last condition was an impossibility for Smuts. Hofmeyr was recognised as his successor. (It would, of course, anyway, have thrown out Lady Duncan's scenario.) Smuts, confident with his majority in the House, did not feel that an alliance with the Afrikaner Party was necessary; he also bore a personal grudge against Havenga for his refusal to support his war policy.[71] He baulked too at the idea of including him in the Cabinet. The approach was 'frisked aside with contempt'.[72]

Politically, it was another terrible mistake. There was another taker – Malan. Although the negotiations between the two old antagonists were protracted, an accord was reached on 21 March stating that since 'no difference existed between the two parties', they had decided on cooperation for the purpose of ousting the 'Smuts-Hofmeyr regime'.

A year later, they would succeed in doing just that.

The following morning, Divine Service was held in Bloemfontein's Anglican cathedral. The Cathedral Church of St Andrew and St Michael, with its brick campanile, dated back to the 1860s. Posies awaited the royal ladies in the new, crown-ended pews which had been carved specially for the Royal Family, together with new tapestry kneelers 'stitched by the women of the cathedral under the direction of Mrs Hugh Wiley'.[73] It was here that the prayer by Dean Tugman for the plight of the British people so moved the King that he would use it in his speech at the State Banquet in Pretoria (see page pp 192–193).

The text chosen by the Right Revd AH Howe Browne, the Bishop of Bloemfontein, for his sermon on that bright, auspicious Sunday morning was 'We are colonists of heaven' (Philippians 3:20). The Anglican Church of South Africa (whose adherents habitually dashed off 'C of E' on official forms where 'religion' needed to be filled in), was becoming increasingly vocal in its opposition to Malan's espoused racial policies. The Nederduits Gereformeerde Kerk openly supported Malan, who claimed apartheid would be fair to all races.[74] This was convenient window-dressing; the Anglicans, however, had come to believe that the NGK's unwavering, neo-Calvinistic ideological justification for apartheid was antithetical to the teachings of the Christian church.

The Church of England used the sermons preached at services attended by the Royal Family during the tour to quietly raise this and other related issues affecting church and state.[75] Many of its clergy felt they were increasingly required to take a stand, and to provide timely wake-up calls for their congregations, who often managed to let moral dilemmas of this sort, confronted in daily life, simply slide.

The sermon at Bloemfontein was a subtle one. *The Friend* printed it in full for the benefit of its readers on the Monday the White Train departed. The Bishop did not, for example, take a confrontational 'render unto Caesar that which is Caesar's' line. Nevertheless, he likened the lot of Christians living in Philippi under the Roman Empire to that of Christians in present-day South Africa, and the moral dilemmas and thorny questions they faced. These the Bishop articulated. How far should a Christian insist on certain standards in the affairs of his own country? How far was he justified in opposing trends and tendencies that were contrary to his belief as a Christian? And was it merely enough to stand apart and condemn?[76]

These were the questions that would confront many South African Christians in the years to come.

Lady Harlech, installed back on the White Train as it steamed on through the Free State towards Basutoland, one of her husband's former High Commission territories, took up her letter to him again. The Bishop's sermon, she thought, had been 'very good'.[77]

CHAPTER 5

Race, Empire, Politics and Agendas: Eshowe, Durban and Currie's Fountain

19 to 22 March 1947

Eshowe, 19 March

On the evening of 18 March the White Train left Pietermaritzburg, after a single-day visit. Instead of going directly on to Durban, the largest city in the province, it bypassed it and the following morning pulled in to Gingindlovu[1]. The final destination, by car, was Eshowe, a town on a branch line, whose pretty Zulu name recreated, onomatopoeically, the sound of the wind sighing through the trees of the natural forest that surrounded it. Before it, as you squinted east into the morning sunshine, lay the marvellous hilly views of the sugarcane fields, heaving and rolling away down to the distant Indian Ocean. At 1 600 feet (488 metres) above sea level, with its golf course, tennis courts and trim gardens surrounding little white houses, Eshowe reminded members of the Household of a hill station in India.[2]

Eshowe was the capital of Zululand and, in what was generally seen as a mark of respect to the Zulu people, had been allotted exactly the same amount of time as Maritzburg, the provincial capital. For all that, every aspect of the morning's programme typified the small, white-run town visits that the planners had envisaged. There was the stop at the refurbished

Old Residency;[3] the tea at the country club, with its sweeping lawns and flower borders, its red-polished floors spread with animal skins lent by Captain Potter of the Hluhluwe Game Reserve; the drive around the cricket oval surrounded by cheering, Union Jack-waving schoolchildren (some of the black schoolchildren setting out at 4 am with their teachers to walk there), together with the representatives of the various Zululand Women's Institutes; and the Umvoti Mounted Rifles (commanded by Lt Col Slatter) lining the route between the Residency and the town hall for the civic lunch. Much commented on were the roses for the royal tea table supplied by Mr Paul, the chairman of the Empangeni Town Council, from his garden. It was a source of local comment and pride that Mr Kerr, who oversaw the 'excellent catering', had previously cooked for the King at a civic lunch in Glasgow in 1919, when he was still Prince Albert.[4]

Yet it was the event planned to take place at the aerodrome in the afternoon that was to be the significant component of the visit here. For days, thousands upon thousands of Zulus from all over Natal and even further afield had been converging on the town; many old white Natal hands had turned up too, keen to be present at the great Zulu *Ngoma Nkosi* dance before the King.

This was essentially a 'Black Show', as Lascelles put it,[5] jointly organised by the Department of Native Affairs and the Zulu people, or, more particularly, their royal house, its chiefs and *indunas*. Both before and after, it was considered alternately as an impressive display of loyalty to the King, or decried as something merely ornamentalist, or even regressive, depending on one's political standpoint. For here, again, simmering just beneath the surface, was a cauldron of politics that threatened to boil over at any moment.

All politicians – not only Smuts and Malan but also the ANC, its Youth League, the tribal chiefs (the Native Affairs department, too), the South African Indian Congress, even the British government through the person of the King himself – sought to attach agendas to the royal tour for their own purposes.

The tour had placed the Union in the spotlight; it was much publicised and photographed. Images and newsreels of its progress through South Africa flew constantly around the world. Though the Smuts government had intended it to put a positive spin on the country, the tour proved to be a double-edged sword. Everyone immediately saw it as a golden opportunity to draw attention to their own issues. In certain instances, for example, identical photographs would be held to support diametrically conflicting claims. Photographs of township life that for the ANC and its liberal white and African-American supporters highlighted the evils of segregation, were believed by the Smuts government to contrast favourably with the familiar slums of Delhi and Mexico City. It all must have been a minefield for the uninitiated. No wonder the Royal Family had felt apprehensive at the start of their African odyssey.[6]

To put the politics of the day into perspective, it is essential to remember that from about 1942, when the tide of war began to turn in the Allies' favour, there dawned an era in which the political possibilities seemed endless, and not, as we might view them now, hopelessly unlikely.[7] No one could be sure what exactly the brave new world would be. A somewhat war-weary Smuts himself must have been aware of this uncertainty as he peered into the future in November 1944: 'The making of blue prints for a world order which may remain unborn [is a] horrid undertaking,' he wrote to Margaret Gillett.[8] Perhaps, having lived through three major wars, Smuts was at last beginning to feel his age. At any rate, he was soon to discover that the post-war future held more nasty shocks for him than for most.

Wearing the spectacles of hindsight, then, the modern reader sees the Nationalist victory of 1948, the establishment of the apartheid monolith, the worldwide retreat from Empire, and the changes in the Commonwealth's make-up and influence as inevitable. But this was not obvious at the time, even to the major protagonists of our story. Indeed, only a year before the fatal election of 1948, South African liberals were actually displaying a cautious optimism. The war years had inevitably seen a general easing of attitudes, and some welfare reforms had even benefited non-whites, while assorted soundbites, heard locally and abroad, encouraged a faith in progress.

Thus, in late January 1947, Margaret Ballinger, one of the three Native Representatives in Parliament, took the opportunity of telling the House of Assembly that 'there was a solid core of liberal opinion in this country that is prepared to take their stand on the basis of recognizing the rights of the Native population of this country to aspire to ultimate citizenship. There is a widening support,' she continued, doubtless seeking a resonance or even an echo within the Union, of the tide now running in international political affairs, as recently evidenced at the United Nations, 'for the principle of equal rights for all civilised men.'[9]

This was barely three weeks before the *Vanguard* docked in Cape Town and was a statement of optimism – at least for those who wanted to hear it. Both Ballinger and Edgar Brookes[10] and other like-minded liberals were to claim to have heard sympathetic royal support for their cause in the King's speech at the State Banquet in Cape Town at the start of the tour.

The Empire, too, in this era, was far from being seen as done for. Having beaten the Germans, the King's second major agenda of his reign was retarding its disintegration and building up the concept of the free association of the Commonwealth.[11] Though the days of the Raj in India were clearly numbered, it was plausibly hoped that India would remain as a self-governing Dominion within the Commonwealth. This body was not then perceived as the *dudu*, or comfort blanket, for the post-imperial British baby that some unsentimental historians have come to see it,[12] but more what Smuts himself described in a wartime letter to *Life* magazine as 'the widest system of organised human freedom which has ever existed in human history'. (Smuts might have had a point in general terms here, but even at that date not many would have cited South Africa as a shining example of human freedom.)

An abstraction, then, rather than a political entity, the Commonwealth was to be held together by a common loyalty to the Crown. Smuts himself and many others saw it as a force for good among its members and in the greater world at large. The sovereigns thought so too. Writing to Lady Duncan in 1943, when the fortunes of the Allies were at their nadir, Queen Elizabeth expressed the hope that after the war 'our people will have a great opportunity ... to show the worth of our system of government'.[13]

This, of course, referred especially to the governance of the many remaining colonies, whether self-governing or not. There was no thought of jettisoning them. Indeed, several of the King's senior Labour ministers, including Ernest Bevin, the Foreign Secretary, and Sir Stafford Cripps, Minister for Economic Affairs, now thought that the focus of the Empire should shift from the East to mineral-rich Africa, which had the potential to ameliorate Britain's chronic balance-of-payments issues.[14]

South Africa, the modern, go-ahead and industrialised hub of the sub-continent, would clearly have a pivotal role to play here. It was rich in minerals – most notably for the nuclear age in uranium – and therefore needed to be kept on side in this new scheme of things. Aiding and abetting Smuts's post-war vision of white-led Dominion-ism against Malan's espoused republicanism, anti-imperialism and apartheid, must surely have been an agenda in itself. This much may be reasonably adduced from Queen Elizabeth's letter to Queen Mary as the tour drew to its close: 'I think that it was high time a visit was paid in South Africa, and if it proves successful, then it is all worthwhile.'[15]

It must be said at once that the royal version of Smuts's dream came with the tentative hope that it could shortly be shown to accommodate some of the political aspirations of its non-whites. This, as the King would note in his Guildhall speech on his return to London, would require breadth of vision, human sympathy and statesmanship (see pp 310–311).

There was, however, a real fly in the imperial ointment, and that was the chronic balance-of-payments situation itself. Britain's power and her ability to maintain and run an empire had been drastically undermined, not so much, it has been recently argued, by the threats within the empire's boundaries, but by rival empires without, namely, Germany (twice) and Japan.[16] Victorious but staggeringly in debt, Britain after 1945 simply had neither money nor manpower to maintain her colonial possessions in the face of nationalist movements within them. Ten years later, the Suez crisis would show it no longer had the united will to do so either.

Moreover, an additional, maverick factor had entered into the impe-rial equation, one that would undermine the very idea of empire in the post-war age. Victory had been won with the vital support of yet another challenging empire – the United States – which had emerged from the conflict as a new superpower. The United States was an ally with whom there was purportedly a special relationship. Yet there was a significant ambiguity to this, economic rivalry apart. For all Churchill's talk about a common language and identity, white, liberal American thought (and later, African-American thought) differed fundamentally on one especial issue: that of Empire.

To white Americans reared on the stories and myths of their own freedom struggle against British oppression, imperial rule over a subject people was unpalatable. And morally wrong. No amount of rhetoric about upliftment of backward people would persuade them otherwise. Indeed, America's entry into the war (finally caused by Japan's pre-emptive aggression and Hitler's declaration of war, not by going to the aid of their beleaguered cousins across the waters), had prompted *Life* magazine to publish an open letter to the people of Britain. Addressed to its British readership, but clearly intended, too, for its much larger American one, it was remarkably forthright, self-righteous and even sibilant in tone:

> One thing we are sure we are *not* fighting for is to hold the British Empire together. We don't like to put the matter so bluntly, but we don't want you to have any illusions. If your strategists are planning a war to hold the British Empire together they will sooner or later find themselves strategizing all alone.[17]

Britain, relieved to have the United States on her side in a war she could not possibly have won on her own, had been in no position to argue. The Atlantic Charter, signed in 1941 by Churchill and Roosevelt prior to America's entry into the war, had been nothing less than a fire-bell in the night for all imperialists (Churchill being an unregenerate one of that number) and a harbinger of a coming, more liberal age, too, for oppressed peoples everywhere in the post-war world.

Indeed, back in England, Churchill had had to reassure Parliament that Article 3 of the Charter, which reaffirmed the right of all peoples to choose the form of government under which they lived, and further stated that the signatories wished to see sovereign rights of self-government restored to those who had been forcibly deprived of them,[18] did not 'embrace the progressive evolution of self-governing institutions in the regions and the peoples which owe their allegiance to the British crown'.[19] In other words, Whitehall would decide on the pace of the colonies' journey towards self-government. Unrealistically, this included India – always foremost in his mind – and of course the African colonies too.

At the time, these anomalies had been allowed to pass. Visiting Washington in 1943, however, anti-imperial sentiments eddied round and round the British prime minister, and Churchill came face to face with this unpleasant feature of his new, long-awaited alliance. The president and his advisors all took much the same view as *Life's* open letter, though they were tactful enough not to press the issue, possibly trusting that post-war economics would bring about the Empire's natural collapse. (At the Tehran Conference later that year, Roosevelt would express his disapproval of Empire in private to Stalin, as a way of ingratiating himself with the Russian leader.) Mrs Roosevelt, who didn't much care for a lot of Churchill's Tory-style politics, far less his capacity for alcohol, was less circumspect on this aspect of Britain's policy; others were even more openly vociferous.

Typically, like many a vociferously held opinion, it was a decidedly blinkered one. While the British prime minister was staying at the White House, among the Sunday lunchtime guests was Mrs Ogden Mills Reid, a future vice-president of the *New York Herald Tribune*, well known for attacking Roosevelt but also for sharing his anti-imperialist views. These currently centred on India in particular, then much in the news, and Britain's supposed oppression of the Indians there. On the porch after lunch, she saw fit to raise the matter confrontationally.

Churchill was in no mood to mollify a strident, self-righteous woman of the Mrs Ogden Mills Reid sort on a subject as sacred to him as British India. Habitually well-oiled by that time of the day and grumpy at the end of yet another indifferent meal (the teetotal and disapproving Mrs Roosevelt was away; her famously under-par cook wasn't), he decided to have a go at her. Was she, he growled, referring to the brown Indians in India, who had multiplied so under Britain's benevolent rule there, or was she speaking of the Red Indians of America, who he understood were almost extinct? Helen Ogden Reid was apparently totally disconcerted by this and furious; the president, kicking for touch, simply roared with laughter. The subject was dropped.[20]

All too soon after the war, Smuts, too, would come up against this new

American-supported, anti-imperial and liberal mindset. South Africa was particularly vulnerable to it. Although he had rewritten the preamble to the UN Charter, when faced with the dichotomy of its sentiments on human rights and South Africa's segregation, he argued that human rights did not equal full political rights and racial equality. Were it to do so, it would mean the end of progress in countries where less progressive races constituted a majority.[21] Like Churchill, he was swiftly to discover that such caveats were becoming unacceptable.

Smuts, as we shall presently see, had gone to the first session of the United Nations in 1946 to press for the formal incorporation of South West Africa into the Union. He had counted on his international prestige and the country's wartime record in getting this through. They availed him nothing. The annexation – against which there had been fairly intense lobbying by the canny regent of neighbouring Bechuanaland, Tshekedi Khama – was disallowed owing to South Africa's racial policies. A second blow, even harsher and more publicly administered, was dealt in the General Assembly a short while later when India, with the support of the United States, censured South Africa for the treatment of its Indian population (see pp 174–176).

Whatever the various agendas behind these two events, one thing was certain: South Africa's race issues were becoming alarmingly internationalised. The policy of non-interference in domestic affairs of member states, so hotly debated in San Francisco the previous year, was now shown to be worthless. Naturally, it could be pointed out that hypocrisy and double standards were involved here. Half a million minority Muslims had recently been massacred by Hindus in Calcutta and Bengal, numbers that would have deeply shocked and been unimaginable to even the harshest, racist-minded Afrikaner member of the South African Police. Writing to his wife from Europe, Smuts expressed his suspicion that at least part of the Indian attack on South Africa was to divert attention from this.[22] Some economists, too, would come to see America's anti-imperialism as having a distinctly self-serving element – ie, a need for cheap natural resources and unimpeded new markets for themselves.

White, mid-century, American liberalism, however well intentioned, was anyway, at that date, comfortably afforded by numerical superiority;

de facto social segregation existed in much of the South, and mixed marriages were banned in 38 of the 48 American states. Such liberalism was not even concerned with the fate of its indigenous people – whose numbers had been systematically decimated in the nineteenth century – and whose final great land dispossession was now not only conveniently forgotten by the many, but actually, at the date of the awkward White House lunch party, being celebrated by default in the hugely popular and quintessentially American Broadway musical *Oklahoma!*, which had opened in March that year.

The musical was much touted as a morale booster for the American armed forces, which it undoubtedly was, and as 'symbolising what we are fighting for and what we as a nation stand for'. This was a widely held opinion. The historical background to it all was rather less edifying. Oklahoma, deemed unsuitable for farming, had been set aside as a catchall area for Native Americans living and resettled there from elsewhere, often inhumanely, before the Civil War. Towards the end of the nineteenth century it was found, due to advances in agricultural methods, to be eminently arable. Dubious legislation, almost all of it to the disadvantage of the Native Americans, eventually resulted in the much-publicised Land Rush or Run, organised for white settlers in 1889. The musical opens to find these settlers happy and making good on a 'beautiful morning', their corn as high as an elephant's eye. Ironic, then, were the famous lyrics: 'We know we belong to the land, And the land we belong to is grand.' Ironic, too, was the meaning of Oklahoma – 'land for red people' in Choctaw.

Liberal white American opinion had tended to draw a veil over these (then) comparatively recent events. Rather, the concern was with African Americans, still called Negroes, and even here, it tended to emanate primarily from whites living in areas where this group was in a decided minority.

In South Africa, Africans were in a minority only in the western and southeastern parts of the Cape. Accounting for roughly 61 per cent of the population, they had no vote and no hope of getting it, any provision for the extension of the Cape's qualified franchise having been glaringly omitted from the Treaty of Vereeniging at the end of the Anglo-Boer War in 1902. There it had been agreed that the decision would be deferred until after the introduction of self-government to the Transvaal and Orange

River colonies. This was a big missed opportunity, for thereafter things went from bad to worse in this vital regard for blacks in South Africa. The two colonies were the former Boer republics, only temporarily vanquished, and were highly unlikely to entertain ideas of even a qualified franchise once they attained self-government.

At the time of Union, nothing more concrete was offered. As the South Africa Bill was debated in the House of Lords in July 1909, WP Schreiner, Gandhi and other liberals had looked down from the public gallery in consternation, alarmed by the lack of protection for blacks, Indians and coloureds. Asquith, while recognising their reservations, claimed that whites would deal more wisely with these issues if they were united rather than divided. Any intervention from the outside world would, he said, be 'in the very worst interests of the natives themselves'.

It was a premise falsely arrived at and argued. The Land Act of 1913, and the Native Trust and Land Act of 1936 contrived to dispossess the African population, who were left with a mere 13.5 per cent of the country's land. The Representation of Natives Act of 1936 removed the small number of Cape blacks from the common voters' roll. The African electorate in the Cape Province were by this law removed from the ordinary electoral roll and placed on a separate roll, with the right to elect three representatives in the Union House of Assembly and two to the Cape Provincial Council. In addition, the African population of the whole Union could designate four senators to represent their interests.

As a population group, the 'Natives' or 'Bantu' clearly fell under Smuts's less progressive races constituting a majority. South African Indians, numerically a much smaller group but generally better skilled and educated, were similarly disenfranchised, and occupied a stratum somewhere above blacks. Following the Pegging Act of 1943, activists of both groups for the first time made common cause with their mutual grievances: dispossession, segregation and thwarted political rights.

When the royal tour was announced, black political organisations had been quick to exploit it to highlight their political issues. By 1946, these were such as to have provided fertile ground for discontent. The rapid increase of black urbanisation occasioned by the war had also led to a greater increase in black militancy. The pass laws were a particular grievance. Strikes, stayaways and teachers' protests, together with the black municipal Advisory Boards, the ANC and the Communist Party, had all played their part in this new era of black consciousness, while popular young leaders such as Oliver Tambo, Walter Sisulu and Nelson Mandela urged more confrontational politics. Indeed, under AB Xuma's leadership, the ANC, referring explicitly to the Atlantic Charter of 1941, had demanded full citizenship rights for all Africans in its document entitled *African Claims*.

At the 24th conference of the African National Congress held in Bloemfontein in December 1946, therefore, Resolution 17 stated: 'As a protest against the barbarous policy of the Union Government of denying the elementary democratic rights to Africans and in view of the fact that these injustices are perpetuated and maintained in the name of His Majesty King George VI of the Union of South Africa, this Conference instructs the incoming Executive Committee to devise ways and means likely to bring about the abstention of the Africans from participation in the welcoming of the Royal Family during its tour of the Union.'[23]

Yet, following on from this, no cohesive front seems to have existed among its members for their subsequent response to the tour. Letters poured into the newspapers suggesting why officials should not appear or arguing why a boycott was or was not a bad idea. The issue rumbled on well into the general timeframe of the tour itself. *Ilanga Lase Natal*, an influential black newspaper, wrote: 'Loyalists will no doubt be perturbed over the resolution ... which has provoked serious heart searchings ... It was generally accepted that a boycott was no longer possible, but that the consensus ... was that Congress as such [never invited officially to take part in the welcome] could not justifiably identify itself with the welcome.'[24]

As with Afrikaner and Indian nationalist movements, there seems to have been a decided disconnect between the politically motivated boycotts planned by black leaders and the response of the people called on to do the boycotting. Indeed, the evidence suggests that there was remarkably little appetite for it; the great majority simply refused to participate in such political gestures.

Even the political leadership started to lose heart once the tour got under way and great crowds of black South Africans everywhere flocked to welcome

Liberal voices: Margaret Ballinger (*left*) was one of the Native Representatives in Parliament. Albert Luthuli (*centre*), the future leader of the ANC and later a Nobel Prize winner, was Representative Chief of the Zulus at the *Ngoma Nkosi*. A B Xuma (*right*) was President-General of the ANC. The painting of Luthuli is by Neville Lewis.

ARCHIVE PL/ALAMY STOCK PHOTO; BY PERMISSION; GALLO IMAGES/GETTY IMAGES

the Royal Family, often having walked miles to do so. Jean Lawrence, travelling in the ministerial carriage en route to East London, three hours ahead of the White Train, describes the winding streams of Xhosa coming over the rolling hills to throng the little stations to see the Royal Family pass by.[25] Bush telegraph must have alerted them; JS Marwick, the MP, pointed out at the time that the great majority did not yet have radios.[26]

It was the same story elsewhere; the boycott hadn't worked. In the face of such populist enthusiasm, it began to look misjudged and unconstitutional. Worse, the situation was being manipulated by extremists. Before the royal party reached Natal, at the February meeting of the Johannesburg branch of the ANC, with AB Xuma presiding in person, there was a vote of 15 to 2 against the boycott (see page 203). And Xuma and his wife, Madie Hall, the social worker, had thereafter pointedly journeyed to Eshowe to attend the *Ngoma Nkosi*, having been exasperated by the Youth League's further calls for a boycott and the Communist Party's skilful promotion of them.[27]

Populism triumphed over politics when it came to the crunch. There were many reasons for this. African journalists never tired of pointing out to their readers that the highlights of the tour for the Royal Family would be when and where non-Europeans would welcome them.[28] The constitutional monarchs were held to be apolitical; this particular family were, moreover, attractive, charming and friendly, the very image of respectability, and, most significantly, apparently colour-blind. In their gowns, jewels, orders and uniforms, they impressed.

Of course, there was also some truth in the theory (naturally embraced by the Native Affairs Department) that traditionalist blacks were susceptible to chiefly and monarchical forms. These were also seen as an antidote to radicalism and communism,[29] especially by the amaRespectables among them. This group had emerged in urban as well as rural areas to form a black middle class, often with a mission-school background, and who prized family life, respectability and conservative politics.

Detractors of the Empire, always dismayed by evidence of cooperation among indigenes and even moderately radical party leadership, where they hope only for anger and rebellion, also forget that, in its day, the Empire looked impressive and *proper*, and that, moreover, on big occasions it glittered. A jamboree is hard for most people to resist, especially for those living in modest, deprived or remote circumstances. A royal jamboree under such circumstances clearly proved irresistible to the majority.

But it is not enough to leave it there. In her detailed study of the black response to the royal tour, Hilary Sapire concludes – convincingly – that the tour witnessed the last genuine outpouring of black loyalism in South Africa.[30] It is all too easy to argue, as some revisionist historians do today, that such loyalism was archaic and regressive in the 1940s, a decade of unprecedented black protest. A close look at the literature suggests, however, a very different picture.

It was not, anyway, the intention of the King or his advisors to ignore his non-white South African subjects. At the very first meeting of the Planning Committee in Durban, the mayor reiterated that the King had expressed a desire to see 'masses of children, ex-servicemen, and non-Europeans'.[31] Nor was it the intention of his Household, the ruling government, the Native Affairs Commissioners or the Central Planning Committee of the tour, though it is probably fair to say that their agendas in not so doing differed widely.

Both the Palace and Whitehall were additionally anxious that meetings with blacks and Indians should be seen to go off smoothly and gracefully, to set a precedent for a trouble-free handover of power in India and

Burma. Significantly, when things became disorganised at events – as they did at the indaba in Pietersburg[32] or the huge gathering of 100 000 blacks at the Durban aerodrome – the Royal Family would be driven away early, lest things got ugly or out of hand.[33]

No such disorderliness was apparent at the *Ngoma Nkosi* Dance that sunny afternoon at Eshowe. Unlike the indabas at Umtata or King William's Town, it was essentially seen as a tribal celebration, organised by the Native Commissioners as a tribute from the Zulu people to the monarch. This was far from being a long shot. Traditional Zulu society was very stratified, its royal family surrounded, since the formation of the kingdom, by an elite of clans.[34] Symbolically, the occasion was subtly designed to underscore the power of the rural chiefs, while at the same time seeking to restate the relationship between them and the ruling house and the House of Windsor. A hierarchical parade of power, in other words, with the King at its apex, ruling through the Zulu royal house, the loyal chiefs and *indunas* (headmen).[35]

Critics of the event complained that the Zulu had not been consulted enough. This was an old liberal grievance, and this time not entirely borne out by the facts. Some radical blacks also felt betrayed by the presence of their senior political leaders at Eshowe and elsewhere, pointing out that 'the essence of the Royal Visit is directly interwoven with the political structure of the country.'[36]

Others, on the other hand, not only the Native Affairs Department, who had urged the tour planners to include as many indabas as possible on the itinerary as a reward for 'steadfast loyalty' of the blacks during the war,[37] but also many of the participants and onlookers, saw it as a great show of Zulu pride and loyalty to the Crown. *The Natal Mercury* naturally put this view of things unhesitatingly, describing it as 'a tribute of loyalty from the Zulu nation to the Person and crown of His Majesty the King'.

That this suited conservative white opinion should not blind us to what it meant to the Zulu people and their pride, hopes and aspirations connected with the event. Tellingly, the next sentence in *The Mercury* reads: 'And that is no insignificant thing in times like the present when so many subtle forces are at work to undermine the faith and goodwill of the Native Peoples.'[38]

That faith and goodwill remained at all was surely remarkable in itself. Yet, there it is; even a white liberal like Leo Marquard acknowledged that it survived, though he believed, as he wrote to Hofmeyr, it was being rapidly forfeited in the political climate of post-war South Africa.[39] Perhaps a unique royal occasion provided an opportunity for displaying this, then, something which by that date would have been almost inconceivable at a purely white-controlled, political event, supposing that one ever presented itself. For despite being dispossessed, despite the disillusionment about the failure of wartime promises within South Africa, it had become very obvious as the tour proceeded that black loyalism to the Crown, which stretched back to the days of Queen Victoria, 'Setori', was far from dead. Her memory, it became clear, was still revered. As the Zulu regent Mshiyeni would say in his address of welcome that afternoon: 'We remember with gratitude, when her armies had conquered our warriors in battle, she generously sent for our King and when he arrived in her august presence, she spoke to him not in words of wrath and vengeance, but in the words of a mother to her erring son, and sent him back to us again.'[40]

Indeed, the Crown was still vaguely understood to have executive powers and was seen as a beneficent protector of rights. The special supplement in the Zulu newspaper, *Ilanga*, published to commemorate the arrival of the Royal Family in Natal, contained a poem by Herbert Dhlomo, known as 'the poet of the ANC Youth League'. Citing the sufferings of black people, the poem went further:

No sham your visit or a sophoriphic
Your presence here we take as a sign prophetic
Of greater things to come; of a new birth
Of freedom, righteousness and peace when worth,
Not race, will be the standard and the law;
When the Union will be a union, not a raw and deceitful sham;
    when union citizens
Will include both black and white and denizens and serfs no longer
    will our people be
And all will join in a Hymn of Unity.[41]

This extended the Crown's perceived role beyond that of upholding democratic principles against white settler rapacity. It was also seen as a conduit of the spirit of a more egalitarian post-war world – witnessed by the election of a Labour government in Britain and the King's cousin overseeing the granting of independence to India. Black loyalty during the war,[42] it was held, deserved to be rewarded, and traditional tribal events such as this, graced by the sovereign in person, were seen as an opportunity to underscore this belief. Renewed claims to the rights and freedoms already enjoyed by his white subjects would surely now be entertained. Mshiyeni again: 'We recall how fear gripped us when, in the Second Great War, your enemies appeared to be gaining ground. But through the air we heard your voice, rallying your people and directing them to put their trust in righteousness and simple living, and so we took courage and we sent our sons to aid your armies in their colossal task ... When it was all over, Your Majesty did not send an envoy to greet us but came in person.'[43]

Against this background and the discouraging calls for boycotting the tour by radical black opinion, then, the Zulus flocked to attend the big dance. A great migration estimated at 80 000 (some reports suggest slightly less) had made their way to Eshowe, by bus, train and lorry. Some had travelled on foot for five days or more, sleeping out in the open at night; their campfires had been seen burning across the countryside for days. Some arrived well after the event.[44] Many were migrant mineworkers who had responded to the call from Prince Cyprian, the 20-year-old Zulu Paramount Designate, who was in Johannesburg having his new uniform fitted, to come and welcome the Royal Family with songs and dances at Eshowe.[45]

It was not a case of princely coercion; the endless surplus footage of Pathé News tells the story of a proud and happy people journeying towards an event of great significance to them. One former Eshowe resident vividly recalls the lasting impression made on her as a (white) child by the extraordinarily happy atmosphere that unusually prevailed in the town as the chiefs and *indunas*, in traditional dress, walked down its streets, waving their shields and spears in greeting.[46] Among their number were even veterans of the great Zulu victory over the British at Isandlwana; one, Mapelu Uzungu, who gave his age as 100, had been awarded the *Umyezawe*, the Zulu equivalent of the VC, only given to warriors who had shown the utmost valour in battle. *The Natal Witness* carried his photograph, proudly wearing his regalia, among its great pictorial accounts of the event.

According to the newspapers, this was the first time in 60 years that the Zulu people would meet and dance as a nation – an event requiring enormous organisation to reform the old regiments. Rehearsals had been taking place for months; old men were consulted over the dance gestures and movements, old women for the details of traditional dress. A fortnight before, councillors and sangomas were sent down from the royal kraal of Cyprian Zulu to make sure that the arrangements were perfect.[47]

The day itself was perfect – almost cloudless and full of bright late-summer sunshine. 'Real King's Weather', said *The Zululand Times*, proudly.[48] The dress of the principal participants was remarkable in its variety. The dancers wore great shows of vulture or *sakabula* feathers on their heads; leopard or monkey skins between their wrists and elbows, and black and white calf skins draped on their bodies. The women wore beadwork, *ubuhlalo*, and a variety of kilts, each one denoting their social status; many of them danced with their breasts uncovered.

There was no such traditional costume for Prince Cyprian, whose uniform ('plum coloured ... with plenty of gold braid', according to *The Natal Mercury*) was based on a British regimental prototype and specially made for the occasion. As with the indaba of the chiefs in Umtata, there was a reluctance to appear in tribal dress 'lest the King think we are native savages'.[49] Not even all the dancers, noted *The Zululand Times*, to its disappointment, wore tribal dress.

The King himself wore his white tropical naval uniform with his medals, Garter and sword. This followed Sir Piers Legh's note, on his return from the recce in 1946, which tendered Sir Evelyn Baring's advice that the King should wear distinctive uniforms at the indabas.[50] Apart from his aide-de-camp, therefore, the rest of the Household wore lounge suits, which showed him to advantage.[51] The Queen was in 'a graceful frock of palest cyclamen' ('Parma Violet', thought *The Natal Mercury*) with long shoulder drapes down to the hem. She wore a hat of balibuntal straw (Aage Thaarup again) with a sweeping Gainsborough brim, cut sharply to the right; the whole movement of the hat, as the Natal dailies lovingly

The Royal Family arrives for the *Ngoma Nkosi* at Eshowe.

described it, was accentuated by a large period bow in a wide taffeta ribbon. Her gloves, bag and shoes had all been skilfully dyed to match. The Princesses were in yellow and white, respectively.

This was not to be an all-black affair. The number of whites allowed to attend the *Ngoma Nkosi* had originally been strictly limited, according to *The Natal Witness*. Thousands of old Natal hands, however, mostly from country families, had managed to obtain tickets and poured into the town to witness the event.[52] There were few hotels in either Eshowe or nearby Melmoth, but local families offered rooms in their houses; many simply slept in their cars or camped by the roadside. It was only after 10 pm on the night before that the Melmoth police finally succeeded in unblocking the tremendous traffic jam headed towards the town.

Their presence represents yet another example of parallel lives lived out in segregated South Africa and the occasional connect that an event such as this afforded. Judith Handley, then a senior schoolgirl, recalls her

The *Ngoma Nkosi* at Eshowe, with the dancers in front of the thatched dais
erected for the royal party. TRANSNET HERITAGE LIBRARY PHOTO COLLECTION

father's insisting on going to Eshowe to be present. For this fourth-generation Natal settler farmer, and many others like him, the Zulu people and
culture were unhesitatingly accepted as an integral part of their everyday
life. Her parents had driven there after the garden party in Maritzburg
the previous afternoon, encountering the appalling traffic along the way.
On the afternoon itself, the Natal farmers were seen to move unaffectedly
among the warriors, ex-servicemen and dancers, happily talking to them
in their fluent Zulu.[53] In the context of the segregated society that was
Natal and South Africa at the time, this purely social moment of genuine
fraternising was probably as close as you could come to a multiracial event.

'All colours and creeds rubbed shoulders in Eshowe,' noted *The Natal
Mercury*, proudly.[54]

The men's wives - the Natal ladies — who sat apart, busy with their
picnics beneath their umbrellas around the wattle hurdles erected on the
perimeters of the great theatre of African grass,[55] wore simple tailored

linens or floral print frocks. Drawn threadwork and Liberty Tana Lawn, canvas sunshades and straw hats or knotted peasant scarves were the sartorial order of the day here.[56] Folding chairs and shooting sticks were produced for those who did not care to sit on the stand erected.

It must, in part, have lent the event a faint whiff of a polo match or gymkhana. And perceived thus, this could only have enhanced the ornamentalist or tourist aspect of the occasion, which aroused the disapproval of the more liberal members of the Household. Tellingly, Lady Harlech had earlier replied rather discouragingly – even snubbingly – to a letter from an Eshowe woman (based on only a slight acquaintance) who sought advice on the appropriate dress for the occasion. As she was not a participant in the event, replied the former High Commissioner's wife, it wouldn't matter what she wore.[57]

The tourist flavour of the event was identified by at least one member of the Royal Family, too, though possibly with Lady Harlech's input. Princess Elizabeth wrote to her grandmother that there were many Europeans there just to see 'the fun of the war dance at Eshowe', so that it was rather like 'a great amusement for everyone who could get there'.[58] Perhaps she felt it slightly demeaned or trivialised the occasion. She cannot have been aware, sitting apart and on the dais, of any of the subtler social nuances, if such they can be described, among some of the participants and white male spectators.

Having driven out to the aerodrome under archways of pale autumn leaves on which '*Bayete*' was spelt out in huge letters composed of yellow mealie cobs,[59] the Daimler made a tour of the arena, finally reaching the specially erected thatched dais at 2.10 pm. Four stout *indunas*, magnificent in their full regalia of peacock plumes, monkey tails and beadwork, formed a guard of honour around it.[60] They were received by the Chief Native Commissioner for Natal, Major Leifeldt, and his wife, who escorted the royal party to their seats; Captain OC Oftebro, MC, Native Commissioner for Melmoth, was the master of ceremonies.

At the commencement, the dancers were seated on the ground, *aya-fola amabutho*, for custom required them to sit, not stand, before royalty. Now the regent Mshiyeni, acting for Cyprian, made his speech of greeting, much of it already noted, which ended with the words: 'Just when the great elephant [the Zulu name for the King was 'The Royal Black Elephant'] stamps his feet, the earth shakes, so when Your Majesty's foot trod our soil, we felt the trembling of it and we said in our hearts: "The Great One has come."'[61]

Thereafter, it was the turn of the Representative Chief to speak. This was none other than Chief Albert Luthuli, the future ANC leader and Nobel Prize winner. His presence at the dais was as close as any ANC leader got to the Royal Family, who had previously only met the non-European white parliamentary representatives, such as the sympathetic Senator Edgar Brookes, who had also made his way to Eshowe to attend.[62] Luthuli's presence at Eshowe and that of AB Xuma, the President-General, was a surprise – even an affront – to some of his more radical colleagues and followers.[63] And since he had openly espoused a wider form of African identity in his politics, what he said seemed somewhat at odds with this stance, reflecting as it did the continued, widespread desire among Zulu intellectuals to preserve, celebrate and display aspects of Zulu cultural heritage: 'Just as when a lion roars, all nature is hushed, as when Your Majesty speaks to us we listen to Your Majesty in silent awe, knowing that only wisdom will come from your lips.'[64]

At 2.30 pm the heir to the Zulu royal house, Cyprian Bhekuzulu ka Solomon ka Dinuzulu, presented an address of welcome to the King and was at the same time presented to Their Majesties and the Princesses.

Five minutes later, the King delivered his reply, thanking those assembled for their loyalty in the two world wars: 'I am proud to say that in both of them your gallant young men at once rushed to fight for King and country.' Carefully crafted by his ministers, it gave little hint of future hopes, which optimists had detected in his speech at the State Banquet on his first night in Cape Town, bar one very vaguely phrased sentence: 'We have heard your Royal salute and it has greatly stirred us. You say that you love your country and I reply that a people who love their country are worthy people who will progress in this their land of birth.'[65]

Thereafter he requested the Chief Native Commissioner to present medals to 40 selected Chiefs on his behalf.

The dance, when it commenced at 2.55 pm, was not a war dance, as many claimed at the time, but a ceremonial one that the Zulu people used to perform for their own royal house in the days (as the official programme noted without apparently any irony[66]) when they were undisputed rulers of the whole territory between the Pongola and Umzimkulu rivers.[67] It was reserved for occasions when the Zulu monarch proclaimed new laws or made statements of national importance. After the affairs of state were over, the whole assembly would perform the dance, the women grouped by age, and the men by regiment, each new one formed from those who had come of age in the preceding four or five years.

It was more than merely a dance; it was meant as a magnificent expression of the spirit of the people – 'The Spirit of Shaka', the Natal papers called it. In some ways it was. It began with the *Ihele*, a serpentine advance by the dancers led by their *indunas* distinguishable by their waving plumes. As they approached they chanted their *Hlabelele*, which gave way to the *Isaga*, the regimental cries – a deep-throated chant, after which several *impis* (regiments) of approximately 6 000 warriors poured forward and, waving shields and knobkerries, spread out into the famous Zulu battle formation of the horn. They were led by the 70-year-old Pika Zulu ka Siteku ka Mpande, a prince of the royal blood, the official 'organiser and leader of the dancers'. The men's ages ranged from 17 to 90.

And so it went on building up, remarkable, as Captain Ritchie, the scribe of the official Tour Diary, put it, 'for its organisation out of what appeared to be a chaotic mob of excited Zulus'.[68] The 'Rumours of War' section saw the regiments limber up, chanting praises of their chief and boasting of their fighting prowess before singing the famous '*Ihube*' song of the Talana Regiment of Cetshwayo.

Then 500 unmarried girls, hitherto lined up behind the male dancers, singing and clapping during their dance, advanced and began a 'pleasure dance' which culminated with the witch doctors leading them in, taunting the men to emulate the great warriors of the era of Shaka and Dingane. The 'whinnying' maidens (Ritchie again; he meant ululating) 'undulating their sleek, shining, black bodies, tended to assert themselves more and more and were in some danger of stealing the show'.[69]

The climax, 45 minutes later, was a final rush towards the throne, the *Ukuqubula*, partly to salute the King and partly to show how they would charge his enemies; despite misgivings on the part of the security police, this was permitted only because Queen Elizabeth had 'begged them to be allowed to come nearer'.[70] At the last second, they prostrated themselves before the dais; there was a moment's silence before they roared a triple 'Bayete! Bayete! Bayete!' The souvenir programme, written with the help of Pika Zulu and EN Braadveldt, an ex-president of the Native Appeal Court, felt obliged to explain that this exciting rush might be frightening to those who misjudged the dancers' peaceful intentions. Not a few of the spectators present wondered if it had been so for the Royal Family.[71]

At the very end, a chieftain lifted his hand and cried: 'Do not forget us when you go away.'[72] Thereafter the official party retired to the adjacent pavilion erected for tea. Prince Cyprian was included, with two Zulu women who brought gifts for the King.

It is evident that many strands of complex South African nationhood were co-joined at Eshowe that afternoon. However popular the tour, and however happy this event made the participants, it could not fail to highlight the underlying political grievances of many of them. And bonding though it might have been between the sovereign and a dispossessed people, it was, therefore, an inherently awkward one. As a constitutional monarch, the King acted on the advice of his government's ministers. South Africa was a thoroughly independent Dominion. It was, moreover, a white Dominion held in place by white minority rule.

Political advancement was not even on the cards for its non-white population; it had, if anything, regressed. This ultimately flew in the face of British imperial thinking whereby even committed imperialists like Baring and Lady Harlech envisaged a moment in the far-distant future when a gradually uplifted people could vote and take part in the ordered administration of their own land. That this was intended to follow the patterns established by their former colonial masters goes without saying.

Events being played out in India were proving that not all former colonial peoples accepted such a slow timetable. What Smuts's timetable was we'll never know. Certain it is that some of the recommendations of the Fagan Commission, then sitting, would have been implemented had he won at the polls in 1948.

Reading the letters from those advocating a boycott– not only from blacks but also coloureds, Indians and even Afrikaners, and all of them with an agenda of political advancement or aspiring nationalism at their core – one cannot help but have a sneaking feeling of admiration for Smuts's faith in the healing, balm-providing powers of the Royal Family.

Its members must surely, at times, have felt that in visiting South Africa, they were entering a hornet's nest. 'So many serious racial problems,' as Queen Elizabeth noted early on to Queen Mary.[73] As more and more opposition to the tour had come to light before they started out, it is small wonder that, as *Vanguard* approached Cape Town, they felt apprehensive about the reception that awaited them.[74]

Princess Elizabeth had privately said as much.[75] Yet the fear of boycott and protest – in the event, a damp squib insofar as the Royal Family, personally, were concerned – must have prompted some formative soul-searching. Royalty, as already noted, is required to be apolitical. This too, must be a double-edged sword, but this time it was to advantage. It avoids controversy, certainly; it must also enable them to free themselves, as individuals, from the spectre of borrowed judgement.

Within her family circle, the Princess would have been aware that her father, to whom she was close, was appalled at not being allowed by his South African ministers to personally pin medals on the black ex-servicemen, far less shake them by the hand, not to be able to personally confer the commemorative medals on the chiefs and elders at indabas and related events such as this, and that he referred, in private, to the white policemen over-zealously guarding them as 'our Gestapo'.

By the time of the Eshowe dance, too, the Princess had travelled across South Africa with a variety of personalities, all expressing their own views. Among them was Major Piet van der Byl, the Minister of Native Affairs, who thought the Eshowe dance was one of the most impressive experiences of the tour.[76] During the royal progress, he had allowed international journalists full access to all Native Reserves, 'to show that we have nothing to hide'.[77] At all events, he was eager to put an acceptable gloss on the South African way of doing things. United Party supporters thought him polished and well turned out; liberals, however, thought him an unimpressive appointment in that important role.[78] An insult, as Leo Marquard went so far as to put it, to fling to the Natives.[79]

Also there at times was Sir Evelyn Baring, the High Commissioner, and (constantly) Lady Harlech, the Queen's Lady-in-Waiting and wife of his predecessor. Both were aristocratic-type intellectual liberals of the old school, wary of South African politicians who were ready to humour the more racist Nationalist opposition in order to win votes, invariably to the detriment of the blacks. And they were always, anyway, keen to demonstrate the superiority of the British way of handling this side of things in the Rhodesias and the Protectorates. Baring was well known for not mincing his words on this front. For example, he would afterwards tell everyone that it was the large numbers of white policemen and officials at Eshowe telling the Zulus what to do that had made them lose their enthusiasm.[80]

Almost constantly with the Princess too, was General Smuts, the senior and endearing statesman-politician, who now found his international and domestic political policies at odds with each other. While wholeheartedly agreeing with the best intentions, as he put it, of the United Nations, he was not, in the final analysis, able to contemplate, as he wrote to Margaret Gillett, handing over everything that had been built up by the whites in South Africa to be 'lost and drowned in the black pool before us'.[81] And finally there was Jan Hofmeyr, the plump, awkward figure, slated as Smuts's successor, who had recently lost Sir De Villiers Graaff the safe seat of Hottentots-Holland for simply replying to a question from the floor at a political meeting what he in his heart believed to be true – that 'Natives would be represented in Parliament by Natives and Indians by Indians'.[82] All had had their say.

Some of the Princess's personal thoughts about empire, race and politics must therefore have been just beginning to crystallise. Her letter to her grandmother, Queen Mary, gives a small hint of this. It is the writing of a young woman, maturing through experience, and not the *jeune-fille*-style holiday letters her younger sister wrote from South Africa.

Possibly echoing Baring, she contrasted Eshowe to the *Pitso* at Maseru and the indaba in Swaziland (also behind her by the time she wrote the letter), which evidenced greater freedom: 'no one thought of telling the Swazis not to get too excited'.[83] She went on: 'The Zulus nowadays are a broken people, not at all what one expects to see after hearing about the "huge Zulus" [of British military folklore].' 'The Union Government,' she continued, pointedly, 'has been very ruthless with them, which is sad, and have removed a lot of their customs ...'[84]

More than one of her biographers have seen the experiences of the South African tour as formative for her. Although this is naturally conjectural, they point to her continued concern for the region throughout her reign, her distancing herself from Mrs Thatcher's stance on Rhodesia, and her friendship with Nelson Mandela.[85] In her later life she would confess, 'South Africa is in my blood.'[86]

Baring and the Princess were not the only ones who regretted signs of restraint in the dancing. At one stage Prince Cyprian himself was reported looking 'glum', possibly for this reason. Perhaps the movements were not so well-remembered after all the intervening years. The more traditionally-minded Zulus had been reluctant to take part in the rehearsals, claiming that their dance was 'for the Great Black Elephant and that no other eyes shall see it before he does'.[87]

And among the many postmortems held after the event, on the traffic-bound and appallingly grey-dusty roads that led from Eshowe on that windless evening,[88] some spectators were heard to confess that they had expected the ceremony to be more primitive and abandoned, and that the presence of royalty might have been the inhibiting cause. Most thought it spectacular, however, 'better than Hollywood', as one journalist noted, 'not quite Chaka [sic], but perfect Rider Haggard'.[89]

* * *

Durban, 20–24 March

Having staged the night at the siding at Fraser's, via a stop at Stanger, the next morning the White Train finally approached Durban. Like Cape Town had become, and like Port Elizabeth and East London had been since their beginnings, this was another British city built in Africa. It was the largest port in South Africa (vital in wartime) and the industrial centre of the province. It was very prosperous. Handsome official buildings stood in its centre and along its elegant Esplanade; West Street, with its arcades and awnings, was considered by many to be the best shopping street in the Union, and the great, airy private houses of the well-off stood in their lush gardens on the Berea, whose streets and avenues were lined with Flamboyant trees. It was also the number-one seaside resort of the country, with many good hotels, its subtropical climate and the surf of the warm Indian Ocean washing its white beaches making it a mecca throughout the year.

Noticeably English in atmosphere, as Princess Elizabeth put it to Queen Mary,[90] and completely English in its ways and rhythms, Durban was a quintessentially imperial port city, part Bombay,[91] part Liverpool, part Blackpool and part, too, Bournemouth and Cheltenham. Of its white population (117 228), 109 994 were English-speaking, and only 16 618 were Afrikaans. The black population was slightly less than the white – 104 584. The majority were Zulu (94 310), generally municipal, office or factory workers who lived apart in the locations, or domestic servants who lived in, in servants' quarters provided. In addition to this mix was an equally large Indian population (106 604),[92] who, with their temples, curries, saris and Indian market, gave a distinctive, exotic overlay of the Raj to the prevailing pink-gin, bridge, chintz-covers and hibiscus-hedge atmosphere of the (white) city.

The Englishness was a source of local pride. A Durbanite was far more likely to speak Zulu, or even French, fluently than to speak Afrikaans. As with Pietermaritzburg, no one therefore doubted the reception the Royal Family would get in Durban as they pulled into the King's Park siding. Natal, which had been slightly reluctant to join the Union in 1910, had viewed with dismay the republican elements now rising so prominently at national level. Though the province loved South Africa, it was – almost to a man – fiercely imperially patriotic. A Natalian, as Mervyn Ellis, editor of *The Natal Mercury*, put it 'was proud to be a South African ... but he is not only a South African, but a British subject, with all that that privileged and honoured title implies'.[93] This, then, was going to be the day to demonstrate this.

On the platform to meet them was Major Piet van der Byl, back as Minister in Attendance, together with Senator CF Clarkson, Minister of the Interior, and the Administrator of Natal, and Mrs Mitchell. Rupert and Clare Ellis Brown, the impressive wartime mayor and mayoress of Durban, and specially re-elected that year in order to appropriately host

Arrival in Durban: the scene in front of the City Hall, showing the crowds and
the school cadets presenting arms.

TRANSNET HERITAGE LIBRARY PHOTO COLLECTION

the royal visitors, were presented. Mr Ellis Brown's family owned the
West Street-based business that made the coffee of that name then widely
drunk throughout the Union.

Clare Ellis Brown, the handsome, well-dressed[94] and energetic mayoress,
had, together with several other formidable matrons of her ilk, overseen
much of Durban's considerable civilian, financial and material contribution
to the war effort.[95] In addition to South African troops, they entertained a
quarter of a million Allied servicemen and women who had poured through
the port on their way to and from the battlefronts in the Middle and Far East;
they also sent parcels and raised funds specifically for the British war effort.

One such had been the 'Speed the Planes' fund set up during the Battle
of Britain, which aimed to purchase Spitfires, each then costing £6 000 to
£7 000. Conceived by Horace Flather, editor of the local *Daily News*, Clare

Ellis Brown took it over as her special project. An appeal went out and Durban and the Natal province rallied with a will. Within the first day, £50 000 was donated and money, heirlooms, jewellery, wedding rings and more continued to pour into its coffers. Within one month the fund topped £200 000 and later pushed through £250 000, enough to equip and maintain the RAF's 222 (Natal) Squadron, which had a wildebeest at the centre of its crest (approved by the King) and a Zulu motto, *Pambili Bo* (Go Straight Ahead).[96]

Having inspected the Guard of Honour of the Natal Mounted Rifles, the 1st Royal Durban Light Infantry and the 2nd Royal Durban Light Infantry, the royal party entered the waiting Daimler. The processional route that morning led along the Marine Parade, up West Street to the City Hall, a fine, unmistakably English imperial edifice. Like the majority of Durban's public buildings, its architects had seen no political or aesthetic reasons to accommodate Cape Dutch architectural conceits in its design, as their colleagues had in public buildings elsewhere in South Africa.[97]

All Durban wore its heart on its sleeve that morning, thought *The Natal Mercury* in its report the next day. It was hot and humid; only a light breeze from the northeast made the sea of flags and bunting flutter.[98] Some 300 000 people had turned out to cheer the Royal Family on their eight-mile (13-kilometre) drive, many having spent the night in the open and in the light rain that fell to be sure of good front-row positions. All Active Citizen Force (ACF) units and certain cadet detachments had been turned out to line the route.

Everyone seemed to have a Union Jack to wave; only occasionally was a South African flag to be seen.[99] The surviving newsreel footage shows the tremendous cheering crowd. It was a multiracial crowd, too ('no colour bar in Durban yesterday', the press reported, perhaps meaning only in contrast to the norm), with people hanging out of windows and balconies, cheering and cheering 'as if they would never stop'.[100]

In front of the City Hall a great mass of humanity had been waiting patiently for hours in the subtropical heat. Suddenly they caught sight of an ample, dumpy and familiar figure in a white dress and red hat standing on one of the crowded balconies. This was none other than Perla Siedle Gibson, Durban's 'Lady in White', a trained concert singer who had won wartime fame throughout the Commonwealth and Empire.

Perla Gibson, Durban's famous 'Lady in White',
sings to an Allied troopship during wartime.
DITSONG NATIONAL MUSEUM OF MILITARY HISTORY

According to one account, while she was serving in the canteen set up at the docks for the Commonwealth forces early on in the war, an Irish seaman, whom she and her family had entertained at their home the day before, caught sight of her from his departing ship, and called out to give them a song. Mrs Gibson (or Madame Perla as she preferred to be known professionally) had obliged with 'When Irish Eyes Are Smiling'. She had a powerful voice, London-trained, employing an open-throat technique; several of the greats of the day had conceded its abilities.[101] The troops on board and everyone on shore were moved by this emotionally charged scene and Madame Perla suddenly found for herself a new and vital role added to her civilian war work. She also found a new identity; for hundreds of thousands of Allied troops she now simply became 'The Lady in White'.

Shipping movements were kept strictly secret in wartime, but whatever the weather and whatever the hour, troopships arriving at Durban docks or departing into U-boat-infested seas would find the lone, distinctive figure standing on North Pier, where the harbour entrance narrowed, singing the patriotic or sentimental songs of that era, all belted out in her rich soprano. Instead of cupped hands she was now aided by a black vulcanite megaphone, presented to her by the grateful survivors of the *Llandaff Castle*, torpedoed and sunk 'by the Japs' one day out of Durban.[102] 'Rule, Britannia' (for all warships) and 'There'll Always Be an England' were particular favourites, as was 'Now is the Hour', popularly believed to be of Maori origin.

Of course, some sophisticates scoffed, but neither illness, exhaustion nor bad weather ever deterred her; 'I sang a song into the air,' as she put it ingenuously in her autobiography, 'and the song, from beginning to end, I found again, in the heart of a friend'.[103] She even sang on the day she heard that one of her sons, Roy, had been killed while fighting with the Black Watch at Monte Cassino in 1944.

That evening, as the departing troopship headed out into the open seas, all on board, unaware of her personal tragedy, heard not the anticipated, rollicking finale to the sendoff, but the hymn 'Abide with Me', the increasingly faint, famously rich soprano voice quavering, most atypically, at the final, poignant verse.[104]

It's no exaggeration to say that she became a legend for many. Now invited to meet the Royal Family, it was not surprising that someone in the waiting crowd below called out, 'Give us a song, Perla!' Under normal circumstances she needed little encouragement; on this unique, royal occasion, she needed none. Within seconds she stepped briskly out onto the portico, her megaphone conveniently to hand, and launched into 'Land of Hope and Glory', with the Durban Philharmonic strategically stationed on a dais close by and the crowd accompanying her.

As the clock in the Post Office tower reached 10.35 am the royal cars arrived and the roars of the crowd — *oorverdowend* and *byna histeries* (deafening and almost hysterical), according to a rather sour piece in *Die*

Volksblad[105] – were such that they sent clouds of pigeons wheeling into the air. The playing of 'God Save the King' was followed by such cheers that it drowned out the first part of '*Die Stem*', to which no one seemed to be paying much attention. The Afrikaans press were quick to notice this.[106]

The mayor presented the city's address of welcome. Much was made in it of the Royal Family's war record: 'Our sincere admiration of the courage and example given to our people by yourself and other members of your Royal House during the years of long and bitter struggle through which humanity has so recently passed ... your inspiring example which contributed in large measure to the overthrow of the forces of evil.'[107]

The King replied in kind:

> We have looked forward to this day, having heard so much about your city and the hospitality of its people from the men and women of our armed forces who during the recent war passed this way, to and from the battlefronts of the world ... We ourselves have now had experience of your warm-heartedness and in thanking you I am taking the opportunity of thanking you also on behalf of those thousands of fighting men and women who bear such happy memories of their visits here.[108]

As always, it was the Queen who was the particular crowd-pleaser. 'We want the Queen, we want the Queen!' they chanted, and when she looked up, smiled and gestured with her gloved hand, the result was deafening.[109] Tea was taken inside, where councillors and dignitaries were presented; among them were several prominent Indian couples,[110] the men in their smartly cut English-style suits, the women in their saris.

Mrs Ellis Brown insisted on presenting Madame Perla first. So flustered was the Lady in White by this honour that she tore her glove in hastily drawing it on (she later claimed she had been applauding their arrival too hard), and had to frantically borrow another,[111] before curtsying to the Queen, who greeted her publicly with the words 'for your work, of which I have heard from so many sources, I thank you most sincerely'.[112]

Leaving the City Hall by another entrance, the royal party returned to the Daimler for the short drive to the Cenotaph. The commission for this monument to the fallen of the First World War had been won in competition by HLG Pilkington. For a conservative, traditionalist city, its design was noticeably modern. A granite pylon soared skywards with two long-winged angels in white and lapis faience Poole tiles bearing the soul of a dead soldier heavenwards, the figures executed in the Arts and Crafts style. On the summit, vaguely recalling the shape of the cenotaph at Whitehall, the words 'TELL IT TO THE GENERATION FOLLOWING' were boldly carved.

At its base was a recumbent figure of the Unknown Warrior in bronze; a horizontal stone cross, two great Art Deco lions symbolising the courage of the men of Durban in the First World War, and a wooden cross made from one of the few trees left standing at Delville Wood after the battle (considered the South African equivalent of Gallipoli) completed the overall concept.

It is fair to say that the great majority of Natal men who joined up for the Second World War had, like those in the First, gone off to fight for King and Country. None of the reasoned, non-jingoistic arguments Smuts had used in the parliamentary debate against Hertzog's motion of neutrality would have been necessary. Nor had there been the soul-searching common in other parts of the country about answering the bugle call in 1939. Had Hertzog won his neutrality motion, a great band of South African volunteers would still have undoubtedly been raised in Natal.

They thought themselves as Englishmen, 'hewn from England's rock', as they had been taught in their nurseries, and lived in South Africa as if in another part of England, like a distant county. Of all South Africans, perhaps, they were closest to the Southern Rhodesians in this respect. Many of them, however, were already the fourth generation of the second or third sons of yeoman farmers or local gentry who had emigrated from (mostly) Yorkshire and Derbyshire in 1848, after the agricultural slump that followed the repeal of the Corn Laws. In the farming Midlands the gene pool was so tight that the odd Yorkshire inflection was still detectable in their speech.

Here, then, was unabashed, unexpurgated Empire still at large in South Africa. It was a sentimental attachment; the hands-across-the-sea spirit was perhaps more alive in Natal than in any other province, the relatively small size of the Afrikaner community doubtless being a contributing factor.

One of the most patriotic songs of 1939, 'There'll Always Be an England', had become even more popular as the war progressed. If England had its Vera Lynn and Gracie Fields, Durban had its Perla Gibson and any number of vocalists, pianists and string orchestras belting it out at the Playhouse, the Royal Grill, the tearoom at Greenacres and the Country Club. Those seated here would sing along to it; schoolchildren, soldiers and families gathered around a piano did so too. Often a certain lachrymosity would accompany such sing-songs. The words were unashamedly understood to be a rallying cry:

> There'll Always be an England
> And England shall be free
> If England means as much to you
> As England means to me!

It contained too, lines especially aimed at colonials:

> The Empire too, we can depend on you.
> Freedom remains. These are the chains
> Nothing can break
> There'll always be an England, etc.

The Queen picked up on this loyalism at once, writing in a letter home to her niece, Elizabeth Elphinstone, 'They [the people of Durban] are very English and Scottish there & cling to the old links with Great Britain'.[113] Indeed, Natal proudly considered herself 'an outpost of the Empire' well beyond the creation of the republic in 1961, though a move towards separatism in the 1950s had come to nothing.

The dates of the Second World War had been added to the Cenotaph and the Durban branch of the Memorable Order of Tin Hats (MOTH) had erected handsome bronze memorial gates at the entrance. A strong and immediate protest had been sent by telegram from the Durban Committee to the prime minister's Interdepartmental Committee, when it was learnt that their opening by the King had been deleted from the official programme.

The Opening of Parliament by HM King George VI in 1947, oil painting by Robert Broadley. The King reads the speech from the throne, while the Princesses watch with Mrs Van Zyl, wife of the Governor-General, from the middle bay above. PARLIAMENT OF THE REPUBLIC OF SOUTH AFRICA

Cape Town's Civic Welcome, 18 February. The Queen stands next to the Administrator of the Cape, JG Carinus; behind them are Cape Town mayor Abe Bloomberg and his wife, Miriam.

Leaving Cape Town on the White Train, 21 February. From left: Jan Smuts, Mrs Van Zyl, Princess Elizabeth, Queen Elizabeth, the King and Governor-General Brand van Zyl. Behind them are Princess Margaret and Wing Commander Peter Townsend.

Waving goodbye to Cape Town from the White Train.

Pulled by two locomotives, the White Train chugs across the veld.

The royal receiving line on a station platform during a stop on the tour.

Bloemfontein cheers the Royal Family.

The King accepts greetings at the great *Pitso*, or national gathering, held at Maseru, Basutoland (Lesotho), on 12 March. Sir Evelyn Baring, High Commissioner for Southern Africa, stands behind Queen Elizabeth.

The Royal Family relax for the cameras at Natal National Park in the Drakensberg.
Smuts (with camera) stands behind.

The *Ngoma Nkosi* at Eshowe, on 19 March, was organised as a tribute by the Zulus to the King,
'The Royal Black Elephant'. ROLLS PRESS/POPPERFOTO/GETTY IMAGES

At the gathering of *oudstryders* (Anglo-Boer War veterans) at the Union Buildings, the Queen examines Ouboet Viljoen's hat, worn in the field during the war.

A young girl in Voortrekker dress presents a bouquet to Princess Elizabeth at an event in Pietersburg (now Polokwane).

In Johannesburg, 23 000 ex-servicemen march past the Royal Family, who are on the Harrison Street saluting base. *We Have Won the War!* was a constant subtext of the tour.

Princess Elizabeth arrives to take the salute at the military parade by the Cape Command at Youngsfield on her 21st birthday.

Moving towards the gangway of HMS *Vanguard* on departure.

While the crowds on shore sing 'Land of Hope and Glory', the Royal Family wave from *Vanguard*'s saluting platform, which replaced the anti-aircraft mount on the battleship's 'B' turret.

Rupert Ellis Brown, the mayor of Durban, watches Queen Elizabeth open the new war memorial gates. Piet van der Byl stands between the Princesses.

TRANSNET HERITAGE LIBRARY PHOTO COLLECTION

As with the attempted cancellation of the march-past of ex-servicemen by the British Empire Service League in East London,[114] and the discarding of other proposed events to be held under similar aegises, there is an indication here that occasions such as this, tinged with overtly imperial sentiments, were initially recommended by the Smuts government as best avoided, fearing that they would open up the old divisive wounds of the war years. Organisations like the Royal Victoria League and the British Empire Service League were, not surprisingly, the particular bugbears of many republican-minded Afrikaners.

Removing the gate-opening ceremony at the Cenotaph, however, was a step too far for the greater Natal public. Significantly, the Durban telegram declared that this event, which commemorated those who had given their lives during the war, was considered the most important of all in the Durban programme.[115] The point was quickly taken. Two days later, a statement was issued from the Administrator of Natal to the effect that the King had conveyed through the government that he had agreed to open the gates.[116]

So it was that the King and Queen and Princesses now alighted before them and the cheering ceased. As planned, it was just before noon that the King opened the gates and he and the Queen passed through them. The sovereigns stood side by side before the stone cross and the Cenotaph in the blazing midday sun while the buglers sounded the Last Post and a two-minute silence followed. When the Reveille sounded, the Queen noticed that one of the heavy gates had remained closed, and she now turned and swung it open. This spontaneous gesture – described by the press as the Queen's personal tribute to the soldiers who had died in battle – greatly pleased the crowd and all who read of it afterwards.

Now the King and Queen bent to read the inscription on the gateposts:

> I said to the man who stood at the gate of the year
> 'Give me a light that I may tread safely into the unknown' and he
>   replied
> 'Go out into the darkness and put your hand into The Hand of God.
> That shall be to you better than a light and safer than a known way.'

This came from a previously little-known poem by Miss MK (Minnie) Haskins quoted by the King (at the Queen's suggestion) in the first Christmas broadcast of the war to the Empire in 1939. It was a brilliant choice, designed not only to allay the fears of what the new year would almost certainly bring, but also seeming to reflect the simple, low-church, everyman faith and stoicism of the sovereign. And this found a broad resonance around the English-speaking world. Christian, middle-class Durban had wanted this sentiment recorded.

The King and Queen now met Charles Evenden, the founder of the MOTH, and the leaders of other ex-servicemen's organisations and then Mrs Swales, the mother of Captain Edwin Swales, VC, DFC, who had been killed over Pforzheim, Germany, in February 1945. After six years of war, the sovereigns were adept at talking to the bereaved. Mrs Swales stood rigidly quiet and, except for a faint smile, showed no emotion.[117] Afterwards, she quietly told the reporters that both 'had spoken with simplicity and quiet sincerity about Edwin ... He was so nice, and she was just as beautiful as I imagined.'[118]

Across the street, and afforded a direct view of the proceedings, stood a long row of other bereaved mothers, widows and next-of-kin, all wearing the medals of their dead. Several were Indian women wearing saris. The King and Queen walked over and, in the relentless heat, slowly moved down the line exchanging words with them. 'We feel very deeply for you,' said the Queen. Sixty-three-year-old Mr Norrey told the Queen he had taken 'fifteen years off his age' to enlist with the 2nd Transvaal Scottish; the Queen expressed her sorrow that his son, Sergeant J Norrey of the 1st Natal Mounted Rifles, had been killed with the 6th Division in Italy.[119] One mother reflected sadly afterwards that she had had to lose her only son in order to meet the King and Queen of England.

Then they walked back to their car. As they were climbing into it, they were told that there was an elderly woman who wanted to speak to them. This was Mrs Jacobs, who had lost her 25-year-old son, Captain DJ Jacobs, DFC, killed in Italy. Without hesitating, they walked back to where she was standing, all in black. This was not an easy meeting. So overcome was Mrs Jacobs by their gesture that she wept uncontrollably and was unable to answer, while the Queen spoke quietly to her. Finally, after they had said goodbye, ambulance men had to take the distraught Mrs Jacobs away.

The Durban visit lasted for four days, each of sticky, subtropical heat that never let up. It was four days when, as the *Natal Daily News* proudly claimed, the city had been 'the centre of the Commonwealth.'[120] It included a garden party at Mitchell Park, a race meeting at Greyville, a rally of 100 000 blacks, matins at St James Anglican Church (a typical stone parish church found in the colonies, lovingly embellished with gothic detailings and set in lush vegetation) and a mixed-race pageant performed by schoolchildren. A pleasant feature of this, Ritchie felt compelled to record, was the applause the white children gave to the black children as they marched in proudly to take their places. There was also an impressive march-past down West Street of 23 000 MOTHs from the Natal regiments. The King

The Princesses enjoy the warm breeze off the Indian Ocean in the garden
at King's House, Durban.

took the salute from the dais in front of the City Hall for over 40 minutes,
with a giant Union Jack stretched out over the building behind him.[121]

The visit also included a civic ball at the City Hall. As at all these
events, the Durban crowds arrived en masse to cheer, anxious to savour
the unique treat of having the Royal Family, who were housed at King's

House on the Berea, living among them. They were not disappointed. On the night of the ball, the family in their jewels, orders and ball gowns made a spectacular appearance on the City Hall dais beforehand. Such was the 'fairy scene' that they created under the arc lights that there was a collective intake of breath from the crowd of 10 000, followed by a hush, and only, it was reported, when Their Majesties had raised their hands to wave did a roar of appreciation break out.

The iconic, royal image they created was everything Durban wanted to see and believe in. Cheer after cheer erupted from the throng. According to Major Van der Byl, who was standing behind them (and this was subsequently corroborated by Dr Mears, who was in the crowd), when they turned to go back inside, one could sense the feeling of dismay in the crowd as the royal magic, so long and dearly anticipated, was about to vanish. 'Don't break the spell ... we know it's a dream – but don't wake us up – let us dream a little longer,' they seemed to say. With her skill at empathising, the Queen apparently sensed this atmosphere, and with one of her typical gestures, she half turned and gave a final wave to the crowd before finally disappearing inside.[122]

* * *

Currie's Fountain, 22 March

On Saturday 22 March, the Royal Family went to meet the city's Indian community at Currie's Fountain. There a massive crowd – 65 000, more than half of Durban's total Indian population[123] – had turned out before a raised dais which boasted a 20-foot-high (6-metre-high) representation of the Taj Mahal positioned behind it. There were vociferously cheering crowds, Loyal Addresses, salaams and presentations of baskets of flowers by curtsying little girls dressed in saris. The King and Queen descended from the dais and made their way through lanes opened up through the tightly packed crowds, stopping to talk here and there, often to Indian ex-servicemen. Many of these, it was reported, had tears in their eyes. Later, the King took the salute at a march-past.

Populist loyalism had once again manifested itself, triumphing over

Currie's Fountain: over half of Durban's Indian population greeted the
Royal Family here. AI Kajee, chairman of the Reception Committee,
who had defied a planned boycott, is to the left of the King.
TRANSNET HERITAGE LIBRARY PHOTO COLLECTION

Receiving Indian civic dignitaries on the dais at Currie's Fountain.
TRANSNET HERITAGE LIBRARY PHOTO COLLECTION

calls for boycotts from politicians. The crowd – as at other Indian receptions, almost all waving Union Jacks alone[124] – had sung 'God Save the King', 'Die Stem' and 'There'll Always Be an England'.

It must have been most encouraging. AI Kajee, chairman of the Reception Committee, had welcomed the Royal Family on behalf of Durban's Indian community. His committee did not have the support of radical politicians; in view of the numbers there on that day it is hard to believe he felt he needed this.

'Our hearts are filled with joy that you are in our midst,' he said. 'May merciful Providence bless and protect you and your family.'[125]

A month earlier, the morning's event would have seemed unlikely in several respects. After the tour was announced in early November 1946, the Natal Indian Congress had called on all South African Indians to boycott the visit. This had been immediately cabled to London and passed on, via Lascelles, to the King.[126] Gandhi himself had supported the call with a cable from Hamica in East Bengal.[127]

The Guardian, the radical South African newspaper regarded as the mouthpiece of the Communist Party, put the matter empirically: 'To the majority of South Africans, "Rex" symbolises oppression. It is Rex – the Crown – who charges them with being passless, shelterless, moneyless – with all the hundred and one petty "crimes" which arise out of South Africa's racial laws ... In this knowledge the African National Congress and the Indian Congress and Passive Resistance Movement have requested that the Royal visit be postponed to a day when Rex is a less unhappy symbol.'[128]

Not all Indians had seen it thus, viewing the King as being above party politics, and the moderates resented decisions being taken on their behalf by the more radical. Kajee had actually gone to Johannesburg with PT Pather and A Christopher in February to plead against the boycott which had been decided on, arbitrarily as it seemed to them, by Dr GM Naicker and Dr YM Dadoo, leaders of the Natal and Transvaal Indian Congresses, respectively. Kajee's appeal was harshly rejected with the accusation that they 'once again desired to play the role of arch-collaborators'.[129]

However, it was again apparent that there was a disconnect between the wishes of politicians and the people called on to boycott. Kajee, Pather and Christopher were well aware of this. Even the fairly hard-hitting black newspaper *Inkundla Ya Bantu* agreed that the coming of the King gave the Indian moderates a magnificent opportunity to challenge the Natal Indian Congress's campaign.[130] Although Gandhi had originally supported the boycott and in February 1946 endorsed it in writing,[131] Nehru himself had by now intimated to the Natal Indian National Congress, through the High Commissioner's office, that he was personally of the opinion that a boycott of the royal visit was inadvisable, and in particular, any demonstration was 'undesirable'.[132] Perhaps he viewed the royal tour as providing an unworthy battleground for the moderates to score victories.

This counter-response had, in fact, initially started in Pretoria, when wealthy Indian merchants decided to form a committee of their own to welcome the King, and even to make a presentation. Northern Natal followed suit, the Indian merchants there stating bluntly that they would welcome the Royal Family whatever the Congress said. Ladysmith, the first town visited in Natal, had been seen as a litmus test; to the relief of the tour organisers, the Smuts government and the Palace itself, the Indian community turned out in force to cheer, with flags and banners of welcome strung across the route.

Thereafter the counter-movement against the boycott only gathered momentum. There was a riotous meeting in Maritzburg when Dr K Gooman, vice-president of the Natal Indian Congress, was howled down while attempting to address the crowd. 'Traitors!' she screamed back at her audience and pandemonium followed, with the Gandhi caps worn by the Resisters as a political insignia snatched from their heads and set alight.[133]

The Indians of South Africa had originally been imported in the 1860s to work in the sugar fields; they had stayed on, again living apart, with some civic but no national political influence. Many had risen to prosperity. Legislation discriminating against them, however, had long angered their kith and kin in India. Whitehall had remained deaf to this and was supported, in the early 1900s, by the attitude of imperialists such as Alfred Milner and Lionel Curtis, who saw the danger of mass Indian immigration 'polluting' the white Commonwealth. By the 1940s, segregation and political rights, or rather the lack of them, had become burning issues to politically motivated Indians in South Africa.

In a very real sense, however, the wider issues at stake here were represented by two political giants of twentieth-century imperial history, who had met and clashed in South Africa. A political thread ran through the careers of Gandhi and Smuts. Gandhi, a British-trained barrister, had come to South Africa in the early 1900s to fight a court case on behalf of some friends of his brother's. Finding institutionalised racialism at every turn, he deployed a new kind of revolutionary action – *satyagraha*, or passive resistance. Smuts, in his capacity as Colonial Secretary of the Transvaal, had arrested and imprisoned him. As historians have often pointed out, had they but known it, those who humiliated Gandhi then were driving him into political activism, with incalculable consequences for South Africa, India and the world.

Though they met ostensibly on opposing sides, the two had a strange respect for one another. Perhaps their spirituality was a bond; it is possible they recognised greatness in one another too. Smuts sent Gandhi religious books in prison; Gandhi returned the compliment by sending him a pair of sandals he had made while incarcerated. Smuts, pleased by the gesture, wore these every summer. When Gandhi left South Africa in 1914, Smuts remarked: 'The saint has left our shores,' adding, with a dry wit he had clearly picked up from the English, 'I sincerely hope for ever.'[134]

It was for ever but only technically, for Gandhi's subsequent career in India would make him the very real symbol of anti-colonial, nationalist and independence movements there and elsewhere. Moreover, this was about to find fulfilment on the Indian subcontinent in the very year on which we are focused. In the intervening years, Gandhi and Smuts had met again once, and cordially, in London in 1931, when Smuts was asked to intervene in negotiations between him and the British government. Smuts had been critical of British policy in India, but regarded Gandhi as an honest man to deal with, 'despite his vagaries'. He came to see that Gandhi's exceptional spiritual qualities made him the single most powerful force in Indian politics.

It was partly to avoid exacerbating problems in India that a hostile boycott would have been most unwelcome during the tour, for just as the Natal papers gave front-page coverage to the warm reception the King received at Currie's Fountain, a small headline elsewhere on the same page recorded that the Viceroy Designate, Lord Mountbatten, and Lady Mountbatten had arrived in New Delhi.[135] While royal speeches during the tour hinted at a reshaped, more multiracial Commonwealth, it was also hoped that a successful, trouble-free tour would be reflected in the orderly transformation of India and Burma into Dominions. Even the Washington-based *World Review* commented: 'There is hope that continuing loyalty in South Africa will be impressive to India and Burma. Indeed the King might even strengthen the Government's hand in maintaining order.'[136]

No wonder, then, that the King looked pleased by the crowds who had gathered to cheer him, as they had in Ladysmith, Pietermaritzburg, Stanger and other towns with sizeable Indian populations.

Yet the South African government and its supportive newspapers had equally good reason to be thankful for the collapse of the Indian boycott. It appeared, temporarily at least, to confound India's opinion of South Africa. Towards the end of the previous year, as we have seen, Smuts had been thwarted when he had gone to the UN to press for the inclusion of South West Africa into the Union. This was another attempt to fulfil his long-held vision of South Africa's geopolitical destiny by expanding northward into Africa.[137] It actually had the support of the Labour government in Britain. It did not, however, have the support of Tshekedi Khama, the Regent of Bechuanaland, or AB Xuma, President-General of the ANC, who were in contact.

Smuts, aware of Khama's opposition, had urged the Labour government to muzzle him and prevent his going to the United Nations. This was achieved. Nevertheless, Khama continued to lobby from his dusty territory against the annexation on the grounds of South Africa's racial policies; he must also have feared for the sovereignty of his own country and the other two Protectorates should South West Africa be successfully incorporated into the Union. The King and Baring (*in absentia* due to tick-bite fever) appear to have reassured him on this issue when the White Train stopped on Bechuanaland soil in April 1947; Senator Major Richards, whom we shall meet in Chapter 6, in a handwritten postscript in one of his letters to Lady Milner, indicates that Morrah had assured him too that there would be no surrender of the High Commission Territories.[138]

During a stop at Lovedale College, the King talks to DDT Jabavu (*above*), the pioneering educator and founder of the All-Africa Convention. Tshekedi Khama (*left*), Regent of Bechuanaland, encouraged opposition at the UN to Smuts's proposal to annex South West Africa. Here he talks to an American journalist in front of the White Train during a stop at Lobatse in Bechuanaland.

TRANSNET HERITAGE LIBRARY PHOTO COLLECTION

The annexation was turned down, the British government finding itself embarrassingly isolated on this issue in the General Assembly. It was again seen to be out of step with the spirit of the post-war world, where international opinion was hardening against the idea of colonial rule in general.

There was, however, something fundamentally more to it than that. What had happened at the UN had also shown that this reformist spirit could be expressed by non-colonial powers acting within the Assembly. This extended into the directorate itself. It was something the Soviet Union could and would now exploit for their own ideological-political ends, as indeed would America, at least in areas she regarded as not strategically essential.[139]

It was a blow for the man who had hoped to bank credit for South Africa's war effort and secure the country's post-war position as the guarantor of Western interests in Africa.[140] Worse, however, was to come just a few weeks later.

Khama had been successfully kept away from the United Nations. Who *was* making his way there now, much to Smuts's chagrin, was AB Xuma. The President-General of the ANC led a delegation across the Atlantic comprising HA Naidoo and Sorabjee Rustomjee of the Indian Congresses; they were joined there, to their surprise, by Senator Hyman Basner, the most radical of the four white senators appointed to represent the Indians and Africans in the South African Parliament.[141] He despised Smuts and had hitherto had little time for Xuma and the rest. But he was taking no chances of their missing the opportunity to beard Smuts internationally in his role as philosopher-statesman and humanitarian. Smuts himself had always refused to meet Xuma on home ground. Now there was no escaping it. And there would be no muzzling of the delegation in America, where they were much fêted by radical bodies and African Americans.

The multiracial South African delegation – fairly remarkable in its composition for the day – met up in New York in late October. This was well timed, for not long afterwards, South Africa's racial policies again surfaced at the United Nations, this time with far more adverse publicity. This was the result of the handiwork of the delegation from not-quite-independent India. It was a deprecatory motion, put forward in early December, by Mrs Pandit, Nehru's very determined sister, concerning

South African policies towards its Indian community. To Smuts's surprise and discomfort, the motion was passed with a two-thirds majority and the support of the United States.

Mrs Pandit's 'ambush', as Saul Dubow neatly describes it,[142] was the culmination of years of argument about the status of Indians in South Africa. But her principal target was the 1946 Asiatic Land Tenure and Indian Representation Act – known as the 'Ghetto Act' – itself following on the heels of the Pegging Act of 1943, which sought to restrict the rights of Indians to purchase land except in certain areas, in return for a modicum of political representation. This would involve whites elected by Indians to represent them in Parliament and for Indians to represent themselves in the Natal Provincial Council. Though it was a step in the right direction, it had proved to be a messy piece of legislation, satisfying neither the Indians nor the whites in South Africa. It was now proved to have been a remarkably ill-timed piece of legislation, too.

Jawaharlal Nehru, installed at the head of the interim Indian government in the run-up to independence, had long advocated that Indian nationalists develop an internationalist consciousness, free of the inevitability of the British connection, and of Eurocentrism in general. Reacting to the news of the Ghetto Act, the Natal Indian Congress had urged the Indian government to raise the issue at the UN. This gave Mrs Pandit (in reality, Nehru, by extension) an extraordinary opportunity to prove her country's mettle in the international spotlight. She had taken it with both hands.

Jean Lawrence, who saw her in action at the UN six months later, described her in her diary as 'rabid' and 'vitriolic' and a first-class actress, able to 'squeeze a tear for any cause'.[143] Such was the view of a moderately liberal-minded, white South African Cabinet minister's wife then. Others like her, watching events unfold in the Assembly, might have felt she had a point; the majority, however, supported Mrs Pandit, squeezed tears and all. Smuts's argument, that the social separation of the races in South Africa violated no human rights under the Charter and avoided the bloodshed witnessed in India and elsewhere, simply fell on deaf ears.

Again, it was a portent of things to come. Only five years earlier, after the signing of the Atlantic Charter, Churchill had insisted in the House of Commons that Whitehall would decide on the pace of a colony's journey to self-government. India had here, however, simply bypassed Whitehall, where Smuts and South Africa had good standing, and against accepted Commonwealth practice, taken their much-publicised case directly to a new, alternative international forum: the UN General Assembly.

India thus emerged as the first successful challenger of the doctrine of the European right to rule, and highlighted what would surely be the coming new order in the post-colonial world.[144] This promised to be an uncomfortable one for white South Africa; the policy of non-interference in the internal affairs of its members, so exhaustively debated in San Francisco the year before, had been rubbished. If Smuts was dismayed, Malan and his successors were not. And now they offered the affronted, conservative white electorate in South Africa the old Boer alternative: they could turn their backs on all this, retreat into the laager, and occupy a world of their own devising.

Smuts's world was rapidly falling apart. Typically, Gandhi had told Mrs Pandit before she left India that it was important that, whatever the outcome of events at the UN, she must come back as a friend of Field-Marshal Smuts. It says much for the respect that Gandhi and Smuts had for one another, despite their political differences, that he should have said such a thing. It had not been possible.

Mrs Pandit's attack on South Africa in general and Smuts personally had been virulent and unequivocal. It was met with loud applause from many of the delegates. Smuts had been publicly humiliated in a forum where he expected reverence. At home, his enemies on both sides of the political equation gloated at his discomfort.

Flushed with success, but mindful that, in having won her case, she had failed conspicuously to live up to the high ideals of the Mahatma, Mrs Pandit had made her way over the floor of the Assembly to Smuts to ask his forgiveness. Smuts, seeing all too clearly now the bitter harvest that her actions would cause him to reap shortly, together with his party, his country and indeed, even the South African Indians she sought to help, turned to her and said: 'You have won a hollow victory. This vote will put me out of power in our next elections, but you will have gained nothing.'[145]

CHAPTER 6

A State Banquet in Pretoria: The Transvaal Capital Receives the Royal Family

29 March 1947

There was no State Ball planned for the visit to Pretoria. This may have been a tactful decision on the part of everyone concerned. The administrative capital had formerly been the seat of Paul Kruger's Boer republic. While life in official circles – in the ministerial and diplomatic houses that surrounded Government House in the Bryntirion enclave – was Anglophile and reasonably sophisticated, with its rounds of At Homes, cocktail parties, dinner parties, dances and Sunday tennis parties,[1] it contrasted markedly with much of the rest of the town, which had remained predominantly Afrikaans-speaking, churchgoing and conservative.[2]

Even in the 1940s, many dominees in the Afrikaans churches still took a dim view of ballroom dancing. This had been explained to the Royal Family as they watched *volkspele* at Standerton. It was the only dancing of which the dominees approved, as technically it involved no close embrace. (This was accompanied by the explanation that *volkspele* and other cultural activities were in the course of being rapidly appropriated by the National Party for political purposes.[3] Hence their pointed inclusion, no doubt, as a *divertissement* during the outdoor lunch on the occasion of the visit to Smuts's constituency.)

As with the Methodists, many of the older generation within the Dutch

Smuts and the King lead the royal party on arrival at Pretoria station.
TRANSNET HERITAGE LIBRARY PHOTO COLLECTION

Reformed Church saw dancing as decadent. Even Smuts himself, far from being a regular churchgoer, insisted, when asked, that he had only ever danced with one woman, and that was his wife,[4] and that must have been a long time ago. Jan Hofmeyr, raised by his mother in the Presbyterian Church, didn't dance, saying he would as soon take a pole and swing himself round it.[5] His mother certainly did not dance either. Nor did many others who held senior positions in both government and provincial services.

The State Banquet planned for the evening of 29 March, the day of arrival in the capital, was therefore to be the highlight. It was to take place in the City Hall. Pretoria was a latecomer when it came to building a city hall. A competition for its design had been held in 1926 and won by FG McIntosh. Only completed in 1935, it boasted a 32-bell clarion, donated by George Heys, the former owner of Melrose House, where the Treaty of Vereeniging had been signed in 1902.

Handsome and built of sandstone, with richly varnished teak wood-work, it had strong echoes of Lutyens' and Baker's public buildings in

New Delhi. It chimed with many of Sir Herbert Baker's earlier buildings which, before the construction of many indifferent skyscrapers, dominated the capital's skyline. Together, these made Pretoria the very fine city that the Royal Family much admired. In 1947, the Union Buildings on Meintjieskop remained the architect's crowning achievement; south of the city, however, Moerdijk's monolithic monument to the Voortrekkers was beginning to rise on another hill.

The largest city hall in the country, its auditorium boasted a great organ with two consoles, and seated with ease, at long tables, the 650-odd invited guests at the State Banquet. Its interior, however, was slightly disappointing, being a throwback to the wedding-cake, Edwardian-Baroque style of the country's other late-nineteenth-century city halls. The Council had put its best foot forward for this state occasion. Under the direction of Mr Bruins-Lich, Superintendent of the Pretoria Parks Department, the hall had been amazingly transformed for the '*groot ete*' (literally, the Big Meal or banquet).

The resulting municipal display of plants and flowers, once common enough, was an example of a floral art that has all but vanished from this world. This was a stupendous example of the genre. Careful planning had preceded the big day, and flowers had been grown specially for it. The Pretoria city colours were red and yellow, and this was the colour scheme applied. There were bright, showy, seasonal blooms of tea-plate-sized chrysanthemums and tall gladioli;[6] thousands of red begonias and salvias were massed in raked rectangles on either side of the stage; and bright yellow marigolds, employed to outline the outsize crown in the gallery and the royal cipher emblazoned on its green-draped front.

It didn't end there. The municipal greenhouses and nurseries had been ransacked. Days of potting up, picking, installing and positioning had been organised with military precision. Great quantities of cypresses, palms, pampas grass, ferns and bamboos were imported in their containers and arranged on the stage and in the first-floor boxes; these were swagged festively with garlands of greenery. As was traditional for this sort of display, all exposed earth was covered in damp moss, and it was this smell that pervaded the City Hall that night.[7] None of the flowers had any scent at all.

It didn't look anything like a 'sylvan forest glade', though everyone, of course, loyally said it did. It was a municipal gardener's vision, in pre-war, English provincial taste, conventionally executed to the highest standards, accepted and admired as such. The sovereigns were both keen garden- ers and patrons of the Chelsea Flower Show where this sort of display was, at the time, still pretty standard fare. As she entered the Hall the Queen was seen to gasp appreciatively, stand still and look around her in wonderment, pointing out the horticultural glories to the King as well as to General Smuts,[8] to whom they certainly would have meant nothing. Smuts preferred indigenous flowers, of which there were few out at that season, even supposing Bruins-Lich might have considered using them.

The sovereigns and the Household were also unanimous in their delight in the garden at Government House in Pretoria where they were staying, 'a lovely house with a beautiful garden and we wish we could stay here for a few days', as the King wrote to Queen Mary.[9]

Both house and garden had been designed by Herbert Baker, the archi- tect laureate of the imperial age in South Africa, with Lady Selborne's help; the cost of the initial garden layout in 1906 had been £7 000.[10] It was very much of the Lutyens-Jekyll school, Baker having been a friend of both.[11] Long green *allées*, pergolas and herbaceous borders 'going on for yards' as Princess Elizabeth described them to her grandmother,[12] was the general note here; there were also lily ponds, sundials, rock terraces, paths of gravel and crazy paving, and jacarandas by the score.

The koppie edge, which in those days gave panoramic views 'across Africa' from the great sandstone columns of the *stoep* and atrium, was planted with indigenous plants from all over the Union. Princess Alice ('Aunt Alice' in family letters home to Queen Mary, whose sister-in-law she was) had laid out a Dutch garden and put in a swimming pool and tennis court, much used by the King and his Equerries.

A huge staff of 75 (mostly poor whites) tended these once-famous gardens. The Athlones, Clarendons and Duncans, all keen gardeners themselves, had also looked after them, and the effect, as Queen Elizabeth wrote 'is *enchanting*'.[13] Even Lascelles came round to revel in them, along with the glories of the Middleveld climate in which they flourished, rising early on his last morning there to enjoy the beauties of the gardens – 'full of flowers though it is now late-ish autumn'. It was just before sunrise

Imperial Pretoria: Herbert Baker's great columned *stoep*, which fronted Government House, with its views 'across Africa'. Here the royal party stayed for nine days.

NATIONAL ARCHIVES AND RECORDS SERVICE OF SOUTH AFRICA

on the 'most perfect early morning imaginable', as he wrote to his wife, knowing, he added, 'that such mornings are a certainty for 300 days out of 365 – if not more ...'.[14]

Altogether, the nine-day stay in what Lady Selborne, its first chatelaine, would recall as 'that beautiful house,'[15] would be a success. Although it was often described as being 'in the Dutch style', it was essentially an English Arts and Crafts mansion, whose architect had, in addition to dormers, battered eaves, Kentish beams and gentlemanly chimneys, incorporated both imperial and Cape Dutch elements. In the drive towards unification in the early 1900s, it had been thought tactful to include the latter.

Government House, Pretoria, had cost a huge £95 000 to build. To receive the royal visitors, it had been enhanced by the skills of Mr Terry, the state decorator. The Glamis Castle linen toile he used (from Donald Brothers in Dundee) and the popular 'Wine Stag' design from Liberty's were much commented on in the press.[16]

New curtains of damask and velvet hung from stylish, shaped pelmets in the Lenygon & Morant taste, and pretty glazed chintzes were used in the bedrooms and private sitting rooms. New bathrooms had been installed, too, in accordance with the advice given 'about the routine of Their Majesties' lives' and the general comfort requirements of the Royal Family, as provided by Sir Piers Legh, Master of the Royal Household, during the recce in 1946.[17]

The great rooms were further garnished with monumental arrangements of flowers in Linn Ware vases for which the head gardener, Mr Hose, had stripped the great picking gardens. Hose had actually written in advance to his former employer, the Earl of Clarendon,[18] Governor-General of the Union in 1931–1937, to ask what the Queen's favourite flowers were. The question was often asked. Lascelles had given the Earl the standard answer, viz, that the Queen liked all flowers and had no favourites.[19]

Having driven from Government House in their finery, the royal party arrived at the City Hall at 8.40 pm. A crowd of 4 000 braved the rain to cheer them on and greet their appearance on the balcony outside. Was the rain responsible for these modest-sounding numbers? Possibly. Pretoria was, however, a fairly small city of 'public servants and of quiet, sober demeanour', as the *Rand Daily Mail* put it.[20] The weather cannot but have been a contributing factor. Indeed, it had been damnable all day. It had drizzled intermittently during the arrival and State Entry into Pretoria that morning and positively poured in the afternoon, all but washing out the Administrator's garden party.

As always, the Queen was the centre of attention. She arrived for the banquet in a Hartnell crinoline of ivory duchess satin, its wide panniers and bodice heavily embroidered with pearls and gold sequins. It was her most glorious dress of the tour; Pretoria, stated the *Cape Times* categorically, had never seen so magnificent a gown. A diamond and sapphire tiara and a great diamond and sapphire necklace and earrings set off her colouring and the Garter sash.[21] The King also wore his Garter with white tie and miniatures. As always, Smuts too was faultlessly attired on such occasions. Typically, however, the prime minister tactfully avoided wearing his miniatures at such functions. Wearing *die vyand se medaljes en uniform*

Arriving for the State Banquet, Pretoria. Queen Elizabeth in sapphires and diamonds and one of Hartnell's crinolines, with the Princesses at right. Smuts has his back to the camera.

COURTESY OF BRITISH HIGH COMMISSION, SIR ANTHONY REEVE

(the enemy's medals and uniform) had caused outrage among his political detractors in the past. That evening, he wore the Order of Merit alone around his neck.

Around 630 guests attended. The tables were laid with 15 000 pieces of silver and 6 000 glasses, a great array of which would have stood empty throughout the meal before the many teetotallers among the guests. One mile (1.6 kilometres) of damask had been used to make up the tablecloths and napkins. More than 100 paste bowls had been ordered for the table

The State Banquet at Pretoria City Hall, showing the Council's floral decorations.
MARTIN GIBBS / AFRICA MEDIA ONLINE

decorations, whose composition of red and blue salvias, cockscombs, French marigolds, roses, heliotrope and ageratum[22] suggests results that were colourful verging on the *bont* (garish or overly bright).

The City Hall kitchens had been completely refurbished at a cost of £3 000 with what *Die Vaderland* described as *'sommer 'n plaat stowe'* (a veritable bank of stoves). Twenty chefs – *'die beste in die hele land'* (the best in the whole country) – and 140 waiters garnered from every hotel on the Rand as well as from the SAR had been employed. Restaurants in those days were few. The local Afrikaans press noted approvingly that all the staff for this function would be white.[23]

The service was excellent, and the food and plates, when they needed to be, were hot. The lessons of the strung-out State Banquet in Cape Town had been learnt. The menu was the most elaborate so far and was written in English and Afrikaans; French, which every smart hotel then would have employed, was deliberately avoided.

They ate:

Caviar

French Goose Liver in Jelly [*Pâté de foie gras*]

Beef Tea with Celery in Cup [*Consommé*]

Poached Cape Salmon [our old friend Geelbek]
Hollandaise Sauce

Lamb Cutlets, Royal Style
Fresh Buttered Peas
Fried Potatoes

Water Ice

Roast Duckling
Orange Salad

Ice Cream Sandwich
Fruit salad
Biscuits

Fruits

Coffee

The actual wines are unremembered, but there were dry and dark South African sherries (which had come to the fore during the war), white and red wine, port and liqueurs, as well as an 'imported champagne of the type South Africans normally drink to mark special occasions', as the *Rand Daily Mail* put it evasively.[24] Newspapers in those days went to great lengths to avoid giving out venue or brand names, as this smacked of free or partisan advertising.

Pretoria still had at that date a sizeable English-speaking minority, partly owing to their presence in the government, military and civil service, which would have accounted for what was the surprisingly large number of English names on the guest list. This included Cabinet ministers, judges, high-ranking officers of the UDF, members of the Senate, Parliament and the Provincial Council, and representatives of the churches and of public and industrial bodies.[25]

It was, however, disproportionate. There were twice as many Afrikaans-speakers as English in the city.[26] Indeed its mayor, DP van Heerden, who was host to the royal party, had actually been interned during the war as a member of the Ossewabrandwag. This astonished Princess Elizabeth, for she wrote to her grandmother describing this movement as 'the Communist Party here'. She meant, of course, republican, wrongly assuming (on the basis of the Russian Revolution) that all anti-monarchists were communists. The mayor had, she said, 'been interned during the war. He confided to Mummy [Queen Elizabeth] that he had been shut up without evidence, and that he had never even cut a telephone wire or blown up a railway line!'

Van Heerden was apparently not without a sense of humour, for he continued with his piece to the Queen, unabashed, saying that having been a 'guest of the King for nine months [in jail]', it was now his turn to entertain His Majesty for six days, and that 'he had arranged the programme himself'. He had certainly put his best foot forward; Pretoria's decorations were magnificent. Princess Elizabeth decided to give him the benefit of the doubt, telling her grandmother that she understood a great many were shut up 'just in case, and I imagine he was one of them'.[27]

The speeches were slated to precede and follow coffee. Both the BBC Overseas Service and the SABC were on standby to broadcast them.

The State Entry into the administrative capital: the royal Daimler arrives in Church Square.
TRANSNET HERITAGE LIBRARY PHOTO COLLECTION

Smuts spoke first. He was technically on his home ground in Pretoria (although his constituency was Standerton); his farm, Doornkloof, near Irene, where he stayed when Parliament adjourned to Pretoria, was just south of the capital.

The reception in Pretoria had not been as muted as the Nationalist press had tried to predict or assert afterwards; indeed, Princess Elizabeth thought the crowds of 30 000 'tremendous and noisy'.[28] Heartened by this, Smuts now tried to drive his agenda home. The welcome the Royal Family had received in South Africa – in city, town or wayside station, on farm or the veld, as he put it – did not merely derive from the traditional hospitality of our people (he meant here the *volk*). This was a firm attempt to refute the argument put forward by the Nationalist press to explain away the (to them) distressingly large and happy crowds who had turned up to cheer the Royal Family even in predominantly Afrikaans-speaking areas. It [the welcome] also sprang, Smuts said, 'from a deeper sentiment and devotion for the Royal Family.'

While there might be some truth in this, Smuts was really grasping at straws here. He wanted to suggest that at least his one-third support (that is, from the so-called Waverers) among the Afrikaners had comprehended the virtues of a constitutional monarchy. It followed, he trusted, that they did so because they saw it as the force that bound the British Commonwealth together and ensured its place in the world order, and South Africa's place within it.

Perhaps he hoped that more could be persuaded to believe in this too. He ploughed on, therefore, mentioning Kruger and Louis Botha as part of Pretoria's glorious past and stating that, in spite of past wars, mutual experience and mutual understanding had 'healed the wounds of the past and enabled the two great races to come together and to go forward to their united destiny'.

This was Smuts's post-war dream. In fairness, the war and the election of 1943 appeared to have shown it was possible. A generous view of the tour's success would seem to endorse it further. In the event, racist politics would dominate the following election, and utopian dreams of this sort would be consigned to oblivion.

The King's reply was lengthy. It had given his speechwriter, Morrah, 'some turmoil' in its composition. (Lascelles was not present; he was in bed for 24 hours at Government House with what he described as a 'chill on my stomach'.[29]) He was, of course, aware he was addressing a rather different audience to the one at the State Banquet in Cape Town on the first day of the tour. He needed to reach out to the Afrikaners, specifically. No general sop was here included for the non-white population and their hopes for a better future.

The speech was preceded by a slight hiccough. According to one account, Smuts, in Lascelles's absence, had had to coerce the King to speak sooner than planned – before having his coffee – and, most unusually, the King's displeasure at this was heard around the world as the microphone had not been switched off in between the speeches. The full exchange, partly picked up by some of the newspapers, was set out, purportedly verbatim, by Major George Richards, a senator and correspondent of Lady Milner, Lord Milner's widow, as follows:

SMUTS: You are to follow me now, Sir.

KING: I'll speak when I've had my coffee and the waiters have left the room.

SMUTS: They're waiting for you now in England, Sir.

KING: Well, let them wait. I have said I will speak when the waiters have left the room.

PRINCESS ELIZABETH: Can we be heard?

A MAN'S VOICE: No.[30]

Richards was to claim that there was more besides. The reason for Smuts's opening line of the exchange was surely simple enough. The BBC was on the air waiting to relay it. It was a Saturday night and the BBC had had to forego relaying some of their most popular programmes of the week to accede to what amounted to a royal command that the important speech be broadcast. Sarah Bradford, King George VI's excellent biographer, however, implies that the King's grumpiness, as reported to Violet Milner, resulted from a growing general feeling that he was 'part of a side-show, a totem in a travelling circus, marking time to Jan Smuts's tune'.[31]

Many liberals abroad, who later felt the tour had squandered royal time and misplaced effort on what they, in retrospect, came to regard as simply another white supremacist South African government, have similarly sought to try and explain away the sovereigns' efforts in South Africa. Dancing bears and monkey-and-organ-grinder analogies are again and again hinted at.

Such a reported exchange and the interpretation readily placed on it cannot, however, be taken at face value. It emanated from a now largely forgotten but equally die-hard strand in South African politics in that era, this time an English-speaking one which had hitherto been voiced at the polls through the Dominion Party, under Colonel Stallard. Though they espoused the more enlightened and paternal racial policies of the Empire, they were hardly a liberal body. Essentially, they were imperialist, with a strong anti-Afrikaner nationalist bias. And they resisted all attempts to placate it.

Clearly, they had a political agenda too. Major Richards, a Natal senator, with a farm, Summerhill, at Mooi River, in the Midlands, personifies this type. No liberal himself, in any accepted sense of the word, he is a slightly shadowy figure, appearing to have been something of an *éminence grise* flitting between the various Empire Leagues and Victoria Leagues, which survived as para-political bodies and which aimed to continue to foster Milner's vision for the British Empire among like-minded, English-speaking South Africans.

Smuts sought to distance himself from these bodies, which served to highlight for his opponents the issue of divided English-speaking loyalties. He saw this as especially necessary in the context of the tour, as we have seen in East London and Durban (see pp 162–164). There was a vaguely perceived sort of freemasonry among the heads of the different organisations which he and others found both annoying and slightly sinister. Richards, for instance, describes their eventual audience with the King and Queen as being 'behind locked doors' and 'getting to know each one in his or her particular role'.[32]

While bodies such as the Victoria League undoubtedly had their practical uses, in wartime especially, they conveyed a blimp-ish image that sat ill with mainstream mid-twentieth-century South African politics. They were slightly absurd too. Describing his meeting with Morrah, Richards saw it as letting the *Times* know and understand 'the manner of men we are, what we stood for and what we are up against', the *Times*, he noted testily, 'having been no friend of ours hitherto'.[33]

Even in the 1930s, distinguished visitors to the Union were typically warned on arrival that this network of old-fashioned imperial spirits simply survived as the counterpoint to extremists like the Malans and Hertzogs of the South African political scene. The sovereigns and the Household had been warned of this too.

Richards, a somewhat blimp-ish figure himself, loathed all politicians whose aims seemed to thwart the perpetration of Milner's aims. Although the pro-war coalition had forced him and the Dominion Party to side with Smuts, he was no great fan of the prime minister, who not only kept his distance but, he thought, gave far too much away in the interests of political expediency. Lady Milner, as editor of the *National Review*, kept up a steady barrage along these lines.[34] Richards even suspected Smuts – absurdly – of being equivocal on the vital issue of loyalty to the throne; he believed that Smuts had used the visit for personal aggrandisement and a canvassing expedient for the next election. 'People out here look upon Royalty as something to be used for their own ends,' he wrote irritably to Lady Milner, 'loyalty and gratitude of course [illegible] come into the picture.'[35]

By this stage of the tour, it had become an especial obsession of Major Richards that everyone connected with the tour, not only Smuts, was hobbling the Royal Family to their own inimical ends. The Afrikander [sic] police, he wrote, sleuthed them constantly and never allowed them to move freely among their people. The King's description of them as 'the Gestapo' is naturally mentioned. One gets the distinct feeling he was telling Lady Milner, who had co-founded the Victoria League and much of whose widowhood was spent carrying a torch for her late husband, what she and he wanted to hear.

As for the microphone incident, Richards, not present, was reporting hearsay from 'his informant'; he admits that it does not match up to the press reports of the incident.[36] Certainly, the final exchange between the King and Smuts, as he reports it, looks suspiciously as if it might be an embellishment, designed to be a clincher:

> Shortly after [the initial exchange] the King rises and speaks. On resuming his seat:
> SMUTS: That was very good, Sir.
> KING: Well, I suppose now I might have my coffee.

It certainly doesn't tally with the BBC's Frank Gillard's detailed and more plausible account of what happened.[37]

Are these then calumnies? Smuts, like others, it is true, had been alarmed on several occasions during the tour by the King's outbursts of temper and other signs of being unwell; Van der Byl's claim of a duodenal ulcer would explain much after a meal such as this with an important speech at its end. Nevertheless, the last exchange seems highly unlikely as the King, at the conclusion of his speech, asked the Toastmaster to request the company to sing together 'Sarie Marais'.

The King's speech in Pretoria had proved to be the trickiest speech of the tour; Lascelles's claim of 'some turmoil' was surely an understatement. Thanking the prime minister and the people of South Africa, the King said that he and his family had had to travel through the country to plumb the secret of its great attraction. Now they knew this, they could 'walk on common ground in our love and admiration of this happy land'.

These were expected platitudes. Although the press would make much of such phrases – 'this happy land' in particular – privately, there is evidence that the King was by now thoroughly aware of the unhappiness of many of his segregated South African subjects, and the absence of a firmly stated political intent to alleviate this. We know, too, that he was exasperated by the lack of unity between even the two white races. And although they had enjoyed making 'new friends', as Queen Elizabeth put it, again, privately, the King thought many of them a dissatisfied bunch. 'South Africans live very comfortably in every way,' he wrote to his mother, comparing their current lot to that of his British subjects, 'and are still not satisfied.'[38]

There was a chance here now, therefore, to make this point – to 'rub it in' as he put it to Queen Mary[39] – although in a gentlemanly and very roundabout way. Departing from the upbeat themes invariably employed on such occasions, he now referred to the hardships the people of war-battered Britain had been going through in his absence – especially the very severe winter of 1947. It had indeed had an appalling one, with dire consequences for the economy.

This, his one unhappy memory of the tour and a constant spectre at the feast, much reported in the South African press and often accompanied by shocking pictures, was now swiftly turned to advantage in the context of his Pretoria speech. It was the first time he had mentioned it in public. His anxiety had been easier to bear, he said, because of the sympathy felt by South Africans for the men and women of the British Isles who faced their troubles so courageously. He then quoted in full the prayer offered up by the Dean of the Bloemfontein Cathedral, DC Tugman, during the service the family had attended there on 9 March.[40] In it, Tugman had entreated the Lord to look down with compassion upon

> our brethren in Britain, and lighten the burden of these vigorous
> days – the burden of cold and the burden of shortages, the burden of

industrial difficulty and international uncertainty, the burden of disappointment and of hope deferred ... and grant to us who have lived so gently through all these years that we may have true sympathy with them in their struggle and follow the example of their courage.

It has to be said that South Africans, especially English-speaking ones on the home front, had been very sympathetic to the plight of the beleaguered people of Britain since 1939, donating generously to War Funds, Spitfire Funds and various other relief charities. Even now, as the great thaw began, resulting in tremendous floods and yet more misery, a further substantial amount of £300 000 would be raised for flood relief (see pp 293–294). Possibly, therefore, the King had particularly his intransigent Nationalist subjects in mind as being the dissatisfied ones; this group was unlikely to have donated funds to these causes.

He had quoted the prayer in full, the King went on, because he believed that it symbolised the spirit that must inspire the whole Commonwealth and Empire – 'the understanding of each other's troubles; the wish to help and the determination to solve our problems together'. Pressing home the point, he asked rhetorically: 'And why should this not be so? Are we not one brotherhood – the greatest brotherhood in the whole history of man?'

It was worth a try, and many South Africans, again mostly but not exclusively the English-speaking ones, would have applauded this quasi-religious and decidedly Christian sentiment. Lascelles certainly believed it had gone down well.[41] It found a strong echo in The Star's leader of 1 April 1947, two days later, when the Royal Family entered Johannesburg:

We cannot stand long on the heights and look at a cavalcade passing through fairy land ... Soon it will become merely a pleasant and colourful memory. But what can endure is a renewed dedication to those high purposes the King has set before us: the strengthening of that common brotherhood in which we forget the causes and remember only the lessons of our past differences. The Kingship we acclaim today is not the exclusive prerogative ... of any one group in our midst. It is the common heritage of us all.

The new Commonwealth that evolved, however, would prove less of a congenial brotherhood to some of them and no brotherhood at all to the Afrikaner minority that would rule the country after the election the following year.

At this point the King's speech took a bold step. He now quoted from Paul Kruger, 'the great patriot' as he called him: 'May his immortal words ... "Take from the past all that is good and beautiful; shape your ideal therewith and build your future on this ideal" ever remain the watchword of young South Africans.'[42]

He naturally did not elaborate further. As president of the old Transvaal Republic, Kruger had been Britain's great foe, and consequently the hero and subsequent martyr of the *volk*, having died in 1904, in exile in Switzerland, where he had eventually fled from the advancing British forces during the Anglo-Boer War.

It was, in retrospect, an audacious ploy designed to reach out to traditional Afrikaners. It also showed the royal party's belief in the tour's success thus far, and the Smuts government's continued confidence in its political strength, that the King could be heard to quote from such a patently anti-British, local folk hero. Doubtless the warm reception given to the Royal Family that morning beneath the statue of Louis Botha, on the lawns in front of the Union Buildings, by a crowd of one thousand *oudstryders*,[43] who had answered their old leader's call to meet them, had helped here too.

Not all English-speakers present or listening in can have felt entirely happy about referencing Kruger, even if they recognised the point of the gesture being made. Those such as Major Richards and Lady Milner at their wirelesses must have been apoplectic.[44] *Dirty Ole Kruger* had been the bogeyman of the English in both South Africa and Britain until his defeat, much as Napoleon had been decades before him.

There was, of course, a sizeable group of Nationalist politicians at the banquet. They were seated together at the same tables and were seen to be noisily enjoying themselves. Observing strict constitutional niceties of political impartiality, Jansen, who had recently won the Wolmaransstad by-election for the Nationalists on a very racist ticket, was seated at the top table. So too was Havenga, of the Afrikaner Party. Perhaps this

Greeting the large gathering of *oudstryders* (Anglo-Boer War veterans)
below the Union Buildings.

TRANSNET HERITAGE LIBRARY PHOTO COLLECTION

was a significant gesture born out of Lady Duncan's political prognosis
for the United Party, as espoused at the dinner at Government House
in Bloemfontein three weeks previously (see pp 126–127). If so, it was
now too late. For, only eight days earlier, Havenga had formed a pact with
Malan that would prove critical in the 1948 election.

The King's speech duly went out on the airwaves. Many in South Africa
and elsewhere thought it excellent and conciliatory; those young South
Africans, however, who revered Kruger's memory and heeded his words
had a very different future South Africa in mind.

For now, the well wined and dined audience of mixed political backgrounds who made up the company that evening applauded the gesture
and the King's speech in general, which ended with him asking, charmingly, not to say goodbye 'but, if I may, *totsiens*'. Through the Toastmaster
(then a feature at such occasions), the King then asked the assembled
company to sing 'Sarie Marais'. This popular Afrikaner *liedjie* of the late

nineteenth century, sung to the tune of the American Civil War-era ballad 'Ellie Rhee', itself a version of the Irish folksong 'Foggy Dew', had been elevated, especially during the recent war, to a popular national song. It now stood almost on a par with 'Waltzing Matilda', the evocative, unofficial Australian anthem, and many were the Afrikaner women who came forward claiming to be the eponymous Sarie. Were its words not in Afrikaans, a language generally unknown outside South Africa, it would have been almost as widely known around the English-speaking world. The tune certainly was.

In an age of community singing, asking guests to sing at the end of a State Banquet was not the surprise it would certainly be nowadays. It was, moreover, a clever gesture on the part of the King, as it engaged with Afrikaner folklore sentiment and a much more broadly-based South African sentiment resulting from the war.

The request almost certainly bears the hallmark of Queen Elizabeth. Senator Conroy, Minister of Lands and Irrigation in the War Cabinet, stood and conducted from the top table. The Royal Family had assiduously learnt the song in advance, onomatopoeically, and joined in enthusiastically:

> *O bring my terug na die Ou Transvaal*
> *Daar waar my Sarie woon*
> *Daar onder in die mielies by die groen doringboom*
> *Daar woon my Sarie Marais*

> Oh take me back to the Old Transvaal
> Where my Sarie lives
> Down there in the mealie fields, by the green thorn tree
> That's where my Sarie Marais lives.

Indeed, at its completion, the Queen, ablaze with her diamonds and sapphires, bowed radiantly across the top table to the loudly applauding company, applauding them too,[45] almost as if she had been performing a solo with an accompanying chorus.

As the Royal Family departed, the guests spontaneously burst into 'For

They Are Jolly Good Fellows' and cheered and clapped. They left slowly, chatting to many of the guests on their way out, some of whom stood in the hallway outside to see them leave. Finally the Daimler moved off.

Smuts, who disliked late nights, was pleased to find his official car quickly for the longish drive out to Irene. As was always understood now, Mrs Smuts had not accompanied him to this sort of official event. At the last minute he had thought to ask old Mrs Hofmeyr to accompany him, knowing that, complicated and difficult though she was, it would secretly give her great pleasure to do so.

This was undoubtedly so. But it backfired horribly. For in the general melee surrounding the departures, Smuts forgot all about her. Presumably, owing to the last-minute nature of the gesture, the driver of his official car forgot about her too. In the upshot, she was left behind at the City Hall and had to make her way home into the rainy night as best she could.

Everyone in Pretoria knew her reputation as a termagant, and her prickliness about what she felt was her due, as the mother of an important (bachelor) Cabinet minister, with whom, although in his fifties, she still lived, ran his house and still went about with him everywhere. In many ways she still treated him as a minor; she was intensely protective and proud of her boy.

Hofmeyr, slated as Smuts's successor, was widely believed to have 'run South Africa' during Smuts's frequent wartime absences, a view his mother did nothing to discourage. The prime minister's visits to London, where he was seen to hobnob with the great and good, were an especial grievance to his many small-time detractors in political South Africa. Old Deborah Hofmeyr ranked foremost among these. Perceived slights were almost a nourishment for her, and everyone habitually tiptoed around her. When the word got round about what had happened to her after the banquet, official Pretoria collectively held its breath.

They were right to do so, but the immediate blow did not fall as directly on Smuts's head, as was generally anticipated. Instead, she entered the fray with gusto, making of it one of her amusing stories, told repeatedly, at every opportunity, heavy with irony, invective and innuendo. 'Of course, I am n-not important,' she would declare roundly, typically fixing her interlocutors with a basilisk-like stare that brooked no comeback, 'You s-see, I'm n-n-not *R-r-royalty*.'[46]

CHAPTER 7

꿁

Johannesburg: 'Becher's Brook, Second Time Round'

April Fool's Day 1947

The first of April was to be a particularly gruelling day. This was Johannesburg's day, and it was 'the most exhausting day of the whole trip,' as Lascelles put it to his wife.[1] Smuts once famously remarked to Princess Alice, who with her husband, the Earl of Athlone,[2] had been South Africa's much-loved gubernatorial couple of the 1920s, on the toughness of royalty. 'They have to be,' she answered crisply, and clearly here including herself, 'otherwise they would not last the course.'[3]

The Royal Family were certainly going to need all their toughness on this day, for it would be crammed with a non-stop programme lasting from nine in the morning until well after midnight, interspersed with nearly 120 miles (192 kilometres) of car travel.[4] Afterwards, so amazed and exhausted were the courtiers by what had been accomplished in a single day that they referred to it as 'Becher's Brook, Second Time Round'.[5] There was a good reason for likening it to the notorious fence that has to be jumped twice in the steeplechase that is the Grand National: Johannesburg, the biggest city in the Union, had, to general astonishment and indignation, only been allotted one full day in the itinerary. A huge programme, therefore, had to be got through. The second day was only a part-day for the city, and included long drives out to the East and West Rand.

Despite the apparent snub (it was nowhere suggested that the Royal Family was to blame), there had been a tremendous build-up to the visit in the Rand's English-language press. In its leader of 28 March 1947, *The Star*, Johannesburg's evening newspaper, told its readers: 'The royal visitors are now approaching the greatest city in Southern Africa. In a few days they will see what many of us, with some justification, regard as the greatest marvel of all – a large, modern city in the heart of what was till recently the dark continent: a fantastic silhouette, like a single many-turreted castle, dominating a wide plain and built on a rock of gold.'

This was not solely a Eurocentric view; black writers too spoke of it as a 'throbbing giant'[6] and of their fascination with 'the garish lights ... the colour and rumble of the city.'[7] The writer Es'kia Mphahlele, gazing out of his not-yet-electrified house in Orlando, contemplated 'the beauty of distant electric lights ... [that] blink and tease the spirit of the night: little sparkling fires, so unearthly, so inorganic.'[8]

Not everyone connected with the royal tour, however, regarded Johannesburg as the greatest marvel of all. The Central Committee and the Transvaal provincial sub-committee had all along felt that Pretoria, 30 miles (48 kilometres) to the north, the administrative capital of the Union and the headquarters of its Defence Force, with Church Square at its heart and fine public buildings and tree-lined avenues, had deserved first priority – and by far the greatest number of days allocated.

Nor was there a Government House in Johannesburg to house the Royal Family; as we know, it was situated in Pretoria. A mere 400 yards (365 metres) away too stood Libertas, the prime minister's residence, which the Smutses never used, preferring to live on their farm at Irene. Even the extended Household could be housed there with ease. The entire royal party could therefore have nine days in comfort off the White Train.

There was, as we have already seen, almost certainly another factor, never actually expressed, at work here: Pretoria was also the old capital of Kruger's Boer republic,[9] and it was essential that the Royal Family should be seen to give it its full due and earn a warm reception there.

With all that in mind, the committee had therefore contrived to give Johannesburg merely one day of the itinerary. For the city that was the largest and richest in South Africa, this was clearly absurd. But the courtiers and even the Palace Advance Party seem to have gone along with this from the start – almost certainly also for old-fashioned, snobbish reasons. Like many visitors to the country at that date, they viewed Johannesburg as a brash, vulgar and unruly city – a 'modern Babylon if ever there was one', as Lascelles (who didn't like it and all he felt it stood for) himself described it.[10]

It was planned that the royal party would drive out from Government House, and that Johannesburg and the Reef towns would be visited on two consecutive days, with the party returning to Pretoria each night. At that date, even on pre-cleared roads, this involved a journey of an hour.

Everyone seems to have got this one wrong. Pretoria, with a white population of twice as many Afrikaans- as English-speakers, was conservative, sleepy and increasingly Nationalist. Lascelles, who prided himself on being the King's brother-in-law's first cousin once removed, might privately profess to prefer the Free Staters of Bloemfontein and its neighbourhood 'who are as different from the Jo'burgers as a West Country Yeoman is from a Birmingham stockbroker',[11] but neither they nor the Pretoria Afrikaners were likely to vote for General Smuts in the next or any other election. Johannesburg – modern, moneyed and go-ahead with a vibrant cultural life – had more than twice as many English-speakers as Afrikaans-speakers, and they were a great source of votes and financial support for Smuts's party. So too, potentially, were the towns of the West and East Rand, which had been given even shorter shrift in the scheme of things on Day Two.

Not surprisingly, the citizens of Johannesburg were outraged when they learnt of the arrangements. How had East London (total population 76 105) and Bloemfontein (total population 67 196) been given three days each, and their city, with a population of 606 016, only one? There were questions asked, aggrieved articles and letters in the press, and even cartoons showing Johannesburg getting short commons at the dinner table of the royal visit. The local committees protested, as did Mr Welsh, Honorary Co-ordinating Officer for the Transvaal leg of the tour, who liaised with them,[12] and eventually even the King was made to see that this was a glaring error. To Queen Mary he admitted: 'The Transvaal people are angry (the officials I mean) that there were not enough days given to

Sean Coughlan's cartoon in the *Sunday Times* (9 March 1947), which highlighted
Johannesburg's indignation at being allotted less than two full days of the royal itinerary.

BY PERMISSION OF THE *SUNDAY TIMES*

them. Two days allowed for the largest city in South Africa is really too
stupid.'[13]

At last, on 10 March, Mr Welsh was able to tell the people of
Johannesburg that, following a series of specially convened meetings
involving everyone from the Tour Manager, the Transvaal Committee
and the Witwatersrand Command, the Royal Family had agreed to give
up a day of leisure over the Easter weekend and give Johannesburg an
extra day: 'While many people would doubtless prefer even more opportunity of paying homage to the royal guests,' as he put it, evenly, to the
press, 'they will, nevertheless, be ready to concede that the plan does mark
a great improvement on the original.'[14]

The King remained very displeased. By the second day of the visit, he
was aware that conservative (and possibly snobbish) forces, even within
his Household, must have been at work here. In addition to the tumultuous welcome, a great contrast to the polite applause of some of the Pretoria
crowds, he was clearly impressed by the vigorous, progressive, go-ahead

city and the leading citizens he had met. Doubtless, they were a refreshing change from the conservative and often intransigent Afrikaner politicians and civic personalities he had come across again and again elsewhere. At the second civic luncheon on the following day, therefore, he decided to make an impromptu speech.[15] Given the strains of the two crowded days and his dislike of public speaking, his breaking with the careful advanced planning suggests that there was something he particularly wanted to say. There was, and it went well beyond the usual platitudes expressed on such occasions: 'There is an atmosphere here that I find very encouraging and stimulating,' he told the assembled guests, with the skill of appearing to make a personal aside, and adding, significantly, 'it is, I can assure you, a pleasure to be among this progressive and friendly community.'[16]

Yet another protest about the proposed programme had come in, this time from the black townships – Alexandra to the north, and Orlando to the southwest. By 1947 their populations, greatly increased during the war as result of Smuts's policy to relax influx control to supply manpower for the factories contributing to the war effort, were, officially at least, 52 000 and 57 660, respectively. In reality, they were almost certainly significantly higher. The inhabitants lived in vibrant squalor with a nascent overlay of civic 'black Britishness' which the authorities hoped to further extend. There were schools attended by simply uniformed children who might also be Pathfinders, Wayfarers and Sunbeams, a post office, bus services, an overworked clinic, and so on. On the day of the visit itself, for example, black members of the St John's Ambulance and the Red Cross stood by in both townships to offer first aid to the crowds. The Rand's English-language press, at least, noted this approvingly.

For now, however, at the planning stage of the visit, the inhabitants objected strongly. If the Royal Family were driving over from Pretoria, and practically skirting Alexandra, how was it that they were to be bypassed? Over 50 000 people lived here, almost all black, and was it because of this, they wondered? Threats of non-cooperation and boycotts hung in the air.

The Royal Family, by now all too aware of the sensitivities within a sharply segregated society, and the whites-only tour organisers' keenness to show a town's more attractive aspects at the expense of large communities, agreed readily to depart earlier from Government House and make a detour into Alexandra. They may by this stage have been encouraged by the meeting of the executive committee of the Johannesburg branch of the African National Congress in February (presided over by the President-General, AB Xuma, in person), where, by 15 votes to 2, it was agreed not to boycott the royal visit. Smuts, who tracked these developments carefully, was certainly aware of this.[17]

The royal party reached Alexandra at 9.45 am. Like many stops in townships or locations, the organisation was not particularly good and the decorations humble, but, delighted at being the first welcome of a crowded day,[18] the numbers and enthusiasm made up for this. An estimated 60 000 turned out to cheer the King and Queen and Princesses along the two-mile (3-kilometre) route through the township, lining the road five to ten deep on each side.[19] The Native Affairs Department had had to hurriedly allocate £500 to buy meat pies to feed children waiting for the procession to pass. This was in response to the many collapses from heat, thirst and exhaustion which had marred the great rally of black loyalists in Durban. There was a pause during which a children's choir sang 'Nkosi Sikelel' iAfrika' and a black pipe band wearing kilts of Royal Stewart tartan played Scottish airs,[20] said to be in honour of the Queen.

As always, the visitors were glad they had agreed to the detour, but members of the Household were struck by the sad contrast, as it seemed to them, between the cheerful herdsmen they had seen in the countryside and the often miserable-looking urban blacks 'in grey flannel trousers, shiftless and outcast'.[21] Many black South Africans of that date, who were keen to modernise, would have resented this unfavourable comparison; the image of picturesque native rustics was not the collective image they sought to project in the mid-twentieth century. The contrast between the two ways of life was, nevertheless, an almost inevitable part of the process. Britons and Afrikaners alike, as convulsive industrialisation changed their countries, had had to grapple with the unfamiliar new freedoms and insecurities that came with urban life. There was a significant difference here, of course. However poor a poor white was, he still had the vote.

The cheers of Alexandra's township dwellers were but a curtain-raiser of what was to come. Back on Louis Botha Avenue, then the main road linking Pretoria and Johannesburg, the Daimler pressed on across the veld at a steady 60 mph (96 kph), occasionally slowing when groups of waving people had gathered at dusty crossroads, and occasionally glimpsing the marvel *The Star* had promised on the horizon ahead. Every so often, to the east, a mine dump could be seen peeping over the ridge.

Johannesburg really was a marvel in many respects, a city that had replaced a mining town on the barren veld in 60 short years, 'within the lifetime of many of you', as the King was to put it shortly in reply to the city's Loyal Address, 'when this Ridge of White Waters was but the home of wandering buck and the lonely, soaring eagle'.[22]

What had been created since was essentially an English, or, more technically, a British city. British or Anglo-South African identity had both a civic and ethnic dimension to it, expressed in municipal government, businesses and institutions and even recreational facilities. And the people who had built the city were mostly British by birth or descent.[23]

Others were merely British by aspiration or osmosis. There was, for example, a large and increasingly influential Jewish community in Johannesburg – greatly swollen by refugee immigrants from Lithuania and Germany up until the 1930s. Ready and indeed keen to assimilate (though not in matters religious), they rapidly adopted an increasingly English identity, and more and more lived like their fellow neighbours of British descent. Other nationalities did too. Accents were ironed out; mannerisms and styles of dress were subtly altered. Helen Suzman, the leader of the Progressive Party, whom we shall meet in Chapter 11 and who in her adult life might have reasonably passed in manner and voice for the owner of the large house outside an English market town, had as a father Sam Gavronsky, a self-made Lithuanian immigrant who spoke with a Yiddish accent.[24]

Nationality, as has been pointed out elsewhere, may become defined by citizenship and that can be acquired through naturalisation, birth and residence in the territory of the nation-state.[25] Many immigrants to Johannesburg at this date saw the English South African identity as the means of trading up, some of their less successful co-immigrants wryly referring to these efforts, often achieved in the face of social anti-Semitism and related prejudices, as 'trying for white'.[26]

Education was the strongest factor in starting off this process. Where permitted, children were sent to private schools, modelled on English public schools. Where it was not, for there was considerable resistance from within these schools until the 1960s, the government schools available – King Edward VII, Jeppe, Parktown, and so on – all strongly imitated this prototype. Here, children one generation out of the shtetl, Balkan village or Greek island were duly attired in school ties, boaters and gymslips. They were taught to play cricket, rugby, tennis, hockey and lacrosse; they learnt about the kings and queens of England, and about Drake, Nelson and Rupert Brooke; they sang in carol services and in Gilbert and Sullivan operettas and ate the watery-smelling food of English institutional cooking.

The *South African Jewish Times* of April 1947 ran pages of pictures of prominent Jews at royal events – 'Among the select and representative gathering invited to the official functions were many well-known personalities in South African Jewry,' reads a typical heading.[27] It indicated the prominent positions in South African society they filled, such as MPs, MPCs, judges, KCs, mayors and mayoresses, St John's nurses, the Red Cross Jewish Guild Detachment, and so on. Chief Rabbi Rabinowitz appears smilingly, 'snapped in the rain' at the Pretoria Garden Party. There is a special article on Gerald Woolfe – celebrated as 'Baragwanath's Florence Nightingale' for his voluntary work among TB patients at that hospital[28] – who had been presented to the King.

There is an additional subtext here suggesting that, expressed loyalism apart, this was an occasion to record not only that due honour had been shown to Jews of standing within the community, but also how, increasingly, they themselves identified with important aspects of civic and national official life within the Dominion. The only mention in the *Jewish Times* of the thorny situation regarding the British in Palestine concomitant with its reportage of the royal visit is on 2 May, well after the tour's completion. And in accordance with a policy to live in concord with the governing authority dating back to the Roman Empire, it was firmly ring-fenced from the loyalism being espoused, '… testimony to the fact that whatever may be Jewish grievances against the British administration in Palestine, these do not derogate from the bonds of friendship between

Jewry and the British people as such, and the loyalty of the Jews through-out the Empire to the British Crown'.[29]

All over Johannesburg, in the weeks leading up to the visit, a great sea of Union Jacks (and some of the St Andrew's Cross to honour the Queen) had been raised. Many were over public buildings and skyscrapers, where they were flown jointly with the South African flag, giving the impres-sion from a distance of the 'many-turreted castle' that *The Star* said the city's skyline now presented to welcome the Royal Family. Many more were raised over private homes, in both richer and more modest suburbs. Fluttering in the Highveld breezes, they made an impressive sight, and symbolised a shared social and political identity. For many families, keen to follow the example of their Anglo-Saxon neighbours, this was a first, and one or two journalists felt obliged to point out, drily, that some of the Union Jacks were being flown upside down.[30]

There was also in Johannesburg a large poor white Afrikaner popu-lation, mostly living to the south of the city centre and in some of the less salubrious areas along the Rand, whose lives were – unintentionally – becoming more English, though certainly not in politics or senti-ment. (The same could be said for many Afrikaners of that era.)[31] Not many flags were raised in these areas; none of them were Union Jacks. Urbanisation had not been easy for these people. One of the many Nationalist grievances was that the business world was almost exclu-sively in the hands of the English-speakers and the Jews. As late as 1937, *Die Transvaler* estimated that there were only 20 Afrikaans enterprises in Johannesburg.[32]

Significantly, English surnames predominate in the long guest lists for Johannesburg's Administrator's Banquet, the two civic lunches and the Princesses' ball. There is a fair smattering of Afrikaans names, no more, and some presumably belonged to people who had anglicised. The names of prominent Jewish families appear too. The leading Johannesburg baronet and knight, Sir George Albu and Sir Ernest Oppenheimer, respectively, and their wives, whose names both appear just under the titled courtiers and civic officials, were both of Jewish descent, though by this date practising Christians.

The weather, until now at any rate, had remained glorious, with all the snap and sparkle of a Highveld autumn morning, the finest air in the world – the much-vaunted 'champagne air of the Highveld' (as the newspapers and travel agents were still able to claim) – sweeping up to meet them as the open tourer drove steadily onwards and upwards along the made-up dual carriageway. Finally the procession passed under the triumphal arch that marked the then boundary of the greater city (near Bramley); the route led on through some of the suburbs which by that time were spreading rapidly north, east and west of the city and boasted names like Orange Grove, Yeoville, Dunkeld, Rosebank, Houghton and Parktown, all essentially conforming to the English garden suburb prototype on the lines originally envisaged by Ebenezer Howard.

This replicated further the very English ideal of *rus in urbe*, which had been introduced to the Cape in the early nineteenth century and remained the pervasive vogue in urban South Africa.[33] At this date, there was more than a hint of WASP California thrown into the mix too. Here, jacaranda'd avenues were lined with comfortable houses of mostly unremarkable architectural merit, set in intensely gardened plots that benefited from a marvellously repaying horticultural climate, and often boasting a tennis court and, increasingly, a swimming pool.

By now the crowds on the pavements were thick and continuous, and augmented here and there by phalanxes of schoolchildren in their uniforms: the boys of King Edward VII School, the girls of St Andrew's and Roedean. The King Edward's boys had strung a welcoming banner across the road and gave the school war cry ('Gigamalayo Gee! Gigamalayo Gee! Teddy Bears, Wha! Who are we: *Teddy Bears!*') as the Daimler passed. Marist Brothers and their band were stationed on the crest of Orange Grove Hill; nearer the city, the boys of St John's College lined the road. Among the spectators, too, standing side by side with their employers, were many domestic workers (uniformed too, but quite differently, of course) and given the morning 'off'; many responded to the cavalcade with waves, ululations and cries of 'Hau!'[34]

By 9.50 the Daimler had reached Clarendon Circle,[35] the elegant circus that was considered the entrance to the city proper. On this day it boasted a mammoth crown at its centre, designed by the architectural branch of the City Engineering Department and installed by the Parks and Estates

Department;[36] its outer circumference was ringed by the helmeted city constabulary, standing smartly to attention in uniforms identical to those of London bobbies.

The Jeppe Boys' High Pipe Band and the St John's Ambulance Brigade Boys' Band were stationed to play at the Circle; the King saluted as he passed and the crowd of 6 000 (the northwest side of the Circle being 'lined with natives', as *The Star* reported)[37] cheered wildly. At this point, the colour scheme of the civic decorations, which had been a patriotic red, white and blue since the Bramley arch seven miles (11 kilometres) back, changed abruptly to green and gold, the colours of the city. By then, the full extent of Johannesburg's incredible reception must have begun to dawn upon the Royal Family and the Household. One million people in all were there to cheer the Royal Family that day; this would prove to be the greatest South African welcome of them all.

Months of meticulous planning and organisation had gone into this, and Johannesburg's citizens had read of the correctly phrased and worded details of the preparations in its daily papers with a mixture of patriotic and civic pride. The Council had lined the ten-mile (16-kilometre) route to the City Hall with 1 000 shields, 2 000 flags and 500 banners, the huge order having being placed months before by the Controller of Stores.[38] Buildings and shops had bought their bunting, flags, royal photographs, streamers and banners bearing the words 'LONG MAY HE REIGN' from shops like Herbert Evans[39] and E Lindsay Smithers, who had specially imported these from England.

The large department stores, such as John Orr, Ansteys and Cleghorn & Harris, had vied with each other with their displays of loyal greetings. The undoubted winner, however, was the OK Bazaars (proprietors: Messrs Sam Cohen and Michael Miller), which had erected above the store's street canopy a fully articulated model of the Coronation Coach, with figures of the King and Queen waving from the inside; it was drawn by six Windsor Greys, with footmen, postilions and outriders and even a Life Guard on a rearing black charger, all one and a half times life size, and executed locally (it was proudly said) in *papier mâché* which had been heavily lacquered.[40] Crowd control had been necessary in front of it on the night the city's lights were first switched on.

These lights were magnificent. The City Electricity Department had worked 'night and day' to complete its schemes and floodlighting using 65 pylons and 10 miles (16 kilometres) of coloured fairy lights. As the weather had by now clouded over, with the suddenness of the Highveld climate, promising an electrical storm, the lights had been switched on for the arrival, creating a 'highway of fairy light and loveliness' all the way to the city centre. By night, and already seen since the big switch-on of 29 March, 30 000 lamps floodlit the main buildings, the handsome Supreme Court, for example, being suffused in a soft pink glow with an enormous crown surmounting it.

Much of the design work had been carried out by Norman Yule, who told the *Rand Daily Mail* on 25 March that he had survived on three hours' sleep a night for the previous month. The total cost of decorating the city was a whopping £250 000.[41] The City Hall alone was outlined in 12 000 white lamps with a 7 000-candlepower illumination on top of the dome.[42] All the lights remained on until Princess Elizabeth's birthday three weeks later, attracting crowds of motorists, nightly, from all over the Rand.

The City Hall itself – the ultimate royal destination – was still, by civic planning and design, the heart of the city. Its sandstone columns had been hung in green and gold bunting, cut and stitched by workers in the Social Welfare Department (whose members included a one-legged ex-serviceman) and proudly fixed in position by the city's Fire Department, deploying their longest ladders.

Despite the enthusiasm of the general public, brought to fever pitch by press reportage, these preparations had not gone ahead without criticism. At the council's monthly meeting on 25 March, Colin Legum, later the celebrated Pan-Africanist political journalist on David Astor's *Observer*, but then a Labour Party councillor, said the City Hall should be undraped as soon as possible. 'Anyone who had any aesthetic appreciation would be appalled by the appearance of the City Hall,' he said, though he admitted that the street decorations, especially around Clarendon Circle, were creditable. The City Hall's pillars, he went on, rather over-egging the pudding, 'gave the impression of a fat woman's legs attired in green, yellow and blue stockings'.[43]

This was apparently a signal for all other malcontents on the Council to get their oars in and have a good spat. Miss Hilda Watts (Communist Party) said she had objected *all along* to the expenditure on decorations for the royal visit. This indeed, was the tenor of her party, who had inveighed in their local mouthpiece, *The Guardian*, against the 'luxury spending and vulgar ostentation' that the tour had occasioned.[44] In addition, she added, warming shamelessly to Legum's theme, she objected to them on the grounds of taste. This apparently went down particularly badly: 'Well, but what about Red Square on May Day?' swiftly interjected a councillor, indignantly.

Actually, Miss Watts's real issue, it soon transpired, was not so much the decorations as 'the hysteria being worked up in the advance of the visit'. Making such political capital out of the royal visit was the final straw for many of the councillors, almost all of whom were loyally disposed monarchists. 'We are tired of the cheap communist propaganda [she brings] to these meetings,' roundly declared another of their number, adding menacingly for good measure, 'and the sooner the Communists are prepared to leave this country [presumably for the joys of Red Square] and leave us to ourselves, the better!'[45]

It cannot be said that any of this criticism served in any way to dampen the enthusiasm of the many. The ovation that greeted the Royal Family at Clarendon Circle had been picked up by radio and relayed across to the dense crowd of 100 000 that packed the square in front of the City Hall, where they whiled away the hours of waiting by singing patriotic songs from 20 000 song sheets, distributed by the police. They were accompanied by the UDF and SAAF bands, and led by a choir of 400 Philharmonic, ASFAS and opera members, under the baton of Joseph Connell, Johannesburg's Director of Music. Connell, the man who had persuaded Sir Thomas Beecham and Dr (later Sir) Malcolm Sargent to come out to raise the standard of symphonic music in Johannesburg (see page 278), was resplendent in formal dress with a red rosebud in his lapel. Girl Guides, members of the Red Cross and St John's Ambulance distributed water and gave first aid. The laconic commentary broadcast about the approaching procession and the cheering from Clarendon Circle onwards was received with roars of anticipatory excitement.

Ahead of the Royal Family still lay a three-mile (4.8-kilometre) drive and a half a million flag-waving spectators, many of whom had slept out overnight to be sure of securing a good position, and who had been given tea and coffee by flat-dwellers from the early hours when they had all been rudely awakened by the testing of the new loudspeaker system hastily ordered at the last minute by the Council (at a cost of £390.)[46] Others had made use of the specially laid-on 240 trams and 110 buses which had been running since an unheard-of 3.30 am from their farthest terminals.[47]

Determined that no bad behaviour or disorderliness still widely associated in the popular imagination with Johannesburg's crowds should mar the day, a tremendous security system had been put in place. The city's regiments, the ACF, all duly presenting arms as the procession came into view, had been deployed to line the route. There were six units of the Imperial Light Horse, as well as the 1st Battalion Transvaal Scottish, the Rand Light Infantry, the Witwatersrand Rifles, the South African Corps of Signals and the 1st Battalion Railways and Harbours Brigade. The Transvaal Horse Artillery, the 3rd Field Artillery and the South African Irish were deployed to cordon off the Cenotaph in front of the City Hall.

In addition, all through the night roped cordons and in some cases wooden barriers had been erected by municipal workers, 2 000 policemen, 162 traffic officers, 700 members of the Civic Guard and 1 000 Boy Scouts. All the city's special security men had been deployed, augmented by others brought up from Cape Town and Durban. Each body had to man several stations on the royal route during the day and thus be rapidly moved from one section to another. At Wits University, ex-servicemen alumni had mounted guard over the campus all night and assisted the police and other authorities during the morning.[48] Standing by were 700 members of the St John's Ambulance and the South African Red Cross, and the Noodhulpliga (roughly the Afrikaans equivalent of the St John's Ambulance) manned 148 first aid stations, 8 casualty clearing stations and 13 ambulance posts.[49]

Johannesburg had never witnessed or heard anything like it. The Royal Family's arrival seemed to have had a unifying effect on the city, thought the *Rand Daily Mail*: 'For once the teeming, cosmopolitan city was bound by a common purpose – to pay homage to the sovereign.' So it would have appeared that morning as the roars became deafening and the crowd seemed to be 'swallowed up by a gigantic wave of sound'.[50]

The procession turns into Eloff Street, showing the great cheering crowds ahead. In all, one million people turned out to cheer the Royal Family in Johannesburg.

Even Lascelles, inclined to dismiss the city unfavourably, was astounded: 'We left Pretoria at 9 am and [have] been yelled at by vast crowds, black and white, ever since. It has been a remarkable, popular success – I've never seen larger and noisier crowds since perhaps in Montreal in '39.'[51]

It has to be said, however, that the Afrikaans-language newspaper *Die Transvaler* took a different view. Under the editorship of Dr HF Verwoerd, the future prime minister and main architect of apartheid, it had refused to comment on the visit at all, merely advising readers to avoid the city centre on that morning as the arrival of foreign visitors would make the roads impassable. On that day, in the light of such a tumultuous welcome, such a comment must simply have seemed like sour grapes. Even Strijdom, another future prime minister and a board member of *Die Transvaler*, disagreed with Verwoerd here, arguing that the readership would go elsewhere for news of the visit. He suggested that small items should be published, together with an editorial saying what a waste of money the visit was.[52]

Down Hospital Hill the procession went, past the General Hospital, with its nurses and patients in dressing gowns, some in wheelchairs and some on stretchers, who had all turned out to cheer (they included staff and patients from the Transvaal Memorial Home, Tara, the Otto Beit Home, the Non-European Hospital and many others), on down Klein Street, King George Street, on into Eloff Street and into the great chasm of Commissioner Street with its enormous banners 'like the chapel of the Garter at Windsor' thought the reporters. The cheers seemed to roll, bouncing back and forth from the many high buildings.

High up in one of these with her nanny stood the ten-year-old Princess Elizabeth of Yugoslavia, whose parents were then living in exile in a house near the Inanda polo ground (see Chapter 8), and who still recalls the tremendous noise of the cheering and the excitement.[53]

In front of the City Hall stood the Cenotaph to the Johannesburg fallen of the First World War. In accordance with general South African policy that memorial donations should rather be spent on more practical causes, a simple inscription to those of the Second World War, with dates, had been added to its northwest and southeast corners, and lay waiting to be unveiled. Four thousand ex-servicemen and women had paraded through

Cheering the Royal Family, standing beneath the great ruby velvet canopy
in front of the City Hall.

'Wave after wave of cheering such as Johannesburg has never heard before,' said *The Star*.

the streets and were now seated with next of kin on a platform reserved for them west of the Cenotaph.

To a great fanfare sounded by the trumpeters of the Imperial Light Horse, the Royal Family alighted at the Harrison Street entrance to the City Hall at 10.35 and the Royal Standard broke from its mast. They were greeted by the Administrator of the Transvaal, General and Mrs Pienaar, and the mayor and mayoress of Johannesburg, Mr and Mrs James Gray, on whose shoulders the organisation of this day and the next had largely fallen. Mr Gray was popular enough;[54] his wife was another matter. Straight-talking and undistinguished-looking, Ethel Gray was not generally beloved. 'You did what you were told with her,' remembers one of the young ladies playing a minor but not insignificant role in the day's proceedings.[55] No one doubted, however, but that she was a very good organiser; *capable*, is what everyone allowed.[56]

There were bows and curtsies and then the anthems were played. The King went over to inspect the Guard of Honour of the Transvaal Scottish, proudly carrying the new colours he had presented to them at the ceremony at Voortrekkerhoogte (as Roberts Heights had been renamed in 1939) the day before. He then unveiled the new inscription to 'OUR GLORIOUS DEAD – ONS ROEMRYKE DODES 1939–1945'. Four members of the Guard of Honour stood at each corner, their arms reversed. At once a hush fell upon the crowd. The Last Post was sounded followed by the Reveille. The King and Queen bowed their heads to the Cenotaph and, as a warm, approving round of applause broke out, the band struck up the familiar opening chords and within seconds 100 000 voices sang out 'Land of Hope and Glory'; at its conclusion great waves of cheers once again surrounded the Royal Family.

The party now entered the City Hall, where presentations to local senators, MPs, MPCs and councillors were made in the Selborne Hall and a stupendous tea was provided. This was at 10.50. The beautifully inscribed Loyal Address was handed over. Outside, however, the waiting crowds grew impatient and had begun to chant 'We want the King! We want the King!' with an increasing intensity. Soon enough the Royal Family reappeared to stand beneath the pride of Johannesburg's decorations: a truly magnificent, outsized ruby velvet canopy bearing the royal coat of arms with a glittering crown surmounting the dome above.

As they smilingly acknowledged the crowd, 'wave after wave of cheering such as Johannesburg had never heard before rose from the assembled multitude'.[57] Four little girls in English poke bonnets and period frocks, whose design might have come straight off a tin of Quality Street toffees, and all of whom had lost fathers in the war, presented the customary bouquets: red roses for the Queen, and Cecile Brunner roses and white flowers for Princess Elizabeth and Princess Margaret. Inside each nestled gold brooches bearing the city's coat of arms; the Queen was seen sportingly to fix hers beneath the great diamond corsage shoulder ornament she was wearing. The King got a gold tiepin.

By 11.25 the Royal Family had taken their place on the scarlet-draped saluting base in Harrison Street, as 20 000 servicemen and women marched past, commanded by Colonel E F Thackery, CMG, DSO, C de G (with palm) and led by Pipe Major W Scott-Crichton of the Johannesburg Caledonian Society to the Scottish tune of 'Cock o' the North'. They had been urged to appear by the Johannesburg branch of the South African Legion (affiliated to the British Empire Service Legion), which had put out this appeal in the press: 'It is our earnest desire that every ex-Volunteer who can march will assist in paying this homage to our Sovereign on a scale worthy of our city ... TURNOUT!'[58]

The threatening rain had held off. Fifteen abreast they marched, swinging along down Harrison Street. Among them were blind soldiers who had to trust their comrades on either side to guide them. Some marched on crutches. The Cape Corps (Coloured) and Indians all took part in this too, and a wonderfully smart body of the Native Military Corps brought up the rear, smiling proudly and receiving a great ovation.[59]

As always on the South African tour there was an element of a victory parade here: *We Have Won the War!* Fighter ace Sailor Malan took part, as did Prince Alexander of Yugoslavia, with a detachment of the RAF, which he had joined while his family were exiled in Kenya.[60] His participation had been arranged, after some difficulty (see Chapter 8), by Wing Commander Ian Hay, a friend of his parents, Prince and Princess Paul.[61] The crowds cheered their local regiments with pride and delight, some even calling out to their fathers, husbands and sweethearts when they

The King and Queen inspect the prize cattle, after having opened the
Rand Easter Show at the Milner Park Showgrounds.
TRANSNET HERITAGE LIBRARY PHOTO COLLECTION

recognised them in the ranks. What can have been the emotions of the
widows and bereaved families among the seated ex-servicemen west of
the Cenotaph is not recorded.

After it was over, the Queen and Princesses walked across and pat-
ted the regimental mascots – Hussar, the Shetland pony of the Imperial
Light Horse, prancing restlessly in the storm of cheering, and the Alsatian
dog of the RAF who barked excitedly. Then the Queen, in a spontaneous
gesture, walked over and laid her bouquet of red roses at the base of the
Cenotaph. For a moment, the crowd was caught by surprise at this and
were nonplussed and silent. Then, taking in that she was honouring the
dead, they clapped and cheered with approval.

It had taken 22 minutes since tea, and the Royal Family now departed
in the Daimler, many of the crowd rushing to reline the onward route for
a second view. This route ran out of town and through the campus of Wits
University, reached at noon, where the Principal, members of the senate

body and staff, all gowned, and 5 000 students cheered them on their way to the Milner Park Showgrounds. Here they arrived just after noon to find the main arena packed to capacity with 40 000 people wanting to hear the King open the Rand Easter Show. This then was a highlight of the Rand's calendar. Royal agricultural shows were anyway regular fixtures in the royal year, and the King and Queen in their roles of a landowning squire and his lady were able to inspect the prize-winning cattle knowledgeably, while the Queen further endeared herself by inquiring about the standard of exhibitions in the Home Industries section.

There was no time to visit these. The organisers could not afford to let the pace slacken for a minute; indeed, the whole day's proceedings had been enacted out a week before as a full rehearsal, with all the players, even General and Mrs Pienaar, dutifully going through the motions of the day's plan, and Joseph Connell, the musical director, standing in for the King and Judy Welsh for the two Princesses.[62] The timetable was exacting:

> 12.45 Depart from Showgrounds via Empire Road
> 1.05 Arr Carlton Hotel
> 1.25 Leave Carlton Hotel
> 1.30 Arr Harrison St entrance to City Hall for the Civic Lunch
> 2.30 Leave City Hall for Orlando (via Fordsburg)

The menu for the Civic Lunch was a seven-course affair, but fairly light by the standards of catering of the day, and mostly cold. In view of the day's hectic programme and the Royal Family's by then much-publicised fastidiousness about too much food, it had been submitted beforehand to the Queen and approved. Lady Delia, the Queen's Lady-in-Waiting, was tickled by the Afrikaans translation of lobster (really Cape crayfish) – *kreef* or 'krief' as she recalled it spelt in old age. There was no translatable equivalent for Charlotte Russe.[63]

The menu was as follows:

Fruit Juice cocktail

Fried Fillet of sole and sauce tartare

Lobster Mayonnaise

Iced Asparagus and capered mayonnaise

Cold meats, Poultry and salads

Charlotte Russe

Iced Neapolitan Preserve and Coffee[64]

It must have been served in record time, as the Royal Family were now running late. As always, this does not seem to have concerned Queen Elizabeth. Coming out of the City Hall, her elder daughter drew her attention to a group of blind people, some with a relative in attendance, for all of whom Joseph Connell had thoughtfully arranged seats in a prominent position.

Her Majesty, it was later reported, walked straight over to the group and a general silence fell upon the whole crowd who watched with fascination. 'This is the Queen,' she said softly to them, and immediately eager hands stretched out to reach her. Without hesitation she grasped the hands of an elderly woman. 'God bless you, Your Majesty,' said the old lady. Every eye witnessing this was apparently misty now. 'Thank you, thank you all,' replied the Queen. The King joined her and asked: 'Who is in charge here?' Mrs Nolan, President of the South African Society for the Civilian Blind, stepped forward and curtsied. ('I never thought this would happen to me,' she said later, 'this has been the proudest day of my life.')

Relatives were seen explaining what was happening to the blind who were standing further back, and when they heard they beat their white sticks and clapped with delight. Although the royal party was far behind schedule, typically the Queen seemed to be in no hurry as she chatted quietly to the group. Finally she said: 'I really must go now. Goodbye and thank you all for coming to welcome us.'

As they left for Orlando, the cheers from the crowd broke out anew and the blind group, beaming, joined in and waved their Union Jacks.[65]

Orlando, reached via Fordsburg, was the largest black township south of Johannesburg and at that time reckoned to be the seventh-largest town in the Union. Here there could be no question of the 'invented traditionalism' and the regressiveness claimed by critics of the so-called Black Shows – the indabas and the Eshowe Dance, for example. Indeed, far from answering calls to boycott the visit, urban African communities had demanded their fair share of the Royal Family, and by threatening non-cooperation, the advisory boards of Orlando, like those of Alexandra, had compelled the white-controlled Civic Welcome Committee to revise their timetable.[66]

Thus the planned, brief drive through Orlando had been changed into a proper visit. The King, it had been announced in advance, 'had agreed to stop'.[67] The courtiers, by now already exhausted by 'being yelled at all day',[68] saw at once that the change had been worth it.

'The road was lined,' reads the Tour Diary, 'almost entirely with Natives in hundreds of thousands, almost frenzied in their excitement and loyalty.'[69]

At 3.20, the royal party, with General Smuts in attendance,[70] drew up and ascended a decorated platform in front of the Community Centre to find before them another 'wildly cheering' crowd, estimated at between 100 000 and 130 000 (the combined attendance in Alexandra and Orlando was 200 000, the biggest non-white turnout in South Africa), many of them domestic or factory workers released for the day, their numbers swollen by others from neighbouring areas brought in by buses and by 5 000 schoolchildren brought from Vereeniging, Evaton and Krugersdorp.[71] Many among them were simply squatters. Again, the numbers made up for the poverty of the decorations. Nor had black officialdom boycotted this event. Thirty members of Johannesburg's various advisory boards and two Witwatersrand members of the Native Representative Council were present,[72] and while the King inspected black ex-servicemen who had not taken part in the march-past that morning, a choir of 6 000 children, led by the Witwatersrand Native Labour Association Band, sang to them.

The stop had been brief and, like many during the tour, far too fast for many of those present. The Orlando Boy Scouts (Pathfinders), whose band had practised the Royal Salute for days to honour the King, their

Part of the crowd of 130 000 people who greeted the Royal Family during
the brief stop in Orlando.

MARY EVANS PICTURE LIBRARY/JEAN HOILE COLLECTION

international patron, were bitterly disappointed to be unable to play it for
him. Other royal viewings had been obstructed or very fleeting. Indeed,
among the one or two of the less effusive postmortems, it was felt that
the organisers had considered the next event on the itinerary – the race
meeting – to be more important than the populace of the largest native
township in South Africa.[73]

Nevertheless, the fact that the visit had transcended all colour discrimination[74] and that the Royal Family had visited 'their place of residence'
was a source of great personal pride to the people of Orlando. As the
Daimler left, the Queen, realising the difficulties imposed by the numbers
and the timetable, motioned to the King, and the royal couple stood up in
the back of the car in an effort to give the cheering crowds a better view
of them.

Like a hailstorm, as one of the black newspapers put it, he had suddenly
come and gone.[75]

Desperately trying to make up for lost time, the royal progress now headed on towards Turffontein, then as now the big racecourse southwest of Johannesburg. No greater contrast could have existed between the two juxtaposed stops, separated by only a few miles – dusty, impoverished, teeming Orlando with its shacks, squalor, shebeens and vibrant nightlife, and Turffontein, with its mown lawns and flower beds, its paddocks and bookmakers, its members' enclosure and tea tents. Racing was then still habitually referred to as 'the sport of kings'. The King had not inherited the family passion for it, but had dutifully carried on its traditions and maintained the royal stud; indeed, as an owner, he was mildly successful. Both the King and Queen, however, encouraged their eldest daughter's very evident keen interest in the turf; attending fashionable race meetings was, anyway, seen as part of the royal social round.

Turffontein, therefore, offered an outing of real interest to the whole family, and since race meetings were then social, dressy affairs, a royal meeting was as close as Johannesburg got to a garden party. Thousands turned up; long before noon the enclosures and stands were packed.[76] The afternoon presented a scene gay with fashion and bright colours, said *The Star*,[77] and the columnists of the 'ladies' pages' commented endlessly on the styles of the hats and outfits, the Rand women, it being noted, having seized the opportunity to dress 'gaily and smartly'.

The Royal Family were given a 'tremendous reception', as they arrived at 4 pm; a little later they walked through applauding spectators to enter the paddock where the horses were being paraded. The King's Cup was presented to Mr A Ellis, the owner of Cape Heath, and the jockey Basil Lewis was duly congratulated ('I could never imagine that royalty could be like the King and Queen were,' the delighted jockey told the press afterwards).[78] The following morning Mr Ellis called on Mr Gray and presented his winnings of £1 000 to the mayor's Britain's Flood Relief Fund, later subsumed in the general countrywide Flood Relief Fund as a birthday present for Princess Elizabeth (see pp 293–294).

The party left the royal box for tea with the chairman of the Johannesburg Turf Club and the stewards, and then watched the Queen's Cup. By now the strain of the day was beginning to show and 'Amelia', the Ladies' Page columnist of *The Star*, thought the King and Queen 'looked frankly worn out'.[79]

Yet the day was nothing like nearly over. At least they didn't have to change at a hotel or face the hour's drive back to Pretoria at its end. Having rejected the Administrator's proposal for them to stay at the Carlton Hotel[80] (which had unwisely garnered some pre-publicity with pictures of the specially redecorated royal suites), and having viewed the day's programme with some alarm, Lascelles had wisely had the White Train brought to a siding adjoining one of the Crown Mine's mine dumps.[81] There they drove to bath and dress for the evening's events. Of course, their valet and dressers would all have been standing by and at the ready, clothes pressed, jewels and orders laid out and baths drawn. Even the ladies-in-waiting had their personal maids – Miss Bamford and Miss Geach – to assist them. Nevertheless, they cannot have had much more than an hour to collect themselves before they were off again.

At 7.30 the cars left the train for the (old) Carlton Hotel, the city's most prestigious and elegant commercial venue. There the King and Queen were to attend the Administrator's Banquet while the Princesses were entertained to a private dinner for 24 young people on the floor above, before going on to their ball at the City Hall. The crowds had not dispersed. Johannesburg, always energised at an altitude of nearly 6 000 feet (1 800 metres), bathed in the unaccustomed fairy lights and flood-lighting and by now thoroughly keyed up by the day's events, was looking forward to witnessing the royal glamour the evening promised. Its streets remained packed with people in gala mood.

At the hotel, the Princesses were persuaded to make a balcony appear-ance on their own, shyly waving to the cheering throng below, who were enchanted by their appearance – Princess Elizabeth in an orchid-pink faille crinoline with a white fox cape, Princess Margaret with an ermine cape over a gown of frothy white tulle with posies of sequins. Indeed, it was said that the King's younger daughter, who had seemed to mature and grow more lovely as the tour progressed, and now sported a becoming tan for the first time in her life,[82] appeared to walk in a sea of twinkling foam. Both wore their pearl necklaces to which it was understood the King and Queen had added each birthday.

Mr Welsh's daughter, Judy, of an age with the Princesses, was the host-ess at their dinner. After the balcony appearance, the Princesses retired to

The old Carlton Hotel's Art Deco ballroom is set for the Administrator's Banquet. Queen Elizabeth is wearing Marie Antoinette's five-strand diamond necklace.

their appointed cloakroom and Judy thought to use the break to quickly powder her nose. These were the days of loose powder compacts, and to her horror she found that, in her hurry, she had spilt powder down the front of her hand-painted, magenta taffeta ball gown. To her amazement Princess Elizabeth reappeared and, taking in the situation, used her gloves to expertly flick the mess away.[83]

Down below, the King and Queen with General Smuts and the Administrator and Mrs Pienaar ('Uhuhuh rough, you know, *and rough looking too*,' as someone there still recalls)[84] passed through the famous palm court of the Carlton Hotel, cleared of furniture for drinks beforehand, three of its corners banked with chrysanthemums and the fourth accommodating the Marine Band from HMS *Vanguard* who had arrived well before 1 April and had been playing to the citizens of Johannesburg and the Reef towns. During cocktails they played a selection of Strauss waltzes; now they played Fletcher's 'Spirit of Pageantry' march for the

The Princesses arrive and pass beneath the gladioli-bearing guard of honour made by the young ladies of Johannesburg at the Youth Ball at the City Hall.

TRANSNET HERITAGE LIBRARY PHOTO COLLECTION

royal arrival. Other music included songs from the Hebrides in honour of the Queen, a potpourri of Afrikaans melodies and, perhaps most evocatively for that era, Eric Coates's 'By the Sleepy Lagoon'.[85] Inside the ballroom, all was set for the Administrator's Banquet. The guests were in full evening dress presenting, according to the papers, 'an animated canvas of splendour and vitality'. They included the Transvaal Division of the Supreme Court and their wives, and many of Johannesburg's leading citizens.

Johannesburg, a very prosperous city, has never been known for dressing down. A royal banquet, therefore, was naturally destined to produce an array of splendid evening gowns; much jewellery was worn and even a few tiaras, here and there. 'Amelia', back on duty and busy with her notebook and pencil, was so carried away by the sight of it all that she thought that the sumptuousness of the beautifully dressed guests 'took one back to pre-war days of plenty'.[86]

Nothing, however, could compete with the Queen's appearance. Fully re-energised since Turffontein ('all the fatigue seemed to have vanished by the time they arrived at the banquet', noted the beady-eyed 'Amelia')[87] and in her cyclamen ball gown ('petunia satin' said *The Rand Daily Mail*), she wore the Cartier honeycomb tiara, and the magnificent five-strand diamond necklace that by repute once belonged to Marie Antoinette. Both had been inherited in 1942 from Mrs Greville, the acerbic pre-war society hostess who left her fabulous collection of jewels 'with my loving thoughts' to Queen Elizabeth. It is possible that the King had vetoed her wearing these in the age of war and austerity; others at the time suggested, inaccurately, death-duty considerations. At any rate, they were brought to South Africa and worn for the first time on the tour, possibly by way of sending up a kite on these thorny issues.

This was the first time she had worn the necklace in public and only the second time she had worn the tiara. The combination of the two was dazzling. Arc lights switched on for the benefit of Pathé News and the Killarney Studios cameras flashed back the fire of the necklace as she stood beneath the mock-ermine corona and gold lamé curtains with which the hotel management had draped the wall behind her. As she inclined her head to acknowledge the spontaneous, gloved applause and cheers that her appearance had brought forth, they caught too the diamonds in her tiara and jewelled Order of the Garter. 'Never,' said the commentator of the official film made of the tour, 'has the Queen looked more radiantly lovely.'[88]

The Princesses had meanwhile finished dinner and proceeded to the City Hall. Ever since the civic luncheon that afternoon, the building had been a hive of activity. Tables and chairs had been removed, the floor swept and sprinkled with French chalk for dancing, and the Selborne Hall and Upper Gallery had been rearranged for the supper buffet. SAWAS members were on duty in the cloakrooms. Those reserved for the Royal Family had new curtains of grey-blue damask.

The stage had remained unchanged since lunchtime with its massed municipal displays of trees (flanking the organ), palms, pampas grass and garlands of greenery. The yellow chrysanthemums and asters, the bright gold marigolds outlining the royal cipher and the banks of tulips and gladioli, created under the direction of Mr JC van Balen, director of the city's Parks and Improvements Department, all composed the fairyland of burning colours referred to by the press.[89]

The gladioli, chosen 'not only for their statuesque beauty but because they last well and lend themselves to arrangements on a grand scale',[90] were now to be elevated to a crucial part of the arrival proceedings. Widely grown by florists, they were originally hybridised from wild South African flowers at the end of the nineteenth century. Needless to say, the blooms which so delighted the florists and matrons of London, New York, Melbourne and Johannesburg bore little relation to their fragile cousins in the veld. It was as if they were on steroids.

Their procurement had not been achieved without some difficulty. Like the tulips banked to some depth below the royal dais, the gladiolus bulbs had been ordered in good time from the Netherlands. Unfortunately, there had been a fire on the ship transporting them, and in the end they only reached Johannesburg, by rail from Cape Town, on 9 January. Ground had been prepared in advance for their immediate planting in four different places, exhibiting varying microclimatic conditions. No one was taking any chances here. A Dutch gladiolus expert was actually flown out to inspect their growth and potential. He was most discouraging. 'You can forget about the gladioluses [sic],' he said, bluntly, 'they won't be ready on time. Better make other arrangements.'

This was a bitter blow for all concerned, and all the resources of the department were now brought into play. Every gladiolus being grown commercially for miles around Johannesburg was swiftly secured and purchased in advance, just in case the Dutch expert was proved to be correct.

Only Van Balen remained reasonably sanguine. 'I don't think he was right,' he told the press, whose readership (then almost all gardeners at some level) were following these developments anxiously. 'As you can imagine, I have watched these plants like children. We have had some wonderfully warm nights lately and these have helped us. Already I can feel the spikes inside the foliage and I am pretty certain [that] at the last possible moment picking the flowers will be perfect.'

Johannesburg held its breath.[91]

Van Balen was proved right, and 6 000 gladioli and 3 000 tulips were in full bloom and on display on the big night at the Princesses' Ball. (The tulips had been planted in the back of lorries, driven backwards and forwards between sunlight and shade to encourage their blooming on the right day.) The ball was to be the highlight, the feeling of fantasy that had assailed Johannesburg all day culminating with it in the evening. The Princesses were met at the City Hall by the mayoress and John Connell, and Mrs Mason Gordon and Mrs PM Anderson (the 'matrons', as social custom then still required, responsible for the proceedings and the unmarried young ladies attending the dance).

Entering the hall, they now found the young girls and their partners formed in a concentrically reducing guard of honour. As the Princesses processed along the lanes so created, each girl held aloft a coral gladiolus in the manner of regimental crossed swords. They curtsied, lowering the coral bloom as they did, and the men bowed as the Princesses passed, finally arriving at the heart-shaped centre of the pageant, meant to symbolise Johannesburg's position as the industrial heart of the Union. This now unfolded and from its centre emerged two little girls, both of whom had lost their fathers in the war, this time dressed in Voortrekker costume, who presented flowers – a spray of pink nerines for Princess Elizabeth and a spray of white lilac for Princess Margaret.

Horribly stagey though this all sounds to us today (it was apparently the mayoress's ingenious concept, carried out with Connell's assistance, as she later proudly put it out to the press),[92] the whole complicated choreographed set piece was apparently performed without a hitch and widely praised as 'charming' at the time. There had, however, been great difficulty training the Afrikaans girls to curtsy, something all English girls had been taught to do at school.[93]

All the coral gladioli were now immediately handed in by the young ladies, collected by nurses from the Voluntary Aid Detachments and given to Miss MC Borcherds and Miss C Hose, the formidable matrons-in-chief of the Johannesburg and Baragwanath Hospitals, respectively, who stood by in their starched uniforms with two nurses each in attendance to take them back to decorate the wards. The SAAF Band then struck up and the Princesses were partnered by two ex-servicemen. Everyone took to the floor. For the hungry, a magnificent supper buffet of whole suckling pig and salmon had been laid out in the adjacent Selborne Hall.

Fantastic rumours had been circulating about the expense some Johannesburg ladies had gone to for their dresses, and prices of up to 500 guineas mentioned. (A fox fur cape would then have cost 21 guineas at a Johannesburg furrier; 500 guineas would have purchased a very elaborate ball gown from one of the great Parisian couture houses.) More likely the figure, including shoes, long gloves and hair ornaments (and the required perm) would have been between 20 and 50 guineas, possibly up to 100 guineas, at the outside,[94] more modest outlays being achieved by buying good materials and using couturiers' patterns on sale in all department stores, and the services of talented dressmakers, who, at that date, existed at most levels of society.

Meanwhile, back at the Carlton Hotel, the King and Queen were still eating their way through another seven-course banquet. This was as follows:

Fruit Cocktail

Clear chicken soup or Cream of tomato soup

Fillet of sole with button mushrooms and white wine sauce

Roast saddle of lamb with breadcrumbs and parsley

Fresh garden peas with mint; Cream of spinach; Potatoes French style;

Sherbet

Transvaal capon with cream sauce and goose liver

Lettuce and pineapple salad

Pawpaw ice cream

Dainties in sugar baskets   Coffee[95]

By the time they got to the pawpaw ice cream the courtiers were becoming restless. Everything was again running late and the King and Queen were due to be reunited briefly with their daughters on top of Escom House, one of the tallest skyscrapers in the city.

This was to witness the biggest fireworks display of the tour and indeed the greatest display of fireworks ever seen in South Africa. It had been organised by the Chamber of Mines and was imaginatively conceived by a subcommittee set up by all the gold producers, with much help from the pyrotechnics expert HT Brock, who had come out to the Union to give advice for displays during the visit. The plans, together with a map, had been presented to the King at Buckingham Palace in advance, so that he fully comprehended the vast scale of the display.

Huge bonfires 50 feet (15 metres) high had been built on 61 of the mine dumps of the Witwatersrand which then crowded the skyline south of the city, from the Nigel Mine in the far East Rand through Blyvooruitzicht to Western Deep, Klerksdorp and St Helena 100 miles (160 kilometres) away across the Vaal River in the Orange Free State and just visible, when burning, as pinpricks, to the elegant diners who packed the Old 400 and His Majesty's roof garden[96] to witness the spectacle.

On the Witwatersrand proper, 48 mines took part. Each mine had a special bonfire team and another for the fireworks. The fireworks team each had a captain (who lit the fireworks with a cheesa stick), a supply controller, a shell aimer and a rocket carrier. Aerial maroons, flares, quarter-pound and one-pound rockets, mortar shells and roman candles were all employed. In the spirit of the bonfire chain lit to warn of the approach of the Spanish Armada up the English Channel, the bonfires and their accompanying displays began at the outer mines and slowly spread from the east and west towards the central focal point – Johannesburg – meeting, as it was put, in a 100-mile (160-kilometre) horseshoe of flame.

The whole thing was designed to last 25 minutes.[97] 'The keynote of the operation will be zero hour when the Royal Family appear on top of Escom House,' said The Star, 'and watches will be synchronised and fires lighted at extreme wings first, gradually getting nearer.'

What happened next is slightly shrouded in mystery. No one noted the exact time the King and Queen left the banquet; it was said to be later than planned, and yet at 9.20 pm, a crowd of firework viewers at Van Wyk's Rust, eight miles (13 kilometres) south of the city as the crow flies, heard, carried on a gentle north breeze, a faint burst of cheering,[98] and this must almost certainly have been one of the royal cars proceeding to Escom House. No one knows how much of the display they saw – it had certainly started well before they reached the top of the building.

According to Ted Groves and Captain Ritchie, the official tour diarist, it was over by the time the King and Queen – escorted by large numbers of people – reached the tenth floor.[99] Yet the Johannesburg and Reef public saw it all right, and it caused the biggest traffic jam in Johannesburg's history, with cars parked or simply abandoned solidly across streets leading to the best vantage points, for three miles (4.8 kilometres).[100] The climax was a general launching of a massive 1 000 rockets from the central area.

There seemed little point in going back to the Carlton Hotel for coffee and the dainties in sugar baskets, and the King and Queen resolved to accompany their daughters back to the City Hall. Everyone seems to have gained a second wind by now. Maybe it was due to the unaccustomed, energising high altitude, maybe it was the excellent wine (Meursault 1937, Nuits-Saint-Georges 1942) and vintage champagne (Pommery 1937) that had been served,[101] perhaps it was just the wonderful welcome that seemed to constantly roll back at them, whenever they appeared, from all Johannesburg's citizens.

Opera-goers in evening dress attending a gala concert in the vast auditorium of His Majesty's Theatre, for example, had earlier resisted being coaxed inside to take their seats until it was announced that the royal banquet had been prolonged and that the King and Queen would not leave the Carlton Hotel for some time. During the interval their obedience was duly rewarded when they poured outside to see the King, Queen and Princesses driving down Commissioner Street, late, on their return to the City Hall, and they cheered along with the vast throng of people who already packed the pavements.

Back inside the City Hall, the youthful guests foxtrotting around the floor were delighted by the unscheduled appearance of the whole Royal Family in the box high up to the right of the stage; while their daughters once more went below to dance, the King and Queen watched for a while before making their way back to the White Train. The dance music was broadcast outside the hall and, in the warm night air, couples danced happily in the streets.

Every ball organiser on the tour claimed afterwards that the Princesses stayed longer than expected. Sometimes this was true; more often it was simply a case of the courtier's spin. It is clear, however, that they were enjoying this one, just as they had the private dinner for the young before it. Princess Elizabeth wrote to her grandmother, Queen Mary:

> We have met remarkably few young people since being out here, I suppose because we never stayed long enough in one place. We did go to a ball in Johannesburg, which was fun, and it gave us an opportunity to meet people of our own age, and to exchange views and ideas on life in general.[102]

According to the programme, they were due to leave the Ball at 11 pm, which, after a long day, was fair enough. As it was, they eventually left at 12.15. Johannesburg's day had been a triumph.

* * *

The day after it was all over the mayor had it put out in the *Rand Daily Mail* that he was 'delighted at the manner in which Johannesburg rose to the royal occasion', adding that 'it was both a revelation and an inspiration to me as chief citizen of this great city'.[103] *The Star*, under the heading 'Rand's Lesson in Good Manners', went one further. No incident worth mentioning had occurred to mar the happy spirit of the occasion.[104] Crowd control had been admirable, no wolf whistles had followed the attractive Princesses, no cries of '*Vrystaat!*' had lowered the tone; even pickpockets tempted by such enormous throngs, and burglars by almost uninhabited suburbs, had held off.

The King, too, had remarked to the mayoress on the crowd's 'enthusiastic but orderly acclaim'.[105] Despite the area having a dubious reputation for rumbustiousness and disorderliness – a 'university of crime' as someone once called it – the critics had been silenced; it had all gone without a hitch or unpleasantness, and much credit, it was said all round, was due to the police, the Civic Guard and the other bodies involved.

The mayor and mayoress, basking in the happy afterglow of the royal visit, fed royal titbits to the press. 'Amelia', the indefatigable columnist from *The Star*, seems to have been the useful conduit here. Watching the dancing from the royal box, the King had apparently said how impressed he was by the demeanour and deportment at the ball. And the Queen had said, 'I am so pleased to see my daughters so happy among the young people,' while her Lady-in-Waiting apparently asked how the Queen could get a letter to Mr Van Balen to congratulate him on the floral decor.[106]

Typically, Mrs Gray contrived to deliver the parting shot. Apparently, over coffee at the second civic luncheon, the King, seated next to her, had lit up a cigarette and relaxed. 'After that,' as Mrs Gray imparted to 'Amelia', 'we had a very personal conversation and had I been a life-long associate of His Majesty, I could not have been placed more at ease.' (Here 'Amelia' felt obliged to point out to her readers that these details had been 'extracted' by her from the mayoress, without the slightest wish for publicity on Mrs Gray's part, but because she realised her privileged position had given her a unique opportunity.) 'It is only fair,' concluded the mayoress, in words that must surely have nettled her detractors, along with many a less privileged lady of the Rand, 'that the people of Johannesburg should know second hand what I had the great good fortune to experience.'[107]

Despite these pleasantries, the King remained suspicious about the origins of the unfortunate snub administered to Johannesburg and the Reef towns in the tour's planning. Who was responsible, he now asked the mayor privately, 'for allocating only one day of the itinerary to the city?'

'If you ever find out, sir,' returned Mr Gray robustly, 'I wish you'd let me know.'[108]

Johannesburg did get its extra day after all. On Easter Saturday, the Royal Family drove over from Pretoria and reviewed 26 000 schoolchildren from the northern suburbs at the Zoo Lake and another 11 000 from the poorer, more Afrikaans southern suburbs at Pioneer Park. They went down Crown Mines (something the Princesses had wanted to do since the tour was first mooted)[109] and visited Baragwanath Hospital, which they found full of military patients recovering from tuberculosis contracted in Burma and India[110], and other convalescent imperial troops waiting to be repatriated.[111]

꘍꘎꘏

CHAPTER 8

Tea with Ouma

Irene, Easter Sunday 1947

A few miles south of Pretoria lay the village of Irene, from where, at the time of writing, a dirt road twisted southeast across the veld, crossed the Hennops River and some lucerne pastures watered by it, and so on up to the farm Doornkloof. This was where the Smutses lived while Parliament adjourned for six months and moved to the administrative capital.

The farmhouse itself was an architecturally undistinguished prefabricated wood-and-iron affair, with a narrow verandah all round, of the sort exported all around the Empire at the end of the nineteenth century. Its exterior presented a rough, colonial charm of the late-*Picturesque* school. Originally a British officers' mess, the Smutses bought it cheaply for £500 after the Anglo-Boer War, transported it to the farm and had it erected on stone foundations. It had many rooms; being prefab these could expand and contract like a Meccano set, as their son later put it. Indeed, by South African farmhouse standards it wasn't small, containing several living rooms, some barely used, and eventually 14 bedrooms, though many were quite pokey. There were two bathrooms, two indoor lavatories and an improvised outdoor shower, with no screening, connected to a garden tap next to the garage. Smuts, who suffered from no inhibitions, would often use this.

The newly erected farmhouse at Doornkloof, formerly a British officers' mess.
By the time of the royal visit it was surrounded by trees.

It was comfortless and devoid of pretty things, though the hall later contained two oils of the Pyramids by Churchill and a dinner gong made of two enormous elephant tusks on an ebony base, with two brass shell cases. This had been presented to Smuts by his imperial staff in 1916 after the success of the East African campaign; the shell cases were off the German light cruiser, *Königsberg*, which had been trapped and sunk in the Rufiji River delta in 1915. No flowers were permitted to brighten the house's dingy rooms; even Christmas trees and birthdays were non-events in the Smuts family, being dismissed as of no consequence.

The house's construction made it hot in summer and freezing cold in winter; bees swarmed in the space between the corrugated-iron outer skin and the matchboarding of the inner. It contracted and expanded with alarming reports in the extremes of the Middleveld climate. The roof leaked perpetually during heavy thunderstorms, and Mrs Smuts would rush around placing a variety of containers strategically to catch the drips. The floors were uniformly covered in brown linoleum, which the gardener, Jeremiah, would scrub once a week.

There was only water for a hot bath on Sundays when the boiler was lit. Otherwise it was cold baths or cold showers. Lord Harlech claimed there was not one comfortable chair or sofa to sit on. Smuts himself slept on the verandah off his bedroom, on an iron bed with a hard coir mattress; an old kitchen chair, pulled up, served as his bedside table. In the interests of security this arrangement was curtailed during the war. (So lax, indeed, was the wartime security at Doornkloof that Robey Leibbrandt, the Nazi-trained South African traitor, actually had Smuts in his sights on the dummy run of the assassination attempt.)

The only room of any merit was the well-stocked library at its heart (the old billiards room of the officers' mess), its walls lined with flags and Zulu shields, assegais and guns. This was largely out of bounds to all but the Oubaas himself, and occasional guests. Off it was an enclosed *stoep* which housed his botanical specimens, neatly stored in their presses. Botany was one of Smuts's enthusiasms. Dr Pole Evans, a leading South African botanist of the day, was a near neighbour in Irene, and he and Smuts enjoyed a close friendship.

Smuts and his wife spoke Afrikaans to one another, but it was a completely bilingual family. Indeed, when filling out official forms, the Smuts children were unable to decide which language to give as their first. The house was cleaned by a pint-sized housemaid, Annie Mofakeng, though everyone had to make their own beds. In the kitchen, James, the cook, produced quantities of very plain food; Mrs Smuts sometimes saw to the baking herself.[1] Unusually for Afrikaans-speaking country households at the time, the servants were referred to as 'Natives' or *Naturelle*, and the children were brought up to be polite to them. After Mrs Smuts died, James went to work for Sylma, one of the daughters; Annie was given a pension and a small legacy in Mrs Smuts's will.

Outside, there was no garden to soften the setting in that unpromising, dolomite-studded terrain, which encouraged frequent lightning strikes in the summer thunderstorms. Smuts was an early enthusiast of indigenous gardening, discouraging his wife's efforts with seed packets of annuals (though they did plant many trees on the property). It appeared as if the sparse veld came right up to the front steps.

Many distinguished visitors from South Africa and abroad who made what almost amounted to a pilgrimage to Doornkloof were privately appalled that a man of Smuts's stature should live in such surroundings. Its very nickname, *Die Blikhuis*[2] (the tin shanty), indicated its unsuitability, the more so as such buildings had rapidly gone out of fashion in the decades that followed Union, and were regarded as inherently jerry-built and dilapidated. Lady Moore, the Brits-born wife of the Governor of Ceylon, and one of Smuts's close female friends during the last decade of his life, referred to it as a 'tin hovel'.

The Smutses, however, loved it; even Daphne Moore saw that.[3] It was always filled with their children and later their grandchildren, all of whom remembered it with affection. The basic, frugal, happy-go-lucky and austerely functional aspect of their dwelling appealed to the couple far more than the beauties and comforts of Libertas, the official house for prime ministers built in the Bryntirion Estate. When in Cape Town for the parliamentary session, living at Groote Schuur, the mansion left to the nation by Cecil Rhodes, was a trial for Mrs Smuts, who found its grandeur overwhelming; she said she felt as if she was inhabiting a museum.[4] Doornkloof, more reflective of their personalities, was, as their son Jannie aptly described it, 'a refuge for stoics'.

Mrs Smuts — Isie to her family — was a fairly remarkable personality herself. Indeed, she was as unexpected for the distinguished visitors as the wife of the famous statesman as the house was as his habitat. Stellenbosch born and raised (a Krige), she was something of a bluestocking. The couple had met at the university there. Later on, her unaffected love of detective stories and romance serials from the *Women's Home Journal* disguised an intellectual ability that must have appealed to Smuts in their cerebral courting days. Hancock records how once, at breakfast, Smuts had quoted a verse from the New Testament, whereupon Ouma recited the whole chapter back to him in the original Greek.[5]

Blonde, blue-eyed and pretty like all the Krige women in her youth, she was a stranger to vanity from her early middle years and cut a slightly comic figure in pre-war parliamentary and diplomatic circles. A teetotaller, she wore homemade dresses that owed nothing to fashion, cut her own unruly mop of curls and seldom wore a hat. Her shoes were either of the flat, black 'Little Girl' variety worn with black stockings, or takkies; at home, she often padded around the house barefoot. She wore no make-up.

Frugality was raised almost to an art form; nothing was thrown away.[6] She shopped for bargains at Hack's Stores, the general dealer in Irene, and at Pearce's and Henshilwoods, the somewhat joyless suburban department stores in Claremont's Main Road, as well as at Mr Davenport's Second Hand shop, next to the Herschel service station. Even her own children were sometimes mortified by the remarks her homespun appearance caused in public.[7] Loyal friends and associates adopted the 'dear old Mrs Smuts' (Lady Duncan, Jean Lawrence and others), 'the essence of cosy, solid Dutchness' (Lady Delia Peel)[8] or 'the dear old lady' (Princess Paul) line. Others were exasperated by her inability to rise, as they saw it, to the role of consort to an internationally great man. 'A *peasant woman*' is what they said in private,[9] evincing no surprise that Smuts, away from home, sought and found alternative feminine company among beautiful or grandee women. It is a telling aside to human frailty that when Isie Smuts discovered these friendships and the often-intimate correspondence they had involved down the years, she burnt the love letters he had written to her in their youth.

Nevertheless, Mrs Smuts did step up to the mark at one particular juncture of her husband's political career. That was during the war. As wife of the prime minister, excoriated by many of his fellow Afrikaners for taking the country into Britain's war, she pinned her colours to the mast and organised a massive campaign to provide gifts and comforts for the South African forces. This led to heroic fundraising drives,[10] national lecture tours and even took her north to Cairo. The troops – 'her boys' – adored her and she became a maternal, generic grandmotherly figure to them all. They called her Ouma (grandmother or even granny) and the name stuck; even Queen Mary wrote to her using that sobriquet.[11] South Africa's Africa Service Medal was actually nicknamed 'Ouma's Garter' or 'Ouma's Fruit Salad' by the wartime volunteers.[12]

Many fell for her original personality along with her charming face, which radiated sweetness – like a bunch of bright cherries on an old black hat, it was said. British war artist Simon Elwes, who came to South Africa to paint an official portrait of Smuts, could not resist doing one of her too; in the end, she reluctantly sat for him in Cairo. It remains one of his finest. Noël Coward, who toured South Africa triumphantly, giving concerts to raise money for her Gifts and Comforts Fund,[13] was enchanted by her; so too were Sybil Thorndike, George Formby and many others. Princess Paul of Yugoslavia said it was a tonic to be in the company of one so naturally outspoken; conventional social filters were absent from Ouma's speech.

In early 1943, just as the war news started to get better, Mrs Smuts had a minor stroke or heart attack which curtailed almost all of her public appearances. In some ways, this must have suited her, for conventional social occasions, where she did not necessarily shine, had always been something of an ordeal. Perhaps she preferred not to compete; she did not, for instance, even attend her adopted daughter's wedding reception. It was therefore announced that she would take no part in official events during the royal visit. The stroke story may even have helped here; Jean Lawrence, usually a reliable witness in her diaries, speculates, in a book written in her old age, that it was a residual anti-British feeling dating from the Anglo-Boer War, when she had been placed under house arrest on Milner's orders, that caused her to stay away.[14]

This is not the claim of her family. Her wartime speeches stated unequivocally, 'We are proud to stand by Great Britain,' and referred glowingly to the 'good King and Queen of England', seeing them as 'the force that bound the Commonwealth together'.[15] And certainly a letter survives that suggests she was fully aware of the political importance of the royal tour – so carefully denied at the time by all the major protagonists – to her husband and his party. Writing to Margaret Gillett, one of her husband's chief correspondents, she said:

> I think here the visit is going to do us a lot of good, esp. after UNO [India's motion of censure] and our loss of the seat at Hottentot's Holland [the safe seat narrowly lost in the by-election by Sir De Villiers Graaff]. And they must be very tired after all this fuss, even though it is all a great success and they have won all hearts wherever they go, esp. the Queen with her friendly smile and kind words to each and all.[16]

At all events, it was essential that no Old Boer snub should possibly be perceived, despite the fervent hopes of Afrikaner die-hards. To avoid such a scenario, the Royal Family had already made a point of calling on Mrs Steyn, the widow of the last president of the Orange Free State in Bloemfontein (see Chapter 4), conferring on her the distinction of being a great lady of local consequence. This was represented as a gracious act on the part of the sovereigns and a mark of singular honour. In similar vein, the visit to Irene was arranged for Easter Sunday.

Naturally, there was a subtext here too. In a famously unforgiving matriarchal society, time, it needed to be shown, had healed the wounds carried by the wives of the Boer leaders, whose husbands and children were now co-opted within the Dominion forged in the aftermath of the Anglo-Boer War. The timing of the call, at the end of the successful Pretoria visit, was therefore perfect. According to the Tour Diary, the Royal Family took along only the King's detective, Superintendent Cameron[17] – 'no court', as another eyewitness put it[18] – but it would appear that Lady Delia Peel went with them too.[19]

Smuts himself had already left Pretoria for Cape Town, where Parliament was sitting, but Mrs Smuts had filled the house with her four daughters and two sons and almost all their offspring, down to the latest two grandchildren of six months. It was a family affair, 'very parochial and cosy', as one guest wrote afterwards, and the numbers – 24 in all[20] – astonished the royal visitors. 'What a rather large family you have,' commented Princess Elizabeth, laughingly, when she met Kathleen Mincher, the Smutses' adopted daughter,[21] at her 21st birthday two weeks later.[22]

It evidently went well, though the house was overcrowded and to start with the King 'looked lost with so many members of that big family to talk to'.[23] Queen Elizabeth, by nature more adept on such occasions, was much more at ease, and her daughters talked easily to the Smuts family members, though later admitting they found the farm 'an extraordinary sight'.[24] Mrs Smuts, the King reported to his mother, was 'a wonderful old lady, surrounded by all her children and grandchildren'.[25] No one detected any signs of the supposed stroke. 'Very much on the spot,' noted Princess Elizabeth.

They talked about many things, apparently, Mrs Smuts comfortably referring to the two Princesses as 'you girls'. Tea was served in the formal sitting room or parlour, seldom used, with two of her daughters presiding. Sylma Smuts had brought over from her bushveld farm her frankly ugly Mappin & Webb 'Cellini' pattern tea service, and Santa Smuts, her sister, her best tea set. Mrs Smuts, who did not see herself in the chatelaine role, did not habitually pour the tea when they had visitors, even in her own house, leaving the task to her daughters;[26] she did, however, dispense the food.

Twenty-nine in all sat down, 'a lovely mix-up and all so nice'. 'There was our family and Ouma and her family,' wrote Princess Elizabeth. 'Hers outnumbered ours easily.'

Since the Royal Family numbered only four, this curious comment may now be explained. On arrival, they had been greeted in front of the house by the Smuts family, 'all dressed up and in a flutter'.[27] Mrs Smuts waited to receive them up on the verandah. A swarm of policemen and detectives had preceded them and were deployed behind trees and bushes. After the greetings and introductions, they went inside to the formal sitting room, to the left of the hall, where there was indeed family backup, comprising some of their Continental royal cousins, waiting to greet them. This was Prince Paul of Yugoslavia, his wife, formerly Princess Olga of Greece, and their two sons, Prince Alexander and Prince Nicky, and their daughter, Princess Elizabeth, aged ten.

Prince Alexander was in his RAF uniform, Prince Nicky in a new suit. Princess Paul wore black for her cousin, George II, King of the Hellenes, who had died unexpectedly that week,[28] throwing the tour organisers and the Pretoria ladies into a panic. Would the King order court mourning, which would have necessitated black being worn at all the functions planned in the capital? In the end, court mourning was ordered for a week in England, but not in South Africa – a typical compromise of that family, as Lascelles put it drily to his wife.[29]

They embraced all round and seemed happy, as Princess Paul put it to her mother, that the meeting had come off after all. They hadn't seen each other since London in the summer of 1939 and much water had flowed under the bridge since then.

This part of Tea with Ouma was Top Secret and it appears to have been treated thus ever since. None of the Smuts family ever mentioned it publicly. Even today, in their old age, some of the grandchildren present were unaware of who these people were, assuming them to have been part of the 'entourage',[30] and when they sold the Cellini pattern tea service at auction recently, it was incorrectly stated in the catalogue to have been used at a tea party to entertain the English Royal Family and Prince Paul and Princess Frederica of Greece.[31]

The Yugoslavs had been motored over from Sandown in their Ford, which

Cecil Beaton's portraits of Princess Paul of Yugoslavia (*left*) and her sister, Princess Marina, the Duchess of Kent (*right*), who with Smuts contrived the exiled Yugoslav royal family's presence at the Irene tea party.

LEFT: © THE CECIL BEATON STUDIO ARCHIVE AT SOTHEBY'S
RIGHT: © CECIL BEATON/VICTORIA & ALBERT MUSEUM, LONDON

was on its last legs.[32] Their presence adds another dimension to the tea party at Irene. Prince Paul had been Regent to his nephew, Peter, since 1934. A great Anglophile, he had known the Queen before she married; the Duke and Duchess of York had attended his wedding in 1923 to the beautiful Princess Olga of Greece, and the King was godfather to their eldest son, Prince Alexander, actually born under the Yorks' roof; Princess Olga's equally beautiful sister, Marina, would later marry the Duke of Kent, the King's brother.

Come the outbreak of war, however, the Regent's position looked precarious. Although pro the Allied cause by nature, Yugoslavia was geographically vulnerable and had declared its neutrality in 1939. By 1941, his position looked more ominous still. King Peter was now 16; the regency had only until September of that year to run. Kingship when it came would surely prove a poisoned chalice to his nephew. Prince Paul knew that none of the Balkan countries was strong enough to withstand Hitler for long; the chance that they would receive help from Britain at that date seemed very remote. Moreover, the country lacked arms and it could not even rely on its separatist Croats to fight against the Germans. Realpolitik must have beckoned and, under pressure from Hitler, Paul signed a Tripartite

Pact with the Axis Powers, though with significant caveats appended.

If this sat badly with elements of the Yugoslav military, it sat very badly with Churchill and Eden, the Foreign Secretary. Britain supported the military; two days later Prince Paul was removed and sent into exile in Cairo and Peter was declared of age. An awkward situation was thus created: what was to be done with the Duke of Kent's sister-in-law and her family? Churchill, Eden (and Lascelles) and indeed the English press and much of the English public now regarded Paul as a 'treacherous quisling',[33] their opinion being largely based on unanswered attacks at Westminster, and Rebecca West's best-selling book on Yugoslavia published during the war.[34]

The family were first sent to Kenya as little more than prisoners, and then, with Smuts's connivance, to South Africa. Their life in Kenya had been made particularly unpleasant. In South Africa, it was considerably improved; Smuts and his wife called on them the day after their arrival.[35] As a result, they referred to the Oubaas as their 'Protector', which he undoubtedly was, smoothing their stony path in exile in many ways. Pitus (Greek for broadly denoting the qualities of an alpha male) was the code name they used for him in correspondence. By 1946, Princess Paul would also include it in her prayers – 'Pitus will protect us!' This was at the time the Nuremberg trials were getting under way, and it was suggested in some quarters – erroneously as it turned out – that Prince Paul might be called to face trial.[36]

Although Smuts was convinced of the Prince's innocence, it is not surprising that not everyone considered them worthy royal refugees. This was in contrast to Princess Paul's cousin, Crown Prince Paul of Greece, and his wife, the beautiful, German-born Crown Princess Frederica who, after the Nazi invasion of Greece, had been officially housed in Cape Town and made much of. (Indeed, such was the friendship between Smuts and the 22-year-old Princess Frederica during her husband's frequent absences that fashionable wartime Cape Town was consumed by gossip as to whether they might be having an affair.)

The Greek royals had long since left South Africa; with the death of King George II that very week, the couple were now suddenly summoned to the Greek throne. The fact that Prince and Princess Paul and their family were in semi-disgrace meant that they were required to live an altogether quieter and more retired life at Atholl House, near the Inanda

Polo Club, and were not, as the King put it to Queen Mary, 'able to go about much'.[37]

Post-war political and social retribution, together with mischief-making, nevertheless swirled round them, even in Inanda, and the coming royal visit was used as an opportunity to expose the pariah status that more than a few preferred to think they now enjoyed. Lady Oppenheimer, considered the leading hostess of Johannesburg, was one of several who refused to receive them; Sir Ernest did meet them, but only when his wife was away in England, and then at his son Harry and daughter-in-law Bridget's table ('both loyal friends of ours', as Princess Paul described them).[38] He was kind to the princes.

The family was insulted when they took communion at the Greek Orthodox Church,[39] and their children were not immune to other hurtful slights. There was an incident in the playground at St Andrew's School, where Princess Elizabeth had been sent to school, when another little girl accused her of having a father who was 'a friend of Hitler'; this she can only have heard from her parents. In retaliation, the Princess punched her in the face.[40] Her brothers, the two good-looking princes, were pointedly not invited to the ball held in Johannesburg for their cousins, Princesses Elizabeth and Margaret (see Chapter 7).

Deliberate trouble had further been made by Alex Geddes and Sir George Albu ('known for his conceit and small mind', according to Princess Paul), which reached a climax at a dinner party at Little Brenthurst. Harry Oppenheimer, appealed to in private afterwards, would later make Geddes apologise, which he did, but he continued to spread his views around the BBC on his return to London. The Yugoslavs, it was said, should be pointedly excluded from any official entertainments connected with the tour, and, indeed, should leave Johannesburg during the two days the Royal Family were due to visit it.[41]

Smuts, who enjoyed playing Mr Fixit in royal intrigues and dramas, especially ones on his own doorstep, was clearly annoyed that the matter had now got out of all proportion, and, further, that the King and Lascelles appeared to have fallen in with Geddes' line, which now appeared to represent official South African opinion. Lascelles had gone so far as to arrange through Harold Nicolson for them to absent themselves from Johannesburg on 1 and 2 April.[42]

On this issue Smuts put his foot down, writing to the King that as they lived eight miles (13 kilometres) out of town they should simply stay quietly at home. Lady Moore, then staying at Groote Schuur, possibly helped arrive at this solution. The mischief, however, was done. Indeed, the local Communist Party mouthpiece, *The Guardian*, subtly kept up a barrage against them. Under the headline 'PRINCE PAUL AGAIN', and reporting from Belgrade on 2 April, it stated:

> A witness in a war crimes trial here recently said that Goering had ordered Belgrade's White palace to be spared because it was the home of Prince Paul of Yugoslavia 'with whom he was on cordial terms'.
>
> Witness was General Loehr, one of the German officers on trial before a Yugoslav court at Belgrade. Prince Paul is now living in South Africa, where he is reported to be on cordial terms with cabinet ministers and other dignitaries.

Under the circumstances, it seemed that there was every chance that they would not meet their royal cousins after all; Attlee, Churchill and Lascelles thought it best they should not. By now Princess Paul's sister, the war-widowed Duchess of Kent had entered the fray, writing letters to both Smuts and Queen Elizabeth.[43] This was a shrewd move on her part; Smuts, who had a penchant for beautiful women (certainly in his later years), would regularly seek out the Duchess at London receptions, claiming that she was one of the most beautiful women he had ever met.[44] Princess Marina's letter must have set his mind working. Besides, he was also aware that the King and Queen took a more understanding view of the situation. Queen Elizabeth, who famously took a very firm line concerning ex-Nazi collaborators or sympathisers, even within the family,[45] had told Princess Marina before they left England that they were determined not to pass through South Africa without seeing them.

The minor furore had clearly set Queen Elizabeth's mind working too. She was adept all her life at circumventing political thwarters when their motives and reasons did not suit her purposes, and it is apparent that she and Smuts now hatched a plot together. As soon as she arrived at

Government House in Pretoria, she penned a very charming letter, written, as Princess Paul noted, 'with a lot of heart and affection':[46]

> My Dearest Olga
>
> Here we are in Pretoria & longing to see you both! This little note is just to bring you our dear love & to say that General Smuts is going to arrange a meeting in some quiet place – I promised him that I'd tell you that he has it in hand – It will be lovely to see you, & I am looking forward *so so* much to a talk.
>
> With love to you & Paul, ever yours affect.
> Elizabeth[47]

Smuts personally delivered the letter to Atholl House on 1 April, arriving with outriders and a car full of detectives on his way back from the Orlando visit (the Royal Family went on to Turffontein without Smuts, who, like Hofmeyr, disapproved of all forms of gambling, horse racing included)[48] Most unusually, he had telephoned the night before from Irene with the words 'Everything is all right for both of you'.[49] The plan was for everyone to meet at Doornkloof on Easter Sunday. Strict secrecy was, however, to be maintained. They were to travel to Irene early, to avoid detection on the road. This now involved lunch at Doornkloof too, as they would arrive well beforehand.

The Queen's letter must have dispelled the anxiety felt by Princess Paul, even if only for her husband's sake, as she claimed. It is hard to believe that it did not affect her too. It was of the utmost importance for them to be received, even very privately like this, as part of a gradual royal rehabilitation process; it would 'do much to clarifie [sic] D's [her husband's] position', as Princess Paul put it in a letter to her mother.[50] It would also, it was hoped, restore the friendship on a personal level.

Moreover, Prince Paul was suffering from depression brought on by living in exile in Johannesburg. It was hoped that the King's gesture in overriding his politicians would not only be a clear indication of royal favour, but would have a lifting effect on his spirits. Before he could ever

The Royal Family pose with Mrs Smuts in front of the house after tea.
Their Yugoslav royal cousins were obliged to remain inside, out of sight.

SMUTS HOUSE FOUNDATION

return to Europe, he needed to feel that, as his biographers have put it, at least in the opinion of his friends, he had not behaved with dishonour.[51] Indeed the religious, family-minded Yugoslavs had even foregone the memorial service held on Easter morning for the late King of Greece, Princess Olga's cousin, in order to be at Doornkloof.

Prince and Princess Paul remained indoors out of sight when, after tea, the phalanx of photographers and newsreel cameras captured the Royal Family smiling charmingly with Mrs Smuts, who had been persuaded by her daughters into a new dress; the black stockings and 'Little Girl' shoes, however, remained. Both the Princesses stand behind her, informally bareheaded. Returning to the house, ostensibly because of the crowded room, the Royal Family took the Yugoslavs into Smuts's study, in accordance with his suggestion, where they were able to talk in private. There the King finally relaxed and laughed; the whole atmosphere was very cordial and easy, 'like old times' thought Princess Paul.[52] 'Both were looking well,

Olga very pretty and Paul hardly changed at all. They were very pleased to see us, but their life is dull,' wrote the King to Queen Mary. Princess Elizabeth added that Nicky and Alexander were both huge boys, and adding, 'They are going to be mining engineers, I think. Elizabeth, the little girl is very naughty and she is also remarkably like Alexandra [Princess Alexandra of Kent, the Duchess of Kent's daughter].'

As for the Yugoslavs, they were so delighted by the way the meeting had gone that Princess Paul immediately sent a coded cable to her mother, Princess Nicholas of Greece for, as she later wrote, 'I knew it would give you pleasure to know that the meeting did take place after all.' Princess Nicholas (formerly the Grand Duchess Helen of Russia) was a first cousin of the last Tsar, murdered by the Bolsheviks, and as such set great store by solidarity among the extended Royal Family. In the letter following the cable, Princess Paul added that it had happened in the best and easiest way and that 'B & E [Bertie and Elizabeth] couldn't have been nicer or more genuinely glad to see us'.

This display of faith and loyalty marked the beginning of a process of reinstatement that continued to gain ground for the rest of Prince Paul's life. King George and Queen Elizabeth and their daughter, Elizabeth II, would treat him as a friend, royal prince and Garter Knight for the rest of his life.[53]

As for Yugoslavia, Germany had invaded and dismembered her anyway in 1941. Two resistance movements emerged – the Chetniks, led by Mihailović, and the communist partisans, led by Tito. Initially the Allies supported the Chetniks, but later switched to Tito, who established a totalitarian communist government there in 1944. The monarchy was abolished in 1945; Mihailović and other loyalist officers were summarily executed the following year. It was not until 2012 that the remains of Prince and Princess Paul would be reburied in Oplenac, the royal mausoleum outside Belgrade.

The Royal Family left Doornkloof at 5 pm, having been there an hour and a half. They were attending evensong (the first time the Princesses had ever attended this service) and due to leave early in the morning by air, for Southern Rhodesia, the next leg of the tour.

⇒⁑⇐

CHAPTER 9

Tea at Vergelegen

Somerset West, 22 April 1947

On 23 April, a cryptically worded telegram was delivered to Cynthia Barlow, the owner of Vergelegen, in her suite at Claridge's. Away from home and doubtless fearful of a crisis, she tore it open and read:

GEORGE AND ELIZABETH HAD AFTERNOON TEA HERE TODAY
SEND YOU THEIR LOVE STOP AM RINGING YOU 10 AM SATURDAY
LOVE AND ALL VERY WELL = DORIS[1]

She must have been astonished. Vergelegen was one of the oldest Cape estates and its beauty was held to be unequalled. At that date, almost all visitors to the Cape of any standing sought an invitation to visit it. But this was extraordinary. She knew no George and Elizabeth. If they were visitors at the Cape with an introduction, it was fair enough that they should be given tea. But why should they send her their love and why should Doris Trace, the wife of their agent there, send her a wire about it, far less book a trunk call about it for later? A letter would have done just as well.

In the event, it took several days before the mysterious telegram was explained. This is what had happened. At 3.20 pm on 22 April, the afternoon following Princess Elizabeth's 21st-birthday ball, Doris Trace had just come in from a ride. She had been accompanied by Tom, the Barlows' eldest son, Crispian, her own son, and Susanne Bailey-Southwell, who was staying with them. As was customary when the Barlows were overseas, the Traces had moved into the main house.

Garth Trace, bluff and popular, formerly of the Fleet Air Arm, had been invited by industrialist Charles Sydney (Punch) Barlow[2] to come south from Rhodesia and manage the estate, which his wife had purchased in 1941. Vergelegen suited the Traces and it quickly became apparent that Garth Trace's wife, Doris, who before the war had run Government House in Georgetown, British Guiana, as a secretary-cum-lady-in-waiting to the Governor's wife there, was every bit of an asset as her husband. Much of the domestic side of things at Vergelegen – the food, the flowers, and so on – was soon left to her.[3] Her talents in this regard were exceptional.[4]

Young Tom Barlow and Crispian Trace were due back at Western Province Prep that evening and were told to go and have a bath and change into their school uniforms, ready to leave at 4 pm. With that, Joseph, the white-coated major domo inherited from the Phillipses, came in to say that the local police sergeant was at the door, and asking for the lady of the house.

Thinking it must concern the then frequent Cape country incidents involving a drunk or yet another minor assault among the farm workers, Mrs Trace said he could wait and finished seeing to the children before going to the front door. There stood the village bobby, whose recorded cockney accent now adds an authentic Agatha Christie-like period touch to what Somerset West was then – a village with a narrow, oak-lined main street that still boasted hurdles before some of its shops to which riders could tie their horses.[5] Both Somerset West and the surrounding district were predominantly English-speaking. Comfortably smiling at the lady in front of him, the bobby announced blandly: 'Afternoon, Mrs Trace, I've just 'ad a message to say Their Majesties will be here in five minutes!'[6]

Crispian Trace, who was present, thinks his mother overdramatised the story after the event; he recalls 20–30 minutes.[7] Nevertheless, pandemonium broke out immediately. By her own account, Mrs Trace did not wait to hear another word. She fled down the long passage that, 30 years before, the architect CP Walgate had created leading north to link the old Dutch *gaanderij* (long gallery) with the Phillipses' new bedroom wing, calling out to Eileen, William (Billy) Barlow's white nanny, to dress her charge in his best as 'the King and Queen are coming NOW!' A more practical matter then suddenly occurred to her, and she ran back along the vaulted passage opposite it that led south to the extensive domestic offices, shouting after the rapidly retreating figure of Joseph: 'Tea at once – about eight cups!'

Distinguished visitors were a regular occurrence at Vergelegen, but this naturally was quite exceptional. So was the lack of warning. Word had spread like wildfire among the numerous staff (there were eight indoor and twenty-six outdoor staff employed at Vergelegen)[8] and in the ensuing panic, and to her very great relief, she caught sight of Mrs Hanson, the head gardener's wife, rushing in from their cottage to take charge in the kitchen, muttering, 'God help us, God help us, God help us!' under her breath all the while.

It was not a good day for an impromptu visit, far less one from the King and Queen. Spring cleaning was being carried out in the Barlows' absence; Mrs Trace had to give orders to stop the hoovering of rugs right away. Even worse was the sight that awaited her outside on what was known as the verandah – in reality a shady terrace with old pear trees and a freestanding sun awning, which faced east onto the lawns of the octagonal garden.[9] This was where tea was customarily served in fine weather. Mrs Trace stared out of the high, many-paned Cape sash window, aghast. There before her was a scene of desolation, as she put it later. In the middle of it all stood Mr Hanson, the Phillipses' English gardener whom the Barlows now employed. He had his braces down and was repotting the great terracotta pots with geraniums for a spring show. There was black soil everywhere.

Hanson, a brilliant gardener, was well known to have a temper; everyone, even Doris Trace, was careful in their dealings with him.[10] 'Wow, Mr Hanson, they want to find us just the way we are,' was all she dared venture.

'Madam, they certainly will,' came the dour reply. It was the closest Hanson came to making a joke.

There was no time to change her clothes (besides, Doris Trace always knew she looked rather good in her jodhpurs) and she merely slashed a comb through her hair. In the general hubbub, Tom and Crispian had meanwhile emerged looking neat and shining in their school uniforms, every hair in place, and were arranging for the Union Jack and the South African flag to be raised on the twin flagpoles that stood in front of the house. Another police car now drove up – this time, to the boys' delight, a more important-looking Buick from Cape Town and bearing a hasty scrawl from Peter Townsend.

The royal Equerry had visited Vergelegen the previous day on the strength of a local introduction. Tired and stale (in his words) by this stage of the tour, and in his heart of hearts 'longing for the *Vanguard*', he had been taken for a ride over the estate and shown the house, the library and the garden. Like many before him, he was captivated. His whole attitude, he wrote later, changed under the refreshing and happy influence of 'that lovely house and its particularly nice inhabitants'.[11] He had told the King and Queen about this enchanted place[12] at lunch the next day[13] and they had asked to be taken to see it. That meant that very afternoon. He had tried to telephone from Government House, but had had no luck in getting through, and instead sent the hasty note on ahead.

It proved to be only just ahead. Doris Trace barely had time to instruct the boys on how to address the King when up drove 'a socking great Buick' (Doris Trace again) bearing Major-General Palmer, the Commissioner of Police, and seconds behind it came the royal Daimler, incognito, with no royal standard flying. In those days the driveway still came up to the front door. The cars stood in the shade of the great camphor trees planted by Van der Stel, the builder of the original house 250 years before, and which, Arthur Rackham-like now, were one of the wonders of the garden.

The King and Queen alighted. Doris Trace and Sue Bailey-Southwell both curtseyed in their riding clothes, and the boys were presented, Billy being brought up by his nanny from the croquet lawn where they had been waiting, wearing his best blue and white smock, the very image of Christopher Robin. He put out his little hand and was not at all shy, wrote his nanny proudly afterwards. For Eileen, that moment and the rest of the afternoon that followed it, was, quite simply, 'the biggest thrill I ever had'.[14]

They all went into the homestead.[15] In the few sentences she would add to the King's farewell speech at the Civic Luncheon at City Hall on their last day (see Chapter 11), the Queen would refer, with evident pleasure, to the times she had been fortunate enough to go into some of 'your homes' in South Africa. By this she meant private houses. Yet in reality there had been very few of these visits. We have now followed them into two, and surely no greater contrast can have existed between the atmosphere of Vergelegen, with its house and setting, and that of Doornkloof at Irene. No greater contrast could have existed, too, between Isie Smuts and Cynthia Barlow, or indeed the previous incumbent, Florence Phillips, whose ghost seemed a constant, if somewhat unrestful, presence looking on from the shades. It was another example of parallel lives lived out in South Africa, even though in this case the Smutses had been friends of the Phillipses.

Smuts, at least, had always seen beyond the battle-axe image conjured up by Lady Phillips's many detractors; he was a great admirer of hers. He and his wife were regular guests at Vergelegen where, even as prime minister, he was accustomed to being chided and lectured to by her. In the end it was he who would give the noble eulogy over Lady Li Phi (as they called her) when her coffin lay in the great library, deserted in her last days by those she had helped and sponsored, and even the many who for years had warmed their hands before the roaring blaze she created, the glittering, cosmopolitan world in which she had played such a prominent part being almost in eclipse at the time of her death in 1940.

Vergelegen had been built by the Dutch governor Willem Adriaan van der Stel (son of Simon) at the start of the eighteenth century, when it was the finest private house at the Cape. Van der Stel had been banished from the Cape on charges of corruption and peculative gain and the estate had suffered many vicissitudes over the years.[16] Its restoration had been effected by Sir Lionel and Lady Phillips at the end of the First World War, when they had purchased what was generally considered to be 'an uninhabitable ruin', albeit one in a marvellously romantic setting.

Sir Lionel, one of the leading Randlords, had retired to settle in the Cape. Creating and living in beautiful houses was the very breath of life to Lady Phillips, who was dubbed the Queen of Johannesburg by the press. Their magnificent home there, the Villa Arcadia, designed by Herbert

Country Life at the Cape: post-war Vergelegen. Lady Phillips's aesthetic legacy, maintained and enhanced by the Barlows, delighted the sovereigns.

BARLOW FAMILY PAPERS

Baker very much in conjunction with Lady Phillips, was sold up and its contents conveyed to the Cape. Now she would turn her attention to Vergelegen.

Baker had already left South Africa and was designing New Delhi with Lutyens. Lady Phillips had originally entrusted the restoration to her protégé, Joseph Solomon, a talented but troubled Paarl-born architect, for whom she had secured the prestigious University of Cape Town commission. Overwhelmed by the scale of that project, he had committed suicide; colonial society being what it was, it was darkly hinted in some quarters that Lady Phillips had *driven him to it*. Before this tragedy, however, Baker had sent CP Walgate from New Delhi to assist him. It was Walgate's task now to draw up the plans for Vergelegen. Under Florence Phillips's guidance he learnt about Cape Dutch architecture on the trot; the schemes and ideas were undoubtedly hers.

A place of rare beauty emerged. What Walgate (and his assistant

Ellsworth, who also came out from New Delhi) and Lady Phillips achieved was a restoration in the South African Arts and Crafts tradition. Much was renewed, replaced, replastered or simply added onto in the general spirit of the Cape Dutch revival that Herbert Baker had initiated at Groote Schuur some 30 years before. New doors, new windows and new floorboards were all put in; fireplaces with bolection mould chimneypieces were installed to add cheer in winter, and herringbone brickwork, electrified 'Knole' chandeliers and much more that simply came under the heading of Good Taste in 1920, was employed.

The great bedroom wing, with its bathrooms, was added to the north and the extensive domestic offices to the south. In addition to a large kitchen, there was a servants' hall, a butler's pantry, a china pantry, a silver safe, a flower room, a linen room, a valet's room, rooms for white indoor staff and the other offices considered essential to running the house of an Edwardian hostess.[17] They were added on without the tiresome concerns of modern restoration purists, anxious to adhere to what they believe is the original, early-eighteenth-century plan of a house. Fortunately, perhaps, the additions were largely hidden by the existing screen walls to the left and right of the front façade. At any rate, they have stood the test of time.

At the start of the project Lady Phillips had typically fired off a letter to her old secretary-companion in England, imperiously demanding that she 'Find Hanson!', their former, talented head gardener at Tylney, the Phillipses' large country house near Basingstoke. Hanson, duly found working for Lord Warwick, answered the summons and came out to the Cape in 1921. The octagonal garden, so visible in the two eighteenth-century drawings of the property, was recreated, now, however, embellished with paths, pergolas, Italianate urns and statues, and bisected by great twin herbaceous borders.

Filled with the treasures and furnishings of Tylney and the Villa Arcadia to which had been added some superb Cape pieces, it is difficult to see the end result as anything else but an Edwardian Cape house with a Cape Dutch house of long ago buried at its centre. Nor should this matter. It was beautiful; Florence Phillips had a genius for arranging furniture and choosing just the right stuffs and old needlework to enhance

Two South Africas meet: Ouma Smuts (*left*) and Lady Phillips (*right*),
unlikely fellow travellers.

SMUTS HOUSE FOUNDATION

the rooms.[18] Cynthia Barlow brought to bear similar, related skills on the aesthetic legacy she had inherited.

What the King and Queen now saw was a monument to Anglo-Cape taste created by the house's two succeeding owners. Even the aesthetically unaware Smuts, who had known the estate in its former, less palmy days, had seen it as standing proof of Lady Phillips's sense of beauty, together with something rather more, suggesting that she had created what he called 'this expression of the human spirit'.[19]

In the flesh, Lady Phillips was a tornado of a woman. Her energy, enterprise and patronage had encompassed an extraordinarily wide range of South African endeavour. The Johannesburg Art Gallery, the establishment of the Kirstenbosch Botanical Garden, the preservation of the Old Town House, the Koopmans-de Wet House and the Martin Melck house, the Rand Regiments' Memorial, the Witwatersrand Agricultural Show, Marloth's *Flora of South Africa* – all were projects that she and her husband initiated and helped finance. There were many more besides. She freely spent her husband's money on her projects and bullied his less public-spirited colleagues into parting with theirs. However, her mercurial moods (her 'April temperaments' as she herself called them) and lifelong gynaecological and related health problems made her famously tricky; she lacked what would nowadays be called 'people skills' and was unbeloved by the generality.

'Fearless and tactless in pursuing her aims,' wrote her biographer, who knew her in old age, 'she saw only what needed to be done and forthrightly attacked her projects with an ardour that scorched her beholders. A great and emotional visionary, she envisaged a glorious future for her country which was in many ways too immature to accept her ideals.'[20] Yet few of her contemporaries would have denied her remarkable achievements; she had an exceptional claim to having played a significant part in the evolution of modern South Africa.

Cynthia Barlow (née Butcher) was an altogether different sort of woman.[21] A considerable Natal heiress, several times over, she was far more retiring by nature. Kind though unmaternal, as was typical of many women of her background in that age, she was in other ways generous to a fault; no charitable request or begging letter went unanswered. According to her son Willy, her husband, in intelligence during the war, had warned her after Dunkirk that if the Nazis invaded England they would make two important strikes thereafter – one on the Persian oil fields, then under British control, the other on the Rand goldfields. The latter would be effected, possibly with Japanese assistance, through a seaborne invasion via Durban. She was to buy an estate at the Cape and get out of the firing line.

Lady Phillips had died three months after Dunkirk. She had been a terrible mother in many ways to her wayward and eccentric children, and much of Sir Lionel's fortune had been lavished on Vergelegen. The estate was put up for sale by her heirs, who wanted no part of it.[22] In 1941, Cynthia Barlow purchased it for a rock-bottom wartime price of £40 000, with most of the contents thrown in too. Bought with Butcher rather than Barlow money, it was the real estate buy of the century.[23]

For the property, this was considered a happy outcome. Cynthia Barlow had superb taste too, and now addressed herself to enhancing the homestead and the estate. Slowly some of the fashionable 'Curzon Street Baroque' elements of the immediate post-First World War era, for which Lady Phillips had displayed a decided penchant, were weeded out; the Jacobean patterns, woodwormed carvings and parchment yielded to the Chippendale and chintz of the succeeding generation, along with her fine collection of English silver. Despite the presence of children, and the skill employed of not making it all look too perfect, the atmosphere remained formal, with uniformed servants and the regular, upper-class Anglo-Saxon domestic routines of that date. Trout fishing in pools created and duly stocked in the Lourens River, polo, croquet, squash, bridge and later Scrabble, and the tea table and drinks tray, provided recreation and relaxation. The Cape Hunt met annually on the lawn in front of the house, and the Barlows dressed for dinner.

The royal couple were perfectly at ease in this milieu. As they entered the *voorkamer* (front room), the King ragged the boys, like a gay, light-hearted schoolboy (and so different, thought Doris Trace, from the 'tired, worn look' he had recently shown in public). They were fascinated by the house's history. They too had enjoyed restoring and adding to the stunted remains of the Royal Lodge, the Prince Regent's great *cottage orné* in

Windsor Great Park, where they had made their home in the early 1930s. The Queen gazed at the sea of beefwood and stinkwood and Cape silver escutcheons before her, the monumental arrangements of hydrangeas[24] now in their autumnal green and russet, and on through the handsome screen or *porte de viste* that Lady Phillips had found in an attic and restored to its rightful place. 'What a lovely house and how beautifully cool,' she said, quietly, before walking on and asking questions about the building's date, and so on. This was not exactly Doris Trace's strong point; she answered as best she could and, as she admitted later, simply made up what she didn't know.

Having admired the house, the royal couple passed out onto the terrace beneath the beautiful, east-facing gable – a replica of the one on the recently demolished Paarl Parsonage, which Lady Phillips had caused to have erected to replace the simple eyebrow gable that survived there – and surveyed what was considered one of the great horticultural *coups d'oeil* of the Cape. Two life-size lead statues of buck, copies of the celebrated pair unearthed at Pompeii, stood guard over the twin herbaceous borders that bisected Van der Stel's octagonal garden, whose walls Lady Phillips had had restored from a few crumbling foundations. The borders were Hanson's pride and joy, especially in November when the masses of delphiniums, their imported seed sown in an annual ritual every New Year's Day,[25] were at their height, their blue colouring matched by the great mountain peaks that stood behind them.

Passionate about gardens, neither Lady Phillips nor Cynthia Barlow had green fingers themselves – Hanson did – but Cynthia's sister-in-law Pam, another Natal heiress, married to Punch's brother Peter, had them all right and was creating, from scratch, a garden of almost greater beauty at Rustenburg beyond Stellenbosch, very much in the Hidcote/Sissinghurst school. The two sisters-in-law spoke daily on the telephone. Two or three times a week an agricultural vehicle would make the journey between the two estates bearing promised seedlings and cuttings each way. There developed a healthy horticultural rivalry, Pam Barlow privately describing Vergelegen as 'a gloomy old house with those big trees in front of it', and Cynthia Barlow retaliating in kind with 'Pam's garden is really quite nice once you get into it'. The idea of a garden with 'rooms' was unheard of then in South Africa. The two met perhaps twice a year.[26]

On the day of the royal visit, the Vergelegen borders were in their autumnal splendour with dahlias, Michaelmas daisies, zinnias and other late-flowering annuals. It was a perfect, windless, golden Cape afternoon, when late summer merges into autumn. Slanting shadows lay across the lawns. Order had been miraculously restored on the terrace. The cushions were arranged on the chairs and the swing seat, the tea table with its Madeira-work cloth and its silver tea kettle and pretty china was all in place, and Joseph and Charlie standing by. Doria, the parlour maid, had donned her new uniform. A great cascade of the then rarely seen mauve bougainvillea flowered above them.

Mrs Hanson's prayers in the kitchen had apparently been answered. In record time she had prepared a batch of miniature scones and wafer-thin slices of bread and butter; some cakes had appeared too, seemingly as if by magic. 'Such a good tea,' as Doris Trace would write afterwards, with relief. Eileen, the nanny, was meanwhile regaling General Palmer and the ten police and plain-clothes detectives with a somewhat lesser tea in Punch Barlow's study.[27]

By now, clusters of the Barlows' indoors and outdoors staff were peeping in awe and wonderment from various vantage points and gateways into the garden. The Queen spotted them and, without pausing with her tea or her conversation with Doris Trace and the children, smiled and waved at them, a scone deftly between her fingers. Pierre, the dog, who had happily retrieved a stick thrown for him by the King, now, in the hopes of the airborne morsel, put a dirty paw on the Queen's lap, soiling her dress. She was completely unfazed by this. The little boys were fascinated by the fact that she addressed the King as 'Bertie'.[28]

They asked to see the library. This had been converted out of the old wine cellar to house Sir Lionel Phillips's fine collection of books, the tail of its T arranged as the billiards room. It was a magnificent room with a marvellously authentic, mouldering atmosphere. Lined with bookcases, it had two fireplaces down its length and great comfortable sofas and easy chairs.

Lady Phillips's Sunday luncheons, always packed with visiting celebrities, and where her unbridled tongue transfixed the faint-hearted, had been legendary at the Cape. To his library Sir Lionel would retire, as soon as it was decently possible after the meal was over, to play his organ, which filled the west wall, or to read or nap on a specially designed daybed at the opposite end. The uncharitable at the Cape said he hid there from his wife's nagging and tantrums. Now the library was Punch Barlow's pride and joy, and he would add many important volumes to it; a Gobelins tapestry replaced the organ, which was donated to Michaelhouse.

After that the visitors toured the farm. They were shown the prize Frieslands and Jerseys by Van der Vyver, the cowman, with whom they discussed farming, and were driven high up to the Korhaan Vlakte, the road black with guinea fowl with the odd buck leaping across it. The King and Queen kept asking to stop to get out and admire the view and breathe in the air, saying how like Scotland it all was and how peaceful and beautiful.

Typically for little boys, Tom and Crispian asked for a ride in the Daimler, and the King sent them back in it with instructions from Doris to ask Molyneux, the estate arborist (known to all as 'Molly'), to collect acorns from the oak now growing in the garden. This tree was itself grown from an acorn gathered by Lady Phillips while staying at Blenheim in 1928, from an ancient oak in the park known as 'Alfred the Great's Oak'. When the party got back to the house the boys were waiting with smiling faces and handfuls of acorns (later planted in Windsor Great Park), and Molyneux brought in Lady Phillips's little commemorative plaque for the wording to be copied down by the sovereigns. They intended, they said, to ask the Marlboroughs all about this when they got back to England.

They left, or 'sped away' as Doris Trace put it, at 5.45 pm. Hanson, Molyneux, Eileen and Doris fell on the drinks tray to pour themselves the stiffest whisky and sodas they had ever knocked back, only to find they had no effect. Adrenaline was running high in the aftermath of the surprise royal visit. Sleep proved impossible that night, and all Doris Trace could see in front of her was the vision of the Queen's beautiful blue eyes and 'that staggering complexion'. Mrs Hanson took to her bed for two days.

The lady on the Somerset West exchange who had so blunderingly failed to put through Townsend's call to Vergelegen had not been idle. (Callers had to ask for 'Somerset West 42'; those answering had to compete with

Lady Phillips' African Grey in his cage, close by the instrument, who, in a finesse not dreamt up by Daphne du Maurier, gave a spirited imitation of the deceased chatelaine's peremptory: 'Hello? *Hello*? HELLO!' – and then chuckled uproariously at any sign of exasperation). She had been ringing the news, gleaned from the police station, all around the district. Doris Trace would say that she did not dare to show her face in the village for weeks after; no one believed her story that she had not known about the visit in advance, and all thought she had selfishly kept the news to herself. By the time the Daimler reached the lodge gates, they found Muriel Anderson, the Barlows' colourful neighbour and owner of yet another lovely Cape estate, Buzenval (now Fleur du Cap), had been waiting for over an hour to see them drive by. From then on an endless, vociferous throng seemed to line the road all the way back to the village.

Of the journey back to Government House, Townsend wrote later that he had seldom heard the King and Queen give vent to their feelings so readily and warmly about the afternoon and all the things they had seen. They had really loved the visit. He felt that the King and Queen or the Princesses, or all of them, might 'sooner than any of us expect', get a chance of seeing Vergelegen again.[29] Only Princess Elizabeth ever did, as Queen, and that would be fifty years later. By then, Vergelegen was much changed, its once fabled beauty overlaid with corporate taste.

The Coming of Age of the Heiress Presumptive: Gently Towards a New Multiracial Commonwealth

Cape Town, 21 April 1947

Monday 21 April 1947 was, for the courtiers and politicians, the climax of the tour – the 21st birthday of Princess Elizabeth. The day's programme would involve four major events: a military parade suggesting her future role as head of the armed forces; a Youth Rally attended by those who would be her future subjects; the broadcast of dedication; and the celebrations – the public ball and fireworks and the ostensibly grander, more glittering ball at Government House.

That this was to be celebrated in South Africa was significant at several levels. Firstly, it emphasised the importance placed on the Commonwealth and the Union's place within it, for South Africa was seen to be elevated in a very real sense to equal status with Britain where, in previous generations, the birthday might more reasonably have been expected to be celebrated. It represented a very visible evidence of the equality that lay at the heart of the Statute of Westminster and it gave added truth to the claim, now being made again and again, that the monarchy functioned wherever the King happened to be in his Dominions. As *The Times* put it, 'no part of the Commonwealth now, in theory, is better or has better title to his presence and services than another'.[1]

Added to this was the charming notion, now frequently espoused, that the King and his family were just as at home in Cape Town as in London, Ottawa or Canberra.[2] This would be reiterated clearly and early on in his elder daughter's radio broadcast that evening: 'For although I am six thousand miles from the country where I was born ... I am certainly not six thousand miles from home. Everywhere I have travelled in these lovely lands ... my parents, sister and I have been taken into the heart of their people and made to feel that we are just as much at home here as if we had lived among them all our lives.'

For a decade or so, until jet air travel enabled overseas royal visits to be frequent and truncated, and the concept of the Commonwealth changed way beyond the idea of a group of Little Englands flourishing around the globe, this was an encouraged and cherished hypothesis. Thus it would be that the new Queen would spend Christmas 1953 at Government House in Auckland, New Zealand, and the first annual Christmas message since her crowning would be broadcast from there by the New Zealand Broadcasting Corporation.

Of course, the day had constitutional as well as financial implications for her. She would now be able to assume the powers of a Regent if the King became incapacitated; her annual income rose from £6 000 to £15 000. But it must also have brought home a significance that existed on another, much more personal level. For the ball given to celebrate her coming of age would be peopled with strangers, and however much they wished her well and were thrilled to be present, going through the motions of appearing to enjoy such a personal milestone far from home, extended family and friends, must surely have highlighted – if indeed highlighting was still required – what a lifetime of duty would demand again and again: to put personal happiness and pleasure second. 'I felt sad when I realised that I would not spend my coming of age at home, but now I think it forms a very happy link with South Africa,' as she was to put it to Queen Mary after describing the events of her big day.[3]

Naturally, this aspect was not dwelt upon by the politicians or the press, even if it had occurred to some of them. Having alighted on the novel expedient of the celebration's taking place in Cape Town rather than London, it was understandable that the courtiers and the Smuts government should want to make the most of it. It was a very busy day. Planned was an 'almost unbroken round of engagements', as *The Cape Argus* put it,[4] during all of which the Heiress Presumptive was brought exclusively to the fore. These were not her first solo engagements, as has sometimes been made out, even in South Africa. On 3 March she had, for example, opened the Princess Elizabeth Graving Dock in East London, where, before a vast concourse of citizens of the eastern Cape seated in serried rows, and battling to hold onto her notes and hat in a brisk southeaster with an aplomb that would have pleased her grandmother, Queen Mary, she had unfurled the maritime signal flag allowing the first ship to enter the dock.

The day began with her calling tray – brought to her as always by her 'dresser', formerly her nurserymaid, Miss MacDonald, known in the family circle as 'Bobo', reportedly the first word the Princess uttered – and the reading of some of the mountain of telegrams that had been pouring in during the last week.

There were 500 alone that morning,[5] including those from her family (such as her grandmother), from politicians (such as Mr Attlee and Mr Churchill), from organisations with which she was connected (such the Girl Guides Association of Britain and the Welsh Corgi League). This selection was now widened and captured a South African flavour. There was one, for example, from the mayor of Pretoria (the former member of the Ossewabrandwag who had been interned during the war), one from the South African Hindus, and one from the Jewish Community of South Africa. Added to this were a slew of others from people and bodies that had encountered or simply glimpsed her somewhere along the route of the tour and now felt they wanted to be part of her life on such a day. There was one, for example, from four typists in Johannesburg, another from someone who signed himself as 'Old Bill' from Kimberley,[6] and yet another from the *volkspelers* of Standerton, which was said to have given especial pleasure.[7] Answering these was taxing for the ladies-in-waiting. Princess Margaret later recalled Lady Delia doggedly listing them and starting on the seemingly endless task of answering them late into the long hot nights.

This too must have set a pattern that was growing and would continue to do so throughout her life; not merely with letters of congratulations on anniversaries which enabled their senders to feel they could thereby share in a small part of the royal happiness, but also from people who felt they wanted to tell her something they felt strongly about. Indeed, the telegraph and post office on the White Train had been so swamped by the deluge of telegrams and letters such as these that towards the closing days of the epic railway journey, arrangements had had to be made to divert them to the General Post Office in Cape Town for delivery to Government House.[8]

Breakfast was taken to the accompaniment of the carillon at the City Hall nearby, where the bells pealed out 'Happy Birthday' and 'Twenty One Today', at the same time – it was noted to much gratification, locally – as the bells of St Paul's Cathedral.[9] It was here that the family presents were exchanged privately. This was the last of the planned private moments in the day. Other gifts, however, had rained in. A six-petal spray brooch subscribed to by all the royal households in Britain, a diamond badge surmounted by a crown from the King's Flight, a diamond Guard's badge from the Grenadier Guards of which she was colonel, a diamond rosette spray from the Diplomats of the Court of St James's, a silver inkstand from Queen Mary's Household. There was an ostrich feather cape and fan from the people of Oudtshoorn, and the *oudstryders* of Potchefstroom sent a cake in the shape of a Voortrekker woman in national costume. This was personally delivered by Mrs Pienaar, the wife of the Administrator of the Transvaal, along with a songbook of her favourite Afrikaans *liedjies*.[10]

That morning, the autumn mists that herald the changing season at the Cape had spoilt a planned trip up Table Mountain in the cable car, depriving the world press of a marvellous photo opportunity of the Heiress Presumptive with the capital city of one of her future Dominions quite literally at her feet. (In the event, the trip took place in perfect weather two days later.) Typically, as it invariably did, the mist burnt off. At noon a 21-gun salute was fired from Signal Hill; it was answered by HMS *Vanguard* in Table Bay and the cruiser *Nigeria* and the sloops *Nereide* and *Actaeon* at anchor off Simon's Town. In the windless weather these cannonades echoed back and forth around the Peninsula's rocky mountain faces.

At 3 pm, and in now perfect, still autumn sunshine, Princess Elizabeth arrived to take the salute at a great military parade at Youngsfield, the aerodrome next to the Kenilworth Racecourse, that had become a military

The 21st-birthday military parade at Youngsfield. General Sir Pierre van Ryneveld
greets Princess Elizabeth; Field-Marshal Smuts is on the right.

TRANSNET HERITAGE LIBRARY PHOTO COLLECTION

base during the war. Nine thousand troops of 31 units – representing the
whole Cape Command – took part, under the command of Brigadier
HG Wilmott, known to his friends as 'Whisky Wilmott'. She arrived
wearing her favourite wheat-coloured dress ('beige-pink', said the *Cape
Times*), draped at the neck and waist with bow catches, and one of Aage
Thaarup's hats of straw, with veiling tied behind it. She was accompa-
nied by her Lady-in-Waiting, Lady Meg Egerton, and the Queen's Private
Secretary, Major Harvey.

The Princess was met by Smuts in his field-marshal's uniform and
General Sir Pierre van Ryneveld. Also on the reviewing dais was a local
South African VC and the family and relatives of two others. The heroes –
both the living and the dead – were always honoured on such an occasion.
There was seating provided for 4 000 members of the public; in adver-
tisements placed in the Cape dailies beforehand it was trusted 'that all

Children representing all races present a birthday tray of wild flowers arranged by
the Curator of Kirstenbosch. Behind the Princess is Jan Hofmeyr, with Miriam and Abe
Bloomberg (with mayoral chain) at centre and Bishop Sidney Lavis at far right.

TRANSNET HERITAGE LIBRARY PHOTO COLLECTION

Western Province Ex-Servicemen will make a special endeavour to attend
this parade [which] confers a singular honour on Ex-Service personnel'.[11]
They did. She inspected the units standing up in a slowly moving jeep and
later stood on the saluting dais as all the men marched past.

'It took a long time,' she wrote to Queen Mary, 'as there were about
8 000 people on parade, but it was very impressive to see the Permanent
Force, the cadets and the ex-servicemen march past, as a sort of symbol of
the past, present and future.'[12]

Such a parade, while undeniably quietly triumphalist in the immediate
post-war world, was also designed to emphasise her future role as head of
all the armed forces in the Commonwealth.

At 4.15 pm, in a marvel of traffic control that would surely defeat the
traffic police of present-day Cape Town, the Princess was greeted by the
mayor of Cape Town at the United Youth Rally staged at the Rosebank

Showgrounds, where children of the Afrikaans, English, coloured and Malay communities presented her with a tray of autumn wild flowers, arranged by the Curator of Kirstenbosch Botanical Garden. The rally included the massed bands of the Boys' Brigade, a Floral Ballet by the Eoan Group (a coloured ballet and opera company) and more *volkspele*.

After a choir of over a thousand had sung 'Happy Birthday Dear Princess', the Princess spoke. Having reminded her youthful audience that they too, one day, would turn 21, she said: 'I shall always remember this day and the welcome you have given me and I hope that the time will not be too far distant when I can visit you again.' This was greeted with deafening cheers – the hope of the speedy return of the Royal Family to South Africa was one that was repeated constantly by (non-Nationalist supporting) speech-makers in the last days of the tour, and the entire assembly sang 'Land of Hope and Glory'.

It was now time to make her broadcast. Although this was ostensibly to be made from Government House, it had in fact been rehearsed during a hot weekend at Victoria Falls, with instruction from Frank Gillard of the BBC, the King and Queen participating,[13] and then prerecorded and filmed, under the trees on the lawns of the hotel, the proceedings watched with intense curiosity by a troop of baboons.[14] Although at that date, prerecorded speeches by royalty were considered to be *not on* – 'a fraud on the listener', according Sir John Reith, the former and influential Director General of the BBC – discs had in fact been cut and immediately sent to London lest the unreliable radio beam between Cape Town and London prove faulty on the night.[15] Maintaining pretence of a live broadcast, however, was an absolute necessity for the courtiers, for it was important in the context of the speech that it was made 'speaking from Cape Town'. (It was only later admitted that a prerecorded version had existed 'in case'.) Naturally this would also have allowed for splicing in the event of hesitations and error, and removed any anxiety she might have felt about it beforehand, during her busy day.

This much, at any rate, was an unnecessary precaution. The Princess suffered none of her father's difficulties when it came to make a speech; she was observed by Gillard to be composed and confident throughout.

Rehearsed and considerably rewritten, the 21st-birthday radio broadcast is recorded and filmed at the Victoria Falls Hotel, standing in for Westbrooke.

The filmed version that comes down to us is obviously the prerecorded one. In it, the columned verandah and steps of the famous Victoria Falls Hotel double very well for those at Westbrooke (though not so convincingly for Government House in Cape Town), even the hint of a bed of cannas in the background providing evidence of plausibly similar horticultural efforts.

As noted, early on in her speech she charmingly claimed that she and her family had been so taken to the hearts of the people 'and made to feel that we are just as much at home here as if we had lived among them all our lives'. Such a claim would have had more than a kernel of truth back then; parts of South Africa, Rhodesia and the Protectorates[16] were very English in their ways and manners, as we have seen, and many other parts that really were not had appeared warmly welcoming too. It certainly deeply gratified many of her future subjects who lived there to hear this.

Having made the point, however, she now pressed home the advantage: 'That is the great privilege belonging to our place in the worldwide Commonwealth – that there are homes ready to welcome us in every continent of the earth.' This, of course, was music to the ears of all old colonial hands, imbued then with the sentiment of hands-across-the-seas which, as we have repeatedly seen, was certainly reflected in the spirit of the old white Commonwealth. The war had proved it to be a very real truth. 'Before I am much older,' she continued, 'I hope I shall come to know many of them.'

Here, then, was an important platform for this extraordinarily profound dedication by a young woman. The Commonwealth – its growth and its progress – was to be a significant factor in her life and future reign. That it was not to be a white-run, white-only affair was now gradually being made clear. Significantly, the opening sentence of this speech, 'I welcome the opportunity to speak to all the peoples of the British Commonwealth and Empire, wherever they may live, whatever race they come from, and whatever language they speak,' had suggested this. And suggested too, perhaps, in that more class-bound and racist age, was a gradual embracing of a multiculturalism that looked forwards rather than backwards.

In a prominent article opposite the leader page in *The Times* that morning, and possibly coordinated by the Palace beforehand, Viscount

Templewood (Sir Samuel Hoare) had extolled this aspect to her advantage: 'I believe that the inheritance awaiting the Princess will be greater in a real sense and richer in example than any to which an heir apparent has previously succeeded. More and more, the Crown will be recognised as the bond of Union in a Commonwealth of many dispensations ... It may well be that the Crown will make possible a Commonwealth of free peoples and many races far more varied than any that may exist today.'[17]

Next in her broadcast, the Princess addressed herself to the youth of the day 'born about the same time as myself [and who] have grown up like me in the terrible and glorious years of the Second World War'. Asking that they allow her to speak on her birthday as their representative, she called on them to join her in taking some of the burden off the shoulders of elders who had 'fought and worked and suffered to protect our childhood'.

Admitting that the war had left behind anxieties and hardships, she added: 'We know these things are the price we cheerfully undertook to pay for the high honour of standing alone, seven years ago, in defence of the liberty of the world.' This aside was fair enough. It carefully explained away Britain's present troubles resulting from embarking on a costly socialist experiment in her state of bankruptcy in the immediate aftermath of the war. There might also, perhaps, have been a little dig here at the United States, so rich and prosperous, for becoming a global power on the back of a late entry into the war. It was now dawning on many that there had been very few prizes handed out for High Honour and Duty.

Be that as it may, she now returned to the main theme of her speech. The British Empire had saved the world first and now had to save itself after the battle was won: 'It is for us, who have grown up in these years of danger and glory, to see that it is accomplished in the long years of peace that we all hope stretch ahead.'

Lascelles is widely held to have written the speech. This is incorrect. It was initially drafted by Dermot Morrah, a speechwriter to the King and Queen, who was travelling with the party. Morrah, an Arundel Herald of Arms Extraordinary, was a man of considerable intellectual distinction: a mathematician and a classicist, he was also a Fellow of All Souls, and had shared rooms with TE Lawrence while at Oxford.

Lascelles made this fact perfectly clear in his letter to Queen Mary – 'I have had no hand in the composition of the draft'[18] – and in a letter on White Train stationery of 10 March, in which he explains that the valuable pages containing the draft wording had actually gone missing, but had turned up in among, of all places, the steward's bottles of booze in the bar on the *Protea* dining car. 'I have been reading drafts now for many years,' he wrote to Morrah, 'but I cannot recall one that has so completely satisfied me and left me feeling that not a single word should be altered.' This was high praise indeed from the Private Secretary. 'Moreover,' he continued, 'dusty cynic though I am it moved me greatly.'[19]

To begin with, not everyone had agreed with Lascelles, even supposing he didn't mean to flatter. Like all important royal speeches, it would anyway have been subject to a rewrite, with input from the speaker; in this instance, from the King and Queen too. Both saw it as the most important speech of their daughter's life. After a church service on Low Sunday held in the Victoria Falls Hotel, the King, Queen and Princess, together with Frank Gillard, took deckchairs and went and sat in a tight circle on a back lawn.[20] According to Gillard, both he and the King found the original too pompous and full of platitudes; it was now up to the four of them to make it perfect. They spent two hours reworking it.

That the final wording when she came to deliver it would prove to be a triumph has never been disputed, and it had certainly made all the royal ladies cry when they read it over.[21] From here on, then, the speech gathered momentum inexorably, its content and phraseology alike masterly:

> If we all go forward together with an unwavering faith, a high courage, and a quiet heart, we shall be able to make of this ancient common-wealth, which we all love so dearly, an even grander thing – more free, more prosperous, more happy and a more powerful influence for the good in the world – than it has been in the greatest days of our forefathers.

Here now, at the speech's climax, was the moment to invoke the romance of the Arthurian legend which the modern monarchy still conjured up. It was seized and delivered to tremendous effect:

To accomplish that we must give nothing less than the whole of our-selves. There is a motto which has been borne by many of my ancestors – a noble motto, 'I serve'. Those words were an inspiration to many bygone heirs to the Throne when they made their knightly dedication as they came to manhood. I cannot do quite as they did.

But through the inventions of science I can do what was not pos-sible for any of them. I can make a solemn act of dedication with a whole Empire listening. I should like to make that dedication now.

This was the knightly or almost nun-like vow that many feel came to define her reign.

It is very simple. I declare before you all that my whole life whether it be long or short shall be devoted to your service and the service of our great imperial family to which we all belong.

But I shall not have the strength to carry out this resolution alone unless you join in it with me, as I now invite you to do:[22] I know that your support will be unfailingly given. God help me to make good my vow and God bless all you who are willing to share in it.

The speech was heard by an estimated 200 million around the globe. Even in the United States, where, as in England and to the great satisfaction of the technicians, the reception was loud and clear, men and women in offices and bars stopped to listen. Many, many who heard it were moved. Indeed, as a rallying cry, it had strong echoes of the first Queen Elizabeth's speech to her troops at Tilbury in 1588.

'Who is so indifferent,' commented the editor of The Star, Johannesburg's evening newspaper, the following day 'or faint-hearted that he will not, according to his ability, carry some of the burden that belongs not to the leader alone but to all who compose the Commonwealth?'[23]

Understandably, her grandmother was among those moved. 'Of course I wept,' wrote old Queen Mary in her diary, after listening to it on the Marlborough House wireless.[24] Winston Churchill wept too.[25] It also brought tears to the eyes of the King and Queen.

'We realise so well the big responsibility that has now fallen on our daughter's shoulders,' explained Queen Elizabeth with disarming frankness to a young guest, unknown to her, at the dinner party held immediately afterwards. 'Still, as a family we enjoy things so, and have that saving gift of laughter which lightens any burden.'[26]

More moving still, when viewed from 70-odd years on, is a lifetime of unfailing sense of duty toward the new entity that was emerging from the old Empire and transforming into the new Commonwealth. Had she, in the course of her first overseas tour of a very divided, multicultural and multiracial country (and during which, and concurrently, her father's cousin, 'Uncle Dicky' Mountbatten, was granting independence to India – the brightest jewel in the old imperial crown) glimpsed into the future and seen a way forward that was both honourable and worthwhile? Had the particular journey to South Africa, so soon to be proved to have been such a waste of time in the short term, been a formative one anyway, as more than one royal biographer has hinted?

Certainly, her commitment to it has never wavered. Of course, the world has changed since then. Britain, though a prosperous nation once more, is no longer the world power that her empire and its navy assured. The Commonwealth of 54 members that has emerged comprises not a few independent countries where democracy and high ideals can hardly be said to flourish. Yet it survived, defying the image of a face-saving organisation for a declining world power that some sceptics saw it as.[27] Indeed it has grown and revitalised, as a network of nations who find common cause in an ever widening field.[28] Queen Elizabeth II justly sees it as a major legacy of her long reign.

The broadcast, which began at 7 pm,[29] was no sooner relayed – it went out 'live' from Government House after all, as the beam radio service behaved well[30] – than it became apparent that reaction to it would be excellent and that it was already being widely acclaimed around the world. The rest of the evening's celebrations could finally get under way. Unfortunately, there now occurred a hitch in the carefully planned proceedings. Ten minutes after the broadcast's completion, all the lights at Government House fused,[31] plunging the house in darkness and causing great difficulty for all those dressing for dinner. The hastily restored lights kept tripping,[32] and this put back an already crowded schedule by half an hour.

Dinner at Westbrooke was the first casualty. It did not exactly prove to be everyone's idea of 'dining quietly with Their Excellencies', as the Cape papers had described it beforehand. In an effort to dispel the atmosphere of stiff formality and dullness that hung like a miasma around the Governor-General's summer residence, Mrs Van Zyl had rounded up a party of young people. These included Sylvia Sandes, daughter of the Professor of Surgery at Groote Schuur Hospital and who was the resident, stand-by royal surgeon in Cape Town during the visit; Priscilla and Michael Waterson, Sidney Waterson's children; Dick Hennessy, youngest son of Sir Alfred and Lady Hennessy; and Winsome Wollaston, whose father was Secretary for Justice. Lex Sales, who was the handsome young Officer Commanding of the Dukes at the Castle, appeared after dinner to act as the Princess's military escort.[33]

They were a good-looking lot, and Winsome and Lex, who would shortly marry, made an unbelievably glamorous couple. 'Who is that beautiful woman?' the King was overheard to ask, almost wistfully, a little while later, looking down the table at Winsome.[34] Protocol had saddled him with Mrs Van Zyl, who had almost no small talk,[35] on his right, and Miss Ena van Coller from Cathcart (daughter of the Speaker of the House of Assembly) on his left. Others invited to dine included Sir De Villiers and Lady Graaff and Gerry and Moira Henderson – she a Duncan Baxter (of the well-known Cape philanthropic family), he Sir Evelyn Baring's secretary.

Also present were Dorothea and Colin Lang, a niece and nephew of Mrs Van Zyl's. The Governor-General and his wife were childless. Colin, by his own admission a callow, immature and extremely self-conscious 19-year-old medical student at Wits, struggling there 'on a shoestring', was unsurprisingly a figure quite unknown to the busy editors of the social pages of the South African newspapers of the day. His arrival on the Skymaster from Johannesburg had, therefore, triggered a flurry of press speculation, and it was momentarily believed that Lieutenant Mountbatten, as Prince Philip was then styled, had arrived from London for the party.[36]

After a prolonged and alcohol-free general chat in the drawing room to make up for the hastily revised timetable, the Van Zyls finally went out into the hall to receive the royal party, and the guests were formed up into two horseshoes around the room. Suddenly the doors were flung open and the major domo announced, 'Their Majesties'. Everyone bowed and curtsied deeply. They presented a dazzling family group; everyone, even Colin Lang, was overcome by the splendour and beauty of Queen Elizabeth and her daughters. 'One felt it must be a dream,' wrote Ena (Polly) van Coller effusively of that particular moment and the dinner party that followed: the royal ladies' jewels and ball gowns, the dining-room table 'with the King's silver, lovely glassware and flowers' – roses, orchids and gladioli (much favoured by Mrs Van Zyl) – all 'to take one's breath away'.[37]

This was the work of Brand van Zyl's gentleman's gentleman, the aptly named Mr Hurcombe, whose valeting skills apparently ran to doing the flowers ('Hurcombe's flowers *simply* lovely,' as Lady Harlech noted, approvingly, on arrival[38]). He had gone out to South Africa with the Harlechs and remained there, eventually passed on as a good turn to the Van Zyls. As the centrepiece of all this, however, stood Mrs Van Zyl's *pièce de résistance* – a terrible-looking birthday cake, most unwisely 'ordered from a Cape Town confectionery',[39] as she proudly told the press, and upon whose 'glassy' surface (supposed, in a vague allusion to the well-known ballet, to represent a lake) swam an arch-looking white swan, pulling an open nautilus shell that contained a golden key. It was all in pink icing.

As a further touch, each guest had received a spray of artificial flowers with their place card. The King swiftly passed his on to Ena ('here's something for you') and he gamely kept the conversational ball rolling throughout dinner, often talking across and down the table to draw in the Queen, Smuts and the Princesses,[40] while Mrs Van Zyl ('Aunt Marie' as opposed to 'Uncle Manny' to Colin and Dorothea) was observed by her nephew 'trying hard to elicit a smile out of the King'.[41]

Further down the table, Colin was scarcely doing much better with the beautiful, blue-eyed and auburn-haired Princess Margaret, next to whom his aunt had ambitiously placed him. Keen on classical music, but shy and awkward and ill at ease in his new evening tails and boiled shirtfront, and with the additional drawback of a serious nick in his chin – self-inflicted while shaving beforehand – he tried telling her of the wonderful advances Dr (later Sir) Malcolm Sargent had achieved since the war, transforming the standard of symphonic music in Johannesburg and Pretoria. 'That all sounds rather heavy going,' replied the 16-year-old, party-loving Princess, then already experiencing the early throes of love for her father's good-looking Equerry, 16 years her senior.[42]

After this, the party set out back to Government House, stopping on De Waal Drive, the scenic route into Cape Town along the lower slopes of Table Mountain, where a specially erected dais enabled them to watch the last, great fireworks displays of the tour. These were let off from the Eastern Mole of the docks. The quays of the Duncan Dock had been all strung about with coloured fairy lights which reflected prettily in its calm waters.

Cape Town was all lit up again; 25 000 light bulbs outlined its lovely buildings, and many of these were floodlit too. Kingsway was a 'river of light' and Table Mountain's floodlighting had been greatly improved since the first part of the tour. Thousands of Capetonians poured into the city and its docks on that hot, still April night. Still others crowded vantage points on De Waal Drive and Signal Hill to watch the spectacle, which had, as its climax, tableaux of vast portraits of the King and Queen and Princesses outlined in blazing gunpowder.[43]

The scale of the display was immense, but it had been delayed too, for the faulty electricity board at Government House had had a domino effect on the timetable, and not only for the royals and their invited guests. Many ordinary citizens were to find that they had missed the last bus and had to walk home. In the end Mrs Van Zyl, tightly permed and equally tightly encased in duchesse satin, was only able to start receiving at just before 10 o'clock. As the guests had been informally bidden by word of mouth for 9 pm 'to avoid crowding in the cloakrooms', the marquees that flanked the covered way leading from the gates on Government Avenue – two designated as cloakrooms, one as a 'sitting-out lounge' and one for the buffet supper to be served later – were by then already packed with guests who had been unable to get a drink for an hour.

Having at last greeted their host and hostess – 'shaken hands with Their Excellencies', as it was put at the time – the expectant and by now thoroughly keyed-up throng passed on and into the house. This was still substantially the Regency Government House that Lord Charles Somerset had created out of the old Dutch Tuynhuis 130 years before, his ballroom having been extended and redecorated later for the arrival of Sir Harry Smith in 1848.[44] As Lascelles noted, it contained some fine rooms, among them the beautiful drawing room, normally hung with oils of past governors, where the Royal Family were now ensconced, 'smoking and drinking'.[45] Somewhat awkwardly, they were in full view of the young guests as they filed through the interleading anteroom (the old breakfast room of Regency era), which connected eastwards to the white and gold ballroom through pairs of great double doors. As in the days then still fondly recalled in historical novels, these had been taken off their hinges in anticipation of the crush.

And what a crush it was. Well over 500 attended (Captain Ritchie says 600 in the Tour Diary)[46] – many guests regarded as rather random choices by the fashionable Cape who, their offspring now invitationless, may, on this evening, have regretted not making themselves more civil to Mrs Brand van Zyl. In a clumsy attempt to cope with the numbers, the Governor-General's wife had had issued to all the men either a red or blue ribbon, and an exceedingly 'common-looking' robot device, as more than one shocked guest recalled,[47] displayed these alternate colours in lights, indicating who could dance and who could not.

At least none of those invited had heeded the instruction put out by the King and Queen that they did not want any guests to go to unnecessary expense on their clothes.[48] Clothes rationing, such as it was in South Africa, had ended, more or less, within a year or two of the war, and other more stringently rationed items were declared off the ration by Hofmeyr in Parliament during the tour.[49] The young women all wore new or certainly their best evening dresses in white or pastel shades. June, the new Mrs Reggie Hands, for example, wore her beautiful two-week-old wedding dress, designed and slightly altered according to plan by Rejeane, then one of the smart dressmakers who had a shop in Cape Town.[50] It was noticed on this evening that the ugly, upswept hairstyles of the war years had been abandoned; almost all the young women now copied the Princesses, who wore their hair neatly arranged, softly framing their faces with curls at the sides and back. And, despite black tie being an option, all the men wore white tie or mess dress.

Meanwhile, after dropping her parents and sister off, Princess Elizabeth had been driven down to the City Hall where a great, second-tier civic ball, open to public subscription, was in progress. Again, the crowd was enormous: 3 000 people thronged the floor, bays, corridors outside and

In a Hartnell gown, Princess Elizabeth arrives for her 21st-birthday ball.

NATIONAL LIBRARY OF SOUTH AFRICA

The crowded 21st-birthday ball at Government House. Princess Elizabeth dances with
Sir De Villiers Graaff, Princess Margaret with Arthur Falconer. Lucia Vintcent
stands just beyond.

IAN SHAPIRO COLLECTION

the seats in the gallery.[51] Around 10 pm the word went round, *She's Arriving*, and the crush on the floor became insupportable. Suddenly the Princess appeared in the mayor's box, her beautiful fur cape flung back from her shoulders to reveal a magnificent Hartnell evening gown of white tulle lightly sprinkled with paillettes and sequins arranged in diamond-shaped patterns to catch every movement of light. Mayor Abe Bloomberg spoke, saying what was surely the truth: that Cape Town must that night be the envy of every town, village and hamlet in the British Empire.

He then presented the Princess with a golden key to the City, 'as a token of Cape Town's enduring loyalty, and the freedom to the hearts of all Capetonians which [she] had already captured'. It was felicitously put and everyone cheered. Indeed, as the *Cape Times* noted, the guests were so carried away by the radiant picture the Princess presented, standing in the box above them, that the cheering was almost continuous and frequently interrupted the mayor's speech.[52]

Everyone sang 'For She's a Jolly Good Fellow' and then Vic Davis's band – the best in Cape Town, its members all famously good-looking, and which played regularly at Kelvin Grove and The Waldorf[53] – immediately struck up that year's very popular number, 'Open the Door, Richard'. The Princess laughed delightedly. However, this now presented something of a nightmare for Major General Palmer, the Commissioner of Police, for it was essential that she should be seen to have a dance on the packed floor. She took the crowd pressing forward for a closer view 'in good part', it was noted, but in the end, 'his charge' as *The Cape Argus* put it, and her partner, Lieutenant Commander MG McLeod of HMS *Nigeria*, only briefly managed to dance around the outskirts of the floor, surrounded, as she wrote afterwards, 'by 4 000 [sic] people all trying to wish me many happy returns of the day',[54] after which they both escaped upstairs, counting themselves lucky that they had not been crushed to death.[55] There followed a balcony appearance looking down on the Grand Parade, now packed with citizens who had moved on there after the fireworks in the hope of seeing her.

And so it was back to Government House. Regrouping with her parents and General Smuts, they processed through the crowded ballroom, the guests parting like the Red Sea, bowing and curtsying as they passed – like a fairy tale come true, said *The Cape Argus*[56] – and on up the narrow stairs (not kind to crinolines) to the orchestra balcony. There stood the Van Zyls, Jan Hofmeyr, Minister in Attendance, and his old mother – this latter's presence there a move on the part of Smuts in an attempt to mollify the old battle-axe after the unfortunate contretemps that we witnessed at the end of the State Banquet in Pretoria a week before (see page 197). As he should have well known by now, such a gesture would avail him nothing. He was not forgiven. Her response to his greeting, delivered evenly and colloquially, given the occasion, with the charming Malmesbury bray that invested his speech, '*Ja, naand, mevrou Hofmeyr*' (Ah yes, good evening, Mrs Hofmeyr), was frosty, and her smile positively glacial.[57]

Ignoring this iceberg of disapproval towering to his left, it was now Smuts's duty and pleasure to present the Union's gift to the Princess – 21 flawless diamonds of modern cut, each with 52 facets, to maximise their brilliance, and all of top colour 'D'. She would ever afterwards refer to them as 'my best diamonds'.

Alas, the night had not cooled down one bit. It was now a stultifyingly hot, airless Cape autumn evening. Though all the doors onto the veranda were open, the heat in that overcrowded ballroom was intense;[58] up in the gallery, where there was no ventilation, it must have been intolerable. It was the end of a long and tiring day. This, it is true, was her party, but it was unimaginatively planned and here she was now, surrounded by over-eager strangers, thousands of miles away from the man she loved.

Keen to be seen to do the right thing, Mrs Van Zyl had engaged a cobbled-together band of ex-servicemen (the city's two best dance bands had been secured months before by Abe Bloomberg for the City Hall). And although the crystal chandeliers installed by Princess Alice 20 years before did indeed sparkle down on the dresses as the dancing commenced below – Princess Elizabeth opening with Sir De Villiers Graaff, and Princess Margaret with Arthur Falconer – by now the flowers alighted on by her hostess and specially grown by the Parks and Gardens Department (red zinnias and golden chrysanthemums to go with Mr Terry's new curtains and not looking at all like Fairyland, whatever *The Cape Argus* later said) and arranged by Helen Addison, Lady Duncan's former Lady-in-Waiting,[59] were beginning to smell musty and wilt in the heat.

Also beginning to wilt was the principal guest, who had been suffering from a headache since the afternoon;[60] more than one of those present felt she struggled to convey the enthusiasm that such a ball in her honour might have produced.[61] Despite the occasion and the red-white-and-gold metropolitan court setting, here faintly reproduced in the colonies, the long-anticipated party was ominously beginning to exhibit the ingredients of being a little bit of a flop.[62]

Standing nearby the dancing Princesses, in her first evening dress hastily run up by her mother's dressmaker out of 'good family lace', but with the addition of two precautionary, sequined straps which were now cutting cruelly into her shoulders, was a very young Lucia Vintcent, a last-minute invitee and who we first encountered with her family on De Waal Drive watching HMS *Vanguard* enter Table Bay (see pp 7–8). Suddenly feeling like a wallflower, she was determinedly persuading herself, as she surveyed the glittering scene around her, that adult life might, after all, have a lot to offer; this was, it had to be said, a long way, she reasoned to herself, from her hometown of Mossel Bay.

Just behind her, a beady 'very Afrikaans-looking' girl off Mrs Van Zyl's guest list, was eyeing her and her mother's dressmaker's ill-advised resourcefulness with her needle contemptuously, and remarked loudly: '*O Eina! Daardie meisie se skouers raak seer!*' (O! Ouch! that girl's shoulders are getting sore!). This proved the cold spoon in the soufflé as far as Lucia was concerned; she was brought down to earth with a bump.[63] Others present that night, apparently, were beginning to feel a similar, gnawing, deflating sensation, despite themselves, as the evening wore on.

Nothing seemed to go entirely smoothly. According to Lucia Bolus, her good-looking, rugby-playing brother Nellis, a dazzling lock-forward but 'a hopeless dancer' with size-13 feet, not only trod on the royal toes but also succeeded in dancing Princess Elizabeth into the fender in front of the ballroom chimneypiece.[64] Deborah Duncan recalls the curiously over-braided and -frogged mess dress of Ian Smith's future foreign minister, PK van der Byl, causing Townsend, the Equerry on duty, to cancel his preassigned dance with the Heiress Apparent with an icy 'Improperly dressed. No 6 Please!'[65] And just before he was due to dance with Princess Margaret, Colin Lang developed an 'intestinal hurry' which compelled him to hastily seek a lavatory in the marquee area. It was a quick Viennese waltz, and although it was accomplished with no toe-treading, his second conversational gambit – was she not overawed by the great portraits of her ancestors staring down on them? – was no more successful than his first at dinner. 'Not a bit,' answered the Princess, shortly, and her ordeal (as he related it, years later) 'was swiftly over'.[66]

True to form, and by now only too aware of the limitations of their gubernatorial representatives, Queen Elizabeth, magnificent and coruscating in her sequined tulle and lace crinoline, and her tiara and necklace of rubies and diamonds, moved tirelessly among the young guests, typically giving the impression that this was the party she had waited all her life to attend.[67]

According to Morrah, the Princess saw her parents off to bed at midnight, and then danced 'on into the small hours'. This, at any event, was the official, recorded, version.[68] Others recall Mrs Van Zyl stopping the band shortly after 1 am, and the last Colin and Dorothea saw of the royal sisters was the two of them sitting on the staircase, giggling, while removing their dancing slippers to relieve their sore, bruised feet. Even the Household were in bed by 2 am.[69]

CHAPTER II

꘡꘡꘡

Gone with the Southeaster

Cape Town, 24 April 1947

Thursday 24 April was the day of departure. The preceding five days, since the White Train had, after an epic journey of 6 942 miles (11 172 kilometres), finally halted for the last time back on the Foreshore, been a whirl of activity – 'unprecedented gaiety' as the *Cape Times* social editor put it happily, 'on all of which glorious Cape autumn weather had smiled'. Again, it had held. There had been two royal balls, a garden party at Leeuwenhof, the Administrator's residence, a royal symphony concert in the City Hall, the great military parade at Youngsfield, and innumerable official and private cocktail parties. 'Cape Town has never been richer in distinguished visitors,' purred Ann Page, 'for, besides South African people of importance, every list of guests included names which would have been found in the impressive lists of pre-war Mayfair parties'.[1]

There had been matins at the Cathedral and also tea at the Castle, a trip up Table Mountain – 'the finest view in the world', said Lascelles, who, along with the royal party, had enjoyed a walk followed by the obligatory tea and scones in the pretty tearoom on the top with the chairman of the Cableway Company, Sir Alfred Hennessy, and Lady Hennessy.[2] Smuts, who loved the mountain, had climbed it to join them up there. There had also been a great South African Girl Guide Rally on St George's Day at

On top of Table Mountain. From left: Jan Hofmeyr, the King, Smuts, the Queen.
In the background is Sir Alfred Hennessy, chairman of the Cableway Company.

NATIONAL LIBRARY OF SOUTH AFRICA

the Rosebank Showgrounds (Princess Elizabeth was the Chief Ranger of the British Commonwealth), a private shopping expedition in Adderley Street and a private visit to Vergelegen (tea and scones again), pronounced 'a dream of beauty' by the Queen (see Chapter 9).

There had been other less social events. The countrywide heads of all the SAWAS divisions had been bidden 'to wait upon Her Majesty' at Government House (Lucy Bean seems to have been particularly keen on employing this courtly phrase with its Arthurian ring). They were led in by their National Secretary, the formidable Mrs Edith O'Connor,[3] and were thanked, over tea and scones, yet again, for their contribution to the war effort. The Queen told them that before they had left England she and the King had received countless letters from soldiers, sailors and their wives, asking that their thanks be passed on to South Africans for the kindness shown to them in wartime transit in South Africa.[4] This was the swan song of the SAWAS, which wrapped up its impressive wartime and post-war work that week.

At the King's request, there was a gathering in the Queen's Hall outside

The great Girl Guide and Boy Scouts Rally at the Rosebank Showgrounds.
From left: Mrs Lizzie MacNeillie, Chief Commissioner of the Girl Guides in the Union,
Princess Elizabeth, Chief Ranger of the British Empire, Lady Margaret Egerton (behind)
and Princess Margaret.

SCOUT HERITAGE CENTRE, SCOUTS SOUTH AFRICA

the Senate Chamber to meet members of both Houses of Parliament who had so far not been presented. This was especially to accommodate the many Nationalist politicians who, with their wives, now apparently regretted boycotting events in the early days of the tour and subsequently, as its success had ballooned across the land, had bombarded the Governor-General's office for invitations during the five-day return stay in Cape Town.[5]

There had been a late-afternoon parade of 9 000 ex-servicemen on the Grand Parade, after which the King had shaken hands with and spoken personally to 40 soldiers blinded during the war who stood quietly by the saluting platform. And on 22 April, while the King presided over a meeting of the Executive Council, Queen Elizabeth had received an honorary degree of Doctor of Law from the University of Cape Town to a standing ovation inside the Jameson Hall and lusty cheers from what seemed the entire student body as she walked down the famous, heroic flight of steps outside it.

During those days, as it dawned on organisations throughout southern

The King with his South African prime minister and Cabinet after a meeting
of the Executive Council, 22 April, 1947.

At the University of Cape Town, following the conferring of an honorary degree of
Doctor of Law on Queen Elizabeth. From left: Prof T Le Roux (Vice Chancellor), Queen
Elizabeth, Dr TB Davie, Mrs Le Roux, Jan Smuts (Chancellor).

Africa that time was running out, Loyal Messages had been pouring in. Even a selection of the organisations and bodies listed in the Royal Archives throws a spotlight on the energies and endeavours of that era. There was one from the Nyasaland African Congress, and others from the Pretoria Indian Association, the Coloured Community of Swaziland, the Pretoria Islamic Society, the Nyasa Council of Women, the London Missionary Society (Lobotsu), the Caledonian Society of Southern Rhodesia, the Victoria League (OFS and Basutoland Branch), and a Prayer from the Hebrew Congregation of the Great Synagogue. More Loyal Messages came from the Christelike Vrouevereniging, the Gazaland Farmers Association, the Chipinga Women's Institute, the Chiefs and African People of the Melsetter District, the Citizens of the Strand, the Association of the Law Societies of the Union of South Africa, the Que Que Farmers Association, the Municipality of De Wetsdorp, Orange Free State, the Mayor and Councillors of Fish Hoek and many others. All these received gratifying acknowledgements.[6]

Meanwhile, *Vanguard* was being packed to the gunnels with acquisitions not to be sent back to England on one of the Vickers Viking aircraft used to convey the Royal Family on long distances in the subcontinent. Safely stowed on board after the farewell luncheon were the Union's official gifts: for the King, the 399 specially cut diamonds, a drop diamond and 230 rose diamonds, which, with the nine rubies he was to supply, were to be made up by Garrard, the Crown Jewellers, into his Garter star. They were all contained in a gold casket with a diamond springbok on its lid.

For the Queen, there was a solid gold tea service in a George II melonised style, plus the large 8.55-carat solitaire marquise diamond presented to her by the Union;[7] this was in addition to the diamond presented to her by Sir Ernest Oppenheimer in Kimberley. At the visit to the sorting room in Kimberley, De Beers had only planned to present diamonds to the two Princesses. A story did the rounds that Princess Margaret innocently asked, 'But what about Mummy's?', and Sir Ernest had had to smartly dip into his private collection for something suitable for Queen Elizabeth. Unlikely as it sounded, it was confirmed years later as 'a rather embarrassing incident' by the nonagenarian Queen Mother herself, who wore the diamond as a ring when she entertained Nicholas Oppenheimer to lunch at Clarence House.[8]

The sorting room at De Beers, Kimberley. From left to right: Bridget Oppenheimer talks to the King, Queen Elizabeth to Mary Oppenheimer, Princess Margaret to Mayor Orr, Sir Ernest to Princess Elizabeth. Behind them are Harry Oppenheimer and Sir Alan Lascelles.

COURTESY OF DE BEERS CONSOLIDATED MINES

For Princess Elizabeth, there was the Union's 21st-birthday present of 21 graduated diamonds plus their settings for a necklace, the Namaqualand diamonds presented by the SAR&H when she opened the Graving Dock at East London, the perfect 6½-carat brilliant-cut pure blue-white diamond from De Beers, and the enchanting diamond brooch in the shape of a flame lily subscribed to by all the schoolchildren of Rhodesia. The *Gloriosa superba* was the colony's national flower, and blooms had been repeatedly sent to Messrs A Sidersky, jewellers in Johannesburg, who made up the brooch. '*Very* beautiful ... which has delighted me very much,' as she put it to her royal grandmother.[9] And for Princess Margaret, there were 19 graduated pure white diamonds for setting into a bracelet, along with the 4½-carat blue-white from De Beers.

There were 540 stones in all, worth £200 000. 'Papa, Mummy and

Margaret were all given diamonds on the last day, so we shall all be very grand when we come back,' wrote Princess Elizabeth to Queen Mary, who had always had an eye for beautiful jewellery. 'I think there are no more beautiful diamonds left in South Africa.'[10] Everything was carefully and hurriedly sealed up by Lascelles and Van der Poel for the voyage.[11] And this, it should be noted, was not the most valuable part of the cargo; £15 million worth of gold bullion had been loaded, to be transported thus as part of the gold loan from South Africa to Britain.[12] Naturally, no publicity was attached to this.

There was more cargo besides. There was the art chosen by the Queen for her collection – an Irma Stern of dahlias, 'Mouille Point' by Terence McCaw and 'Basutos on a Hilltop' by Nerine Desmond. The selection was held to be a triumph for modernists among South African artists. There were other offerings too, some less solicited than others: a SAWAS recipe book, sold for war funds, from its Cape Town branch; a collection of Afrikaans *liedjies*; a copy of Miss Margaret Beth Cuthbertson's *Rhodesian Rambles*; *A History of the De Wet Family* ('which might interest Their Majesties on the eve of their departure'); 'Princess Elizabeth Waltz' by Ralph Trewhela (composer of 'So Long, Sarie'), accompanied by a newspaper cutting showing Mrs Trewhela and their children, Bev and Paul; two of a Miss Fisk's watercolours of the Keimans River and the Ebb and Flow;[13] and a Mr Groenewald's home-made riding crop for the King, which evidently had a copper component ('Only use Brasso for polishing,' advised Mr Groenewald helpfully[14]). There was also a knitted dress for the Heiress Presumptive, from the Women of the South African Police; the woman who had made it presented it to her on the station platform at Beaufort West.[15]

There were the ostrich feathers from Mr and Mrs Basie Meyer, whose farm near Oudtshoorn they had visited, and an ostrich cape and fan for Princess Elizabeth's 21st birthday from the ostrich farmers of Oudtshoorn. Considering the lukewarm ('undemonstrative' is how the Tour Diary puts it) reception given by the fiercely Nationalist town,[16] it is no surprise to discover that this was the result of a private initiative of Mr Max Rose, a Jewish pioneer of the ostrich industry, who had been presented during the visit there.[17] There were 16 silk scarves chosen from a selection brought by request by Stuttafords to Government House and which were to be given away as presents, a model of an ox-wagon from an *oudstryder*, records made of African choirs singing '*Nkosi Sikelel' iAfrika*', and countless spears and trinkets from African chiefs. The royal ladies had all purchased nylon stockings, then still rationed in England, and all three had had copies made of Jean Lawrence's cork-soled platform shoes, much admired on the day of arrival, and which had duly been delivered to Government House in velvet-covered shoe boxes.[18]

Foodstuffs for a rationed England from the land of plenty were crammed into every corner of the hold: 200 cases of sweets for the sugar-deprived children of Britain collected by the patriotic ladies of the South African Victoria League; presents of food ordered by Queen Elizabeth as gifts for family and friends (the order had been quadrupled by CPO Pinfold of the *Vanguard*, on Her Majesty's command, at the last minute); glacé fruit ordered for Queen Mary;[19] *obeletjies* from Mrs Annie Roux of Paarl (the King had said he liked them when they were served at tea there); pots of the sweet-tart Cape gooseberry jam (Mrs AH Short's homemade variety had been a great hit during the Natal National Park weekend, especially with Princess Margaret) and a case of early oranges sent by the Mayor of Rustenburg in the Transvaal.

The Royal Household had similarly stocked up at the urgent entreaties of their families back in England; Lascelles, for instance, returned with 12 pairs of 'slap-up' English socks, silk dress lengths and nylon stockings for his wife and daughters, four pairs of sheets, 48 pounds of marmalade (cost: 1 guinea), guava jelly, six cases of wine, two cases of sherry, two hams, one bag of rice, a cheese from the Bishop of Pretoria, a large tin of salad oil, a quantity of butter, etc.[20]

The idea, repeated again and again in speeches during the tour, of mutual, friendly assistance between Commonwealth countries had not gone unheeded, nor had the sufferings of the British people during the worst winter in living memory. In addition to the parcels of woollen comforts, the South African public now came forward handsomely with a magnificent cheque for £300 000 for flood relief for the many British people rendered homeless as the tremendous snowfalls of the winter of 1947 began to thaw.[21]

The money raised as a 21st-birthday gift to Princess Elizabeth was achieved as follows: a whopping £140 000 from Johannesburg (where Mr and Mrs Gray, the mayor and mayoress, had personally been among those shaking boxes on street corners; the amount was diplomatically stated to have been raised on behalf of all the people of the Transvaal); £33 000 from Cape Town (where students from UCT had gone among the traffic with their collection boxes); £2 400 from Germiston; £2 000 from Potchefstroom; £1 140 from Queenstown; £1 452 from East Griqualand; £1 000 each from Boksburg and Vereeniging; £500 from Barkley East; and so on. Perhaps tactfully, the *Cape Times* draws a veil over the sums collected in Pietersburg and Oudtshoorn. And East London's contribution of £1 000, it should be noted, was only able to be hastily sanctioned after some 'unpleasantness' caused by Meneer De Lange – an atypical but very strident Nationalist city councillor (and later mayor) who strenuously objected to such a gesture – had been skilfully *dealt with*, doubtless amid many pursed lips and meaningful looks exchanged within the council chamber.[22]

Vanguard also carried a variety of plants that the royal gardeners had seen, admired and asked for. Plants noticed at Natal National Park, including bulbs of the Berg lily, were sent by Colonel Shearer from Pietermaritzburg, which for years boasted the country's best nurseries. Like all such gifts, these were addressed 'HMS *Vanguard*, Duncan Dock, Cape Town', with the extra cachet now contained in the handwritten label attached, as per instructions: 'Send to the Head Gardener, Sandringham, Norfolk.' There were also cuttings sent by Davis, the head gardener at Government House, Salisbury;[23] nerine bulbs from Mrs Selma van Rensberg of Kroonstad (admired by Queen Elizabeth, this gift was rewarded at a future date with tickets for the Chelsea Flower Show);[24] seeds of granadilla[25] and *spanspek* (cantaloupe), both of which had been enjoyed on the tour, the latter eaten iced with Van der Hum. There was the brown paper bag of acorns collected from the oak growing at Vergelegen (see Chapter 9). There was additionally, for the Queen, a basket of autumn flowers together with a loyal note, written in pencil, that the flower sellers, then as now a feature of Adderley Street in Cape Town, had requested permission to present.[26]

The farewell State Luncheon at the City Hall began at 12.45. There were 480 guests and everyone agreed it was much better organised than the State Banquet held there on the night of their arrival.[27] The proceedings started 15 minutes late, something startling in an age where official and certainly royal events ran on time and like clockwork. Up in the gallery, Major Dunn of the *Vanguard*, who had sportingly stepped in at the last minute owing to the indisposition of the conductor, kept the Cape Town Municipal Orchestra hard at it with their repertoire.

Word soon got about as to what had happened. The royal party had arrived as scheduled. There, waiting near the door, by arrangement, was Dr Malan and his wife. The couple and the Royal Family had at once repaired to the mayor's parlour and closed the door behind them. After ten minutes, to everyone's amazement, the King himself appeared at the doorway and asked for a tray of sherry to be sent in. Abe Bloomberg personally carried this in and, together with the prime minister, joined the party for another five minutes. Clearly, it was believed, the courtiers had orchestrated this last-minute rapprochement. As the word got round at the banquet, the City Hall buzzed with happy conjecture. Had the Royal Family broken the ice and succeeded in charming the republican Malans too?

Of course, this was too much to ask. It later transpired that the King had sent Malan a personal message, asking to see him just once.[28] Charming the Malans at this stage would have been a tall order; however, as the King intended, it would bear some fruit in later years. Afterwards Malan was firm that the conversation was 'informal and friendly. As was only right, nothing of any political meaning was discussed.'[29] And he was later to castigate the press for implying that it was.

After this the State Luncheon got under way. Smuts spoke first, saying, as he clearly believed, that 'never in the history of this, your South African Dominion, has there been such wave of personal and national emotion as your visit has stirred amongst us'. Yet again underlining the spirit of Commonwealth friendship, he sent South Africa's greetings to the British people and sympathy in their present trials, as well as faith in their victory 'in peace as they have won it in the war'.[30]

In his reply, the King said that the curtain was being rung down on a visit almost unique in the history of the British Commonwealth but which

The farewell State Luncheon: 'I feel as if we are leaving behind friends
we have known all our lives.'
TRANSNET HERITAGE LIBRARY PHOTO COLLECTION

he hoped would be less unusual in the future. Clearly he was thinking of
future, similar tours planned to Australia, New Zealand, India, Ceylon,
and so on, to thank them for their loyalty in the war. Alas, none of these
was meant to be. He went on to mention the frank and sincere friendliness of South Africa's peoples who had welcomed them, the beauty of
the land, and 'the evidence of progress and the unlimited possibilities
for the future'. This is exactly what a post-war audience wanted to hear.
'Your people,' he went on, 'pride themselves on their European stock from
which they are descended,' carefully avoiding singling out either race of
the squabbling (white) community, and adding, 'they are imbued with the
high principles and standards which they have inherited from their ancestors.' Then came the valedictory sentence, possibly suggested by Lord
Harlech, the former High Commissioner, via his wife,[31] which liberals and
non-whites alike heard with some hope: 'May South Africa advance from
strength to strength in justice and righteousness and in happiness to all
its peoples.'

Then the Queen rose to make an impromptu speech. She was a better speaker than the King, but was careful not to upstage him on such occasions. Limiting herself to her particular, feminine sphere, it was a return to the tenor of her wartime speeches: 'When I have been fortunate enough to go into your homes I have been truly happy to feel the good and lasting influence of family life, with its strong religious background in which your young people grow up. That surely is the foundation of all happiness and all progress.'

Then switching into Afrikaans, with a pronunciation she had mastered with some proficiency, she said: '*U het ons hier verwelkom as vriende en U het ons U harte gegee* [You welcomed us here as friends and you gave us your hearts]. For all that I say thank you, and God bless you all. Good-bye.' And then she added '*Totsiens*' (meaning, literally, till we meet again). It was an expression Queen Elizabeth liked and would use all her life.

Almost all present were moved; everyone, thought Princess Elizabeth, had a big lump in their throat[32] and the crowds on the Grand Parade and down Adderley Street, to whom these speeches had been relayed on a loudspeaker system, cheered. As the party left the table, the guests sang for the last time the song which was at once a great accolade and, in that era, a great leveller, 'For They Are Jolly Good Fellows'. There was a final appearance on the balcony of the City Hall.

There were tears in the Queen's eyes as she left the building. 'I feel as if we were leaving behind friends we have known all our lives,' she said, with the consummate skill she had for saying just the right thing at the right time; 'I do hope we will be able to come back again.'[33] It was certainly exactly what Cape Town and, indeed, all English-speaking South Africa wanted to hear. At this date it is likely that many other South Africans wanted to hear this too.

There were even greater crowds (100 000 said the *Cape Times*) to see them off than there had been to welcome them, as they drove down Adderley Street and Kingsway to the docks. Now, however, it was nearly autumn. One of the last black southeasters of the waning summer blew a pall of cloud over the mountain; it was an overcast, dull day with a definite chill in the air. All the wives of officials gathered for the last time on the royal pavilion to say goodbye wore fox furs with their tweeds or woollen winter suits. As he had done during the last days in Cape Town, the King was again seen to have discarded his tropical whites and was wearing his winter naval uniform.

After they had said their goodbyes and thank-yous ('Goodbye and thanks awfully for everything; I have so enjoyed it,' Princess Elizabeth was heard to say to Mrs Van Zyl; to the Lawrences the Queen said, 'I do wish we had seen more of you,' the King adding, 'I hope you will come and visit us soon'),[34] the party turned and faced the guard of honour of the Duke of Edinburgh's Own Rifles, one of the crack old Cape regiments. The guard presented arms and the Royal Family heard 'Die Stem' played together with 'God Save the King' for the last time. While the King inspected them a massed choir of 480 – drawn from all races – sang the moving old Scotch song 'Will Ye No' Come Back Again?' accompanied by the bands of the South African Permanent Force. In that age of community singing, almost everyone in the crowd would have been familiar with the words and those of the melodies that followed, all learnt at their mothers' knee or around the family piano or at school. As intended, they joined in.

Meanwhile the Queen walked over to say a final word of thanks to Major General RJ Palmer, Commissioner of the South African Police, who had accompanied them on the White Train (and who had personally vetted every horse provided at each stop for the Princesses to ride), together with Major Cilliers, the Officer Commanding of the Railway Police, for the manner in which both forces had carried out their duties during the tour. Mrs Van Zyl sank and rose again in her final curtsies.

Then at 4 pm, the traditional departure time of the weekly mailboat service run by the Union-Castle Line between South Africa and England, up the gangway went the King, followed by the Queen and the two Princesses, the bosuns piping them on board.

The Royal Standard broke from the masthead. The South African Artillery fired a 21-gun salute from Signal Hill; the Royal Marine Guard on board were inspected to another Scotch favourite, 'The Skye Boat Song', now played by the Marine Band, while the crowd sang along:

> Carry the lad that's born to be King
> Over the sea to Skye ...

Up the gangway at 4 pm, the traditional departure time of the Union-Castle mail boats.
Mrs Van Zyl, in the foreground, makes a final curtsy.

TRANSNET HERITAGE LIBRARY PHOTO COLLECTION

Everyone was crying.[35] At 4.20 the gangway was removed and the last hawsers slipped. Then, with the Royal Standard fluttering from the masthead in the brisk prevailing trade wind, the flag of the Lord High Admiral of England flying proudly from the main mast and the Union Jack and the White Ensign at the stern, the great battleship, appearing a darker grey now under the lowering skies, was eased from the quayside by two flag-bedecked tugs, who pointed her bows out towards the open seas. Homeward bound! High above, on the balcony made from one of the gun turrets, the Royal Family appeared and waved a final farewell. The bands and choir, with the crowds joining in, burst into 'Land of Hope and Glory'; overhead, a formation of aircraft of the SAAF commanded by Colonel Moll dipped their wing tips in a final salute.

With that, the police cordon holding back the crowds was broken and a mass of humanity surged forward to the quay edge to cheer and wave goodbye. There was more singing – 'Sarie Marais', 'God Be With You Till We Meet Again', 'There'll Always Be an England'. Finally, as the battleship passed through the harbour entrance came the last of the haunting Scotch tunes – 'Auld Lang Syne'.

> Should auld acquaintance be forgot, and never brought to mind?
> Should auld acquaintance be forgot, and auld lang syne?

The three frigates of the fledging South African Naval Forces – HMSA Ships *Good Hope*, *Natal* and *Transvaal* – took up the escort out into the notorious Cape rollers, which, true to form, the southeaster had whipped up into angry, foam-topped waves, until they were joined, at 5 pm, by HM Ships *Nigeria*, *Nereide* and *Actaeon* of the South Atlantic Station. After two hours of duty, the South African vessels turned around and steamed past *Vanguard*, cheering ship as they came down the starboard side, with the King saluting from the deck, and headed for home. In the gathering dusk, a message was flashed across to them from their sovereign, thanking them for their escort and ordering them to splice the mainbrace. By then the Queen had already gone below, along with the exhausted courtiers; even the apparently tireless Sir Alan Lascelles had retired to his cabin with a bowl of hot Bovril to sleep for 14 hours. Several albatrosses were observed to be following the battleship.[36]

The royal tour of South Africa was over.

Had it been a success? On the face of it, it had been a tremendous success. Lascelles believed it had, writing to Queen Mary from the Victoria Falls Hotel and describing it 'as an outstanding success'. What it has done, he continued, 'is to bring home to the people of South Africa that monarchy, as an institution, and the Royal Family, as individuals, mean a very great deal to them'.[37]

Smuts and his party certainly believed it had, injecting a 'sweeter note into public life' but also in the private lives of the South African people who had seen, however imperfectly, a vision of unity for the first time.[38] The prime minister's reply of early June to the King to thank him for his 'beautiful letter [of thanks]' reads, after he had skilfully exonerated himself for not providing the restful holiday originally promised, almost like a love letter:

The effect of the Visit on South Africa has been unbelievably wonderful. Every day I see this in all directions ... The Crown, not as a
distant abstraction, but as a living, human reality. I cannot conceive
any greater service you could have rendered South Africa than giving
her this intimate opportunity to see what the King and the Royal
Family really are and mean to us. I therefore bless this strenuous
time which has given South Africa such a real insight into the heart
of our Commonwealth system.[39]

Both the British press and the English-language South African press
thought so too. 'No doubt that the Royal Visit, just as it did in Canada,
will serve to cement bonds between the Union and Great Britain at a
crucial period in world affairs,' said *The Daily Representative*.[40] The more
conservative papers firmly upheld their view, expressed at the outset,
that the royal tour would do much to offset the unfriendly ānd dis-
torted publicity that South Africa had received during the past months,
and at the same time make known to the English-speaking world the
attractions this country possessed in such rich abundance.[41] Many now
returned to this theme in their summing-up, creating a false equation
in which there were equal elements of pique and naivety: if the Royal
Family had so obviously liked us, why should the rest of the world not
do so too?[42]

The crowds had been astonishing. Even the dyspeptic Lascelles, 'over-
inured to shouting in streets and kindred emotional manifestations', as he
put it to Evelyn Baring, and which he was inclined to undervalue, had been
impressed 'by the welcome Their Majesties had received everywhere in
South Africa',[43] and felt a bit exhilarated by the tremendous success of the
whole thing.[44] It expressed, he believed, a good deal more than the ordinary excitement generated 'by the circus that had come to town   what
one might call,' as he austerely put it, 'the headline excitement aroused by
a visit from Charlie Chaplin or any other merely popular figure.'

The feared boycotts by the provincial Indian congresses and the ANC
had collapsed, and there had been tremendous and surely reassuring
evidence of black loyalty not only in the country areas but also in the
townships and cities.

As for the Afrikaners – the Nationalists in particular – how had they reacted? When the tour was first announced, the Nationalists had declared that, though they could not be expected to show enthusiasm, they would treat the royal party with that courtesy and respect that is peculiar to the Afrikaner.[45] They had done more than that, of course. The sheer spectacle of it all, in a pre-celebrity, pre-television age, had drawn thousands, even in places like Pretoria, Bloemfontein and Kroonstad. The very simplicity of the family had been disarming. The Queen, especially, it was thought, had charmed the Afrikaners. Even the most hardened republicans had melted before her, Townsend felt.[46] Famously confronted by a hostile Boer who told her that while he was happy to welcome the family to South Africa, he could never forgive the British for what they had done to his people, she is said to have replied, with smiling equanimity, 'I quite understand, we feel exactly the same way in Scotland.'[47]

There had, too, been some notably conciliatory gestures, though these perhaps did not quite equate with those of the King in Washington, DC, in the summer of 1939, when he laid a wreath on the tomb of George Washington. He did not now, for example, lay a wreath at the statue of Paul Kruger (though he quoted him in his speech at the State Banquet in Pretoria); there was no question of a visit to the Vrouemonument in Bloemfontein. The Queen had brought with her the Kruger family Bible, clearly looted during the Anglo-Boer War ('it was brought from South Africa by General Horace Smith-Dorrien in 1901; it was his desire later to return it to South Africa ... but it could not be found and only came to light many years later ... Lady Smith-Dorrien[48] has asked that it be placed in the hands of General Smuts ... The Queen has gladly undertaken to fulfil this request and the bible has been included in Her Majesty's baggage', etc.); with some publicity, this was returned, via Smuts, to the Kruger family.[49]

There had been tea with old Mrs Steyn in Bloemfontein, tea with Ouma Smuts at Doornkloof, meetings with the *oudstryders*, endless watching of *volkspele*. They had endeavoured to identify publicly with Afrikaans culture – playing *jukskei*, attending a service in a Dutch Reformed church in Pretoria ('*Exactly* like the Scotch Kirk,' said Queen Elizabeth). They had eaten *sosaties* at braais. Everyone had lost count of how many times they had listened to 'Jan Pierewiet', an Afrikaans *volkslied* with a particularly lugubrious repetitive rhythm. It had even been put out by the government chauffeurs that the family enjoyed jolly sing-songs in the royal Daimler, singing Afrikaans *liedjies* to pass the time during the long drives out from Government House, Pretoria, and back again.[50]

'Pugh's Farm Letter', a regular feature in *The Daily Representative*[51] and which may fairly stand as indicating the tenor of many English-language papers on this aspect of the tour's success, is a litany of how and where the family had charmed the Afrikaners, who all spoke of the 'wonderful visit' with tears in their eyes, how prominent and poor Afrikaners in Pretoria and Johannesburg had joined in, how it had been a red-letter day in Standerton, and so on.

How is one to evaluate all this? It must in part have been true of those who actually turned up to meet them, and Afrikaners who supported Smuts were of course much more easily charmed. Others may have been, too, by the family's apparent simplicity where snootiness had been expected. According to Lady Harlech, the Nationalists couldn't get over the simplicity and informality of the King and Queen, which was not at all what their papers had led them to expect, and what they 'thought about royalty'.[52] The beauty of the Princesses had helped too – 'O, *hulle is mooi*,' was often heard as they appeared. There had only been one recorded instance of booing; that was in Brakpan and it was understood the crowd had 'dealt with' the perpetrator.

It was easy enough to think then as now, in retrospect, that for one brief shining moment much of South Africa had put their best foot forward and pulled together. Though many people at the time appear to have subscribed to this, it was not quite an unreservedly held opinion. Old Dominion Party supporters peevishly felt that Smuts had appropriated their electoral support, which they held as being less equivocal on such issues as imperial defence and the protection of the Protectorates' independence than Smuts's policies since Fusion had offered. They believed that, in the country districts, the government's policy had been to magnify the social aspect of the tour and dilute a true spirit of loyalty.[53] At another point on the political spectrum, black journalists from the more radical press could not resist pointing out that 'the joy was short-lived' and that it was now, once more, back to business as usual.

'Not a thousand visits,' they opined, 'would remove the national oppression of the Non-Europeans.'[54]

Malan, as leader of the republican opposition, was also far too astute a politician not to see this and the dangers to his political goals that lay barely concealed within such post-tour euphoria. The influential newspapers that supported him – *Die Burger*, *Die Vaderland*, *Die Volksblad* and *Die Transvaler* – had certainly not taken the line of 'Pugh's Farm Letter' in their reportage; efforts to identify with Afrikaans culture were often reported scornfully, if at all, or in an 'about-time-too' manner that awarded few brownie points.

In his summing-up of the success aspect of the tour, Malan firmly divorced the Afrikaners from the equation. He said that English-speaking South Africa 'had given new proof of their respect for an understandable sentiment which they themselves [the Afrikaners] could not share ... 'Now that the tour was over,' he could not resist adding, he hoped other sections of the community would show 'the same respect for Afrikaner sentiment as was shown by the Nationalist and Republican Afrikaners for the sentiment of the English-speaking community'.

In other words, this was your show, not ours.

And that was not all. He concluded by expressing the hope that *'ultimately all would join in showing the same love of and loyalty for all things really South African'* [author's italics].[55]

This was more than a neutraliser or a sideswipe; it was how he saw the way forward.

What did the sovereigns themselves think? On one of the last nights in Cape Town, the family gave a small dinner for Hofmeyr (and his mother), the Van Rynevelds and the Barings for a postmortem. The Barings definitely counted as 'one of us' and there must have been an element of getting down to brass tacks around the dining table at Government House. The Queen asked Baring straightforwardly what he really thought the results of the visit would be. Baring replied what he had thought all along, that he did not believe it would change any votes, but that it would make the Nationalists less extreme and more disposed to be friendly towards the English. Hofmeyr, writing to his friend and long-time correspondent, CJK Underhill, was no more hopeful. He did not feel that 'the political effect would be very great, but we never expected it would be, and actually it will probably be greater than we expected'.[56]

All agreed that in Brand van Zyl and his wife there was a real weakness, well beyond the derision tabled by the fashionable Cape of the *She isn't quite up to it* variety (suggesting she was too provincial or ordinary for that position).

This had been another of Smuts's mistakes. His wariness of his war-time coalition supporters – the Dominion Party and its cohorts, the various Empire Leagues – had caused him to sternly resist their urging of him, following Sir Patrick Duncan's death, to abandon Hertzog's practice of appointing a South African Governor-General, and revert to selecting a more appropriate metropolitan vice-regal candidate. He had made it clear that the appointee should not only be local but that both he and his wife should be bilingual.[57] This put out of the running even capable local men like Van der Byl, Lawrence or even Newton Thompson, all of whom had wives who, though eminently socially suitable, spoke no more than elementary kitchen Afrikaans. The Van Zyls had proved not only a very uninspired choice but one that was now seen to serve to weaken imperial ties.

'One feels the lack of an English Governor-General,' wrote Queen Elizabeth to her sister – 'it is really very unsuccessful to have a local, however nice, because he can never feel free to do things or take a lead, which is badly needed.'[58] The 'dear old Van Zyls', as she put it elsewhere, didn't 'really function'.

The King was far more forthright: 'What's the use of our coming out to buck things up if an old chap like that is going to let it all down again,' he asked, his voice, as always when he was vexed, rising to a crescendo. 'He only has a few old cronies of his own to dinner occasionally and never, never does his job as it properly ought to be done. It is perfectly absurd.'[59]

It had been noticed that neither Van Zyl nor his wife had been able to present by name more than a handful of the guests at the garden party at Westbrooke. Even more telling was that Molly Baring, who found herself seated opposite Dr Malan at the State Banquet in Cape Town, had never, in two years as the wife of the High Commissioner for Southern Africa, previously met him,[60] something an able gubernatorial couple should have been able to contrive socially with ease.

The Kennedys in Salisbury, by contrast, had been a great success. Government House, Salisbury had been 'charming ... the Kennedys were very nice and charming hosts – it was delightful to stay *with* someone! One misses that so much in South Africa,'[61] the Queen wrote, pointedly. Lady Harlech and Lascelles too contrasted Lady Kennedy's well-run Government House in Salisbury – 'it's a comfort to find ourselves, for the first time, in a genuine Government House, efficiently staffed on the traditional lines'[62] ('soothing to be in a house where [everything was] intelligently arranged', was how Lady Harlech put it[63]) – with Mrs Van Zyl's hopeless domestic arrangements, and where a scratch staff 'didn't know whether it was Christmas or Easter'. Mr Terry's new chintzes had apparently only gone so far.

(It should here be noted that a potentially very awkward situation within the Royal Family during this leg of the tour had been inadvertently avoided by Smuts some years earlier. He had firmly vetoed Churchill's idea of giving the Duke of Windsor a 'wider sphere of activity' than that presented by Nassau, in the Bahamas, by offering him the Governorship of Southern Rhodesia, which became vacant in 1942.[64] He cited the effect on Afrikaans and English public opinion, the difficulty of explaining away an ex-King to the blacks and his unsuitable Duchess to a respectable and church-going colony.)

Indeed, Southern Rhodesia (now Zimbabwe) in general had been very much to Queen Elizabeth's taste: 'most attractive and a very agreeable mixture of British and good colonial and a nice feeling of freedom everywhere'[65] (the garden party in Salisbury, for instance, had simply been open to all its citizens, regardless of race).[66] She was to return there several times in the 1950s, delighting in the colony's undoubted progress within the Central African Federation: 'They [the settlers] have all *doubled* in population since we were there, new factories springing up & lots of young people, especially men, looking very tough & happy & prosperous. I am sure that this country has a great future ...'[67]

The King thought that Baring, with his fluency in Afrikaans and African languages, and his socially adroit wife, would be a better candidate as Governor-General. Baring thought David Bowes-Lyon, the Queen's brother, who had had a top wartime job in Washington, would be ideal, cashing in on the Queen's great popularity. It was all, however, a little too late in the day. Although in all her letters she claimed that they had been given charming welcomes by the Afrikaners, 'brought up to hate England', she felt compelled to indicate what had been left too long undone, and that 'it was high time that a visit was paid in South Africa'.[68]

The King felt that if the visit had altered the conception of the monarchy to some South Africans (he was clearly referring really to the Afrikaans-speaking section) 'and has given them a new viewpoint from our personal contacts with them, then our tour has been well worthwhile ...'[69] He must have been heartened by the fact that he constantly met Afrikaners and their wives at wayside stations who had driven a hundred miles or more, 'probably Nationalists from their political point of view, but they will come and see us, which is all to the good'.[70] And even more by other encounters, such as the one at Wonderkop in the Orange Free State, with Mr Posthumus, aged 75, who told him: 'I was your country's bitterest enemy in the war of 1899, but now I am your friend for the rest of my life.' They had then shaken hands warmly.[71] There were many such reported incidents.

And both the King and the Queen, too, must have heard the cries '*Bly by ons*' (Stay with, or abide among, us) and, in Afrikaans accents, 'Leave the Princesses behind!' as the White Train pulled out of remote wayside stations and official stops, and perhaps wondered if, in another sort of world, a longer stay might not have had the more lasting, beneficent effect that Smuts hoped for. Both claimed later, according to Robert Rhodes James, not to have been the least surprised by the events that were soon after to overwhelm the South Africa that they had visited.[72]

Certainly, in its summing-up of things, *The Economist* put an altogether less sentimental gloss on things. Indeed, its leader of 10 May 1947 spelt it out bleakly, as *Vanguard* steamed towards Portsmouth. For having warned against the problems any government that has been in power for eight years automatically faces in a forthcoming election (Churchill's defeat at the polls in 1945 being an obvious cautionary tale), and dispensed with the issue of a monarchy versus a republic for South Africa, it said: 'In any case, next year's election will not be fought over the monarchy so much as over the colour problem.'[73]

Here indeed was the rub. Malan saw it clearly as the Achilles heel in the electorate's armour. If the issue of the monarchy would now no longer be the one to excite the voters in the happy afterglow engendered by the royal visit, with its non-divisive, glittering charm all too fresh in their minds, then that could easily be downplayed, for the time being at any rate. What *would* excite them was the issue of colour. For all around, 'breeding furiously',[74] was an ever-increasing black population that would not, for much longer, be content with no political say in a new, post-war Western world order that saw segregation as incompatible with fundamental human rights. In such a world, white South Africa was liable to be swamped.

The generality of Afrikaners saw this all too vividly; *oorstroming* (swamping), pertaining especially to the cities in the wake of the United Party's relaxation of wartime controls, was then a current, emotive expression among the *volk*. Indeed, even as one million people cheered the Royal Family through the streets of Johannesburg, the electioneering at the Wolmaransstad by-election seemed, as *The Star* remarked gloomily, to have put the political clock back 20 years, reviving the essentials of Tielman Roos's appalling racist slogan, 'the kaffir in his place and the coolie out of the country'.[75]

Whatever it was that Smuts saw in this now vital particular, and however much he deplored such crude racism, he appeared unable to offer the electorate any firm answers – and still less comfort – except to fudge issues of multiracial advancement until after the election.[76] He was on a losing wicket here. Only a wavering third of his own people supported him, as Sarah Gertrude Millin pointed out with a bleak brevity to readers in the *Spectator*, in June 1947, 'and those feel like the other two-thirds about colour'.[77]

And so it was, therefore, all rather left up in the air.

After a day's stop in St Helena, *Vanguard* arrived back in Portsmouth on 11 May, after a fortnight, as Lascelles put it, 'of perfect yachting weather'.[78] As they approached shore, Princess Elizabeth was seen to do a little jig of glee; there would be no delaying the engagement further. In England a great welcome awaited them. It was held that they had done a remarkably outstanding job, and it must be said that it is hard to see how they could have done more. They had travelled 11 000 miles, visited over 400 cities, towns and wayside stops, shaken hands with 25 000 people and been seen by 60–70 per cent of the country's population. Everyone, however, was shocked by the king's gaunt appearance.[79]

The following day they rode in state to the Guildhall, still being restored after its virtual destruction during the Blitz, for a luncheon given by the City of London, then traditionally held as a welcome by the City on the return of the Royal Family from abroad. Such an occasion was a shared experience in the Empire, and reported in detail and in a manner that can only be described as joyful in its newspapers.

English-speaking South Africans, for whom England was another reality, read happily in *The Cape Argus*, the *Rand Daily Mail* and other dailies of the State Landau, the mounted escort, the cheering crowds of Londoners, the ceremony at the Temple Bar, the Aldermen in their robes of scarlet, the judges in their wigs, the Lord Mayor 'portly and magnificent in gold lace', the ministers of the Crown and their wives, the Queen in ice blue and feathers 'looking more radiant than ever'. Blotchy radio pictures helped conjure up these images; just three weeks later these would appear more vividly in black and white in *The Illustrated London News*, which commanded a wide and enthusiastic weekly readership throughout the Commonwealth and Empire.

So much for the ceremonial aspect. As was expected, the King's speech at the end of the luncheon was a carefully drafted piece of statecraft designed to sum up the complicated issues that everyone now perceived South Africa presented, while at the same time endeavouring to put an official royal spin on it all. It was intended to be helpful to the Dominion he had just toured and to the prime minister who had so vitally supported him, and at the same time to be conciliatory within a changing Commonwealth.

This was never going to be an easy one.[80] In a handwritten note waiting for the King to read as soon as they were on board *Vanguard* and on their way back, Lascelles pointed out that there were three versions to work from. The first was a final version of Sir Dugald Malcolm and Lord Altrincham's joint draft, written in London and 'telegraphed to me to-day'. The second was Malcolm's first draft, handed to Lascelles before he left South Africa. The third was not a draft, but the notes given to Lascelles by General Smuts.

'I think there is good stuff in all three,' appended Lascelles, 'which can be worked up into a suitable speech.' Lascelles and the King must have been aware of its importance and the difficulties it presented. 'I'm glad we have got a clear fortnight [ie, the voyage back] in which to do this and put in any other parts Your Majesty may wish to make.'[81]

The final speech differs in content but not intent from Altrincham's. Contrasting the experiences of the tour 'of the wonderful country I have visited ... from the Cape of Good Hope to the Zambezi and back again', the King touched on the differing cultures he had encountered, 'ranging from the fine flower of the British and Dutch civilisation to the still primitive cultures of African tribalism'. There was an attempt here to make South Africa another reality for the British people, too, and to some extent it worked: 'South Africa must be a wonderful country,' the *Cape Times* correspondent duly reported a Londoner in the crowd as saying, compounding this by remarking on how well the Queen and the Princesses looked.

Then he got down to one of the major burdens of his delivery, trying to voice what in his heart he must have begun to perceive was going to be irreconcilable and increasingly unacceptable in the coming decades – keeping an important Dominion with racially segregated practices within the Commonwealth: 'South Africa has now grown to the full measure of manhood. Her future and decisions that affect it must be her own, but she is one of our great family and we in the old country who still sit, so to speak, at the family's head can do much to help her by co-operation, provided,' and here he paused and added for effect, 'and this is most important – *provided that our co-operation is based on knowledge.*' The words shown here in italics were heavily underlined for emphasis in the text. This was, in effect, employing an old white colonial adage, which then still contained some currency but which the promulgation of apartheid would rapidly disqualify. He continued:

> She is engaged on a task which I believe to be unique in the world, nothing less than that of adjusting, almost from day to day, the

progress of a white population of well over two million whose future must always lie in South Africa, and that of a far greater number of other peoples, very different in race and background.

There is no easy formula for the wise discharge of that formidable task. It calls for breadth of vision, human sympathy and statesmanship, based on experience, and it is essentially the task of the people who live there.[82]

This was in general terms a response to the votes of censure at the United Nations and the easy capital the Nationalists were making from them in domestic politics. It was clearly an attempt to take the pressure off Smuts on the thorny issue of race before the forthcoming election. But if he hoped to ameliorate the sting in the criticisms now directed at the country from abroad, and indeed also from within,[83] by speaking thus, he was mistaken. Far from grasping this lifeline flung towards them, the Nationalist press crowed with delight at this statement. You see, they cried, our politics is our business and no one else's. Thus *Die Burger* noted 'it was a refreshing change from normal British opinion. Indeed, they [his words] seem a rebuke to those critics in Britain who have displayed a chronic desire to solve our colour problems for us.'[84]

Die Volksblad went one further: 'In the midst of the prejudices and hate with which we have recently been surrounded, it is heartening to realise that opinion overseas is beginning to acknowledge that South Africa is doing its duty towards its coloured population. [The King's] words are a lesson to General Smuts as well,' it added, with what now seems like shameless gall, 'who has all the while insisted on compromise with the UN regarding our problems.'[85]

Just how much actual comfort Smuts drew from the King's Guildhall speech and the reactions to it one can only conjecture. 'I thank you also for your kind references in your great Guild Hall [sic] speech to South Africa and her problems,' is what he wrote to the King after it. 'This has been a great service to South Africa especially at this time of carping criticism abroad.'[86]

For even as the Nationalist newspapers had a field day with this aspect of the speech, on the other side some of the more enlightened

English-language South African newspapers expressed caution about what his South African ministers had caused him to say. What was the King being drawn into here, it was wondered?

We are here again in the realms of Major Richards' ilk among South African voters (see Chapter 10). While there was general praise for the ideal the King espoused towards the speech's ending, namely, the moral leadership to which he felt Britain and the Commonwealth were entitled to give to the world, following the war in which they had so bravely led and lighted the way to victory (in the event, a role that the United Nations would swiftly assume exclusively for itself), a newspaper like East London's *Daily Dispatch*, in its leader the day after the Guildhall speech, found elsewhere in his words cause for a fundamental disquiet:

> The other conclusion on which His Majesty laid emphasis was that the task of solving South Africa's problems was essentially the task of the people who live in it ... the majority of South Africans will argue that in the Nationalist camp there is neither vision nor the sympathy that alone could produce the statesmanship necessary to a solution of the country's colour problem ... We fear that the visit of the Royal Family, welcome and inspiring as it was to most, will not have the effect on the political character of the country that many may have hoped for. Respect, admiration and even affection for the wearer of the Crown may have been planted in many breasts, but the visit of the Royal Family will not have diverted a single Afrikaner from his desire for a republic.

This was in line with the unsentimental post-tour view already expressed by Baring, and it was proved to be a correct one, 13 years later. Interestingly, however, the *Daily Dispatch* went further still. While acknowledging that South Africa owed a deep debt of gratitude to His Majesty for the Guildhall speech, 'What we doubt is the wisdom of his advisors. Had there been no dispute between South Africa and the United Nations, there could have been no possible objection to an expression of opinion of the King ... but in foreign countries, His Majesty's words relative to the solution of South Africa's problems might be interpreted as an attempt to give advice to UNO or as a warning to that body not to interfere in the domestic affairs of South Africa.'

For an Eastern Province daily, this was startling and very enlightened stuff indeed. For Smuts it must have amounted to nothing less than a shot across his bows, almost certainly originating from Lady Milner or even Lord Harlech. Lady Harlech had met up with Vernon Barber, the paper's editor, in East London and noted him down, in a letter to her husband shortly thereafter, as a friend of 'Aunt Violet's'.[87]

In conclusion, the editorial delivered a fairly lethal parting shot: 'The King should not have been placed in a position where he could be described by foreign commentators as defence counsel for South Africa.'[88]

There was yet another ominous portent in the King's Guildhall speech, one of the longest he ever made. As always, he smoked a cigarette before he stood up to speak, and although his delivery to start with was in a strong, clear voice, he later became hoarse, and coughs frequently interrupted his sentences. It was said he was suffering from laryngitis for which his physicians were treating him. Alas, almost certainly, it was nothing of the sort.

* * *

Back in South Africa, Douglas Mitchell, leader of the United Party in Natal, urged Smuts to capitalise on the success of the royal visit by calling a snap election.[89] He refused, honouring the promise he made to Malan in Parliament before the visit that there would be no election for at least a year after it, so that he could not be seen to be profiting by it.[90]

The election was therefore scheduled for some time in mid-1948. The Lawrences were sent off to Canberra on a recuperative voyage and to attend the Commonwealth Conference, and then on to New York on a charm offensive to secure votes supporting South Africa at the United Nations when the Union again came up for censure. This was not for nothing. Harry Lawrence's niceness and his wife's glamour converted many a Latin and South American delegate, temporarily at least, to the country's cause, which in all likelihood was not very high up anyway at this stage on their particular agendas.

Smuts himself went to London to attend Princess Elizabeth's wedding to Lieutenant Philip Mountbatten in November that year, against all advice picking up Queen Frederica in Athens on the way.[91] Tongues wagged again in Cape Town, Pretoria and London. Old Mrs Hofmeyr had a field day. For a collector of her rank, as Alan Paton put it, this was the find of a lifetime. 'General Smuts has g-gone to G-Greece again,' she would regale the gossips sitting around her tea table, then adding, after an appropriate pause, as if inconsequentially, 'He's having a r-r-royal time over there,' and the company would titter appreciatively.

In the meantime, her son Jannie, the boy genius still tied to his mother's apron strings and slated as Smuts's successor as leader of the United Party, was becoming a target for opposition criticism. It wasn't so much his continued taxes on big business or the slowness of the post-war housing programme. It was his perceived liberalism. Hofmeyr had a long history of this, which had come into focus since the war. The Nationalists now seized on it to peddle their racist point of view to the many waverers in the electorate. Even before the Royal Family arrived, Hofmeyr had declared, in a speech at the Strand – as he had in Parliament in 1946 – that 'Natives will eventually be represented in Parliament by Natives and Indians by Indians'.[92] This almost certainly cost a young Sir De Villiers Graaff the hitherto safe United Party seat of Hottentots-Holland in the by-election that immediately followed.

Thereafter, things ominously gathered pace. Sir Evelyn Baring's prophecy that post-war South African politics would be about race appeared to be becoming axiomatic. Malan came forward and stated categorically that the choice was clear: between equality on the one hand, and separate development of racial groups, each with national pride and self-respect for others, on the other. He said that the best way to achieve the happiness of all South Africans was to maintain and protect the white race. Put neatly like that (the reality of its implementation would prove a travesty, not least on a humanitarian level), it was a policy that had a strong appeal to a white electorate with a large conservative component. The findings of the Sauer Commission (the National Party's responsive commission on the colour question) put the case more starkly: white South Africa faced the choice between 'integration and national suicide on the one hand, and apartheid and the protection of the "pure" white race on the other'.[93]

The Nationalist campaign of 1948 purposely presented a more moderate image than that of 1943. The issue of the republic was hedged, with some skill, to the point that Nationalist leaders often found themselves having to reassure their more radically minded followers that the party had not abandoned this ideal altogether. But from the point of view of the HNP, republicanism was no more useful as a campaign issue now than was the question of South African participation in the war. The draft constitution for a republic published in 1942, almost certainly the work of Malan originally and which, among other things, demoted English to a secondary language, was now strenuously repudiated. Malan was seeking to broaden his political following.[94]

The election was set for 26 May 1948. Smuts could, constitutionally, have waited until later in the year, when many of the typical grievances surrounding post-war demobilisation would have been ironed out. He didn't. In the postmortems after the event, the theory was put forward that he wanted it to be held at that date, and not later, in order to allow him time to go and be inducted as Chancellor of Cambridge University, yet another singularly high honour that had come his way. Far worse than this decision, however, was the one he had taken not to allow a delimiting committee to adjust the disparity in numbers between rural and urban constituencies, as it might legally have been entitled to do.

The vote in South Africa had, under the Act of Union, been heavily weighted by 15 per cent in the rural constituencies. It was not a purely South African arrangement. Several countries in Europe, England included, employed this system at the time it had been written into the South African constitution. Ironically, this was something Smuts himself had fought for at the time of Union, believing that the country vote was a more stable one than that of the towns, then felt to be the home of fly-by-nights, Bolsheviks and other malcontents. By 1945, this hardly pertained any longer.

Smuts's large majority in the House since 1943 gave him considerable power over the rules and customs of delimitation. But when some of his advisors in the party met with him to discuss ways and means of using this power, he cut the discussions short. He felt sentimentally about his *platteland* supporters; this was foolish in seats that were essentially marginal.

'They are a good people,' he would cry out, his voice, as Bertha Solomon (the UP member for Jeppe, a working-class Johannesburg constituency) recorded, rising to a falsetto. 'They will not let me down.'[95] Besides, the existing electoral arrangements, he insisted, damaging though they were to his party, had their roots in the pact of good faith that had created the Union and must still sustain the constitution.[96] He seemed to have forgotten the gerrymandering with the constituencies that had gone on under the Fusion government;[97] it was and would prove to be a favourite industry of politicians not committed at heart to a Westminster system.

It was a second act of good faith and a noble sentiment to espouse; politically, it was another terrible mistake. For now the heavily weighted rural constituencies presented, in effect, many more eager ears into which Malan could pour his dire prognostications about the *swart gevaar* (black peril). Apartheid was peddled here and within the Afrikaans churches as a policy that would be fair to all the races in South Africa. His words fell on fertile ground. The church supported his party, he said, and since the state refused to do so, they would present the policy at the next election.[98]

As noted, the republican issue was cleverly played down. It cannot be said that many of the young firebrand Afrikaners whom we met with Alan Paton at the time of the Voortrekker Centenary (see Chapter 2), who had now reached voting age, had not been antagonised further by the loyalist outpourings that the tour had invoked. They had. But it is unlikely that these alone would have caused a sufficient swing in Malan's favour. The issue of race, however, was another matter entirely.

The country went to the polls. The results shocked everyone. Even Malan was said to be surprised. From a majority in the House of 40 seats over Malan, Smuts's party now had eight seats less than his adversary and their allies. Malan and Havenga together won 79 seats and commanded an absolute majority of five over all comers, including the three Native Representatives. Smuts even lost his own seat at Standerton, the town at which 'Pugh's Farm Letter' had supposedly described the royal visit as having been a red-letter day. It probably was, only Standerton was now voting for apartheid.

To make matters worse, his failure to allow the delimitation commission to sit was now all too clearly shown to have been disastrous. In the popular vote, Smuts actually won by 158 350 votes, 53.49 per cent of the total vote, as opposed to Malan's and Havenga's 39.85 per cent.[99]

The Westminster style of democracy, with its constituency seats and first-past-the-post electoral system, so dearly enshrined in the Act of Union, was now seen to have served South Africa very ill indeed. One of the most momentous elections in the country's history had been won by a minority.

In Pretoria, Malan was given a hero's welcome, driven through the streets where only 14 months before the crowds had cheered the royal Daimler, in a car wrapped in the Vierkleur, the old flag of the Transvaal republic. Men and women wept; some fell to their knees. September 1939, the internments at Koffiefontein, Jopie Fourie, the Anglo-Boer War, the concentration camps, the Jameson Raid, the annexation of the diamond fields and of Natal, Slagtersnek and more – all, all were now to be avenged. Robey Leibbrandt, the Nazi agent and traitor, jailed for life during the war,[100] was released and became a hero of the *volk*. The Afrikaner Ascendancy to which the Centenary of 1938 had given its spurs and the war vote its urgent impetus, had finally triumphed. 'Thank God,' it was said. 'We have got our fatherland back' (*Dankie God. Ons het ons vaderland teruggekry*).

For Smuts, who suddenly appeared to be an old man, it was a crushing blow. He saw it not as one for himself, personally, but one for the country. 'Reaction has struck its roots very deep in this land of ours,' he told the liberal journalist Colin Legum. 'It will take years to overcome it,' he said, presciently, then adding typically, 'but don't tell the people that.'[101]

Over the next 12 years, right up to the end of the 1950s, world events seemed to play into the hands of the Nationalists. The Republic of Ireland became independent in 1949 and left the Commonwealth; India in 1950 and Pakistan in 1956 became republics, although they remained within the Commonwealth, showing that the Crown was an unessential link in the entity.

South African politics, as Baring had predicted, realigned itself; it now became primarily an issue of maintaining white supremacy in the face of black nationalism. The latter grew apace in a South Africa now committed to apartheid, culminating in the outlawing of the ANC and the

Pan Africanist Congress (PAC) in early 1960, following the Sharpeville massacre. It grew apace even more rapidly elsewhere in colonial Africa, threatening white settlers, most notably with the Mau Mau unrest in Kenya. Malan's successors had only to bide their time to get the electorate on their side; the issue of a republic was becoming – seemingly inexorably – linked with that of maintaining white supremacy. From the late 1950s both JG Strijdom and HF Verwoerd saw the achievement of a republic as essential to unite the two white races under their ideology. In the event, this was never to be achieved to the extent they hoped.

For the time being, but only in the short term, this divisive issue was somewhat shelved. Malan, once in the prime minister's office, had something of a change of heart about the Commonwealth. Like Smuts, he retained for himself the portfolio of Foreign Affairs. In 1949, he went to London to attend the Commonwealth prime ministers' conference. As the international criticism of South Africa and the implementation of apartheid mounted, he realised the usefulness of the contacts and connections abroad the body provided.[102] Britain's veto in the UN, especially, might one day prove vital. Metropolitan rumours, too, filtered back to Cape Town and Pretoria, suggesting that Mrs Malan had rather taken to official life when visiting London, and that Commonwealth and diplomatic receptions there, tea with Queen Mary at Marlborough House, and so on, were rather to her liking.[103]

There were fears now expressed in Afrikaner circles that the Malans, too, were being seduced by the English.[104] Whereas stories brought back to South Africa from London by the fortunately placed in diplomatic and military-attaché circles of Palace receptions and garden parties, far less something like an invitation to tea at Royal Lodge, caused the English-speaking at home to gasp and stretch their colonial eyes appreciatively, similar tales were greeted with sour remarks and pursed lips by the majority in Nationalist-voting company. The metropolitan capital, its court and its denizens were perceived as having an allure not dissimilar to that of a house of ill repute. Botha and Smuts had gone the way of all flesh; would Malan now fall too? These suspicions gained extra credence when, the following year, Malan sent a South African contingent to fight with the Commonwealth forces in Korea, in a sense repeating Smuts's action of 1939, which Malan and his supporters had so bitterly contested.

The King died aged 56 in 1952. He had been due, in six weeks' time, to journey to revisit South Africa once more in the *Vanguard* with Queen Elizabeth and Princess Margaret, to convalesce at Botha's House on the Reynolds' sugar estate on the Natal South Coast.[105] This was at Malan's personal invitation, having himself convalesced there. It showed a softening of attitude, if only at a personal level. 'I looked into his face and saw a sick man,' Malan was to recall afterwards. The King may well have felt he was building on the slender bridgehead established at the Cape Town City Hall on the day of his departure, and at subsequent meetings during the Commonwealth Conference in London.

The proposed royal convalescence, however, was criticised openly by the League of Coloured Peoples, and by the Labour MP Fenner Brockway, who formed the Movement for Colonial Freedom two years later. It was suggested that the King had been ill-advised to accept an invitation to the home of a man regarded by millions of Africans and Indians in the Commonwealth as the embodiment of the policy of white racial domination.[106] Other Labour MPs made similar protests.[107] The King's death brought the controversy to an end.

His end was seen all round as tragically premature; experience had made him wise in kingship. On a personal level, it also meant, as Violet Bonham Carter noted in her diary, 'the break-up of such a gay − warm − happy − devoted family unit − who shed their happiness on all around. I should think,' she added, 'Balmoral, Sandringham & even Windsor had never been so full of fun & sunshine.'[108]

The new Queen was crowned in 1953 − again as Queen of the Union of South Africa. Malan attended the coronation. Again, this was not a popular move among some fellow Nationalists, who further resented the rumours circulating that Maria Malan was looking forward to the occasion and to being in London again.[109] He processed with the other Dominion prime ministers, though his carriage was booed by the crowd as it came around Hyde Park Corner.[110] The South African contingents, however, were still cheered as they took part in the last great imperial coronation procession, the band of the Guards playing 'Sarie Marais' as the cavalcade wound its way back to Buckingham Palace.

In the Union, shops and theatres with English-speaking owners, not a few of them Jewish, were decorated, government buildings hardly at all. The new elevated freeway into central Johannesburg was named the Queen Elizabeth Bridge by its City Council, with a handsome stone memorial monolith bearing the flowers of the Commonwealth. Copies of the Wilding, Beaton and later Annigoni portraits of the new Queen were hung in offices, scout halls and even government schools where headmasters were English-speaking. Elsewhere, where government control was tighter, things were different. Police uniforms now had a different design to that of the London bobby, pillar boxes were no longer installed bearing the royal cipher, and the Union Jack was no longer flown together with the South African flag.

In the face of hardening Nationalist ideology and the now open policy of apartheid, centring on the removal of the Cape coloured vote, ex-servicemen organised the Torch Commando. It was led by Sailor Malan and other war heroes; even Perla Gibson was a figurehead. For a while this was a reasonably broad display of white consciousness, and the Nationalist government moved swiftly with its smear campaign to paint its supporters as 'traitors'. Later it floundered on the issue of whether coloured ex-servicemen could be members and also on the involvement of the Communist Party, who saw it as a platform for their political aims. In opposition, the United Party seemed to drift, too fearful that any hint of liberalism might bring on them a repeat of the 1948 catastrophe at the polling stations.

Finally, at the end of the decade, in 1959, a small group broke away and formed the Progressive Party. It championed the rule of law and a qualified franchise. This was to be the party of white racial conscience and it was immediately trounced at the polling stations, sending, for example, Harry Lawrence, then in his late fifties, into the political wilderness and retirement in relative poverty after a lifetime in Parliament. Cabinet ministers did not line their pockets in those days. Only one MP was elected and that was Helen Suzman, who for 13 years sat as the sole but resoundingly liberal voice in the House of Assembly.

Malan retired in 1954. His successor was not the more moderate Havenga, as he had wished, but Strijdom, far more of a northern firebrand, and who, like Verwoerd after him, was fully committed to a republic. They were encouraged by an ever-increasing majority in Parliament. Right from 1948, the National Party had been swift to strengthen its grip on the country. English-speaking names became fewer in the higher echelons of the armed services; certainly many of those with openly non-Nationalist political views were overlooked for promotion. The civil service became predominantly Afrikaans-speaking, and Afrikaans-medium schools were built in previously predominantly English-speaking areas.

Railway workers – by now almost all Afrikaans and thoroughly supportive of a party whose ideology protected their jobs – were dispatched in great numbers to live in marginal electoral districts. The delimitation committee that Smuts had spurned was kept busy at every opportunity redrawing electoral boundaries so that, in the end, their contorted shapes, shamelessly designed to take in pockets of Nationalist voters, appeared on a map to be almost farcical.

All was not everywhere reactionary. There were liberal institutions such as the Black Sash, advice centres in townships run by white women, feeding schemes and charitable organisations working among blacks that were set up chiefly by the English-speaking community, and these flourished despite thwarting or worse actions on the part of government[111] or the police. The Athlone Advice Centre, for example, was run by Moira Henderson (together with Eulalie Stott, whose idea it was, and Noel Robb), whom we encountered as a guest at the dinner party at Westbrooke preceding the ball for Princess Elizabeth's 21st birthday. Moira Henderson would devote her life to this organisation, which helped citizens who fell foul of the apartheid system.

It has to be said that the old spectre of anti-Afrikanerdom, now focused on Nationalist political policy, haunted some, but by no means all, English-speaking South African liberalism.[112] And while many of its proponents would have welcomed the ultimate achievement of majority rule, they would have been equally dismayed by the climate of corruption, graft and incompetence it appears to have brought in its wake.

By 1960 Verwoerd – 'the evil genius', as Helen Suzman described him – felt the time was ripe to call a referendum on the issue of whether South Africa was to become a republic. Verwoerd promised that it would remain within the Commonwealth, as a sop to the waverers among the

English-speaking voters. The country threw itself into a fury of campaigning. YES/NO JA/NEE posters blossomed everywhere. The date was set for October 1960.

The year opened momentously for English-speaking South Africans, as they galvanised themselves for a last great concerted rally as a group. At the start of February, Harold Macmillan, the Tory prime minister of Britain, arrived in Cape Town. On the face of it, Macmillan was exactly what they admired: a clever toff, with an aristocratic wife (Lady Dorothy quickly became a favourite of the English-speaking community and press), and a skilled diplomat. They certainly did not perceive him to be the cold, unsentimental politician who, post the Suez debacle, had shafted Anthony Eden and whose sights were now firmly set on Britain's entry into the European Common Market and establishing a special relationship with America, with himself as the senior guiding figure.

Some saw this, then and later, as personal vanity on his behalf, with no particular gain for Britain. Indeed, after a series of body blows delivered to Britain by the United States, starting with the scrapping of Lend-Lease in 1945, at a moment when Britain was technically bankrupt, and ending with a lack of US support during the Suez crisis, many saw the pressure that the United States was bringing to bear on Britain to decolonise as nothing more than global power opportunism to gain access to resources and new markets.

It made no odds to the march of history. Before coming to South Africa, Macmillan had visited several other countries in Africa. He saw black nationalism as something inevitable, especially perhaps in countries poor in settlers and mineral resources (such as Ghana, the first African colony to gain independence). More significantly, he saw any efforts to support white settlers elsewhere, who had been encouraged by previous governments to go out and make a go of it in those countries, as simply a waste of money.

In Cape Town, Macmillan had been invited to address both Houses of Parliament. He rose to speak and what he had to say shook white South Africa rigid: 'The wind of change is blowing through this continent,' he said, 'and whether we like it or not, this growth of national consciousness is a political fact.'

Macmillan had, in fact, already made this speech a month earlier in Accra. This time, however, the world's press were out in force, and both the setting and the stony silence in which his words were received now made it international news. It was clear that Macmillan included South Africa in his comments; from what he said next it was also clear that there had been a complete shift in British policy towards apartheid:

> As a fellow member of the Commonwealth it is our earnest desire to give South Africa our support and encouragement, but I hope you won't mind my saying frankly that there are some aspects of your policies which make it impossible for us to do this without being false to our own deep convictions about the political destinies of free men to which in our own territories we are trying to give effect.[113]

Barely two months later, the Queen's brave visit to newly independent Ghana appeared to set the royal seal on this new order of things. For, to the outrage and howls of derision from Afrikaner racists and, in truth, to the consternation of many less obviously racist old-guard colonials, the Queen – tiaraed and smiling happily – was to be seen, in a photograph that was published around the world, dancing in the arms of President Nkrumah.

Macmillan's momentous speech was in direct contrast to one of the main platforms of the King's speech in the Guildhall 13 years before. Of course there was no Smuts the great Commonwealth statesman to support any more. British politicians on the whole privately loathed Strijdom and Verwoerd and their ministers as intransigents and embarrassments when they had dealings with them. However, the British prime minister might just as well have said the old Commonwealth was a dodo, and given white settlers in African countries with black majorities a clear warning to make other plans: don't count on us for moral or physical support, he seemed to be saying.

Liberal minds felt it was a timeous and indeed important moment in Britain's post-war journey to have such a distinguished and powerful figure in the Western world admonishing racist practices and encouraging black nationalists to achieve equality and independence.[114] Conservatives everywhere, however, were appalled. White settlers in Kenya spoke bitterly of betrayal, and ministers in the Central African Federation, which had but two years to run, were justifiably alarmed. It's not winds of change blowing through Africa, commented old Major Piet van der Byl drily in his diary, but winds of change blowing through Whitehall.[115] Lord Muir, a member of Macmillan's Cabinet, was to say that 'few utterances in recent history have had more grievous consequences'.[116] For many moderate English-speaking South Africans, it was a body blow aimed at a faith long and assiduously held onto even at an unconscious level and however vaguely it still registered. You're on your own, they were being told. The old colonial dream of hands-across-the-sea, so long and dearly cherished, had ended in a rude awakening indeed.

Or this was how many chose to interpret the speech. If Verwoerd was stunned, as he apparently looked to observers[117] (Macmillan had declined to give him any warning of its content in advance, let alone a copy), he lost no time in turning the situation to his advantage. Leaping to his feet to respond to this bombshell, he remained admirably calm and collected. 'The need to do justice to all, does not only mean being just to the black man in Africa,' he said, 'but also being just to the white man of Africa. We call ourselves Europeans but actually we represent the white men of Africa.' With the referendum in mind, he continued, turning this to his advantage. The Europeans [in South Africa], he said, had no other home. Here he was cleverly including English-speaking South Africans in the same boat, as it were, with the Afrikaner; Africa was now their home too.[118]

Many are supposed to have contributed to Macmillan's speech, most notably Sir John Maud, British High Commissioner in South Africa. It reaffirmed British colonial policy 'not only to raise the material standards of living, but to create a society which respects the rights of individuals'. Others saw there was more to it than that. The speechwriters, they believed, clearly sought to separate the British nation from the British colonies, which they now wished to shed as an embarrassment in the modern age and a potential source of money-wasting should they need to prop up small white minorities. And though this was certainly not intended, nothing could have helped Verwoerd more to achieve the referendum result he wanted. In short, as one commentator on his speech has pointed out, 'the unintended effect ... was to help empower Verwoerd by reinforcing his dominance over domestic politics and by assisting him make two hitherto separate strands of his political career seem reinforcing: republican nationalism on the one hand and apartheid ideology on the other'.[119]

For, not long afterwards, having collected himself, Verwoerd was able to declare harshly in the House of Assembly: 'It was not the Republic of South Africa that was told, "We are not going to support you in this respect." Those words were addressed to the monarchy of South Africa, and yet we have the same monarch as this person from Britain who addressed these words to us. It was a warning given to all of us, English-speaking and Afrikaans-speaking, republican and anti-republican. It was clear to all of us that as far as these matters are concerned, we shall have to stand on our own feet.'[120]

Thereafter, as the year progressed, English-speaking South Africa reeled from one crisis to another. At home, the Sharpeville shootings,[121] the Langa riots and the marathon Treason Trial indicated the mounting, radical discontent among the disenfranchised black population. There was an assassination attempt on Verwoerd at the Rand Easter Show in April. More significantly, in the centre of the continent, the Belgian Congo was given a hasty independence in June and a month later went up in flames. Images of white families with their belongings fleeing south appeared in newspapers, along with horrific stories of murder and rape. Verwoerd made much of this in his campaign for a republic,[122] and certainly a less suitable background to encourage doubtful voters to vote to remain within a more liberal, multiracial Commonwealth would be hard to imagine.

In the upshot, the referendum on the issue of a republic involved less than 20 per cent of the total population of the country. Many English-speakers who had refused to give up their British citizenship under the 1949 South African Citizenship Act were excluded. The coloureds and Malays who had survived on the voters' roll – around 40 000 were registered in 1955 (as compared to 54 000 in 1945, and 80 000 in 1943) – had, in 1958, in a disgraceful gerrymandering of the constitution,[123] been removed from it and were therefore ineligible to vote.[124] 'Hulle kan nie nou vir hul miesies in Londen stem nie' (Now they can't vote for their Madam [ie, the Queen] in London), crudely joked John Vorster, the future prime minister,[125] suggesting an additional, non-ideological and crafty political motive for this move. Vorster had been a general in the Ossewabrandwag, and had been interned by Smuts during the war. Furthermore, one of the Nationalists' collective angry memories of the royal tour was that coloureds (as well as Indians and blacks) had almost exclusively chosen to wave Union Jacks and not South African flags during the celebrations.

Both the United and Progressive parties criticised the government for the exclusion of coloureds from the referendum. Verwoerd swiftly and typically argued that that the republic was an issue between the whites. He knew full well, just as Vorster and his fellow Nationalists did, that were they to have participated, the referendum could easily have been lost and his political career ended.[126] Not participating either, of course, were Indians and blacks, or non-whites, who numbered over 71 per cent of the population in 1960; even the positions of the three Native Representatives who still sat in the House of Assembly were abolished in that year.

In further preparation for a yes majority, Strijdom had, in 1958, dropped the minimum age for white voters from 21 to 18, bringing many more Afrikaans-speakers into the field than English – possibly as many as 46 000 more.[127] Moreover, South West Africa, not technically part of the Union, but with its predominantly Afrikaans-speaking and ethnic German populations in its white make-up, did qualify to vote.

Considering all this and the shocks and alarums of 1960, it was, even so, a near-run thing. A majority of 74 580 of the white electorate – 52.29 per cent of the vote – voted for a republic,[128] hardly a ringing endorsement. The ratio between Afrikaans- and English-speakers then was 18:12, and since analysts believed the pro-republic vote had garnered some unlikely supporters,[129] a good number of Afrikaners must have voted no.

Malan had always said a two-thirds majority would be needed for a republic; nothing near this had been achieved. Verwoerd had said that a majority of one would do it. A 75 000-odd majority was, therefore, more than enough for him. As good as his word, he went to the Commonwealth Conference in London in March 1961 to apply for South Africa to remain a member as a republic, as India, Pakistan and Ghana had done.

To the London press he tried to pass off apartheid not as white supremacy, but actually as good neighbourliness. At the conference he – and

HMS *Vanguard*, at right, heads out into the Cape rollers. Before long, three albatrosses were observed to be following the great battleship.

TRANSNET HERITAGE LIBRARY PHOTO COLLECTION

others – anticipated problems from non-European members, Malaya and India in particular. He felt he was safe with the 'Keep South Africa In' lobby, which included, predictably, Macmillan for Britain, Welensky for Rhodesia and Nyasaland, Menzies for Australia and Holyoake for New Zealand. But to his and others' amazement, he received a broadside from where he hadn't expected it – Diefenbaker, the Canadian prime minister, who might have been expected to side with the old white Commonwealth, but who now proposed a communique that stated racial equality was a principle of the Commonwealth.

This suited Verwoerd's machinations admirably. He withdrew South Africa's application and walked out of the conference, returning to South Africa to a staged hero's welcome. There to greet him at the airport was a crowd of 30 000 to 50 000 cheering supporters (depending on the differing sources), organised by the National Party in conjunction with a great number of Afrikaans cultural organisations. He addressed them triumphantly. What had happened in London, he explained, was not a defeat but a victory: 'We have freed ourselves from the pressure of the Afro-Asian nations who were busy invading the Commonwealth. We are not prepared to let these countries dictate what our future should be. Those who love the Commonwealth and who are perhaps experiencing moments of doubt,' he added, with some skill, 'should realise that the present Commonwealth with its majority of non-European nations is a different Commonwealth to the one we wished to be a member of. In it we are no longer at home. Therefore, we now go forward alone.'[130]

On the 31 May 1961, South Africa became a republic. The day and month were deeply significant in the Afrikaner psyche – the end of the Anglo-Boer War in 1902, the date of the Union of South Africa in 1910, and the date when the South African flag had first been flown in 1928. The carefully orchestrated celebrations were triumphalist where expected; elsewhere the transition was greeted with sullenness and despair. On such a slim margin, South Africa now retreated further into a laager for another 33 years.

On that day, all the pride, hopes and aspirations of a mere 14 years before must have seemed almost to have belonged to another age, its fanfares heard like distant trumpets. Now they belong to two South Africas ago.

Acknowledgements

I wish to thank Her Majesty the Queen for permission to use material held in the Royal Archives at Windsor, and to thank the Earl of Snowdon, Lady Anne Somerset, Lady Susan Hussey, Lord Renwick, Hugo Vickers, Mark Magowan and Richard Steyn for their encouragement with this project, and to Sarah Bradford for hers, at the outset of my researches. Thanks also to HRH Princess Elizabeth of Yugoslavia, who made available to me the letters from her mother, HRH Princess Paul of Yugoslavia, from Johannesburg; to Lady Anne Glenconner, who spoke to me about Princess Margaret; to Jane Rynie (Ormsby-Gore), for permission to use the letters of her grandmother, Lady Harlech, and for sharing her memories of her; to the late Viscount Norwich, for permission to quote from the letters of his mother, Lady Diana Cooper, and from her papers held at Eton College; to Emma Soames, for permission to quote from the papers of her mother, Lady Soames; to Isabell Carden, for permission to use the quotation from her father; and to Rian Malan, for permission to quote from 'Zille's Heresy'.

I am greatly indebted to Lesley Hart, former head of Special Collections, University of Cape Town Libraries, and Felicity Swanson, for their research assistance, and to Renate Meyer, the present head, and the staff at Special Collections UCT.

My thanks, too, to the following: Bill Stockting, Archives Manager at the Royal Archives, and Julie Crocker and the staff of the Royal Archives, Windsor, and Karen Lawson, Picture Library Manager there, and Helen Trompeteler, for their assistance; Debbie Horner and the staff of the British Library, and Stewart Gillies, the News Reference Team Leader there; Hedi Egginton and Natasha Swainston of the Churchill Archives, Cambridge; Caronwen Samuels of the National Library of Wales; Oliver House and Sam Lindley of the Bodleian Library; Melanie Geustyn, Laddy McKechnie and Rhulani Sebopetsa of the South African National Library and Yolanda Meyer of the SAR&H Museum for their endless patience and help; Waseema Sydow of the Sea Point Library; Emily-Ann Krige and Senzosenkosi Mkhize of the Killie Campbell Africana Library; Donald van Wyk, Assistant Director, and Shoeshoe Mofokeng, Archivist, of the Free State Provincial Archives Repository in Bloemfontein; and Dr Hannes Haasbroek, Principal Museum Scientist and Head of Department at the National Museum at Bloemfontein. Thanks also to Mary Slack, for permission to use the Brenthurst Library, and to Sally MacRoberts, its Chief Librarian, and her staff; to Janine Blumberg of the Kaplan Centre, UCT; to Naomi Musiker, archivist of the South African Jewish Board of Deputies; to Hayden Proud, Curator of Historical Paintings and Sculpture at the Iziko South African National Gallery; to Lila Komnick of the Artworks Office of Parliament; to Trevor Moses, film archivist at the South African National Film Video and Sound Archives; to Stuart Ravenscroft, Archivist, Scout Heritage Centre; and to the staff at the Ditsong National Museum of Military History and the General Smuts Foundation.

Further thanks to John Lambert, who has generously shared his knowledge of the period. Professors Christopher Saunders and Keith Hunt and Nick Southey willingly assisted and answered my questions, as did Richard Mendelsohn, Adam Mendelsohn, Hillary Sapire of Birkbeck College, University of London, Timothy Keegan, Alex Russell and the Revd Angus Kelly. Deborah Honoré (née Duncan) spoke to me at some length about her parents, Sir Patrick and Lady Duncan, and life at Government House, and Deborah Lavin, who edited the letters between Sir Patrick and Lady Selborne, provided further insights. Thanks too, to Phillip Weyers, who put me in touch with the Smuts family, and to Dr Nico Steytler, who put me in touch with his mother, Elsa Steytler (née Joubert).

Many have read and commented on the text at various stages, and I am particularly indebted to Nicholas Schofield, whose assistance and knowledge is as always invaluable. My thanks, too, to Bruce Addison, Jonathan Kent, Anthony Skillicorn, Jimmy and Elaine Russell, Geoff Pethic and Barbara and Peter Knox-Shaw. Others who have kindly performed this function include Jane Meadows, Nick Wright, Digby Harris, Dominique Enthoven, Barbara McGregor, Robin Woodhead, Michael Hall, Verne Grinstead, Catherine Raphaely and Des Viney, who have all commented on sections of the text, and Julian Melck, who helped with Afrikaans translations, and Stella Cockburn, who brought the Zulu terminology up to current usage. And Stephanie Getty Waibel for her support.

Thanks are also due to Karl Snater, who first spotted that the 21st-birthday speech was recorded in front of the Victoria Falls Hotel, and to Ryk Melck and Justin Melck, for clarifying the issue of the 'ryk and arm Smutses', first brought to my attention by the late Martin Melck. Thanks too to Jeremy Lawrence, who has published his mother's diaries and memoirs and retains a lively memory of these times, and to Rian Malan and Hélène Opperman Lewis, for their insights into the pre-war status of the Afrikaner. Professor Siamon Gordon and Bob Bradway spoke to me about epigenetics and DNA; Laureen Rossouw spoke to me about her upbringing, and the late David Gevisser and Edna Bradlow spoke to me about anti-Semitism in South Africa.

I am grateful to all those who shared their memories of the visit. Miranda Jennings (née Viney) and Peter Simon, who remembered the State Entry into Cape Town; the late Sir David Graaff, who told me about the Koos van der Merwes at Worcester; Margaret Walton and Ann King (née Skillicorn) and Patty St Leger (née Shannon), who recalled the Queenstown visit; Keith and Rosemary Hunt, who assisted on the Grahamstown visit; Di Schonborn (née Reid), who connected me with those who remembered Kroonstad, together with Carol Anne van Rensburg; Elsa Steytler (née Joubert) recalled the braai at Bultfontein and spoke openly about her Paarl childhood; Wendy Jackson (née Van den Berg), who recalled the Beaufort West visit; Judith Field (née Handley), who remembered Pietermaritzburg, Eshowe (with additions as told to her by the late Veronica Burton) and the *Ngoma Nkosi* at the aerodrome, as did Norma Ellis Brown (née Brockwell), who also spoke about her parents-in-law, the Ellis Browns; and Donal McCracken of the University of KwaZulu-Natal, Adrian Rowe and Hardy Wilson, who were contacts for wartime Durban.

Thanks, also, to Judy Holland (née Welsh), who recalled vividly the White Train from Ermelo and the Princesses' Ball in Johannesburg and the dinner beforehand, as did Basil Hersov; HRH Princess Elizabeth of Yugoslavia, who recalled the arrival in Johannesburg, as did Dame Janet Suzman, my mother, the late Pamela Viney (née Handley), and Robin Wilson, who remembered the fireworks display there; Paul Yule, who told me about his uncle, Norman Yule, who devised the city's decorations; Katusha de Kock (née Smuts), who recalled the tea at Doornkloof; Crispian Trace, who recalled the tea at Vergelegen, and Caroline Menell and Max Cullinan, who helped decipher their grandmother's letter to Cynthia Barlow describing that afternoon, and Charles Barlow, for permission to quote from it; Pieter Bairnsfather-Cloete, for the Peter Townsend letter and his willingness to answer questions about the period; Ilse Barlow, Annabel Townsend (née Barlow), Peter Knox-Shaw, Gys Hofmeyr, Dudley Hopkins and Tony North, who remembered Vergelegen then, as well as neighbouring Buzenval; and Rosemary Smuts, for the loan of the royal tour albums.

My appreciation to John Lambert for letting me see the Colin Lang letter, and to Ian Shapiro for making available to me his remarkable collection of royal tour memorabilia. Thanks to June Commerell (née Green) and to the late Pam Enthoven (née Hockley), Winsome Sales (née Wollaston) and Lucia Bolus (née Vintcent), who recalled the 21st-birthday ball, and to Bob Bolus and Camilla Twigg, and Pippa Sales, who additionally gave me access to Winsome Sales's scrapbook; Suzanne Fox (née Krige), who recalled the dance at the Cape Town City Hall and told me about Isie Smuts; Greg Davis, who told me about Vic Davis's band; Nicholas Oppenheimer, who confirmed the story of his grandfather, Sir Ernest Oppenheimer and Queen Elizabeth's diamond; Rachel Slack; and David Robb, Louise Wood (née Stott) and Elspeth (Mosa) le Roux (née

Henderson), who told me about their mother's involvement with the Black Sash and the Athlone Advice Centre.

Thanks to Lisa-Ann Friederich, who assisted with the typescript, and to Stephen Kirsten, who assisted with the sourcing of the photographs.

Barbara Knox-Shaw, Mac Bisset, Jimmy Mould and Professor Keith Hunt, formerly of Rhodes University, have been invaluable with the editing of the text and with comments, as has Alfred LeMaitre and Amanda Keats.

Finally, my thanks to Jonathan Ball and the directors and staff at Jonathan Ball Publishers, and to Duncan Proudfoot of the Robinson imprint of the Little, Brown Book Group in London, who have seen the book through to publication.

Graham Viney
JULY 2018

Glossary

ACF	Active Citizen Force, the reserve arm of the Union Defence Force (UDF)
ANS	Afrikaner Nasionale Studentebond, an Afrikaner student organisation
Babootie	a popular South African curried meatloaf-type dish, finished with a custard topping, whose recipe has distinctive Cape Malay origins. The modern term is bobotie.
Bloedsappe	Afrikaner supporters of Smuts's United Party (UP)
boerebeskuit	rusks, a typical Afrikaans teatime favourite
boerewors	highly spiced, traditional Boer sausages traditionally served at braais
Bond	Afrikaner Bond, a political organisation founded in the Cape in the 1880s to promote Afrikaner interests
braai/braaivleis	traditional Voortrekker method of cooking food, especially meat, in the open air (similar to barbecue)
burra mem	Indian term for a (white) woman of substance in colonial society. Not in general use in South Africa, though its meaning fully understood.
dankie	Afrikaans for thank you
dominee	pastor or minister in the Dutch Reformed Church, who wielded some power
dorp	Afrikaans for village or small country town

FAK	Federasie van Afrikaanse Kultuurvereniginge, an Afrikaans cultural organisation
goeiemôre	Afrikaans for good morning
HNP	Herenigde Nasionale Party, the unified National Party
indaba	Zulu for gathering
koeksisters	a very sweet, plaited dough confection, fried and immersed in syrup
liedjie	Afrikaans folk song or ditty
naartjies	tangerines; up until the 1960s some English cookbooks and London fruiterers spoke of *naartjties*
obeletjies	old-fashioned Cape recipe for tea cakes
Ossewabrandwag	far-right, pro-Nazi Afrikaner political grouping, suppressed by Smuts during the Second World War. The name means 'ox-wagon sentinels'.
Oubaas	Afrikaans for the older master of the house or farm to the staff, and often to the family and friends, affectionately. Kleinbaas was the eldest son.
Ouma	grandmother or granny
Oupa	grandfather
platteland	Afrikaans for rural country or backveld
SABC	South African Broadcasting Corporation
SAP	South African Police
SAR&H	South African Railways & Harbours, the state railway and harbour administration
SAWAS	South African Women's Auxiliary Services
sinkplaat	corrugated iron
sosaties	kebabs
stoep	raised platform to a building of (Cape) Dutch architecture for sitting on in the open air. Sometimes covered by a pergola or roof supported by a colonnade; in the nineteenth century the term was supplanted by verandah.
takkies	South African colloquial for sandshoes or plimsolls
totsiens	Afrikaans for goodbye and until we meet again

UDF	Union Defence Force
UP	United Party
verandah	Originally made of trellis and later cast iron, supporting a canopy of lead, canvas or, post-1860, cranked corrugated iron to give the effect of an awning. The term was itself supplanted by *stoep* as a South African colloquialism in the era of Herbert Baker.
volkspele	Afrikaans folk dances

A note on currency

In 1947, Africa was part of the sterling area. One pound sterling in 1947 was equal to US$4.03. With the introduction of decimalisation in 1961, one old South African pound became equal to two rands. Today a 1947 South African pound is equivalent to R606 and £34. A guinea was a pound sterling plus 5 per cent. At the time it was accepted that model dresses, hats, antiques, tickets for charity events, etc, were priced in guineas.

Notes

INTRODUCTION

1 *The Star*, 10 March 1947.
2 Diana Cooper Papers, Eton College Library, Enid Bagnold Letters, Box VII, Letter Lady Jones to Lady Diana Cooper, [no date] February 1947.
3 *Life*, 31 March 1947. At this time, the popular and influential US illustrated magazine had a strong anti-imperial editorial policy.

CHAPTER I

1 This, one of a spate of post-war fashionable weddings, is necessarily a fiction.
2 LASL CAM, Letter Lascelles to The Hon Lady Lascelles, 7 February 1947.
3 The royal party were to be much struck by the South African night sky, as, for example, 'The skies are wonderful at night, with a blaze of stars such as I have never seen elsewhere' (LASL CAM, Letter Lascelles to The Hon Lady Lascelles, 23 February 1947).
4 Interview, Lucia Bolus (née Vintcent).
5 This, at least, was the boast; in fact, the Japanese *Yamato* (sunk 1945) and the American *Iowa*-class battleships were longer, but all had a similar displacement.
6 *Cape Times*, 22 February 1947.
7 Interview, Lucia Bolus (née Vintcent).
8 *The Daily Representative*, 24 January 1947; *Africa Travel Magazine*, 'Best of World Travel' edition. They included Ellerslie Girls' High, Sea Point Boys' High and Junior, Ellerton, Kings Road Primary and Camps Bay Primary. The numbers are given variously as between 1 200 and 2 000.

9 *Grocott's Mail*, 18 February 1947.
10 RA QM/PRIV/CC14/141, Letter Princess Elizabeth to Queen Mary, 23 February 1947.
11 *Cape Times*, 29 January 1947.
12 The recce had been led by Sir Piers Legh, Master of the Household, together with Major Adeane, in 1946.
13 Letter Lady Diana Cooper to Viscount Norwich, 22 February 1948, in D Cooper, *Darling Monster: The Letters of Lady Diana Cooper to Her Son John Julius Norwich 1939–1952* (London: Chatto & Windus, 2013), p 264.
14 Information: Jean Lawrence.
15 LASL CAC, Letter Lascelles to the Hon Lady Lascelles, Government House, Cape Town, 18 February 1947.
16 Their livery was dark blue and black, with a red stripe, with interiors of polished English ash and grey upholstery with black piping. At the end of the tour, despite having driven over 4 000 miles (6 430 kilometres), sometimes through mud up to their running boards, these required no more than routine maintenance (information supplied by the Crankhandle Club, Cape Town).
17 NLW, BE&FR, PFC 11/1/43, Letter Lady Harlech to Lord Harlech, White Train, 25 February 1947.
18 Viney Papers, Letter Lt Col John Viney to Pamela Handley, Kelvin Grove, 24 February 1947: 'the biggest crowd I have ever seen'; interview, Peter Simon, who as a schoolboy stood on a balcony overlooking the Parade: 'I have never seen bigger crowds in Cape Town – before or since.' According to Lascelles,

even Smuts was surprised by the numbers (RA QM/PRIV/CC13/166, Letter Lascelles to Queen Mary, Government House, Cape Town, 18 February 1947).

19 *The Sun*, 21 February 1947.

20 Ibid.

21 Diana Cooper Papers, Eton College Library, Enid Bagnold Letters, Box VII, Letter Lady Jones to Lady Diana Cooper, Maseru, [no date] February 1947.

22 *The Star*, 17 February 1947.

23 Terry, who worked in furnishings at Greenacres in Durban, was discovered by the Countess of Clarendon and was offered the job of First Grade Clerk of Works in the Department of Public Works in 1935. He was responsible for 37 official residences in South Africa and abroad. He was assisted by his wife's knowledge of fabrics (Ian Shapiro Collection, Terry Archives).

24 *Milady*, February, 1947.

25 G Viney, *Colonial Houses of South Africa* (Cape Town: Struik Publishers, 1988), p 79, has an image from the South African National Library.

26 LASL, CAC, Letter Lascelles to The Hon Lady Lascelles, Government House, Cape Town, 18 February 1947. Mrs Van Zyl seems to have been serenely unaware of her shortcomings, praising her staff to the newspapers and even inviting people 'of all walks of life' to view the private quarters of the Royal Family during their two-month absence up north, something that would certainly not have endeared her further to Queen Elizabeth.

27 *Inkundla Ya Bantu*, 6 March 1947.

28 The King wore two medals with blank reverses – the Defence Medal and the War Medal 1939–1945, neither yet minted (RA PS 08100/010/01).

29 P van der Byl, *The Shadows Lengthen* (Cape Town: Howard Timmins, 1973), p 17.

30 Letter Clementine Churchill to Mary Churchill, quoted in M Soames, *A Daughter's Tale* (London: Black Swan, 2012), p 213.

31 *The South African Home Pictorial*, April 1947, 'Fourteen Days with the Royal Family', by Mrs Lawrence and Mrs Carinus.

32 SAWAS, the South African Women's Auxiliary Service, under the auspices of its Peninsula Secretary, Lucy Bean, had organised entertainments, hospitality

and much more besides to visiting Royal Navy and convoy vessels during the war. Continuing this war work, they arranged a four days' leave in private houses away from Cape Town for 200 sailors each weekend from the battleship. Getting off the White Train at wayside stops in the countryside, the Royal Family were astonished to find crew members waiting to greet them. The Navy League held dances at the Muizenberg Pavilion (officers 26 February, ship's company 27 February). In the tradition of the Royal Navy, then greatly appreciated by Anglo-South African society in the port cities, *Vanguard* held cocktail parties and a dance on board during the visit, and when the general public were invited to visit the ship, three out of the five queues stretched all the way up to Adderley Street.

33 NLW, BE&FR, PEC 11/1/43, Letter Lady Harlech to Lord Harlech, White Train, 25 February 1947.

34 City of Cape Town, Proceedings of Council for Mayoral Year, September 1946 to February 1947, vol 105.

35 Waterson Papers, BC63, University of Cape Town Libraries.

36 NASA, Smuts Papers (1 444), Letter Smuts to Margaret Gillett, Groote Schuur, 2 March 1947.

37 *Grocott's Mail*, 18 February 1947.

38 NLW, BE&FR, PEC 11/1/43, Letter Lady Harlech to Lord Harlech, White Train, 25 February 1947.

39 Ibid.

40 The King's speech at the State Banquet in Cape Town was reported in full by most English newspapers in South Africa, as well as by newspapers in Britain.

41 *Inkundla Ya Bantu*, 6 March 1947.

42 RA QM/PRIV/CC14/149, Letter Princess Elizabeth to Queen Mary, White Train, 23 February 1947.

43 J Newton Thompson, *The Story of a House* (Cape Town: Howard Timmins, 1968), p 128; this was a much-repeated story over the next few days.

44 J Lawrence (ed), *Vintage Year: The 1947 Diaries of Jean St Leger Lawrence* (Cape Town: Gryphon Press, 2012), p 9.

45 I am indebted to Pieter Bairnsfather-Cloete for this information.

46 LASL, CAC, Letter Lascelles to The Hon Lady Lascelles, 18 February 1947.

47 RA QM/PRIV/CC13, Cypher Telegram, 19 January 1947.

48 Miriam Bloomberg's clothes during the visit were much commented upon, favourably, to her great satisfaction. When fashion-conscious Princess Margaret's royally skilful comment, 'Next to her we look like housemaids,' was repeated to her, as it was intended by her mother it should be, she didn't demur. 'Nonsense,' she replied serenely, 'they *also* have some lovely things.' This was a story much repeated, with raised eyebrows, at the time; Princess Margaret herself told it to Theo Aronson years later; see T Aronson, *Princess Margaret* (London: Michael O'Mara Books, 1997), p 98.

49 City of Cape Town, Proceedings of Council for Mayoral Year, September 1946 to February 1947.

50 D Morrah, *The Royal Family in South Africa* (London: Hutchinson, 1947), p 33; *Daily Dispatch*, 19 February 1947.

51 Your enemies' enemies are clearly your friends. De Valera, the Irish president, made a condolence call on the German ambassador in Dublin the day after Hitler's suicide was reported from Berlin. On VE Day, only a few weeks after Smuts had caused the horrifying footage of the recently liberated concentration camps to be shown in all South African cinemas, many of the students at Stellenbosch University donned black armbands (interview, David Gevisser).

52 *South African Jewish Times*, 21 February 1947.

53 NLW BE&FR PEC/11/1/43, Letter Lady Harlech to Lord Harlech, White Train, 25 February 1947.

54 See, for example, the mayor of Pietermaritzburg's address of welcome. RA PS 08100/07/310.

55 *Eastern Province Herald*, 8 March 1947.

56 Letter Nancy Mitford to Lady Pamela Berry, 20 February 1952, in C Mosley (ed), *Love from Nancy: The Letters of Nancy Mitford* (London: Sceptre, 1994), p 290.

57 Lord Moran, *Winston Churchill: The Struggle for Survival, 1940–1965* (New York: Basic Books, 2006), p 274.

58 *Cape Times*, editorial, 17 February 1947.

59 *Cape Times*, editorial, 18 February 1947.

60 *The Star*, 1 April 1947.

61 P Townsend, *Time and Chance: An Autobiography* (London: Collins, 1978), p 147.

62 Interview, Miranda Jennings (née Viney), who as a schoolgirl stood with her parents on a balcony overlooking Adderley Street, remembers this as a significant component of the tremendous cheers that greeted the Royal Family.

63 RA QEQM/PRIV/CSP/PAL/1941, Letter Lady Duncan to Queen Elizabeth, 1 December 1941.

64 RA PS/PSO/GVI/PS/ VISCOM/08100/07/266, Letter D Sinclair to HM The King.

65 According to the 1946 census.

66 *Cape Times*, 20 February 1947.

67 *The Sun*, 'Convey Our Greetings to My People', 28 February 1947.

68 *The Sun*, 21 February 1947. The numbers who served in the Cape Corps were 45 015.

69 The Cape remained servant-ed on a pre-war English standard, as indeed was the rest of South Africa. Ward Price suggested this was one of the causes for the feeling of English-ness for visitors to the Union. The front door of even a fairly modest house in, say, Rondebosch of that date would have been answered by a uniformed maid.

70 Van der Byl, *The Shadows Lengthen*, p 18.

71 RA F&V/VISOV/SA/1947, 19 February 1947.

72 Townsend, *Time and Chance*, p 170.

73 RA F&V/VISOV/SA/1947, Tour Diary, 19 February 1947.

74 *The Star*, 20 February 1947.

75 According to the 1946 census.

76 H Sapire, 'African Loyalism and its Discontents: The Royal Tour of South Africa, 1947', *The Historical Journal*, vol 54 (March 2011), pp 215–240.

77 Saul Dubow makes this point in 'Smuts, the United Nations and the Rhetoric of Race and Rights', *Journal of Contemporary History*, vol 43, no 1 (January 2008), p 44.

78 C Douglas-Home, *Evelyn Baring: The Last Proconsul* (London: Collins, 1978), p 155.

79 Ibid.

CHAPTER 2

1 *Singer Daily Prayer Book of the United Hebrew Congregation of the British Empire*, p 153.

2 *Cape Times*, 31 March 1947.

3 This verse was sung at the Thanksgiving Service at St Paul's on VE Day in May 1945.

4 RA QM/PRIV/CC13/163, Letter King George VI to Queen Mary, HMS *Vanguard*, off Gambia, 7 February 1947.

5 Pathé News, 'The Royal Family in South Africa', newsreel, 1947.

6 LASL CAC, Letter Lascelles to The Hon Lady Lascelles, 22 February 1947.

7 *The Cape Argus*, 21 February 1947.

8 Ibid.

9 Sales Album, Parliament of the Union of South Africa Ceremonial, *His Majesty Proceeding to Parliament, 21st February, 1947.*

10 NASA Smuts Papers, National Archives, Pretoria, (1 441), Letter Smuts to Margaret Gillett, Groote Schuur, 11 February 1947.

11 RA PS/PSO/GVI/PS/ VISCOM/08100/07/027.

12 RA PS/PSO/GVI/PS/ VISCOM/08100/07/055, Letter Lascelles to Fourie, 13 January 1947.

13 RA PS/PSO/GVI/PS/ VISCOM/08100/07/53.

14 P van der Byl, *The Shadows Lengthen* (Cape Town: Howard Timmins, 1973), p 19.

15 Of the Union's white population 9.3 per cent enlisted, as opposed to 12.5 and 13.2 for Canada and Australia, respectively. Considering the number of Afrikaners who opposed the war, this is an impressive percentage.

16 Van der Byl, *The Shadows Lengthen*, p 51. Van der Byl writes that this was a personal experience; for years, many other South Africans would claim this too.

17 25 South African pilots took part in the Battle of Britain.

18 In the apartheid era, when South Africa's popularity was at its lowest ebb internationally, Roger Bushell and his South African background were swiftly written out of the successful Hollywood film of 1963, *The Great Escape*. Sailor Malan suffered slightly less in the British-made *Battle of Britain* (1969), in which the fictional character of Squadron Leader Skipper, portrayed by Robert Shaw, was somewhat based on him. Sailor Malan earned a DSO and Bar and DFC and Bar and played a leading part in the Torch Commando in the early 1950s, when ex-servicemen protested against hardening Nationalist ideology and legislation. Roger Bushell was shot by his captors on Hitler's orders, ignominiously and unsuspectingly in the back of the head, as he urinated on the side of an autobahn in a German wood.

19 University of Cape Town Libraries, BC294 D5.30.7, Letter Lady Duncan to Lady Selborne.

20 *The Economist*, 10 May 1947, in which the leader article at the end of the tour makes this point.

21 J Lambert, '"Their Finest Hour"': English-speaking South Africans and World War II', *South African Historical Journal*, vol 60, no 1 (2008), p 61.

22 *Hansard*, 4 October 1939.

23 Killed off by the royal tour of all things, where the King and Princess Elizabeth and indeed the London papers had all emphasised that the Royal Family felt and indeed were just as at home in South Africa as they were in England. See Chapter 10. *Daily Telegraph*, syndicated in *The Daily Representative*, 28 April 1947.

24 In the 1890s only 2.3 per cent of Afrikaners were urbanised; by 1924 this had risen to 41 per cent; by 1936 to 50 per cent.

25 Interview, Norma Ellis Brown and many others.

26 Interview, Deborah Honoré (née Duncan, daughter of Sir Patrick Duncan, Governor-General of South Africa, 1937–1943). When the author asked how it worked at official levels, her reply was unhesitating: 'Oh, Good Behaviour was required, of course.'

27 For example, in much of the Orange Free State, Kroonstad being often recalled in this regard.

28 The late Allister Sparks recalls his father, a fourth-generation settler farmer in the Eastern Cape, being unable to speak Afrikaans. His Afrikaans neighbour was likewise unable to speak English – for similar, antipathetic reasons, it has to be said – and when they met to discuss matters of general interest, such as water rights, they spoke in isiXhosa. They never met socially (A Sparks, *The Sword and the Pen*, p 45). At that time, almost all farmers were proficient in the local African language, Natal farmers and their children being famously fluent

in isiZulu. See also J Lambert, 'Keeping English-Speaking South Africans British, 1934–1947, (unpublished paper, 2001, pp 7–8), which reports that 30 per cent of those who filled in a questionnaire admitted that, when growing up, they had no contact with or little knowledge of Afrikaners; the true figure may have been even higher.

29 Information, Sir John Carden.

30 Letter Queen Elizabeth to Lady Mary Elphinstone, 26 April 1947, in W Shawcross (ed), *Counting One's Blessings: The Selected Letters of Queen Elizabeth the Queen Mother* (London: Pan Books, 2013), p 399.

31 Interview, Major Thomas Harvey; see 'Queen Elizabeth, the Queen Mother', BBC documentary, 2016. Available at www. youtube.com/watch?v=SzgU03NaCOg; accessed on 11 July 2018; the story appears slightly watered down in E Longford, *The Queen Mother: A Biography* (London: Weidenfeld & Nicolson, 1981), p 106.

32 R Steyn, *Jan Smuts: Unafraid of Greatness* (Cape Town: Jonathan Ball, 2015), p 48.

33 Paul Kruger, the Transvaal's dour and autocratic president, for example, had come north with the Voortrekkers as a boy at the age of ten. He died in exile in Switzerland, aged 79, still firmly believing that the earth was flat.

34 WS Churchill, *The Second World War. Vol VI: Triumph and Tragedy* (Boston: Houghton & Mifflin, 1953), p 552.

35 P Beukes, *The Holistic Smuts: A Study in Personality* (Cape Town: Human & Rousseau, 1989), p 142.

36 The 1911 Census suggests 58.31 per cent were Dutch-speaking.

37 Natal whites were around 88 per cent English-speaking.

38 At that time these Van der Byls pronounced their name Van (to sound like a small lorry) D'Bile, something akin to Vanderbilt, suggested to be their distant kinsmen who had made good across the Atlantic; Jooste was pronounced with a hard J and rhymed with 'rooster'.

39 Quoted in T Gutsche, *No Ordinary Woman: The Life and Times of Florence Phillips* (Cape Town: Howard Timmins, 1966), p 386.

40 Duncan Papers, University of Cape Town Libraries, BC294C15.4.20, Patrick Duncan's Diary, 27 March 1938.

41 A Grundlingh, 'The Politics of the Past and of Popular Pursuits in the Construction of Everyday Afrikaner Nationalism, 1938–1948', in S Dubow and A Jeeves (eds), *South Africa's 1940s: Worlds of Possibilities* (Cape Town: Double Storey, 2005), p 196

42 Rian Malan, www.politicsweb.co.za/opinion/zilles-heresy, 18 April 2018.

43 Interview, Hélène Opperman Lewis. As an adherent of psycho-history, Opperman Lewis promulgates this and related theories.

44 *The Natal Mercury*, 17 December 1938.

45 D Harrison, *The White Tribe of Africa: South Africa in Perspective* (Berkeley: University of California Press, 1981), pp 110–111.

46 A Paton, *Hofmeyr* (Cape Town: Oxford University Press, 1964), p 302.

47 J Lambert, '"Welcome Home": White English-Speaking South Africans and the Royal Visit of 1947', *South African Historical Journal*, vol 69, no 1 (2017), p119

48 Historic UK, 'The Kings Speech', no date. Available at www.historic-uk.com/HistoryUK/HistoryofBritain/The-Kings-Speech/, accessed on 2 July 2018.

49 'Prime Minister Robert Menzies: wartime broadcast', Australian War Memorial, no date. Available at www.awm.gov.au/articles/encyclopedia/prime_ministers/Menzies, accessed on 2 July 2018.

50 *Hansard*, 4 September 1939.

51 Preparing for such a political denouement (and understanding the importance of dealing with it swiftly), Sir Patrick had telephoned Lady Duncan, who had remained behind in Pretoria, to get her to check various references in his library of constitutional law (which annually followed him to Pretoria with the parliamentary migration), and to arrange for key books to be flown down to him in Cape Town by Sir Pierre van Ryneveld. The Duncans, well used to political espionage, heard the clicks on the line signifying that the Afrikaans female telephone operators were listening in to what they were discussing. The gubernatorial couple at once switched to French and distinctly heard a harsh, exasperated female voice exclaim: '*Nee God, watter taal praat hulle nou?*' (For God's sake, what language are they talking now?) Another version has it

that Esselen was listening in with Smuts's knowledge; he spoke no French either.

52 D Lavin (ed), *Friendship and Union: The South African Letters of Patrick Duncan and Maud Selborne, 1907–1943* (Cape Town: Van Riebeeck Society, 2010), pp 630–631; R Rhodes James, *A Spirit Undaunted: The Political Role of George VI* (London: Abacus, 1999), pp 171-2

53 Duncan Papers, University of Cape Town Libraries, BC 294 E 23.4.1, Letter Lady Duncan to Princess Alice, 3 January 1940.

54 *Hansard*, 17 January 1942.

55 JC Smuts, *Jan Christian Smuts* (London: Cassell, 1952), p 432.

56 Ibid, p 420.

57 M Gilbert, *Winston Churchill: Road to Victory, 1941–1945* (London: Heinemann, 1986), p 159.

58 WS Churchill, *The Second World War. Volume V: Closing the Ring* (Boston: Houghton & Mifflin, 1953), p 132.

59 Lascelles Diary, 20 October 1943.

60 WK Hancock, *Smuts: The Fields of Force, 1919–1950* (Cambridge: Cambridge University Press, 1962), p 381.

61 Paton, *Hofmeyr*, p 451.

62 Killarney Studios, 'The Royal Tour of South Africa', film.

63 Paton, *Hofmeyr*, p 464.

64 F Donaldson, *King George VI and Queen Elizabeth* (London: Weidenfeld & Nicolson, 1977), p 31.

65 K Mincher, *I Lived in His Shadow: My Life with General Smuts* (Cape Town: Howard Timmins, 1965), p 148.

66 Lascelles Diary, 20 October 1943, 'he [Smuts] told me ... that he observed a marked increase in stature in the King in the last few years'.

67 WK Hancock, *Smuts, The Sanguine Years, 1870–1919* (Cambridge: Cambridge University Press, 1962), p 12.

68 NASA South African National Archives, Pretoria, Smuts Papers, (1 443), Letter Smuts to Margaret Gillett, Groote Schuur, 22 February 1947.

69 *Grocott's Mail*, 24 February 1947.

70 *Daily Dispatch*, 24 February 1947.

71 Paton, *Hofmeyr*, p 450.

72 NLW, BE&FR, PEC 11/1/44, Letter Lady Harlech to Lord Harlech, Government House, Bloemfontein, 8 March 1947.

73 It is hard to see why Malan felt chippy about the Smuts family during their schooldays, if that is what Malan Jnr, Koorts and others imply. Jan Smuts's family were not well off. They were, however, a branch of the prosperous and considerably more anglicised Smuts family from Malmesbury and the surrounding district, and the Cape gentry of the Swartland of the day referred to the '*ryk* Smutses' and the '*arm* Smutses' (literally, the rich Smutses and the poor Smutses) (information, Martin Septimus Melck, Ryk Melck).

74 L Koorts, *DF Malan and the Rise of Afrikaner Nationalism* (Cape Town: Tafelberg, 2014), p 5, quoting Danie Malan (son).

75 *Hansard*, 21 March 1947.

76 Stellenbosch University, Malan Archives, 1/1/2280, Letter PW Botha to DF Malan, 3 March 1947.

CHAPTER 3

1 P van der Byl, *The Shadows Lengthen* (Cape Town: Howard Timmins, 1973), p 19.

2 This was apparently no mean feat, and the crack SAR drivers engaged to man the White Train were renowned for their skill in almost imperceptibly converting, with a big steam locomotive, a stationary train into one that smoothly moves forward. Similar skills were needed to bring the train to a halt in line with the waiting red carpet rolled out on the platforms at official stops along the way (L Pivnic, 'The Royal Tour of South Africa 1947', Transnet Heritage Library). A whitewashed line on the platform indicated where the centre of the engine cab window should be when the train was brought to a stand.

3 *Spotlight*, 4 April 1947. Interview with Reg Collard, train manager of the pilot train.

4 R Deakin, *An Intimate Record of the Tour of the Prince of Wales to Africa and South America* (New York: JB Lippincott, 1926).

5 Movietone News, 'Royal Train for South Africa'.

6 Six expert needlewomen in England worked in shifts for 16 hours a day to complete this work, an additional woman standing by to thread their needles (*Grocott's Mail*, 31 January 1947).

7 RA PS/PSO/GVI/PS/VISCOM/08100/33/1, 29 October 1946.

8 Interview, Lady Margaret Colville,

documentary on Queen Elizabeth the Queen Mother.

9 Letter Queen Elizabeth to Queen Elizabeth II dd 7 July 1953, in W Shawcross (ed), *Counting One's Blessings: The Selected Letters of Queen Elizabeth the Queen Mother* (London: Pan Books, 2013), p 471; some sources have this being done at Government House, but it seems to have happened on the train.

10 The sovereign's preference for Earl Grey had caused a flurry in the catering department of SAR&H, where such a blend was unheard of. Strong Indian tea, often slightly stewed, was habitually on offer.

11 RA QM/PRIV/CC13/172 Letter King George VI to Queen Mary, White Train, 9 March 1947.

12 E Joubert, *A Lion on the Landing: Memories of a South African Youth* (Vermont: Hemel & See Boeke, 2015), p 376.

13 Mrs Lawrence and Mrs Carinus, 'Fourteen Days with the Royal Family', *The South African Home Pictorial*, April 1947.

14 *The Cape Argus*, 26 April 1947.

15 *Grocott's Mail*, 24 January 1947.

16 D Morrah, *The Royal Family in South Africa* (London: Hutchinson, 1947), p 45.

17 '... telegrams from the cabinet office giving us the lowdown which are deciphered and typed for me by our admirable cypher office.' LASL CAM, Letter Lascelles to The Hon Joan Lascelles, 1 February 1947.

18 LASL CAC, Letter Lascelles to The Hon Lady Lascelles, White Train, nr Swellendam, 22 February 1947.

19 A Thaarup, *Heads & Tales* (London: Cassell, 1956), p 155.

20 J Lawrence (ed), *Vintage Year: The 1947 Diaries of Jean Lawrence* (Cape Town: Gryphon Press, 2012), p 11.

21 Letter Lascelles to Baring, quoted in Lawrence (ed), *Vintage Year*, p 21, n32.

22 NLW, BE&FR, PEC/1/46, Letter Lady Harlech to Lord Harlech, Mont des Sorces [sic], 16 March 1947.

23 C Elliot (ed), *The BBC Book of Royal Memories* (London: BBC Books, 1991), pp 23–24.

24 Transnet Heritage Library Collection, 'SAR Tour of Their Majesties. Special Instructions Regarding Arrangements on the Cape Midland System', p 35.

25 *The Daily Representative*, 26 March 1947,

syndicating James Cameron for the *Daily Express.*

26 All South African and many British newspapers ran detailed articles on the White Train, which was rightly viewed as a wonder of post-war, state-of-the-art rail travel. See also L Pivnic, 'The Royal Tour of South Africa'.

27 *Inkundla Ya Bantu*, 6 March 1947; see also *The Torch*, 24 February 1947.

28 RA/F&V/VISOV/SA/1947, Tour Diary, 5 March 1947; see note 18 above.

29 This, certainly not intended to be picked up, must have cleverly been turned into a running gag; the King mentions 'our personal Gestapo' in his warm, post-tour letter of thanks to Smuts (NASA, Smuts Papers, vol 82, no 4, Letter HM The King to Smuts, *Vanguard*, 2 May 1947).

30 Letter Lascelles to H Lawrence (undated) quoted in Lawrence (ed), *Vintage Year*, p 19.

31 Allister Sparks, who blossomed academically and socially at Queens College around this date and went on to an outstanding career in journalism, notes that the education at Queens, while it taught of the kings and queens of England, Napoleon, Bismarck and Garibaldi, omitted any mention of the re-emergence of black intellectual leadership at Lovedale College and Fort Hare then taking place not far from the school doors (Sparks, *The Sword and the Pen*, pp 49–50).

32 P Napier, *A Memoir of The Lady Delia Peel, Born Spencer, 1889–1981* (Wymondham: J & J Peel, 1984), p 127.

33 Transnet Library Heritage Collection, 'SAR Running Times of Royal and Pilot Trains, and Special Instructions Regarding Arrangements on the Cape Eastern System', pp 8–9. Three engines were used at times to haul the heavy train up steep gradients, another occasion being the line through the Kei Hills between Komgha and Butterworth, where the 760-ton train climbed 1 600 feet in 20 miles (*The Star*, 21 February 1947).

34 P Townsend, *Time and Chance: An Autobiography* (London: Collins, 1978), p 174.

35 Queenstown was the smallest town in the Union to have its own daily newspaper, known locally as 'The Daily Rep'. It is now a weekly.

36 According to the 1946 census. These

figures fall under 'Town and Village' for
Queenstown.

37 Transnet Heritage Library Collection,
'Visit of His Majesty the King, Her Majesty
the Queen and Their Royal Highnesses,
The Princess Elizabeth and the Princess
Margaret to the Union of South Africa, 1947,
Arrangements'.

38 All South African mayors then dressed like
English mayors along Dick Whittington
lines, with fur-lined robes and a cocked hat;
those in prosperous towns and cities had a
chain too.

39 In adulthood, several of her contemporaries
at a school reunion confessed to one another
that at the time they wished *their* father had
been killed in the war, which would have
enabled them to be chosen for this honour.

40 Despite the segregation of the time, these
movements had proved a popular and
successful means of upliftment since the
1930s (RA QEQH/PRIV/CSP/PAL/1937,
Lady Duncan to Queen Elizabeth,
15 December 1937).

41 *The Daily Representative*, 8 March 1947.

42 I am indebted to the Crankhandle Club of
Cape Town for this information.

43 The mayor, however, duly received a
'clear line' telegram from the King sent
immediately after the stop from the
telegraph office on the White Train,
thanking Queenstown for its loyal welcome,
and engagingly added a bit about the pigeons
which had been seen from the train flying
well northwest from the town, red, white
and blue still streaming behind them: 'Would
be gratified if you could confirm this or
otherwise and telegraph details' (*The Daily
Representative*, 8 March 1947).

44 Much of this information is gleaned from *The
Daily Representative*; I am grateful to Margaret
Walton, Ann King (both née Skillicorn) and
Patty St Leger (née Shannon) for verifying
and adding much to it. Queenstown as
thus described fairly represents a typically
predominantly English-speaking small town
in South Africa of that era. Even towns with
Afrikaans-speaking majorities exhibited
some of this anglicised, *Cranford*-esque flavour
at this date, however. See, for example, H J
Vermaas, *Die Aamborstige Klok*, which describes
Pearston, a Karoo village, just before the war.

45 Beaufort West was then a pretty, if hot and
dusty, Karoo town of mostly verandah-ed
Victorian buildings; the pear trees planted
along the *leiwater* furrows were a sight in
blossom time. Although many of the farmers in
the surrounding district were English-speaking,
the town was predominantly Afrikaans, the
shopkeepers uncompromisingly insisting on
using it, and English farmers' children sent to
the preparatory school hostel there were called
rooineks by their contemporaries (interview,
Wendy Jackson). The triumphal arch
through which the royal Daimler passed was
a resourcefully recycled one, previously used
to welcome the ox-wagons in the Voortrekker
Centenary in 1938.

46 NLW BE & FR PEC 11/1/44, Letter Lady
Harlech to Lord Harlech, Government
House, Bloemfontein, 8 March 1947.

47 LASL CAC Letter Lascelles to 'Wool'
Lascelles, White Train, approaching
Bethlehem, 10 March 1947.

48 Information, Andrew Lamprecht, Summer
School, UCT, 2018.

49 RA QM/PRIV/CC13/172, Letter Queen
Elizabeth to Queen Mary, White Train,
9 March 1947.

50 *The Star*, 11 March 1947.

51 RA F&V/VISOV/SA/1947, Tour Diary,
6 March 1947.

52 Van der Byl, *The Shadows Lengthen*, pp 26–27.

53 *The Friend*, 28 February 1947.

54 *The Cape Argus*, 21 April 1947.

55 RA PS/PSO/GVI/PS/
VISCOM/08100/19/071-072. Maritsane
was then considered to be part of
Bechuanaland although, like its capital,
Mafeking (Mahikeng), it was technically
outside its borders. The letter, forwarded
from her friend Miss Marjorie Polkinghorne,
who lived in Sandown just outside
Johannesburg, must have moved Lascelles to
whom it was passed on, for he filed it, and
it surely would have thrilled Miss Green to
know that it was to be preserved at Windsor.

56 *The Star*, 15 March 1947.

57 RA QM/PRIV/CC13/151, Letter Princess
Elizabeth to Queen Mary, Government
House, Bloemfontein, 9 March 1947.

58 Quoted in Napier, *A Memoir of The Lady Delia
Peel*, pp 130–131.

59 Van der Byl, *The Shadows Lengthen*, p 23.

60 Quoted in E Longford, *The Queen Mother: A Biography* (London: Weidenfeld & Nicolson, 1981), p 105.

61 Private information given to the author.

62 James Cameron, 'Boosting Bertie', in *The Best of Cameron* (London: Hodder & Stoughton, 1981), p 328. Cameron's description – also a reconstruction made years later and much more of a generic one – is less convincing than Aronson's (see note 64 below), though it captures the essentials.

63 T Aronson, *Royal Subjects: A Biographer's Encounters* (London: Macmillan, 2001), p 29.

64 The Athlones had advised the King and Queen that their most successful method of breaking the ice with the Afrikaners had been to go and drink coffee with them in their farmhouses.

65 Interview, Sir David Graaff.

66 T Aronson, *Royal Ambassadors: British Royalties in Southern Africa, 1860–1947* (Cape Town: David Philip, 1975), p 113. Aronson's description is a reconstruction, written years later, of what he witnessed as a schoolboy yet it captures an authentic note of the neo-Georgian court. For example, see the letter from Lady Diana Cooper to her son, John Julius Norwich, circa 10 July 1949, in D Cooper, *Darling Monster: The Letters of Lady Diana Cooper to Her Son John Julius Norwich 1939–1952* (London: Chatto & Windus, 2013), p 395, in which she reproduces the conversation, in a very different social sphere, in the royal receiving line at Buckingham Palace at around this date.

67 Van der Byl, *The Shadows Lengthen*, pp 24–25.

68 Ibid, p 22.

69 Lawrence (ed), *Vintage Year*, p 13.

70 Townsend, *Time and Chance*, p 17.

71 D Rivett-Carnac, 'The Royal Visit to Grahamstown', *Annals of the Grahamstown Historical Society*, vol 2, no 3 [no date], pp 5–6, has a version of this. Another variation of it appeared on the front pages of the *Rand Daily Mail*, 1 March 1947. It was repeated and recalled, possibly embellished.

72 Letter Queen Elizabeth to Queen Mary 16 April 1947, in Shawcross (ed), *Counting One's Blessings*, pp 397–398.

73 Townsend, *Time and Chance*, pp 175–176.

74 Lawrence (ed), *Vintage Year*, pp 14–15

75 Ibid, p 16.

76 RA QM/PRIV/CC13/172, Letter Queen Elizabeth to Queen Mary, White Train, 9 March 1947.

77 Townsend, *Time and Chance*, p 172.

78 Diana Cooper Papers, Eton College Library, Box VII, Letter Lady Jones to Lady Diana Cooper, St James, Cape Town, March 1947.

79 Van der Byl, *The Shadows Lengthen*, p 32.

80 Interview, Major Harvey, in 'Queen Elizabeth, the Queen Mother', BBC documentary, 2016. Available at youtube.com/watch?v=SzgUo3NaCOg; accessed on 11 July 2018.

81 LASL CAC, Letter Lascelles to The Hon Lady Lascelles, 30 April 1947.

82 *The Cape Argus*, 25 April 1947.

CHAPTER 4

1 RA QM/PRIV/CC/14/151, Letter Princess Elizabeth to Queen Mary, Government House, Bloemfontein, 9 March 1947.

2 RA F&V/VISOV/SA/1947, 7 March 1947.

3 J Haasbroek, 'Die Britse Koningsbesoek aan Bloemfontein, Maart 1947', *Narvorsinge van die Nasionale Museum, Bloemfontein*, vol 16, no 8 (2000), pp 213–259.

4 Interview, Elsa Steytler (née Joubert).

5 RA QM/PRIV/CC/13/163, Letter Queen Elizabeth to Queen Mary, White Train, 9 March 1947.

6 *The Friend*, 7 March 1947.

7 LASL CAC, Letter Lascelles to 'Wool' Lascelles, White Train Approaching Bethlehem, OFS, 10 March 1947.

8 *The Friend*, 8 March 1947.

9 This is covered in H Sapire and A Grundlingh, 'Rebuffing Royals? Afrikaners and the Royal Visit to South Africa in 1947', *The Journal of Imperial and Commonwealth History*, vol 46, no 3 (2018), pp 524–551.

10 *Die Volksblad*, 7 March 1947.

11 Ibid, 8 March 1947.

12 Haasbroek, 'Die Britse Koningsbesoek'.

13 *Die Volksblad*, 8 March 1947.

14 *Die Patriot*, no 280, April 1947.

15 *Die Volksblad*, 20 January 1947.

16 Ibid, 15 February 1947.

17 Ibid, 20 February 1947.

18 Haasbroek, 'Die Britse Koningsbesoek'.

19 Ibid.

20 *The Star*, 21 March 1947.

21 D Morrah, *The Royal Family in South Africa* (London: Hutchinson, 1947), p 73.

22 *The Star*, 21 March 1947, quoting a letter to *Die Volksblad*.

23 *The Friend*, 'Talk of the Day', 8 March 1947.

24 RA/QM/PRIV/CC14/151, Letter Princess Elizabeth to Queen Mary, Government House, Bloemfontein, 9 March 1947.

25 Duncan Papers, University of Cape Town Libraries, BC294 D5.30.6, Letter Sir Patrick Duncan to Lady Selborne, Government House, Pretoria, 25 August 1942.

26 RA QM/PRIV/CC/13/172, Letter Queen Elizabeth to Queen Mary, White Train, 9 March 1947.

27 Ibid.

28 LASL CAC, Letter Lascelles to The Hon Lady Lascelles, Government House, Bloemfontein, 7 March 1947.

29 *The Friend*, 'Talk of the Day', 8 March 1947.

30 The 82-year-old Mrs Steyn was the widow of the last president of the Orange Free State. Her son, Dr Colin Steyn, was Minister in Attendance on the Free State leg of the tour; her daughter, Miss Gladys Steyn, also present at the tea, was a Member of the Provincial Council. Some political intrigue had indeed been made about initial plans for Mrs Steyn to be presented publicly in the Fourth Chamber; this visit, however, put paid to any idea of her absence being a snub. The rumour that she was opposed to the Royal Family seems wide of the mark. She had met the Prince of Wales in 1925 and had sent Queen Mary, whom she had met and greatly admired in London when she was Princess of Wales, many messages via Queen Elizabeth (RA QM/PRIV/CC13/172, Letter Queen Elizabeth to Queen Mary, The White Train, 9 March 1947). Indeed, she was dressed for the occasion much like the old Queen – *comme une grande dame* – in a long dress, pearls, fur cape and hat. It is inaccurate to state, as some historians now claim, that she pointedly put on Voortrekker dress for the visit.

31 F&V/VISOV/SA/1947, Tour Diary, 7 March 1947.

32 *Eastern Province Herald*, 8 March 1947.

33 Interview, Elsa Steytler (née Joubert).

34 As children, she and her friends in Paarl would walk out in droves and sing their alternative in the street: 'God save the King, dip him in paraffin, don't let him kick or scream, God Save the King.' Her childhood diary records a 'Bah!' on the day of George V's Silver Jubilee and the fact that the family did not celebrate Empire Day; see E Joubert, *A Lion on the Landing: Memories of a South African Youth* (Vermont: Hemel & See Boeke, 2015), pp 88–89.

35 Ibid.

36 Interview, Elsa Steytler (née Joubert).

37 Joubert, *A Lion on the Landing*, p 373.

38 *The Friend*, 28 February 1947.

39 NLW, BE&FR, PEC 11/1/44, Letter Lady Harlech to Lord Harlech, Government House, Bloemfontein, 8 March 1947.

40 *The Friend*, 'Talk of the Day', 8 March 1947.

41 NLW, BE&FR, PEC/11/1/44, Letter Lady Harlech to Lord Harlech, Government House, Bloemfontein, 8 March 1947.

42 Ibid.

43 RA QM/PRIV/CC14/277, Letter Princess Margaret to Queen Mary, White Train, 10 March 1947.

44 *The Friend*, 10 March 1947.

45 Interview, Elsa Steytler (née Joubert).

46 *The Friend*, 10 March 1947.

47 F&V/VISOV/SA/1947, 8 March 1947.

48 *The Friend*, 10 March 1947.

49 Ibid.

50 Joubert, *A Lion on the Landing*, p 376.

51 M Crawford, *The Little Princesses* (London: Cassell, 1950), p 20.

52 *Die Volksblad*, 10 March 1947.

53 This numberplate, formerly on Hans van Rensburg's official car, would cause consternation in wartime Bloemfontein. Though it represented a Bloemfontein vehicle, it could be taken to stand for Ossewabrandwag 1.

54 *The Friend*, 'Talk of the Day', 10 March 1947.

55 *Die Volksblad*, 10 March 1947.

56 RA QM/PRIV/CC/13/163, Letter Queen Elizabeth to Queen Mary, White Train, 9 March 1947.

57 Information, the Hon Mrs O'Neill (née Cavendish).

58 K Mincher, *I Lived in His Shadow: My Life with General Smuts* (Cape Town: Howard Timmins, 1965), p 152.

59 *The Friend*, 10 March 1947.

60 Ibid.

61 Kew-trained Mr Bates, a 'first-class gardener' (Lady Harlech), had been gassed in the First World War, necessitating a move for a lifetime to a drier climate. He and Lady Duncan must have planned a military-like seed-sowing campaign to ensure a late show like this (PEC 11/1/44, Lady Harlech to Lord Harlech, Government House, Bloemfontein, 8 March 1947). A team of 200 black gardeners ensured this and the other municipal flower displays for the visit.

62 NLW, BE&FR, PEC 11/1/44, Letter Lady Harlech to Lord Harlech, Government House, Bloemfontein, 8 March 1947.

63 When the spirit moved her, Pam Barlow, who we will meet briefly in Chapter 9, would give a spirited imitation of Lady Duncan addressing her from the throne, in a rasping and passably patrician voice, when she made a curtsy to her as a debutante at King's House, Durban, before the war.

64 Duncan Papers, University of Cape Town Libraries, BC 294 D5 30.3, Letter Sir Patrick Duncan to Lady Selborne, 20 June 1942.

65 £13 000 had been spent on the interiors alone (Ian Shapiro Collection, Terry Archives).

66 Lady Diana Cooper Papers, Eton College Library, Box VII, Letter Lady Jones to Lady Diana Cooper, Maseru, [poorly dated] March 1947.

67 The Friend, 8 March 1947.

68 NLW, BE&FR, PEC 11/1/44, Letter Lady Harlech to Lord Harlech, Government House, Bloemfontein, 8 March 1947.

69 Ibid.

70 AG Barlow, Almost in Confidence (Cape Town: Juta, 1952), p 320.

71 NM Stultz, Afrikaner Politics in South Africa, 1934–1948 (Berkeley: University of California Press, 1975), pp 104–105; see also Dr EG Malherbe, Never a Dull Moment: Autobiography (Cape Town: Howard Timmins, 1981), p 283.

72 Barlow, Almost in Confidence, p 320.

73 The Friend, 19 March 1947.

74 L Koorts, DF Malan and the Rise of Afrikaner Nationalism (Cape Town: Tafelberg, 2014), pp 372–373.

75 At matins at Cape Town's Cathedral on the Sunday the White Train arrived back in Cape Town, the Archbishop's sermon deprecated the attitude that prevailed among some in South Africa, and indeed elsewhere in the Empire, which opposed giving education to blacks on the grounds that it gave them (dangerous) ideas above their station. The Smuts government's plans to extend black education were praised.

76 The Friend, 10 March 1947.

77 NLW, BE&FR, PEC/11/1/44, Letter Lady Harlech to Lord Harlech, Government House, Bloemfontein, 8 March 1947.

CHAPTER 5

1 Known as 'double-gin-and-I-love-you' to the officers, sailors and Tommies off wartime convoys, sent via this station to be entertained by the Joan Hunter Dunns of Eshowe for jolly, recuperative breaks by the Durban branch of the SAWAS.

2 LASL, CAM, Letter Lascelles to The Hon Lady Lascelles, White Train Approaching Durban, 19 March 1947.

3 When showing the King and Queen through to the newly decorated bedroom set aside for them, the wife of the Native Commissioner for Eshowe was horrified to see their cat curled up asleep on the new counterpane. 'Oh, hello, Kitty,' said the King, apparently well aware of the old adage about cats and kings, and Mrs Burton's mortification was swiftly turned to smiles (interview, Judith Field, née Handley, as told to her by Veronica Burton).

4 The Zululand Times, 21 March 1947.

5 LASL CAC, Letter Lascelles to The Hon Lady Lascelles, White Train, Approaching Aliwal North, 6 March 1947.

6 P Townsend, Time and Chance: An Autobiography (London: Collins, 1978), pp 169–170.

7 S Marks, 'Afterword: Worlds of Impossibilities' in The Ambiguities of Dependence in South Africa: Class, Nationalism, and the State in Twentieth Century Natal (Johannesburg: Ravan Press, 1986), p 267ff.

8 NASA, Smuts Papers, The Second World War, vol 75, no 211, p 649, Letter Smuts to Margaret Gillett, Doornkloof, 22 November 1944.

9 Hansard, January 1947.

10 Inkundla Ya Bantu, 6 March 1947.

11 D Hart-Davis (ed), King's Counsellor: Abdication and War. The Diaries of Sir Alan Lascelles (London: Weidenfeld & Nicolson, 2006), p viii.

12 J Paxman, Empire: What Ruling the World Did to

the British (London: Viking Penguin, 2012), p 263.

13 Duncan Papers, University of Cape Town Libraries, BC294 E20.1.21, Letter Queen Elizabeth to Lady Duncan, Buckingham Palace, 25 January 1943.

14 R Schuknecht, *Colonial Development Policy After the Second World War: The Case of Sukumaland, Tanganyika* (Münster: LIT Verlag, 2010), p 198.

15 RA QM/PRIV/CC/13/176, Letter Queen Elizabeth to Queen Mary, White Train, Bechuanaland, 16?[sic] April 1947.

16 N Ferguson, *Empire: How Britain Made the Modern World* (London: Penguin, 2004), p 350.

17 *Life*, October 1942.

18 Churchill naturally saw this as applying to countries under Nazi rule. Not so Roosevelt, who was strongly anti-imperialist. It did not, however, prevent Roosevelt from swiftly scrapping the principle when he came to negotiate with Stalin over the fate of Eastern Europe towards the end of the war.

19 L James, *Churchill and Empire: A Portrait of an Imperialist* (New York: Pegasus Books, 2014), p 229.

20 M Soames, *A Daughter's Tale* (London: Black Swan, 2012), p 276; Gerald Pawle, *The War and Colonel Warden* (London: Harrap, 1963), pp 249–250.

21 R Steyn, *Jan Smuts: Unafraid of Greatness* (Cape Town: Jonathan Ball, 2015), p 230

22 Letter Smuts to Mrs Smuts, dd 21 September 1946, in J van der Poel (ed), *Selections from the Smuts Papers, Vol VII: August 1945–September 1950* (Cambridge: Cambridge University Press (2007), p 86.

23 Resolutions of the ANC Annual Conference, 14–17 December 1946.

24 *Ilanga Lase Natal*, 25 January 1947.

25 J Lawrence (ed), *Vintage Year: The Diaries of Jean St Leger Lawrence for 1947* (Cape Town: Gryphon Press, 2012), 1 March 1947.

26 RA F&V/VISOV/SA/1947, Tour Diary, Press Digest, 27 February 1947.

27 SD Gish, *Alfred B Xuma: African, American, South African* (London: Macmillan, 2000), p 155; see also Confidential Report by Brigadier for the Commissioner of the South African Police, 'Indian, Communist and Native Boycott in Connection with the Royal Visit of T M's The King, Queen and the Princesses' quoted in H

Sapire, 'African Loyalism and its Discontents: The Royal Tour of South Africa, 1947', *The Historical Journal*, vol 54 (March 2011).

28 *Imvo Zabantsundu*, 8 March 1947.

29 Sapire, 'African Loyalism and its Discontents', pp 215–240.

30 Ibid.

31 *The Natal Mercury*, 24 July 1946.

32 *Die Burger*, 4 April 1947.

33 RA F&V/VISOV/SA/1947, Tour Diary, 22 March 1947.

34 J Iliffe, *Honour in African History* (Cambridge: Cambridge University Press, 2005), p 143.

35 T Ranger, 'The Invention of Tradition', in E Hobsbawm and T Ranger (eds), *The Invention of Tradition in Colonial Africa* (Cambridge: Cambridge University Press, 2012), pp 220–266, discusses this issue in a general colonial African study.

36 *Inkundla Ya Bantu*, 17 April 1947, Letter Skobela ka Mabaso to Editor.

37 NASA NTS 7618 112/378, Letter Secretary for Native Affairs to Minister for Native Affairs, [date unclear] 1946.

38 *The Natal Mercury*, 20 March 1947.

39 Letter Marquard to Hofmeyr, 25 September 1946, quoted in P Rich, *White Power and Liberal Conscience: Racial Segregation and South African Liberalism, 1921–1960* (Manchester: Manchester University Press, 1984), p 91.

40 *The Zululand Times*, 31 March 1947.

41 *Ilanga Lase Natal*, 15 March 1947.

42 123 000 non-white South Africans joined up to serve in the war; the figures for the whites was 211 000. This contrasts with Southern Rhodesia (now Zimbabwe): 99 927 whites and 14 300 blacks. The figure for Kenya was 98 240, Nigeria 121 650 and Basutoland 21 460, the last three figures being non-racially divided; see D Killingray, *Fighting for Britain: African Soldiers in the Second World War* (Woodbridge: James Currey, 2010), p 44.

43 *The Zululand Times*, 31 March 1947.

44 Interview, Norma Ellis Brown (née Brockwell).

45 *Rand Daily Mail*, 19 March 1947.

46 Interview, Norma Ellis Brown (née Brockwell).

47 *The Natal Mercury*, 19 March 1947.

48 *The Zululand Times*, 21 March 1947.

49 RA F&V/VISOV/SA/1947, Tour Diary, 5 March 1947.

50 RA PS/PSO/GVI/PS/VISCOM/08100 /01D/67. On his return from the recce in 1946, Sir Piers Legh wrote that 'both Evelyn Baring and Forsyth stressed the importance of The King wearing distinctive uniform at Native Gatherings. Should His Majesty wear naval white uniform it is most desirable that He should wear a riband and star'.

51 RA F&V/VISOV/SA/1947, Tour Diary, 3 April 1947.

52 *The Natal Witness,* 21 and 22 March 1947.

53 Interview, Judy Field (née Handley).

54 *The Natal Mercury,* 20 March 1947.

55 Interview, Judy Field (née Handley).

56 *The Natal Mercury,* 20 March 1947; 'Natalie' describes the clothes worn.

57 Private information.

58 RA QM/PRIV/CC 14/148, Letter Princess Elizabeth to Queen Mary, White Train, 28 March 1947.

59 *The Natal Witness,* 20 March 1947.

60 *Rand Daily Mail,* 20 March 1947.

61 *The Zululand Times,* 31 March 1947.

62 Brookes wrote to *Inkundla Ya Bantu* on 6 March 1947, saying, 'We were all pleased' with the King's 'inspiring speech ... which made special and sympathetic reference to the need for finding solutions and ways of life which would produce greater harmony among the many different races and colours which make up the Union'. It also stated that the Native Parliamentary Representatives were seated in the front row at the presentation of the Loyal Address at Government House. The letter was prominently featured on the Letters page.

63 A letter to the editor from Skobela ka Mabaso, in *Inkundla Ya Bantu,* 17 April 1947, headed 'King's Visit, People Betrayed?' deals with this issue, while at the same time reiterating that all Africans respected the King. A subsequent, radically phrased article vented fury on both Xuma and Luthuli for attending the Eshowe dance. (*Inkundla Ya Bantu,* 1 May 1947).

64 *The Zululand Times,* 31 March 1947.

65 *The Natal Mercury,* 20 March 1947.

66 The point was not lost on the editor of *Ilanga Lase Natal,* whose leader of 1 March 1947 ran: 'We welcome their majesties as true and loyal South Africans. But our sweetest thoughts about them are tinged with sorrow.

For who can hide the fact that the event brings back memories of the days of the Black Rulers and of tribal democracy, that today we are not citizens in the country of our birth, that our leaders and national organisations have not been consulted about the King's visit and the programme even in African areas; that our educated and gifted have been ignored; that the story of our progress and achievement will not be told.'

67 Souvenir Programme of the *Ngoma Umkosi, passim,* notes by Hugh Tracey, Killie Campbell Africana Library, Durban. Zulu was traditionally a spoken language and its spellings at this date were variable. I am grateful to Stella Cockburn for helping me bring these in line with current usage.

68 RA F&V/VISOV/SA/1947, Tour Diary, 19 March 1947.

69 Ibid.

70 RA QM/PRIV/CC 14/152, Letter Princess Elizabeth to Queen Mary, White Train, 28 March 1947.

71 Interview, Judy Field (née Handley).

72 RA F&V/VISOV/SA/1947, Tour Diary, 19 March 1947.

73 RA QM/PRIV/CC 13/166, Letter Queen Elizabeth to Queen Mary, Government House, Cape Town, 21 February 1947.

74 RA QM/PRIV/CC14/148 Letter Princess Elizabeth to Queen Mary, *Vanguard,* 16 February 1947.

75 Townsend, *Time and Chance,* pp 169–170.

76 P van der Byl, *The Shadows Lengthen* (Cape Town: Howard Timmins, 1973), p 29.

77 Ibid, p 20; D Morrah, *The Royal Family in South Africa* (London: Hutchinson, 1947), p 71.

78 Marks, *The Ambiguities of Dependence in South Africa,* pp 275–276.

79 Marquard Papers, University of Cape Town Libraries, BC 587. BI 674, Letter Leo Marquard to Nell Marquard, 3 August 1945.

80 S Bradford, *George VI* (London: Penguin, 2002), p 517.

81 NASA, Smuts Papers, Smuts Letter 1444, Smuts to Margaret Gillett, Groote Schuur, 2 March 1947.

82 A Paton, *Hofmeyr* (Cape Town: Oxford University Press, 1964), p 443.

83 RA QM/PRIV CC 14/152, Letter Princess Elizabeth to Queen Mary, White Train, 28 March 1947.

84 Ibid.

85 B Pimlott, *The Queen: Elizabeth II and the Monarchy* (London: HarperPress, 2012), p 565; see also B Pimlott, 'Some Thoughts on the Queen and the Commonwealth', *The Round Table*, vol 87, no 347 (1998) pp 303–305.

86 Information, Sir Anthony Reeve.

87 *The Natal Mercury*, 19 March 1947.

88 *The Zululand Times*, 22 March 1947.

89 *Rand Daily Mail*, 20 March 1947.

90 RA QM/PRIV/CC/14/152, Letter Princess Elizabeth to Queen Mary, White Train, 28 March 1947.

91 'This place is very Bombay-like in climate and appearance' (LASL CAC, Letter Lascelles to The Hon Lady Lascelles, King's House, Durban, 21 March 1947).

92 According to the 1946 census.

93 *The Natal Mercury*, 24 March 1947.

94 Her much-admired clothes for the royal visit came from the Durban-born Victor Stiebel, by then a celebrated English couturier.

95 Interview, Norma Ellis Brown (née Brockwell).

96 R Sweet, *Pambili Bo: The Story of Natal's Spitfire Squadron* (Durban: FAD Publishers, 2006), *passim*.

97 See G Viney, *Colonial Houses of South Africa* (Cape Town: Struik Publishers, 1988), chapters on Lynton Hall and Ellingham, both large Natal houses.

98 *The Natal Witness*, 21 March 1947.

99 Morrah, *The Royal Family in Africa*, p 90.

100 *The Natal Mercury*, 21 March 1947.

101 PS Gibson, *Durban's Lady in White: An Autobiography* (Durban: Aedificamus Press, 1991), p 34

102 Ibid, p 68.

103 Ibid, p 180.

104 Perla Gibson was not forgotten after the war; she was regularly flown to England and elsewhere to sing at armed forces reunions. After her death, the Royal Navy erected a statue to her at Durban Docks; it was unveiled by Queen Elizabeth II in 1995.

105 *Die Volksblad*, 20 March 1947.

106 Ibid.

107 RA PS 08100/07/009.

108 RA PS 08100/07/313.

109 *The Natal Witness*, 21 March 1947.

110 *The Star*, 20 March 1947.

111 *The Cape Argus*, 20 March 1947.

112 *The Star*, 21 March 1947.

113 Quoted in W Shawcross (ed), *Queen Elizabeth: The Queen Mother. The Official Biography* (London: Macmillan, 2009), p 618.

114 'Smuts is anxious that there should be no advance publicity of this arrangement. I hope to goodness that it is now finally settled. For God's sake don't let there be any publicity about this,' is the note penned by an exasperated Lascelles to the original request for the King to take the salute at this march (RA PS 08100/51/1–9). Lascelles discouraged many appeals for royal recognition by similar organisations during the tour's planning by referring them to the official committees: 'I am under a solemn compact with Smuts's people to treat all invitations in this way [getting them passed by his office] and it is, indeed, the only method' (RA PS 08100/19/015-017).

115 *Rand Daily Mail*, 6 November 1947.

116 *The Cape Argus*, 8 November 1947.

117 Van der Byl, *The Shadows Lengthen*, p 31.

118 *The Star*, 20 March 1947; *The Natal Mercury*, 21 March 1947.

119 *The Natal Witness*, 21 March 1947.

120 *Natal Daily News*, 22 March 1947.

121 *The Natal Mercury*, 24 March 1947.

122 Van der Byl, *The Shadows Lengthen*, p 32.

123 *The Star*, 22 March 1947.

124 *The Natal Witness*, 21 March 1947.

125 Ibid.

126 RA PS/08100/19/105, 5 November 1946.

127 See chapter on Royal Visit, 1947, in ES Reddy and F Meer (eds), *Passive Resistance – 1946: A Selection of Documents* (Durban: Madiba Publishers, Institute for Black Research, 1996).

128 *The Guardian*, 23 January 1947.

129 *The Sun*, 14 February 1947.

130 *Inkundla Ya Bantu*, 6 March 1947.

131 *The Star*, 20 February 1947.

132 Ibid.

133 Ibid, and Reddy and Meer, *Passive Resistance – 1946*, chapter on royal visit.

134 Letter Smuts to Sir Benjamin Robertson, 21 August 1914, quoted in WK Hancock and J van der Poel (eds), *Selections from the Smuts Papers, Vol III: June 1910–1918* (Cambridge: Cambridge University Press, 1966), pp 138–139.

135 *The Natal Witness*, 24 March 1947.

136 *World Review*, 11 February 1947.

137 In 1923 Smuts had actively campaigned for Southern Rhodesia to become part of the Union. A majority of around 3 000 of a very limited electorate voted against this, a significant factor being that Rhodesian civil servants did not wish to have to learn Afrikaans. Rhodesia had become a self-governing colony. Had Smuts succeeded in persuading them, his political career in South Africa would have been very different.

138 Bodleian Library, University of Oxford, MS, Violet Milner Papers, V48, Letter Major Richards to Lady Milner, 23 April 1947. Richards was assured of this by Morrah; Baring, significantly, had worked hard to prevent this.

139 M Mazower, *No Enchanted Palace: The End of Empire and the Ideological Origins of the United Nations* (Princeton: Princeton University Press, 2013), pp 156–157.

140 S Dubow, 'Smuts, the United Nations and the Rhetoric of Race and Rights', *Journal of Contemporary History*, vol 43, no 1 (January 2008), p 52.

141 M Basner, *Am I an African? The Political Memoirs of HM Basner* (Johannesburg: Witwatersrand University Press, 1993). In January 1947 Basner called for a national convention of representatives of all racial groups to arrive at a national racial policy, the results of which would be submitted to the UN for its approval. The same day, Senator Van Niekerk (HNP) called for the creation of a joint committee of both Houses of Parliament to devise a comprehensive colour policy for the Union based on the principles of separation.

142 Dubow, 'Smuts, the United Nations and the Rhetoric of Race and Rights', p 65.

143 Lawrence (ed), *Vintage Year*, 18 September 1947.

144 Mazower, *No Enchanted Palace*, p 153.

145 Ibid, p 189. Smuts stopped to congratulate Basner back in Parliament in Cape Town, where the latter was almost a pariah now: 'You have worked hard for your constituents and understand how much the world has changed. We must all change with it.'

CHAPTER 6

1 *Die Burger*, typically, had already deplored the fact in a leader that the King had played tennis in Durban on the King's House court on a Sunday. 'His advisors,' said the editor, 'had been guilty of an unfortunate dereliction of duty.' On Smuts's advice, this was taken to be an obvious political gambit and had been ignored (RA F&V/VISOV/ SA/1947, Tour Diary, 26 March 1947). The Royal Family were, however, given credit when they attended a service in the Groote Kerk in Pretoria. (Smuts broke his rule about churchgoing and attended with them.) Revd J Reyneke said in his address that the people of South Africa had 'noted with admiration and respect that, wherever they might be, the Royal family made a point of attending Divine Service, whether such visits were included amongst their official engagements or not.' Tickets were issued for this service to the regular parishioners; a brisk secondary market was soon established, with the price rising to £30 a seat (*Sunday Times*, 23 March 1947).

2 Information, Jean Lawrence, who went as a young Cabinet minister's wife to live in Pretoria for six months each year in the 1930s and 1940s.

3 RA F&V/VISOV/SA/1947, Tour Diary, 26 March 1947.

4 K Mincher, *I Lived in His Shadow: My Life with General Smuts* (Cape Town: Howard Timmins, 1965), p 151.

5 A Paton, *Hofmeyr* (Cape Town: Oxford University Press), p 85.

6 *The Star*, 19 March 1947. The chrysanthemums grown were Lady Hopeton rose, mauve, double-yellow and bronze dazzler; 10 000 'Gold Dust' gladioli were planted in five separate nurseries.

7 'I can still smell the damp moss,' recalled his daughter, Penny, years later. 'Harry Bruins-Lich', profile by Carolize Jansen, 2011 Available at www.carolizejansen.com/Harry-Bruinslich.html, accessed on 4 July 2018.

8 *Rand Daily Mail*, 31 March 1947.

9 RA QM PRIV/CC/13/174, Letter King George to Queen Mary, Government House, Pretoria, 6 April 1947.

10 G Viney, *Colonial Houses of South Africa* (Cape Town: Struik Publishers, 1988), pp 254–256.

11 Ibid, p 208.

12 RA QM /PRIV/CC/14/153, Letter Princess Elizabeth to Queen Mary, Government House, Salisbury, 9 April 1947.

13 RA QM/PRIV/CC/13/ 175, Letter Queen Elizabeth to Queen Mary, White Train, Bechuanaland, 16[?] April 1947.

14 LASL CAC/14, Letter Lascelles to The Hon Lady Lascelles, Government House, Salisbury, 7 April 1947.

15 Duncan Papers, University of Cape Town Libraries, BC294 D4.30.35, Lady Selborne to Sir Patrick Duncan, 17 November 1936[?].

16 *Milady*, February 1947.

17 *Pretoria News*, 31 January 1947.

18 RA PS 08100/19/023, Letter Earl of Clarendon to Lascelles.

19 RA PS 08100/19/ 021 and 023. Almost certainly the most memorable floral display during the tour (quite marvellous, thought Lady Harlech) was provided by the Cape Turf Club, where the tables within the great red-and-white-striped luncheon marquee erected at Kenilworth, were banked with rare red disas, stripped in numbers unthinkable today from mountain gorges. The Tour Diary also mentions the beautiful flowers at Graaff-Reinet.

20 *Rand Daily Mail*, 31 January 1947.

21 *Cape Times*, 31 March 1947.

22 *The Star*, 19 March 1947.

23 *Die Vaderland*, 27 March 1947.

24 *Rand Daily Mail*, 31 March 1947.

25 *Pretoria News*, 31 March 1947.

26 The 1946 census shows the numbers as English 42 362, Afrikaans 82 710.

27 RA QM/PRIV/CC/14/ 153, Letter Princess Elizabeth to Queen Mary, Government House, Salisbury, 7 April 1947.

28 RA QM/PRIV/CC14/153, Letter Princess Elizabeth to Queen Mary, Government House, Salisbury, 7 April 1947.

29 LASL CAC, Letter Lascelles to The Hon Lady Lascelles, White Train, Johannesburg, 1 April 1947.

30 Bodleian Library, University of Oxford, MS, Violet Milner Papers, VM 48, Letter Maj GR Richards to Lady Milner, 23 April 1947; and S Bradford, *King George VI* (London: Penguin, 2002), pp 517–518. The press reports of this omitted the harsher-sounding sentences.

31 Ibid, p 519.

32 Bodleian Library, University of Oxford, MS, Violet Milner Papers, VM 48, Letter Major Richards to Lady Milner, 23 April 1947.

33 Ibid.

34 See 'Janius', 'In South Africa To-day – Whither?' and 'After the Royal Visit', *National Review*, February and June, respectively, possibly written by Lady Milner herself.

35 Bodleian Library, University of Oxford, MS, Violet Milner Papers, U1599 C554/26, Letter Maj Richards to Lady Milner, 19 March 1947.

36 Bodleian Library, University of Oxford, MS, Violet Milner Papers, VM 48, Letter Maj Richards to Lady Milner, 23 April 1947.

37 C Elliot (ed), *The BBC Book of Royal Memories* (London: BBC Books, 1991), pp 28–29. This has the King, Smuts the Queen and even her Dresser all cooperating to avoid a repeat of the very delayed broadcast of the King's speech from the protracted State Banquet in Cape Town. Despite every effort, including the cancelling of one of the courses, the waiters had burst into the room to replenish the glasses just as the King was about to speak.

38 RA QM PRIV/CC/13/174, Letter King George to Queen Mary, Government House, Pretoria, 6 April 1947. Queen Mary must have cabled or written immediately to the King that his reference to Britain's trials in his speech had gone down well at home.

39 Ibid.

40 RA PS 08100/07/037.

41 LASL CAC/ 13, Letter Lascelles to The Hon Lady Lascelles, White Train, Johannesburg, 1 April 1947.

42 *Grocott's Mail*, 1 April 1947, *Cape Times*, 31 March 1947, and most other South African newspapers covered the speech.

43 Many of these Boer veterans retained their allegiance to Smuts and would turn out at recruitment drives and victory pageants during the Second World War. They were, of course, the vanquished, and some must have lost their women and children in the concentration camps. In their old age, they seem to have carried less animosity than might be expected, even tactfully suggesting the foot of the statue of Louis Botha for the meeting, rather than that of Kruger as originally intended. After this, Van Rensburg's men asked to meet the Royal Family in Mafeking (*The Friend*, 18 March 1947).

44 The reception at Great Wigsell, in East Sussex, that evening, was poor; Lady Milner will have read the speech as reported in the newspapers.

45 *Pretoria News*, 31 March 1947.

46 Paton, *Hofmeyr*, p 451. As with most of the stories around Mrs Hofmeyr down the years, there are several versions of this, varying only slightly. Paton knew Mrs Hofmeyr well. She was a monster in many ways but he contrived to treat her fairly in his outstanding biography of her son. Nevertheless, he felt constrained not to publish it until after her death.

CHAPTER 7

1 LASL CAC 13, Letter Lascelles to The Hon Lady Lascelles, White Train, Johannesburg, 1 April 1947.

2 Governor-General of South Africa, 1924–1930. The Athlones were both very popular and very royal. The Countess was a granddaughter of Queen Victoria; the Earl was Queen Mary's brother. 'People are always asking after Uncle Alge and Aunt Alice,' wrote Princess Elizabeth to her grandmother.

3 P van der Byl, *The Shadows Lengthen* (Cape Town: Howard Timmins, 1973), p 26.

4 RA F&V/VISOV/SA/1947, Tour Diary, 1 April 1947.

5 Ibid.

6 E Patel (ed), *The World of Nat Nakasa* (Johannesburg: Picador, 2005), p 5.

7 L Nkosi, *Home and Exile* (London: Longman, 1965), p 26

8 E Mphahlele, *Down Second Avenue*, quoted in V Bickford-Smith, *The Emergence of the South African Metropolis: Cities and Identity in the Twentieth Century* (Cambridge: Cambridge University Press, 2016), p 237.

9 Kruger would have spun in his grave could he but have read *The Star* on the day of the visit, describing, with apparent insouciance, the way gold had transformed the Transvaal from the 'rustic republic lost in the interior of the continent to an industrial power in times of peace, an arsenal in war'. Doubtless some descendants of his supporters did read this, and ground their teeth in fury.

10 LASL/CAC/13, Letter Lascelles to The Hon Lady Lascelles, White Train, Johannesburg, 1 April 1947.

11 Ibid.

12 Welsh headed the Union Defence Force Liaison Committee, his post-war job being to ensure that returning ex-servicemen had jobs to go to. He and his daughter boarded the White Train at Ermelo (Interview Judy Holland, née Welsh).

13 RA QM/PRIV/CC/13/174, Letter George VI to Queen Mary, Government House, Pretoria, 6 April 1947.

14 *Rand Daily Mail*, 8 and 10 March 1947.

15 Tour Diary, 2 April 1947.

16 RA /PS 08100/ 07/014, and *The Star*, 2 April 1947.

17 NASA, Smuts Papers, vol 166, no 41, South African Police Memorandum: Indian, Natal and Communist Boycott in Connection with the Royal Visit, 7 February 1947.

18 H Sapire, 'African Loyalism and its Discontents: The Royal Tour of South Africa, 1947', *The Historical Journal*, vol 54 (March 2011), p 230.

19 *The Star*, 1 April 1947.

20 D Morrah, *The Royal Family in South Africa* (London: Hutchinson, 1947), p 107.

21 P Napier, *A Memoir of The Lady Delia Peel, Born Spencer, 1889–1981* (Wymondham: J & J Peel, 1984), p 126.

22 *The Star*, 1 April 1947.

23 See Chapter 2 of Bickford-Smith, *The Emergence of the South African Metropolis*.

24 Information, Helen Suzman.

25 Bickford-Smith, *The Emergence of the South African Metropolis*.

26 Information, Michael Feldman.

27 *South African Jewish Times*, 3 April 1947.

28 Ibid, 10 April 1947.

29 Ibid, 2 May 1947.

30 *The Spotlight*, April 1947, and other papers.

31 Interview, Laureen Rossouw.

32 H Giliomee, *The Afrikaners: Biography of a People* (Cape Town: NB Publishers, 2011), p 405.

33 GE Viney and P Simons, *Britain in South Africa* (Johannesburg: Brenthurst Press, 1994), Chapter 8.

34 *The Star*, 1 April 1947.

35 This follows the official timetable; inevitably it fell behind during the day.

36 When the city's lights were first switched on a few nights before, a massive traffic jam developed as people drove from miles to see this wonder of civic decoration.

37 *The Star*, 1 April 1947.

38 Ibid, 12 March 1947.

39 Herbert Evans ('Paintmakers to the Nation') ran a crown-headed advert in most newspapers which read: 'Nearly 60 years of service to the South African public has been crowned ... with the high honour of being granted responsibility for the interior decoration [the painting] of the State Lounge and Dining Coaches of the Royal Train.'

40 *The Star*, 29 March 1947 and 3 April 1947.

41 *Rand Daily Mail*, 25 March 1947.

42 *The Star*, 10 March 1947.

43 Those who remember Legum, the son of Lithuanian parents and with a small-town Afrikaans education in the Free State, will be surprised at his putting himself forward as a taste policeman, whatever his actual motives. He slightly gave himself away by adding, for good measure, that the City Hall was 'anyway a squat, ugly building and that the present decorations added to the ugly appearance'. Both he and his wife attended the Civic Reception and the Administrator's Banquet at the Carlton Hotel on 1 April.

44 *The Guardian*, 23 January 1947; see also *Inkundla Ya Bantu*, 'Royal Tour a Political Weapon', 4 March 1947.

45 *The Star*, 26 March 1947.

46 *Rand Daily Mail*, 24 March 1947.

47 *The Star*, 24 March 1947.

48 Ibid, 1 April 1947.

49 Ibid.

50 *Rand Daily Mail*, 2 April 1947.

51 LASL/CAC 13, Letter Lascelles to The Hon Lady Lascelles, White Train, Johannesburg, 1 April 1947.

52 Institute of Contemporary History, PV93, HF Verwoerd Collection, 1/56/1 Letter Strijdom to Verwoerd, 1 March 1947, and Letter Verwoerd to Strijdom, 4 March 1947.

53 Information, Princess Elizabeth of Yugoslavia.

54 Prosperous Johannesburg seems to have had no problem with their mayor ordering a new Silver Wraith Rolls-Royce, at a cost of £4 750, specially for the visit. It was the first model of its kind to be exported anywhere from England; in view of the occasion, the order had been given priority, so the press smugly reported, over others already in place 'from princes and maharajahs'. It had arrived three days early and was allowed to stand in the window of the Rolls-Royce showroom, where it caused a minor sensation. Mr Edmiston, who owned the dealership and had been to England to supervise the delivery, told the press that the car's performance was 'simply marvellous, terrific in fact, smooth and powerful and a credit to that firm who had built Spitfires and Hurricanes.' Sir Ernest Oppenheimer, it was reported, had immediately ordered one for himself. Thereafter, the TJ1 number plates were affixed. Sam Isaacs, the mayoral chauffeur who had driven Johannesburg mayors over 500 000 miles in his time, was given a new uniform together with a set of 'super polishing cloths and polishes' to mark both the purchase and the royal visit (*The Star*, 26 March 1947).

55 Interview, Judy Holland (née Welsh), who remembered this day for me.

56 Ibid.

57 *The Star*, 1 April 1947.

58 Ibid, 28 March 1947.

59 *Rand Daily Mail*, 2 April 1947.

60 Information, Princess Elizabeth of Yugoslavia.

61 HRH Princess Elizabeth of Yugoslavia Papers, Letter Princess Paul of Yugoslavia to Princess Nicholas of Greece, Atholl House, Sandown, 1 April 1947.

62 Interview, Judy Holland (née Welsh).

63 Napier, *A Memoir of Lady Delia Peel*, p 128.

64 Brenthurst Library, MS/OPP/EO/YA.

65 *The Star*, 3 April 1947. It cannot be said for certain which civic lunch this incident followed. The story, however, still stands.

66 Sapire, 'African Loyalism and its Discontents', pp 230–231.

67 *Rand Daily Mail*, 8 March 1947.

68 LASCL CAC, Letter Lascelles to The Hon Lady Lascelles, White Train, All Fools, 1947.

69 Tour Diary, 1 April 1947.

70 Hofmeyr, Smuts's number two, who had been both principal of the University of the Witwatersrand and Administrator of the Transvaal, was a little peeved that Smuts had not left the Johannesburg leg of the tour to him. While Smuts and half his colleagues were away from Cape Town in attendance on the royal party, he was left behind to 'mind the Parliamentary baby'; see A Paton,

Hofmeyr (Cape Town: Oxford University Press, 1964), p 451.

71 *The Star*, 1 April 1947.

72 Sapire, 'African Loyalism and its Discontents', p 230.

73 *The Guardian*, 1 May 1947.

74 *Bantu World*, 5 April 1947, in Sapire, 'African Loyalism and its Discontents', p 239.

75 *Umteteli Wabantu*, 5 April 1947.

76 *Rand Daily Mail*, 2 April 1947.

77 *The Star*, 1 April 1947.

78 *Rand Daily Mail*, 2 April 1947.

79 *The Star*, 3 April 1947.

80 Tour Diary, 1 April 1947.

81 Ibid.

82 The *Star*, 20 March 1947.

83 Ibid.

84 Private information.

85 Brenthurst Library, MS/OPP/EO/YA.

86 *Bantu World*, 5 April 1947.

87 *The Star*, 3 April 1947.

88 African Consolidated Films, 'The Royal Family in South Africa'.

89 *The Star*, 2 April and 17 March 1947. The bill for the flowers was the largest ever paid by the city. *The Star* noted that no woman played any part in the creation of these floral decorations.

90 Ibid, 17 March 1947.

91 Ibid, 2 April 1947.

92 Ibid.

93 Interview, Judy Holland (née Welsh).

94 Ibid, 29 March 1947.

95 Brenthurst Library, MS/OPP/EO/YA.

96 Interview, Robin Wilson.

97 *The Star*, 25 March 1947.

98 Ibid, 2 April 1947.

99 Tour Diary, 1 April 1947.

100 Ibid.

101 These must have outstripped the South African 'Empire wines' patriotically offered, jointly: Nederburg Riesling and Valkenberg (Brenthurst Library, MS/OPP/EO/YA).

102 RA QM/PRIV/CC14/154, Letter Princess Elizabeth to Queen Mary, Victoria Falls Hotel, 12 April 1947.

103 *Rand Daily Mail*, 3 April 1947.

104 *The Star*, 3 April 1947.

105 Ibid, 5 April 1947.

106 Ibid.

107 Ibid.

108 Ibid.

109 RA PS/08100/010/01-67.

110 RA QM/PRIV/CC/13/174, Letter King George VI to Queen Mary, Government House, Pretoria, undated.

111 RA QM/PRIV/CC14/153, Letter Princess Elizabeth to Queen Mary, Government House, Salisbury, 9 April 1947.

CHAPTER 8

1 She once famously told a startled Princess Alice that she had hidden the fruit cake she had baked in her honour among the chamber pots under the bed, so that the children would not eat it in advance of the royal afternoon call.

2 Mrs Smuts's fond nickname for it.

3 Letter, Lady Moore, quoted in, P Beukes, *The Romantic Smuts: Women and Love in His Life* (Cape Town: Human & Rousseau, 1992), p126

4 K Mincher, *I Lived in His Shadow: My Life with General Smuts* (Cape Town: Howard Timmins, 1965), p 87. Much of the information in this section comes from Kathleen Mincher, the Smutses' adopted daughter.

5 WK Hancock, *Smuts: The Fields of Force, 1919–1950* (Cambridge: Cambridge University Press, 1962), p 342.

6 SG Millin, *General Smuts, Volume I* (London: Faber & Faber, 1936), p 265.

7 Mincher, *I Lived in His Shadow*, p 46.

8 P Napier, *A Memoir of The Lady Delia Peel, Born Spencer, 1889–1981* (Wymondham: J & J Peel, 1984), p 128.

9 Information, Lucy Bean.

10 Many in Johannesburg, where she was wont to address her well-heeled audiences: 'You've got a lot of money here; I want a lot of it too. I know you are generous.' See T Macdonald, *Ouma Smuts: The First Lady of South Africa* (London: Hurst & Blackett, 1946), p 74.

11 Smuts Museum, Letter Queen Mary to Isie Smuts, Marlborough House, 25 February 1952.

12 I am indebted to Mac Bisset for this information.

13 Presentation Programme by African Consolidated Theatres Limited with Message from Field-Marshal Smuts, *Noël Coward*.

14 J St Leger Lawrence, *Hatching Out* (Cape Town: Gryphon Press, 1988), p 54.

15 Quoted in Macdonald, *Ouma Smuts*, p 79.

16 NASA, Smuts Papers, 23/361, Letter Isie Smuts to Margaret Gillett, Irene, 23 February 1947.

17 Tour Diary, 6 April 1947.

18 HRH Princess Elizabeth of Yugoslavia Papers, Letter Princess Olga to Princess Nicholas, Atholl House, Johannesburg, 16 April 1947.

19 Napier, *A Memoir of The Lady Delia Peel*, p 128.

20 HRH Princess Elizabeth of Yugoslavia Papers, Letter Princess Olga to Princess Nicholas of Greece, Atholl House, Johannesburg, 16 April 1947.

21 Almost certainly their eldest daughter's illegitimate child. This is not claimed by all the Smuts family. See R Steyn, *Smuts: Unafraid of Greatness* (Cape Town: Jonathan Ball, 2015), p 180.

22 Mincher, *I Lived in His Shadow*, p 152.

23 HRH Princess Elizabeth of Yugoslavia papers, Letter Princess Olga to Princess Nicholas of Greece, Atholl House, Johannesburg, 16 April 1947.

24 RA QM/PRIV/CC/13/174, Letter Princess Elizabeth to Queen Mary, Government House, Pretoria, 6 April 1947.

25 RA QM/PRIV/CC/13/163, Letter King George VI to Queen Mary, Government House, Pretoria, 6 April 1947.

26 Mincher, *I Lived in His Shadow*, p 72.

27 HRH Princess Elizabeth of Yugoslavia Papers, Letter Princess Olga to Princess Nicholas, Atholl House, Sandown, Johannesburg, 6 April 1947.

28 HRH Princess Elizabeth of Yugoslavia Papers, Letter Princess Olga to Princess Nicholas of Greece, Atholl House, Sandown, Johannesburg, 20 May 1947.

29 LASL CAC, Letter Lascelles to The Hon Lady Lascelles, White Train, 1 April 1947..

30 Interview, Katusha de Kock (née Smuts).

31 Strauss & Co, catalogue, Sale No 2017/3, 16 October 2017.

32 Information, Princess Elizabeth of Yugoslavia.

33 N Balfour and S Mackay, *Paul of Yugoslavia: Britain's Maligned Friend* (London: Hamish Hamilton, 1980), p 295.

34 R West, *Black Lamb and Grey Falcon* (London: Macmillan, 1942).

35 Balfour and Mackay, *Paul of Yugoslavia*, p 293.

36 Ibid, p 296.

37 RA QM/PRIV/CC/13/163, Letter King George VI to Queen Mary, Government House, Pretoria, 6 April 1947.

38 HRH Princess Elizabeth of Yugoslavia Papers, Letter Princess Olga to Princess Nicholas, Atholl House, Sandown, Johannesburg, 23 February 1947.

39 HRH Princess Elizabeth of Yugoslavia Papers, Letter Princess Olga to Princess Nicholas, Atholl House, Sandown, Johannesburg, 16 April 1947.

40 Information, Princess Elizabeth of Yugoslavia

41 HRH Princess Elizabeth of Yugoslavia papers, Letter Princess Olga to Princess Nicholas of Greece, Atholl House, Sandown, Johannesburg, 23 February 1947.

42 H Vickers, *Elizabeth, The Queen Mother* (London: Arrow Books, 2006), p 263.

43 HRH Princess Elizabeth of Yugoslavia Papers, Letter Princess Olga to Princess Nicholas, Atholl House, Sandown, Johannesburg, 11 March 1947.

44 Mincher, *I Lived in His Shadow*, p 74.

45 This included the Duke and Duchess of Windsor. None of Prince Philip's sisters, either, were invited to the royal wedding later that year, the Duchess of Kent and Queen Frederica being dispatched in secret to Germany immediately afterwards armed with wedding cake to placate 'the affronted relations'. (Diary of Sir Henry Channon, 25 November 1947 in R Rhodes James (ed), *Chips: The Diaries of Sir Henry Channon*, p 419).

46 HRH Princess Elizabeth of Yugoslavia Papers, Letter Princess Olga to Princess Nicholas, Atholl House, Sandown, 1 April 1947.

47 HRH Princess Elizabeth of Yugoslavia Papers. Letter Queen Elizabeth to Princess Olga, Government House, Pretoria, 28 March 1947.

48 Both Smuts and Hofmeyr resisted the establishment of a South African sweepstake after the war, deploring its get-rich-quick appeal over honest, hard endeavour. Abe Bloomberg, Cape Town's mayor and a racing man himself, was disconcerted when Smuts frostily cut a visit to the Kenilworth racecourse off the proposed itinerary of the tour. He went over his head to Lascelles, who reinstated it. The Royal Family attended the races at Kenilworth, Greyville and Turffontein.

49 HRH Princess Elizabeth of Yugoslavia Papers, Letter Princess Olga to Princess Nicholas, Atholl House, Sandown, Johannesburg, 1 April 1947.

50 HRH Princess Elizabeth of Yugoslavia, Letter Princess Olga to Princess Paul of Greece, Atholl House, Sandown, Johannesburg, 23 February 1947.

51 Balfour and Mackay, *Paul of Yugoslavia*, p 295.

52 HRH Princess Elizabeth of Yugoslavia Papers, Letter Princess Olga to Princess Nicholas, Atholl House, 16 April 1947.

53 Ibid, p 297.

CHAPTER 9

1 Barlow Family Papers, Telegram Imperial Cable & Wireless Ltd Doris Trace to Cynthia Barlow, 22 April 1947.

2 'Punch' Barlow (the nickname was a childhood one, his sister being called Judy) was at this date poised to rapidly expand the family firm, Thomas Barlow & Son (SA) Ltd, that he and his brother had inherited. The machinery of their Caterpillar agency was to be much in demand as the national road scheme was pushed through after the war. This, an American brand previously unknown in South Africa, had been acquired in 1927, the first tractor being sold to a sugar farmer after Barlow won a wager that it could out-plough a span of oxen.

3 Information, Pam Barlow.

4 All attest to her talents in this regard. She later ran The Court House in Johannesburg for the Engelhardts.

5 Information, Peter Knox-Shaw and Dianne Rawbone-Viljoen.

6 Barlow Family Papers, Letter Doris Trace to Cynthia Barlow, Vergelegen, 26 April 1947 Most of the events of this visit are derived from this lengthy letter. Crispian Trace also remembered that afternoon for me.

7 Interview, Crispian Trace.

8 Interview, Fiona Erskine.

9 Interview, Ilsa Barlow.

10 Information, William Barlow.

11 Bairnsfather-Cloete Papers, Letter Peter Townsend to Doris Trace, *Vanguard*, at Sea, 1 May 1947.

12 P Townsend, *Time and Chance: An Autobiography* (London: Collins, 1978), p 179.

13 Bairnsfather-Cloete Papers, Letter Peter Townsend to Doris Trace, *Vanguard*, at Sea, 1 May 1947.

14 Barlow Papers, Letter Eileen (nanny) to Cynthia Barlow, Vergelegen, 25 April 1947.

15 Thus were Cape farmhouses known at that date. Manor house – not technically wrong, entirely – belongs to estate-agent speak of the 1980s onwards.

16 See Chapter 1 in G Viney, *Colonial Houses of South Africa* (Cape Town: Struik Publishers, 1988).

17 Interview, Ilsa Barlow.

18 Information, Stubbie Stratford (Wethered), a woman of great taste and sometime owner of Stellenberg, who told me that this was one of the great lessons she had learnt from Lady Phillips as a young woman.

19 JC Smuts, Eulogy of Lady Phillips, quoted in T Gutsche, *No Ordinary Woman: The Life and Times of Florence Phillips* (Cape Town: Howard Timmins, 1966), p 394.

20 Gutsche, *No Ordinary Woman*, Introduction.

21 I am grateful to Fiona Erskine, the late Pam Barlow, Ilsa Barlow, Annabel Townsend, Peter Knox-Shaw and Gys Hofmeyr for their memories of this far more elusive personality.

22 Nor of her memory. In an act of filial nullification of her mother's record, her daughter Edie (Lady Nicholson) made a bonfire of the contents of the kist containing all Lady Phillips's private papers, thus rendering her biographer's task a very difficult one.

23 Information, William Barlow.

24 'Flowers on a scale and arranged with a magnificence such as I'd never seen before.' (Interview, Peter Knox-Shaw). This was the era of Constance Spry, and Anglo-South African ladies devoured her illustrated books to emulate her innovative talent in flower arranging.

25 Information, Pam Barlow.

26 Information, William Barlow.

27 Barlow Family Papers, Letter Eileen (nanny) to Cynthia Barlow, 25 April 1947.

28 Interview, Crispian Trace.

29 Bairnsfather-Cloete Papers, Letter Peter Townsend to Doris Trace, *Vanguard* at Sea, 1 May 1947.

CHAPTER 10

1 *The Times* (London), proudly quoted by the *Cape Times*, 25 April 1947.

2 See Victor Norton's editorial, *Cape Times*, 18 February 1947, quoted in Chapter 1.

3 RA QM/PRIV/CC14/156, Letter Princess Elizabeth to Queen Mary, HMS *Vanguard*, 1 May 1947.

4 *The Cape Argus*, 17 April 1947.

5 *Daily Dispatch*, 21 April 1947.

6 *The Cape Argus*, 19 April 1947.

7 Ibid.

8 Ibid.

9 *Daily Dispatch*, 22 April 1947.

10 Ibid.

11 *The Cape Argus*, 17 April 1947.

12 RA QM/PRIV/CC14/156, Letter Princess Elizabeth to Queen Mary, HMS *Vanguard*, 1 May 1947.

13 RA F&V/VISOV/SA/1947, Tour Diary, 13 April 1947.

14 RA QM/PRIV/CC14/154, Letter Princess Elizabeth to Queen Mary, Victoria Falls Hotel, 12 April 1947.

15 C Elliot (ed), *The BBC Book of Royal Memories* (London: BBC Books, 1991), pp 32–33.

16 Thus Princess Margaret to Queen Mary: 'I can't tell you how extraordinary it was,' [crossing from Ladybrand into Basutoland] but we all had the feeling that we were in a kind of England overseas.'

17 *The Times*, 21 April 1947.

18 RA QM PRIV/CC13/175, Letter Lascelles to Queen Mary, Victoria Falls Hotel, 13 April 1947.

19 LASL CAC, Letter Lascelles to Morrah, White Train, 10 March 1947.

20 Elliot (ed), *The BBC Book of Royal Memories*, p 32.

21 LASL CAC, Letter Lascelles to Morrah, White Train, 10 March 1947.

22 The pedantic Lascelles pointed out the error here, saying that she would not be alone if her people had joined her. Morrah refused to budge. He had committed the solecism deliberately, he said, because he had a daughter almost exactly the same age as the Princess, and this was how girls of that age spoke. A grammatically perfect speech, he claimed, would sound wrong. He carried the point (see T Utley, 'Grandad's Words Made Churchill and the Queen Cry', *Daily Mail*, 8 June 2012).

23 Editorial, *The Star*, 22 April.

24 RA QEQM/PRIV/RF, Letter Queen Mary to Queen Elizabeth, 22 April 1947.

25 Utley, 'Grandad's Words Made Churchill and the Queen Cry'.

26 Letter Ena van Coller to her family, quoted by permission, *Daily Dispatch*, 26 April 1947.

27 Interview, Lord Renwick. See also commonwealth.org for the mission statement and other documents pertaining.

28 *The Cape Argus*, 17 April 1947.

29 *The Cape Argus*, 17 April 1947.

30 Elliot (ed), *The BBC Book of Royal Memories*, p 33.

31 P Napier, *A Memoir of The Lady Delia Peel, Born Spencer, 1889–1981* (Wymondham: J & J Peel, 1984), p 129.

32 RA QM/PRIV/CC14/156, Letter Princess Elizabeth to Queen Mary, HMS *Vanguard*, 1 May 1947.

33 Interview, Pippa Sales.

34 Ibid.

35 John Lambert Papers, Letter Colin Lang to John Lambert, 21 May 2014.

36 Ibid.

37 Letter Ena van Coller to her family.

38 NLW, BE&FR, PEC, Lady Harlech to Lord Harlech, White Train, 25 February 1947; Colin Lang also mentions his flower-arranging skills.

39 Wrench Town Bakery, of Observatory. This information comes from Elaine, a caller-in to Cape Talk, whose father made the cake.

40 Ibid.

41 John Lambert Papers, Colin Lang to John Lambert, 21 May 2014.

42 Private information. Malcolm Sargent's efforts on behalf of classical music on the Highveld had evidently been found heavy going by others too. During one of the dramatic silences in the Pathétique Symphony in the Pretoria City Hall, old Mrs Hofmeyr was famously heard to inquire, querulously, in a very audible aside: '*H-h-hoe laat is dit, Jantjie?*' (What's the time, Jantjie?); see CJ Driver, *Patrick Duncan, South African and Pan-African* (Cape Town: David Philip, 2000), p 56.

43 *The Cape Argus*, 22 April 1947.

44 During the apartheid era, architect Revel Fox was asked to restore the building and said he would only do it as it stood – viz, as an (important) Cape Regency building. This was not what Mrs Diederichs had in mind. Highly principled, he refused and Gawie Fagan took the commission, restoring the central block back to its Cape Dutch style, much of it being a recreation.

45 Interview, June Commerell (formerly Hands, née Green).

46 RA F&V/VISOV/SA/1947, Tour Diary, 21 April 1947.

47 Interview, June Commerell (formerly Hands, née Green).

48 *The Cape Argus*, 21 April 1947. This had been a general edict issued in advance of the tour.

49 *The Daily Representative*, 26 March 1947.

50 Interview, June Commerell (formerly Hands, née Green).

51 Interview, Suzanne Fox (née Krige, a relation of Mrs Smuts), who, to her mother's anger, had passed up her invitation to the Government House ball and had gone to the City Hall where she knew her boyfriend, Revel Fox, the future architect, would be. She found him and they later married.

52 *Cape Times*, 23 April 1947.

53 Interview, Greg Davis.

54 RA QM/PRIV/CC14/156, Letter Princess Elizabeth to Queen Mary, HMS *Vanguard*, 1 May 1947.

55 Ibid, *The Cape Argus* and interview with Suzanne Fox (née Krige).

56 *The Cape Argus*, 22 April 1947.

57 Interview, Winsome Sales (née Wollaston).

58 Interview, Pam Enthoven (née Hockley). All those interviewed attest to the tremendous heat.

59 K Mincher, *I Lived in His Shadow: My Life with General Smuts* (Cape Town: Howard Timmins, 1965), p 150.

60 Ibid.

61 Interview, June Commerell (née Green).

62 Interview, Pam Enthoven (née Hockley) and June Commerell (née Green) and others. In fairness, Deborah Honoré (née Duncan) and Kathleen Mincher (née Smuts), possibly not party girls like the others, remember it as being 'a good party'.

63 Interview, Lucia Bolus (née Vintcent).

64 Ibid.

65 Interview, Deborah Honoré (née Duncan). Lt PK van der Byl was seconded to the British Army and served in the 7th Hussars in Italy.

66 John Lambert Papers, Letter Colin Lang to John Lambert, 21 May 2014.

67 Interview, Pam Enthoven (née Hockley).

68 D Morrah, *The Royal Family in South Africa* (London: Hutchinson, 1947), p 125

69 Napier, *A Memoir of the Lady Delia Peel*, p 130.

CHAPTER 11

1 The social editor was referring to the aristocratic members of the Household and the glamorous ADCs, Equerries and naval officers, the tour followers like Sir Roderick and Lady Jones, plus the posh refugees from post-war austerity and Labour taxes like Sir Alfred and Lady Beit, Prince and Princess Radziwill (wartime refugees from Poland), and so on, all with the London polish and assurance then so highly prized by the Anglo-Cape. A photograph of the beautiful Lady Beit, a Mitford, wearing a magnificent tiara at the civic ball on day two of the Tour had duly appeared on the social ('Slosh') page of the *Cape Times*.

2 LASL CAC, Letter Lascelles to The Hon Lady Lascelles, Government House, Cape Town, 23 April 1947; interview, Denis Hennessy.

3 Of whom it was said: 'She ruled this vast organisation with a firm hand and her judgement and wisdom commanded respect and ready compliance by all associated with her in the SAWAS.'

4 Information, Lucy Bean; see also L Bean, *Strangers in Our Midst* (Cape Town: Howard Timmins, 1970), p 227.

5 C Douglas-Home, *Evelyn Baring: The Last Proconsul* (London: Collins, 1978), p 152.

6 RA PS/PSO/GVI/PS/VISCOM/08100/07/133-383.

7 *Cape Times*, 18 April 1947.

8 Interviews, Nicholas Oppenheimer and Gary Ralfe, Rachel Slack.

9 RA QM/PRIV/CC14/153, Letter Princess Elizabeth to Queen Mary, Government House, Salisbury, 9 April 1947.

10 RA QM/PRIV/CC14/156, Letter Princess Elizabeth to Queen Mary, HMS *Vanguard*, 1 May 1947.

11 LASL CAC, Letter Lascelles to The Hon Lady Lascelles, HMS *Vanguard*, 30 April 1947; RA PS 08100/19/001-122, Letter Lascelles to Van der Poel, 31 May 1947 and RA PS 08100/58/001-180; see also *Daily Dispatch*, 19 April 1947.

12 TNA Admiralty, (ADM) 1/20593 Report of Proceedings of HMS *Vanguard*, for period 31 January 1947 to 1 May 1947.

13 These went missing and, alas, unacknowledged, until anxiously asked after; '... they are now in Their Majesties' private apartments at Buckingham Palace ... two delightful souvenirs of The Wilderness', wrote Sir Alan Lascelles, reassuringly and kindly, back at his desk in London (RA PS 08100/58/00153).

14 RA PS/PSO/GVI/PS/VISCOM/08100/58/001-66.

15 RA F&V/VISOV/SA/1947, Tour Diary, 13 April 1947.

16 The Tour Diary records that the Royal Family had countered this by descending the platform and moving among the coloured community gathered to one side, and who, doubtless sensing the reason for this, roared their approval (RA F&V/VISOV/SA1947, Tour Diary, 24 February 1947).

17 *South African Jewish Times*, 10 April 1947.

18 J Lawrence (ed), *Vintage Year: The 1947 Diaries of Jean St Leger Lawrence* (Cape Town: Gryphon Press, 2012), p 2.

19 RA QM/PRIV/CC13/172, Letter Queen Elizabeth to Queen Mary, White Train, 9 March 1947.

20 LASL CAC, Lascelles to The Hon Lady Lascelles, Government House, Cape Town, 23 April 1947.

21 South Africa did very well by a victorious but bankrupt post-war England. By late 1947, the Union's 'Parcels for Britain' scheme was sending 10 000 parcels of food and clothing each month. In addition the 'People of Britain' fund, launched in late 1945, had raised £1 333 000 within a year; a separate fund of £100 000 was raised in Cape Town, and Natal raised £196 625 in a 'Salute to Britain' fund; see J Lambert, '"Welcome Home": White English-Speaking South Africans and the Royal Visit of 1947', *South African Historical Journal*, vol 69, no 1 (2017), p 106.

22 After the Nationalist victory and the flooding of UP areas with railway workers (Interview, John Davis).

23 Letter Lady Kennedy to The Lady Delia Peel, quoted in P Napier, *A Memoir of The Lady Delia Peel, Born Spencer, 1889–1981* (Wymondham: J & J Peel, 1984), p 132.

24 Information from the present Mrs Van Rensberg.

25 WE Shewell-Cooper, *The Royal Gardeners: King George VI and His Queen* (London: Cassell, 1952), p 36.

26 *The Cape Argus*, 24 April 1947.

27 see Lawrence (ed), *Vintage Year*, 24 April 1947.

28 J St Leger Lawrence, *Hatching Out* (Cape Town: Gryphon Press, 1988), p 53.

29 *The Daily Representative*, 28 April 1947.

30 Ibid.

31 NLW, BE&FR, PEC, Letter Lady Harlech to Lord Harlech, White Train, Government House, Bloemfontein, 8 March 1947: 'I also note what you [Lord Harlech] say about the King's Final Speech and if I get an opportunity will make a few suggestions.'

32 RA QM/PRIV/CC14/156, Letter Princess Elizabeth to Queen Mary, 1 May 1947.

33 *Cape Times*, 26 April 1947.

34 Lawrence (ed), *Vintage Year*, 24 April 1947, p 18.

35 LASL CAC, Letter Lascelles to The Lady Lascelles, *Vanguard*, 30 April 1947.

36 RA F&V/VISOV/SA/1947, Tour Diary, 25 April 1947.

37 RA QM/PRIV/CC13/175, Letter Lascelles to Queen Mary, Victoria Falls Hotel, 13 April 1947.

38 Ibid, 24 April 1947.

39 RA PS/PSO/GVI/PS/VISCOM/08100/69/65A, Letter Smuts to George VI, 1 June 1947.

40 *The Daily Representative*, 24 April 1947.

41 *The Natal Mercury*, 11 December 1946.

42 *Die Suiderstem*, 24 April 1947.

43 Letter Lascelles to Baring, quoted in Douglas-Home, *Evelyn Baring*, p 153.

44 LASL CAC, Letter Lascelles to The Hon Lady Lascelles, Government House, Cape Town, 23 April 1947.

45 RA PS/PSO/GVI/PS/VISCOM/08100/68/01-31.

46 P Townsend, *Time and Chance: An Autobiography* (London: Collins, 1978), p 176.

47 No one can quite pinpoint where this very clever riposte was made. Possibly it does not matter. Certainly it did the rounds, cementing English-speaking South Africa's belief that in her they had the perfect Queen.

48 Lady Smith-Dorrien was known to the Queen having, as principal of the Royal School of Needlework, supervised the embroidering of her coronation train.

49 RA PS/PSO/GVI/PS/VISCOM/08100/54/1.

50 *The Cape Argus*, 25 April 1947. Almost 60 years later, when David Rattray, the much-loved personality behind the battlefield tours at Fugitive's Drift in KwaZulu-Natal, was a guest of the nonagenarian Queen Mother, she made him accompany her in a duet of 'Sarie Marais' on the Birkhall piano.

51 *The Daily Representative*, 4 April 1947.

52 NLW, BE&FR, PEC/11/1/44, Letter Lady Harlech to Lord Harlech, Government House, Bloemfontein, 8 March 1947.

53 Bodleian Library, Violet Milner Papers, Letter CWA Coulter to Lady Milner, Cape Town, 25 April 1947.

54 *The Torch*, 24 February 1947; this refers particularly to the aftermath of the Cape Peninsula visit, but the tenor was matched elsewhere at the tour's end.

55 *The Daily Representative*, 28 April 1947.

56 JH Hofmeyr Papers, Historical Manuscripts, University of the Witwatersrand, Letter Hofmeyr to Underhill, 14 May 1947.

57 Bodleian Library, Violet Milner Papers, Letter Col Stallard to Lady Milner, Pretoria, 31 May 1944.

58 Letter Queen Elizabeth to May Elphinstone, 26 April 1947, in W Shawcross (ed). *Counting One's Blessings: The Selected Letters of Queen Elizabeth the Queen Mother* (London: Pan Books, 2013), p 399.

59 Douglas-Home, *Evelyn Baring*, p 155.

60 Ibid, p 152.

61 RA QM/PRIV/CC13/176, Letter Queen Elizabeth to Queen Mary, 26 April 1947, White Train, 16? [sic] April 1947.

62 LASL CAC, Letter Lascelles to The Hon Lady Lascelles, Government House, Salisbury, 7 April 1947, Lady Harlech to Lord Harlech, White Train, before leaving Bulawayo, undated.

63 NLW, BE&FR, PEC 11/1/47, Letter Lady Harlech to Lord Harlech, White Train, before leaving Bulawayo, 9.15 am

64 R Steyn, *Churchill and Smuts: The Friendship* (Johannesburg: Jonathan Ball, 2017), pp 134–135

65 RA QM/PRIV/CC13/176, Letter Queen Elizabeth to Queen Mary, White Train, Bechuanaland, 16? [sic] April 1947.

66 D Morrah, *The Royal Family in South Africa* (London: Hutchinson, 1947), p 113.

67 Letter, Queen Elizabeth to Queen Elizabeth II, In the Train, Southern Rhodesia, 7 July 1953, quoted in Shawcross (ed), *Counting One's Blessings*, p 471.

68 RA QM PRIV/CC13/176, Letter Queen Elizabeth to Queen Mary, White Train, Bechuanaland 16? [sic] April 1947.

69 NASA, Smuts Papers Vol 82 (4), Letter George VI to Smuts, *Vanguard*, At Sea, 2 May 1947.

70 RA QM/PRIV/CC13/170, Letter King George VI to Queen Mary, White Train, Port Elizabeth, 25 February 1947.

71 *The Star*, 11 March 1947.

72 R Rhodes James, *A Spirit Undaunted: The Political Role of George VI* (London: Abacus, 1999), p 295.

73 *The Economist*, 10 May 1947.

74 This was a general expression among whites; Lascelles too employed it.

75 *The Star*, 31 March 1947.

76 Most notably through establishing the Fagan Commission, which reported just before the election recommending the revision of the pass laws, as urbanisation of Africans was an inevitable process. The Sauer Report, prepared for the National Party, shared many of the assumptions of the Fagan Report, but underscored the importance of reinforcing influx controls to ensure the supply of labour to white farmers.

77 SG Millin, 'The King of South Africa', in *The Spectator*, 19 June 1947.

78 RA PS/PSO/GVI/PS/VISCOM/08100/19/112, Letter Lascelles to Van der Poel, 31 May 1947.

79 M Crawford, *The Little Princesses* (London: Cassell, 1950), p 106.

80 RA QM/PRIV/CC13/175, Letter Lascelles to Queen Mary, Victoria Falls Hotel, 13 April 1947.

81 RA PS/PSO/GVI/PS/VISCOM/08100/44/34.

82 RA PS/PSO/GVI/PS/VISCOM/081000/44/29.

83 For example, Mary Attlee, the British prime minister's sister, who had spent 26 years in South Africa championing the cause of

non-whites, chose at this juncture to publish an unflattering article on education and race in the country, which was reported locally (*The Friend*, 28 February 1947). Her name also appeared on a petition signed by 500 students from 53 colleges and universities of the British Isles presented on 1 April at Buckingham Palace for dispatch to the King in South Africa, drawing attention to conditions of racial discrimination in South Africa (*Rand Daily Mail*, 1 April 1947).

84 *Die Burger*, 10 May 1947.

85 *Die Volksblad*, 16 May 1947.

86 RA PS/PSO/GVI/PS/ VISCOM/08100/69/65A, Letter Smuts to George VI, 1 June 1947.

87 NLW, BE&FR, PEC 11/1/44a, Letter Lady Harlech to Lord Harlech, Government House, Bloemfontein, 8 March 1947.

88 *Daily Dispatch*, 16 May 1947. Violet Milner might well have preferred a criticism of the King's speech to be made thus, at once removed. As her diaries show, she clearly savoured being singled out for little chats with the King and Queen at palace receptions she attended and had spent a morning prior to the royal departure for South Africa privately giving the Queen instruction on the country's politics (Bodleian Library, MS Violet Milner 6 (F1/21–23)).

89 T Wilks, *The Biography of Douglas Mitchell* (Durban: King & Wilks, 1980), p 5.

90 *Hansard*, 21 March 1946.

91 Letter Lady Moore to Smuts, 1 October 1947, quoted in P Beukes, *The Romantic Smuts: Women and Love in His Life* (Cape Town: Human & Rousseau, 1992), p 141.

92 A Paton, *Hofmeyr* (Cape Town: Oxford University Press, 1964), p 443.

93 *Verslag van die Kleurvraagstuk-Kommissie van die Herenigde Nasionale Party*, quoted in NM Stultz, *Afrikaner Politics in South Africa, 1934–1948* (Berkeley: University of California Press, 1975), p 136.

94 Stultz, *Afrikaner Politics in South Africa, 1934–1948*, p 113.

95 B Solomon, *Time Remembered: The Story of a Fight* (Cape Town, 1968), p 203.

96 WK Hancock, *Smuts: The Fields of Force, 1919–1950* (Cambridge: Cambridge University Press, 1962), p 506.

97 Bodleian Library, Violet Milner Papers, U1559 C55/2, Letter Major G Richards to Lady Milner, 30 May 1938.

98 L Koorts, *DF Malan and the Rise of Afrikaner Nationalism* (Cape Town: Tafelberg, 2014), pp 372–373.

99 Hancock, *Smuts: The Fields of Force*, p 505.

100 After Smuts had commuted his sentence to be hanged for having attempted to assassinate him, Sir Ernest Oppenheimer and others.

101 R Vigne, Obituary of Colin Legum, *Independent*, 9 June 2003.

102 Koorts, *DF Malan and the Rise of Afrikaner Nationalism*, p 383.

103 Information, Alison Willmott.

104 L Koorts, 'An Ageing Anachronism, DF Malan as Prime Minister, 1948–1954', *Kronos*, vol 36 no 1 (November 2010), p 5.

105 G Viney, *Colonial Houses of South Africa* (Cape Town: Struik Publishers, 1988), pp 190–195.

106 It is not impossible that this was the reason for Townsend's turning down Botha's House, which Malan had offered, as being 'unquestionably too small' for the royal party, following his recce. Lynton Hall, accepted instead, was still owned by the Reynoldses, a family with impeccable United Party credentials, and who, emulating Lord Lee's example at Chequers, had built Botha's House on the beach at Umdoni Park, near Sezela, for the use of South Africa's prime ministers.

107 *The Times*, 1 February 1952.

108 Diary of Violet Bonham Carter, 6 February 1952, in M Pottle (ed), *Daring to Hope: The Diaries and Letters of Violet Bonham Carter, 1946–1969* (London: Orion, 2002), p 108.

109 University of Stellenbosch Library, PA Webber Collection, 296 Letter Geyer to Webber, 16 March 1953 quoted in: Koorts, 'An Ageing Anachronism', p 11. Unlike many other Nationalists, the Malans both accepted Queen Elizabeth II's Coronation Medal.

110 Letter Violet Bonham Carter to Raymond Bonham Carter, 21 Hyde Park Square, 16 June 1953, in Pottle (ed), *Daring to Hope*.

111 Eric Louw, the rabidly pro-apartheid Minister of Foreign Affairs, for example, would make a point of walking down the line of silent, immovable black-sashed women protesting

outside Parliament, as if noting them for future punishment. When he came to Jean Lawrence, he stared at her hard in the face, and then would turn aside to spit. Other leaders would later suffer far worse harassments, and even death, from the security police.

112 Interviews, David Robb and others,

113 Quoted in M Evans (ed), *Speeches that Shaped South Africa: From Malan to Malema* (Cape Town: Penguin Random House, 2017).

114 See diary entry for 6 February 1960, in Pottle (ed), *Daring to Hope*, p 223, among others.

115 P van der Byl, *The Shadows Lengthen* (Cape Town: Howard Timmins, 1973), p 110.

116 D Horowitz, 'Attitudes of British Conservatives towards Decolonization in Africa', *African Affairs*, vol 69, no 274 (1970), p 15.

117 According to Van der Byl, Macmillan had failed to put in an appearance at the tea for frontbenchers of both parties before his speech, as had been expected, spending most of the time before the meeting in the lavatory (Van der Byl, *The Shadows Lengthen*, p 109).

118 AN Pelzer, *Verwoerd Speaks: Speeches 1948–1966* (Johannesburg: APB Publishers, 1966), p 338.

119 S Dubow, 'Macmillan, Verwoerd and the 1960 "Wind of Change" Speech', *The Historical Journal*, vol 54, no 4 (2011), pp 1087–1114.

120 D Harrison, *The White Tribe of Africa: South Africa in Perspective* (Berkeley: University of California Press, 1983), p 163.

121 Colin Lang, Mrs van Zyl's nephew, whom we met Princess Elizabeth's birthday ball, for example, was detained in Pretoria Jail in the emergency following Sharpeville.

122 H Kenney, *Verwoerd: Architect of Apartheid* (Johannesburg: Jonathan Ball, 2016), pp 237–238.

123 According to Elsa Joubert, some Cape Afrikaans academics at the time also regarded this as underhand (interview, Elsa Steytler, née Joubert). Not many at the time seem to have spoken out about this publicly, however.

124 Many coloureds were not aware of the provision of the 1945 Electoral Act that required even those on the roll to re-register. *The Sun* of 16 May 1947 claimed that there was a voting potential of 100 000 coloureds.

125 Interview, John Lambert.

126 Kenney, *Verwoerd*, p 214.

127 K Heard, *General Elections in South Africa, 1943–1970* (London: Oxford University Press, 1974), pp 102 and 114.

128 Kenney, *Verwoerd*, p 238, and David Welsh's preface in the same book, p 40. Davenport's figures are slightly different.

129 For example, many members of the Liberal Party, which included Lady Duncan's son, Patrick, on whom the hero of Alan Paton's *Cry, the Beloved Country* was based, voted for the republic, naively claiming that it was important to end the long-standing grievance that the Afrikaners had against the English and get them to face up to the true challenge facing the country: the issue of black political advancement. Only eight years later the party was banned entirely (information, Eulalie Stott). Such analyses are conjectural. There was also, apparently, a not insignificant pro-republican female vote among a class of English-speaking young wives who saw it as an act of defiance or revenge against snobbish and disapproving parents-in-law.

130 Pelzer, *Verwoerd Speaks*, pp 515–516.

꩜

Sources

PRIMARY SOURCES

Manuscript sources (all unpublished)

Royal Archives (RA):
  Letters to Queen Mary
  Private Secretary Papers pertaining to South Africa Tour
  South African Tour Diary, 1947
  Photograph Albums

Churchill Archive, Lascelles Papers, Cambridge University (LASL CAC)
  National Library of Wales, Brogyntyn Estate and Family Records (NLW, BE&FR, PEC)
  Eton College Library, Lady Diana Cooper Papers

University of Cape Town Libraries:
  Waterson Papers
  Lawrence Papers
  Newton Thompson Papers
  Van Zyl Papers
  Duncan Papers
  Marquard Papers

Transnet Heritage Library Collection:
  Visit of His Majesty the King, Her Majesty the Queen and Their Royal Highnesses, The Princess Elizabeth and the Princess Margaret to the Union of South Africa, 1947, Arrangements.
  SAR Tour of Their Majesties The King and Queen and Their Royal Highnesses The Princesses Elizabeth and Margaret; Running Times of the Royal and Pilot Trains and Special Instructions Regarding Arrangements on the Cape Midland System

University of the Witwatersrand, JH Hofmeyr Papers

National Archives of South Africa (NASA):
  Smuts Papers

City of Cape Town, Proceedings of Council for Mayoral Year September 1946 to February 1947

Bodleian Library, University of Oxford, Violet Milner Papers

St John's College, Cambridge University, Cecil Beaton Papers

SOURCES

HRH Princess Elizabeth of Yugoslavia Papers
John Lambert Papers
Sales Album
Stellenbosch University, DF Malan Archives
Killie Campbell Africana Library, University of KwaZulu-Natal, Souvenir Programme of
    the *Ngoma Umkosi*, notes by Hugh Tracey
Brenthurst Library, Albums Royal Tour of South Africa, 1947
Ian Shapiro Collection
Barlow Family Papers
Viney Family Papers
The Smuts Foundation, Irene
National Museum of Bloemfontein

GOVERNMENT DOCUMENTS

Union of South Africa Census, 1911, 1946
Hansard (SA)
Union of South Africa, Interdepartmental Committee on the Royal Visit
General Manager, South African Railways, Public Relations department, *Their Majesties
    The King and Queen and Their Royal Highnesses The Princess Elizabeth and The Princess Margaret in
    the Union of South Africa, Feb–April 1947* (Pretoria: Government Printer, 1947).

NEWSPAPERS AND MAGAZINES

Africa Travel Magazine
Bantu World
Cape Times
Daily Dispatch
Daily Mail (London)
Die Burger
Die Patriot
Die Suiderstem
Die Vaderland
Die Volksblad
Die Volkstem
Eastern Province Herald
Grocott's Mail
Huisgenoot
Ilanga Lase Natal
Imvo Zabantsundu
Inkululeko
Inkundla Ya Bantu
Life
Milady
Natal Daily News
National Review (London)
Pretoria News
Rand Daily Mail
South African Jewish Times
South African Pictorial
Sunday Times
The Cape Argus
The Cape Standard
The Daily Representative
The Economist (London)
The Friend
The Guardian (SA)
The Independent (London)
The Natal Mercury
The Natal Witness
The South African Home Pictorial
The Spectator
The Spotlight
The Star
The Sun
The Telegraph (London)
The Times (London)
The Torch
The Zululand Times
Umteteli Wabantu
World Review (USA)

Printed primary sources
Resolutions of the ANC Annual Conference, 14–17 December 1946

Interviews and correspondence
HRH Princess Elizabeth of Yugoslavia
Lord Renwick
Sir David Graaff
Annabel Townsend (née Barlow)
Basil Hersov
Crispian Trace
Camilla Twigg (née White)
David Robb
Deborah Honore (née Duncan)
Elsa Steytler (née Joubert)
Fiona Erskine
Hélène Opperman Lewis
Hugo Vickers
Ilse Barlow
Jane Rynie (née Ormsby-Gore)
John Lambert
Judy Holland (née Welsh)
June Commerell
Katusha de Kock (née Smuts)
Laureen Rossouw
Louise Stott
Lucia Bolus (née Vintcent)
Miranda Jennings
Nicholas Oppenheimer
Norma Ellis Brown (née Brockwell)
Peter Simon
Pippa Sales
Robin Wilson
Suzanne Fox (née Krige)

Secondary sources

BOOKS

Airlie, M. *Thatched with Gold: The Memoirs of Mabell, Countess of Airlie*, edited by Jennifer Ellis (London: Hutchinson, 1962).

Aronson, T. *Royal Ambassadors: British Royalties in Southern Africa, 1860–1947* (Cape Town, David Philip, 1975).

Aronson, T. *Princess Margaret* (London: Michael O'Mara Books, 1997).

Aronson, T. *Royal Subjects: A Biographer's Encounters* (London: Macmillan, 2001).

Balfour, N and S Mackay, *Paul of Yugoslavia: Britain's Maligned Friend* (London: Hamish Hamilton, 1980).

Barber, JP. *South Africa's Foreign Policy: The Search for Status and Security, 1945–1988* (Cambridge: Cambridge University Press, 1990)

Barlow, AG. *Almost in Confidence* (Cape Town: Juta, 1952).

Basner, M. *Am I An African?: The Political Memoirs of HM Basner* (Johannesburg: Witwatersrand University Press, 1993).

Bean, L. *Strangers in Our Midst* (Cape Town: Howard Timmins, 1970).

Beaton, C. *The Wandering Years. Diaries: 1922–1939* (London, Weidenfeld & Nicolson, 1961).

Beukes, P. *The Holistic Smuts: A Study in Personality* (Cape Town: Human & Rousseau, 1989).

Beukes, P. *The Romantic Smuts: Women and Love in His Life* (Cape Town: Human & Rousseau, 1992).

Bickford-Smith, V. *The Emergence of the South African Metropolis: Cities and Identity in the Twentieth Century* (Cambridge: Cambridge University Press, 2016).

Bradford, S. *George VI* (London: Penguin, 2002).

Bradford, S. *Elizabeth II: Her Life in Our Times* (London: Viking, 2011).

Calpin, GH. *At Last We Have Got Our Country Back* (Cape Town: Buren Publishers (Pty) Ltd, 1968).

Cameron, J. *The Best of Cameron* (London: Hodder & Stoughton, 1981).

Churchill, WS. *The Second World War. Volume V: Closing the Ring* (Boston: Houghton & Mifflin, 1953).

Churchill, WS. *The Second World War. Vol VI: Triumph and Tragedy* (Boston: Houghton & Mifflin, 1953).

Clark, NL. *Manufacturing Apartheid: State Corporations in South Africa* (New Haven: Yale University Press, 1994).

Conradi, P. *Hotdogs and Cocktails: When FDR Met King George VI at Hyde Park on Hudson* (London: Alma Books, 2013).

Cooper, D. *Darling Monster: The Letters of Lady Diana Cooper to Her Son John Julius Norwich 1939–1952* (London: Chatto & Windus, 2013).

Crawford, M. *The Little Princesses* (London: Cassell, 1950).

Davenport, TRH. *South Africa: A Modern History* (London: Macmillan, 1991).

Deakin, R. *An Intimate Record of the Tour of the Prince of Wales to Africa and South America* (New York: JB Lippincott, 1926).

Dhlomo, HIE. *Collected Works*, edited by N Visser and T Couzens (Johannesburg: Ravan Press, 1985).

Donaldson, F. *King George VI and Queen Elizabeth* (London: Weidenfeld & Nicolson, 1977).

Douglas-Home, C. *Evelyn Baring: The Last Proconsul* (London: Collins, 1978).

Driver, CJ. *Patrick Duncan: South African and Pan-African* (Cape Town: David Philip, 1980).

Dubow, S and A Jeeves (eds). *South Africa's 1940s: Worlds of Possibilities* (Cape Town: Double Storey, 2005).

Edgar, RR and L ka Msumza (eds). *Freedom in Our Lifetime: The Collected Writings of Anton Muziwakhe Lembede* (Cape Town: Kwela Books 2015).

Elliot, C (ed). *The BBC Book of Royal Memories* (London. BBC Books, 1991).

Evans, M (ed). *Speeches that Shaped South Africa: From Malan to Malema* (Cape Town: Penguin Random House, 2017).

Ferguson, N. *Empire: How Britain Made the Modern World* (London: Penguin, 2004).

Ferguson, N. *Colossus: The Rise and Fall of the American Empire* (London: Penguin Books, 2005).

Friedman, B. *Smuts: A Reappraisal* (Johannesburg: Hugh Keartland, 1975).

Gibson, PS. *Durban's Lady in White: An Autobiography* (Durban: Aedificamus Press, 1991).

Gillard, F. 'The First Post-War Royal Tour', in C Elliott (ed), *The BBC Book of Royal Memories* (London: BBC Books, 1991).

Gilbert, M. *Winston Churchill: Road to Victory, 1941–1945* (London: Heinemann, 1986).

Giliomee, H. *The Afrikaners: Biography of a People* (Cape Town: NB Publishers, 2011).

Gish, S. *Alfred B Xuma: African, American, South African* (London: Macmillan, 2000).

Gleeson, I. *The Unknown Force: Black, Indian and Coloured Soldiers Through Two World Wars* (Rivonia: Ashanti, 1994).

Grundlingh, A. 'The Politics of the Past and of Popular Pursuits in the Construction of Everyday Afrikaner Nationalism, 1938–1948', in S Dubow and A Jeeves (eds), *South Africa's 1940s: Worlds of Possibilities* (Cape Town: Double Storey, 2005).

Gutsche, T. *No Ordinary Woman: The Life and Times of Florence Phillips* (Cape Town: Howard Timmins, 1966).

Hajkowski, T. *The BBC and National Identity in Britain, 1922–1953*. Studies in Popular Culture series (Manchester: Manchester University Press, 2013).

Hancock, WK. *Smuts: The Fields of Force, 1919–1950* (Cambridge: Cambridge University Press, 1962).

Hancock, WK. *Smuts: The Sanguine Years, 1870–1919* (Cambridge: Cambridge University Press, 1962).

Harrison, D. *The White Tribe of Africa: South Africa in Perspective* (Berkeley: University of California Press, 1981).

Hancock, WK and J van der Poel (eds). *Selections from the Smuts Papers, Vol III: June 1910–1918* (Cambridge: Cambridge University Press, 1966).

Hart-Davis, D (ed). *The End of an Era: The Letters and Journals of Sir Alan Lascelles from 1887 to 1920* (London: Hamish Hamilton, 1988).

Hart-Davis, D (ed). *King's Counsellor: Abdication and War. The Diaries of Sir Alan Lascelles* (London: Weidenfeld & Nicolson, 2006).

Hartnell, N. *Silver and Gold* (London: Evans Brothers Ltd, 1955).

Heard, K. *General Elections in South Africa, 1943–1970* (London: Oxford University Press, 1974).

Hellman E (ed). *Handbook on Race Relations in South Africa* (Oxford: Oxford University Press, 1949).

Hobsbawm, E and T Ranger (eds). *The Invention of Tradition in Colonial Africa* (Cambridge: Cambridge University Press, 2012).

Hyam, R and P Henshaw. *The Lion and the Springbok: Britain and South Africa Since the Boer War* (Cambridge: Cambridge University Press, 2003).

Iliffe, J. *Honour in African History* (Cambridge: Cambridge University Press, 2005).

James, L. *Churchill and Empire: A Portrait of an Imperialist* (New York: Pegasus Books, 2014).

Joubert, E. *A Lion on the Landing: Memories of a South African Youth* (Vermont: Hemel & See Boeke, 2015).

Joyce, P. *The Making of a Nation: South Africa's Road to Freedom* (Cape Town: Zebra Press, 2007).

Karis, T and S Johns (revised and updated by G Gerhart). *From Protest to Challenge: A Documentary History of African Politics in South Africa 1882–1990* (Johannesburg: Jacana Media, 2015).

Keegan, T. *Dr Philip's Empire: One Man's Struggle for Justice in Nineteenth-Century South Africa* (Cape Town: Zebra Press, 2016).

Keppel-Jones, A. *When Smuts Goes: A History of South Africa from 1952 to 2010, First Published in 2015* (Pietermaritzburg: Shuter & Shooter, 1953).

Kenney, H. *Verwoerd: Architect of Apartheid* (Johannesburg: Jonathan Ball, 2016).

Killingray, D. *Fighting for Britain: African Soldiers in the Second World War* (Woodbridge: James Currey, 2010).

Killingray, D and R Rathbone (eds). *Africa and the Second World War* (Basingstoke: Macmillan, 1986).

Kirkwood, C. 'The 1960 Referendum on a Republic in South Africa' (Unpublished Honours thesis, University of Cape Town, 1980).

Koorts, L. *DF Malan and the Rise of Afrikaner Nationalism* (Cape Town: Tafelberg, 2014).

Lash, J P. *Eleanor and Franklin: The Story of their Relationship* (New York: WW Norton, 1971).

Lavin, D (ed). *Friendship and Union: The South African Letters of Patrick Duncan and Maud Selborne, 1907–1943* (Cape Town: Van Riebeeck Society, 2010).

Lawrence, J St Leger. *Hatching Out* (Cape Town: Gryphon Press, 1988).

Lawrence, J. *Home Fires Burning: A World War II diary* (Cape Town: Gryphon Press, 2011).

Lawrence, J (ed). *Vintage Year: The 1947 Diaries of Jean St Leger Lawrence* (Cape Town: Gryphon Press, 2012).

Lees-Milne, J. *Caves of Ice. Diaries: 1946 and '47* (London: Chatto & Windus, 1983).

Lentin, A. *Jan Smuts: Man of Courage and Vision* (Johannesburg: Jonathan Ball Publishers, 2010).

Lewis, N. *Studio Encounters: Some Reminiscences of a Portrait Painter* (Cape Town: Tafelberg-Uitgewers, 1963).

Longford, E. *The Queen Mother: A Biography* (London: Weidenfeld & Nicolson, 1981).

Macdonald, T. *Ouma Smuts: The First Lady of South Africa* (London: Hurst & Blackett, 1946).

Macmillan, H. *Pointing the Way 1959–1961* (London: Macmillan, 1972).

Marks, S. *The Ambiguities of Dependence in South Africa: Class, Nationalism, and the State in Twentieth Century Natal* (Johannesburg: Ravan Press, 1986).

Mazower, M. *No Enchanted Palace: The End of Empire and the Ideological Origins of the United Nations* (Princeton: Princeton University Press, 2013).

Meiring, P. *Smuts the Patriot* (Cape Town, Tafelberg, 1975).

Millin, SG. *General Smuts*, 2 vols (London: Faber & Faber, 1936).

Mincher, K. *I Lived in His Shadow: My Life with General Smuts* (Cape Town: Howard Timmins, 1965).

Moran, Lord. *Winston Churchill: The Struggle for Survival, 1940–1965* (New York: Basic Books, 2006).

Morrah, D. *The Royal Family in South Africa* (London: Hutchinson, 1947).

Mosley, C (ed). *Love from Nancy: The Letters of Nancy Mitford* (London: Sceptre, 1994).

Murphy, P. *Monarchy and the End of Empire: The House of Windsor, the British Government and the Post-War Commonwealth* (Oxford: Oxford University Press, 2013).

Napier, P. *A Memoir of The Lady Delia Peel, Born Spencer, 1889–1981* (Wymondham: J & J Peel, 1984).

Nasson, B. *South Africa at War 1939–1945* (Johannesburg: Jacana Media, 2012).

Newton Thompson, J. *The Story of a House* (Cape Town: Howard Timmins, 1968).

Nkosi, L. *Home and Exile* (London: Longman, 1965).

Owen, M (ed). *To Set Before a Queen, The Royal Cookery of Mrs McKee* (Leominster: Gracewing Publishing, 2003).

Patel, E (ed). *The World of Nat Nakasa* (Johannesburg: Picador, 2005).

Paton, A. *Hofmeyr* (Cape Town: Oxford University Press, 1964).

Pawle, G. *The War and Colonel Warden* (London: Harrap, 1963).

Paxman, J. *Empire: What Ruling the World Did to the British* (London: Viking Penguin, 2012).

Pelzer, AN. *Verwoerd Speaks: Speeches 1948–1966* (Johannesburg: APB Publishers, 1966).

Pimlott, B. *The Queen: Elizabeth II and the Monarchy* (London: HarperPress, 2012).

Pottle, M (ed). *Daring to Hope: The Diaries and Letters of Violet Bonham Carter, 1946–1969* (London: Orion, 2002).

Reddy, ES and F Meer (eds). *Passive Resistance – 1946: A Selection of Documents* (Durban: Madiba Publishers, Institute for Black Research, 1996).

Rhodes James, R. *A Spirit Undaunted: The Political Role of George VI* (London: Abacus, 1999).

Rich, P. *White Power and Liberal Conscience: Racial Segregation and South African Liberalism, 1921–1960* (Manchester: Manchester University Press, 1984).

Roosevelt, E. *This I Remember* (New York: Harper, 1949).

Sampson, A. *Macmillan: A Study in Ambiguity* (London: Allen Lane, The Penguin Press, 1967).

Sampson A. *Mandela: The Authorised Biography* (London: Harper Press, 2011).

Scholtz, GD. *Hertzog en Smuts en die Britse Ryk* (Cape Town: Tafelberg, 1975).

Schuknecht, R. *Colonial Development Policy After the Second World War: The Case of Sukumaland, Tanganyika* (Münster: LIT Verlag, 2010).

Shawcross, W. *Queen Elizabeth: The Queen Mother. The Official Biography* (London: Macmillan, 2009).

Shawcross, W (ed). *Counting One's Blessings: The Selected Letters of Queen Elizabeth the Queen Mother* (London: Pan Books, 2013).

Shearar, JB. *Against the World: South Africa and Human Rights at the United Nations, 1945–1961* (Pretoria: UNISA Press, 2011).

Shewell-Cooper, WE. *The Royal Gardeners: King George VI and His Queen* (London: Cassell, 1952).

Sitwell, O. *Queen Mary and Others* (London: Michael Joseph, 1975).

Smith, N. *Die Afrikaner Broederbond: Belewinge van die Binnekant* (Pretoria: LAPA Uitgewers, 2009).

Smuts, JC. *Jan Christian Smuts* (London: Cassell, 1952).

Soames, M. *A Daughter's Tale* (London: Black Swan, 2012).

Solomon, B. *Time Remembered* (Cape Town, 1968).

Somerset, A. *Ladies in Waiting: From the Tudors to the Present Day* (London: Weidenfeld & Nicolson, 1984).

Sparks, A. *The Sword and the Pen: Six Decades on the Political Frontier* (Johannesburg: Jonathan Ball, 2016).

Steyn, R. *Jan Smuts: Unafraid of Greatness* (Cape Town: Jonathan Ball, 2015).

Steyn, R. *Churchill and Smuts: The Friendship.* (Johannesburg: Jonathan Ball, 2017).

Strong, R. *Cecil Beaton: The Royal Portraits* (London: Thames and Hudson, 1988).

Stultz, NM. *Afrikaner Politics in South Africa, 1934–1948* (Berkeley: University of California Press, 1975).

Sweet, R. *Pambili Bo: The Story of Natal's Spitfire Squadron* (Durban: FAD Publishers, 2006).

Thaarup, A. *Heads & Tales* (London: Cassell, 1956).

Townsend, P. *Time and Chance: An Autobiography* (London: Collins, 1978).

Turner, J. *Macmillan* (London: Longman, 1994).

Van der Byl, P. *The Shadows Lengthen* (Cape Town: Howard Timmins, 1973).

Van der Poel J (ed). *Selections from the Smuts Papers, Vol VII: August 1945–September 1950* (Cambridge: Cambridge University Press, 2007).

Vickers, H. *Elizabeth, The Queen Mother* (London: Arrow Books, 2006).

Viney, G. *Colonial Houses of South Africa* (Cape Town: Struik Publishers, 1988).

Viney, GE and P Simons. *Britain in South Africa* (Johannesburg: Brenthurst Press, 1994).

Ward, S (ed). *British Culture and the End of Empire* (Manchester: Manchester University Press, 2001).

West, R. *Black Lamb and Grey Falcon* (London: Macmillan, 1942).

Wheeler-Bennett, JW. *King George VI: His Life and Reign* (London: Macmillan, 1959).

Wilks, T. *The Biography of Douglas Mitchell* (Durban: King & Wilks, 1980).

JOURNAL ARTICLES AND PAPERS

Dubow, S. 'Smuts, the United Nations and the Rhetoric of Race and Rights', *Journal of Contemporary History*, vol 43, no 1 (January 2008), pp 45–74.

Dubow, S. 'Macmillan, Verwoerd and the 1960 "Wind of Change" Speech', *The Historical Journal*, vol 54, no 4 (2011), pp 1087–1114.

Haasbroek, J. 'Die Britse Koningsbesoek aan Bloemfontein, Maart 1947', *Narvorsinge van die Nationale Museum, Bloemfontein*, vol 16, no 8 (2000), pp 213–259.

Horowitz, D. 'Attitudes of British Conservatives towards Decolonization in Africa', *African Affairs*, vol 69, no 274 (1970), pp 9–26.

Koorts, L. 'An Ageing Anachronism, DF Malan as Prime Minister, 1948–1954', *Kronos*, vol 36 no 1 (November 2010), pp 108–135.

Lambert, J. 'Keeping English-Speaking South Africans British, 1934–1947'. Unpublished paper presented at The Burden of Race? 'Whiteness' and 'Blackness' in Modern South Africa, conference, University of Witwatersrand, Johannesburg, 5–8 July 2001.

Lambert, J. '"Their Finest Hour": English-speaking South Africans and World War II', *South African Historical Journal*, vol 60, no 1 (2008).

Lambert, J. '"Welcome Home": White English-Speaking South Africans and the Royal Visit of 1947', *South African Historical Journal*, vol 69, no 1 (2017).

Rivett-Carnac, D. 'The Royal Visit to Grahamstown', *Annals of the Grahamstown Historical Society*, vol 2, no 3 [no date].

Sapire, H. 'African Loyalism and its Discontents: The Royal Tour of South Africa, 1947', *The Historical Journal*, vol 54 (March 2011), pp 215–240.

Sapire, H and A Grundlingh. 'Rebuffing Royals? Afrikaners and the Royal Visit to South Africa in 1947', *The Journal of Imperial and Commonwealth History*, vol 46, no 3 (2018), pp 524–551.

ONLINE

Historic UK. 'The Kings Speech', no date. Available at www.historic-uk.com/HistoryUK/HistoryofBritain/The-Kings-Speech/, accessed on 2 July 2018.

Malan, R. 'Zille's heresy', *Politicsweb*, 25 March 2017. Available at politicsweb.co.za/opinion/zilles-heresy, accessed on 9 July 2018.

'Prime Minister Robert Menzies: wartime broadcast', Australian War Memorial, no date. Available at www.awm.gov.au/articles/encyclopedia/prime_ministers/Menzies, accessed on 2 July 2018.

'Queen Elizabeth, the Queen Mother', BBC documentary, 2016. Available at www.youtube.com/watch?v=SzgUo3NaCOg; accessed on 11 July 2018.

OTHER

African Consolidated Films, 'The Royal Family in South Africa'.
Killarney Studios, 'The Royal Tour of South Africa'.
Movietone News, 'Royal Train for South Africa'.
Pathé News, 'The Royal Family in South Africa', newsreel, 1947.
Pivnic, L. 'The Royal Tour of South Africa 1947'. *SAR&H Photo Journal*, Bryanston [undated].

Index

Page numbers in *italics* refer to photos and illustrations.